THE MASTER MUSICIANS

BACH

SERIES EDITED BY R. LARRY TODD

THE MASTER MUSICIANS

Titles Available in Paperback

Titles Available in Hardcover

THE MASTER MUSICIANS

BACH

DAVID SCHULENBERG

OXFORD
UNIVERSITY PRESS

OXFORD
UNIVERSITY PRESS

Oxford University Press is a department of the University of Oxford. It furthers
the University's objective of excellence in research, scholarship, and education
by publishing worldwide. Oxford is a registered trade mark of Oxford University
Press in the UK and certain other countries.

Published in the United States of America by Oxford University Press
198 Madison Avenue, New York, NY 10016, United States of America.

© Oxford University Press 2020

Library of Congress Cataloging-in-Publication Data
Names: Schulenberg, David, author.
Title: Bach / David Schulenberg.
Description: New York : Oxford University Press, 2020. |
Series: Master musicians series | Includes bibliographical references and index.
Identifiers: LCCN 2019055835 (print) | LCCN 2019055836 (ebook) |
ISBN 9780190936303 (hardback) | ISBN 9780190936327 (epub) |
ISBN 9780190936334
Subjects: LCSH: Bach, Johann Sebastian, 1685–1750. |
Composers—Germany—Biography.
Classification: LCC ML410.B1 S273 2020 (print) | LCC ML410.B1 (ebook) |
DDC 780.92 [B]—dc23
LC record available at https://lccn.loc.gov/2019055835
LC ebook record available at https://lccn.loc.gov/2019055836

1 3 5 7 9 8 6 4 2

Printed by Sheridan Books, Inc., United States of America

Contents

Preface

To attempt a biography of one of the great artists in world history, a "master musician" in every sense of the word, is a daunting task. Not only do the life and works of such a figure raise complex issues and hard questions; the existing literature on the subject, in multiple languages, is too vast for any one author to read and master in a single lifetime. The previous volume on Bach in the present series, by Malcolm Boyd, went through three editions, each reflecting changing views and expanding knowledge of the subject. Boyd's effort was, in the judgment of the present writer, ideal for its time and its readers in the balanced presentation of life and works, of fact and opinion. Other Bach biographies appeared during the publishing life of Boyd's book, often providing new data and valuable insights but not surpassing it as a readable source of reliable information and succinct, well-reasoned criticism, for specialists as well as students and general readers.

Nevertheless, outlooks change, as do the interests of readers and authors. Writers of Boyd's generation could assume that his readers shared a general knowledge of Bach's music and European history. Yet Boyd could not have originally expected his book to serve a global readership, who could access scores and recordings of any work by Bach with a few clicks of a mouse. Since 1983, when the first edition of his book appeared, performers have recorded Bach's complete works in "historically informed" interpretations, some reflecting radical new understandings of the scoring of Bach's vocal music. Social and economic systems, historical family structures, gender, non-elite and non-European cultures, and other areas of investigation have been opened up by scholars and are now seen to be relevant to the life and music of a "master" such as Bach. The very word *master* has become suspect, and the centrality of individual composers to the history of music is no longer taken for granted, replaced (in some approaches) by networks that involved also patrons, performers, and listeners.

Yet at least within the tradition that produced Bach, the individual composer remains a nexus within which lines representing culture, society, geography, and political economy all intersect. Somehow a substantial body of work emerged from the mind of a single musician, instructing, inspiring, and moving listeners and fellow musicians from his time to the present. This book aims to explain to contemporary readers how that came about.

It has often been remarked that Bach resembles Shakespeare in that we know very little about the person and a great deal about the works. Indeed it is easy to summarize the biographical facts about both men very quickly; for Bach, most of the essential data were already given in the first published biographies. The scholarship of the past two centuries has tended more toward deepening our understanding of Bach's social and cultural context, rather than revealing new facts about his biography. Scholars have also worked toward establishing a chronology of his compositions, and therefore of his inner life as a musician, although the process is far from complete. Gaps remain in our knowledge of how and when Bach composed important portions of his oeuvre, and we may never know such basic facts as when he wrote his first compositions or how many of his sacred cantatas have been lost. Clearly a reliable biography must avoid ungrounded speculation about such things. On the other hand, the Bach of conventional scholarship might be based too unimaginatively on those sources that happen to survive.

Biographers of Bach have traditionally discussed the life and works separately, in part because so many uncertainties remain about when and where his music was composed. This book follows the wisdom of earlier writers in alternating between chapters on the biography and chapters on the works, discussing the latter at appropriate points in Bach's life story, insofar as possible. It differs from its predecessors in considering Bach's "work" not only as musical compositions but also as study, performance, and teaching. Discussions of individual compositions in the "work" chapters are therefore prefaced by consideration of their function and purpose: their place not only in Bach's life but in the communities that heard them. The life, moreover, is understood not merely in terms of Bach's professional career but in its context of family, court, and city, viewing the composer as a member of a society and culture that underwent profound changes before, during, and after his time.

The titles of the "work" chapters reflect the roles in which Bach functioned during various periods of his life: student, organist, music director, teacher. There is no chapter, however, on "Bach the composer," for, as Daniel Melamed has noted, when Bach was born this "was not an occupation or profession."[1] Bach wrote music while serving in other capacities. Of course he and his professional colleagues understood composition as a distinct and praiseworthy undertaking, as do we. And the central concern of this book is how Bach became the composer of those works we most highly value today, such as the Brandenburg Concertos and the B-Minor Mass. Yet composition was never his primary responsibility, at least insofar as his earthly employers were concerned. Most of his music was written in the first instance to fulfill specific, sometimes fairly mundane purposes. That it might become the subject of thousands of publications containing millions of words would have been unimaginable, perhaps repulsive, to him. Nor could he have imagined that so many people from so many countries, cultures, and backgrounds around the globe would be curious about his life and works more than two and a half centuries after his death.

Like its predecessors, this book is meant to serve students and general readers as well as scholars. It avoids detailed music analysis and specialist lingo. But complex compositional construction is an essential element of much of Bach's output, and some readers of this book will be as eager for technical description as others will want to skip over it. I have included some technical matter in the accounts of individual works, I hope in a way that will allow those uninterested or unversed in such things to skim them quickly and without inconvenience. A glossary provides explanations for some of the technical vocabulary; it is part of an online supplement (at <www.oup.com/us/bach>) that also offers a guide to Bach sources and detailed lists of certain compositions that could not be included in the print version of this book.

Also in the online supplement are expanded versions of the music examples. Those wishing to hear the examples will find audio versions in the supplement; for practical reasons, these take the form of synthesized renderings rather than recordings of actual performances. Except where otherwise noted, Bach is the composer of the extracts shown in the music

1. Melamed (1999, 346).

examples. These examples have been checked, where possible, against original sources. They are, however, for illustration only and do not present critically edited texts. The notation has been altered in the interest of legibility, economy of space, or clarification of the point illustrated. In general, measure numbers and readings are those of the most recent scholarly edition. In citations of measure numbers, small letters (e.g., 5a, 27b) indicate the first and second halves of measures, respectively. Large letters (5A, 27B) refer to first and second endings.

No author could complete a book of this type without the assistance of others. It is a particular pleasure to acknowledge the advice and aid of many readers, both named and unnamed, who have contributed in various ways, beginning with Professor R. Larry Todd, who first approached the author about the project, and ending with the editorial staff of Oxford University Press, especially Suzanne Ryan, who have ushered it on its way from start to finish.

About the Companion Website

www.oup.com/us/bach

Oxford has created a website containing the following supplementary material for *Bach*:

audio versions of the music examples
longer versions of certain music examples
Appendix D: A Brief Guide to Sources
Appendix E: Glossary
supplements to Appendix B (list of works), including alphabetized lists of chorale settings.

Users are encouraged to consult the glossary (Appendix E) and to listen to the audio versions of the examples while reading the book. Some readers will also want to explore longer versions of the music examples, available only online. Those who wish to know more about the manuscripts and other documents cited in the book, or who seek suggestions for further reading, will want to consult the guide to sources in Appendix D.

BACH

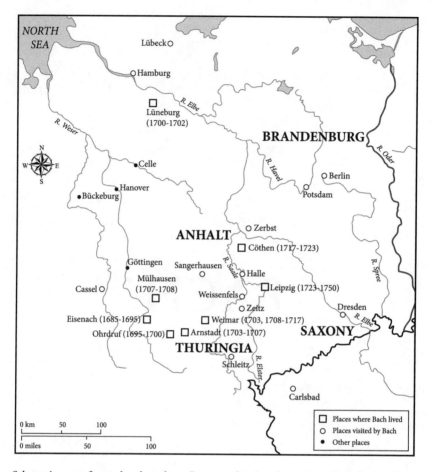

Schematic map of central and northern Germany, showing places where Bach lived and visited.

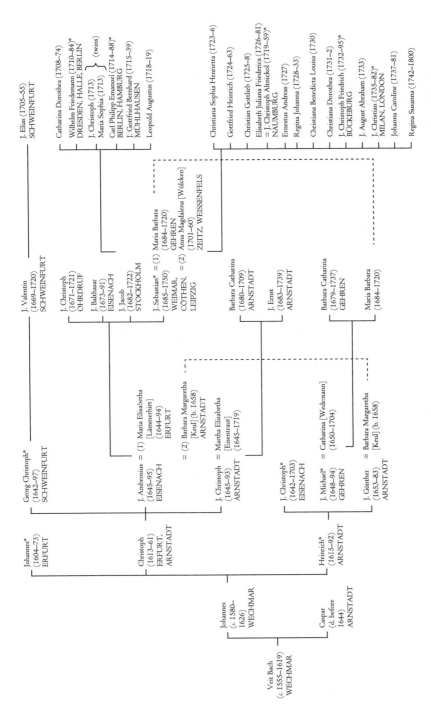

Family tree showing members of the Bach family closely related to Johann Sebastian. City names (in capitals) are those with which each figure is most closely identified; those known to have been composers are signified by asterisks. Names of women before marriage are given in square brackets. "J." = Johann.

CHAPTER ONE

Bach in History

GEOGRAPHY, SOCIETY, CULTURE

JOHANN SEBASTIAN BACH WAS ARGUABLY THE GREATEST MUSICIAN TO have lived in the Western world, perhaps anywhere. Composer, keyboard player, and ensemble director, he excelled in every aspect of his professional life as a musician. He was also father of twenty children, four of whom became significant composers in their own right, and he was the teacher of two generations of students whose influence reached across northern Europe. Today his music, although relatively obscure during his lifetime, is performed worldwide, and Bach himself is viewed by many as an ideal musician. Indeed, more than any other figure in Western music history, Bach has become an icon with whom untold listeners and musicians identify, albeit for reasons that sometimes have little to do with historical reality. Performers may imagine that they play Bach "as he did" while employing instruments or types of ensembles that did not exist in his day. The religiously minded may identify with Bach as a preacher in tones who struggled for his faith, whereas those of other persuasions may imagine him as a kindred spirit who transcended parochial or denominational boundaries.

That Bach might attain such status would have astonished him and those who knew him, despite their high regard for him. Living in a time and place in which musicians and other creative artists were just beginning to be respected as professionals, Bach could not have understood music as having a history in the modern sense. The first genuinely historical writings about European music, incorporating limited amounts of

Bach. David Schulenberg, Oxford University Press (2020). © Oxford University Press.
DOI: 10.1093/oso/9780190936303.001.0001

biographical information about composers of the past, began to appear during his lifetime. Bach himself would be the subject of one of the earliest stand-alone biographies of a musician, although this appeared more than half a century after his death. The very idea that a composer might merit such attention emerged only during the second half of the eighteenth century—an era different from Bach's own and one that, although treasuring his music, did so for its own reasons and in its own ways.

Today we know far more than the Romantics of the later eighteenth and nineteenth centuries did about Bach, music history, and the society and culture into which he was born. Yet our views of Bach and his music continue to be influenced by those who wrote about him in the past. The earliest biographical writings portrayed him as an ideal musician and teacher, and also as a specifically German composer.[1] Certain later writers depicted him as having been especially inspired by religion— a fifth evangelist or a preacher in tones.[2] Others, reacting against such idealizing treatments, have attempted to portray him in a more objective manner but at the risk of underplaying the truly exceptional aspects of his career or character.[3] In fact, Bach may have been fired by an unusually strong motivation to compose and perform music as an expression of religious commitment. That this could have produced a not entirely attractive personality may be irrelevant to Bach's music, yet it would explain certain conflicts that arose in the course of a long and varied career.

That diverse portrayals of Bach are possible reflects how little we know for certain about him. By comparison to European composers of the next generation, or to political figures, scientists, and religious leaders of his own, Bach left few of the types of documents from which

---

1 The earliest important biographical writings about Bach are his Obituary, written by his son C. P. E. Bach and his pupil J. F. Agricola (BD 3:80–92 [no. 666]; partial trans. in NBR, 297–307 [no. 306]), and the biography by Forkel (1802), trans. in NBR, 419–82. For a key to abbreviated citations, see the Bibliography.

2 J. Smend (1921, 6), borrowing a phrase from the Swedish bishop Nathan Söderblum, called Bach not only "der fünfte Evangelist" but "unser Helfer und Prophet," in a sermon that depicted the composer as possessing biblical stature; Germany, defeated in the recent world war, could hear in his music the voice of God their "commander" (Kommandant, p. 8).

3 A famous example was Friedrich Blume's (1963) "new image of Bach" based on a revised chronology of the church music, which downplayed the significance of his sacred works.

historians reconstruct a full picture of a past life. His letters and other writings are mostly short and unrevealing, and writings by those from his immediate circle are not much more numerous or forthcoming. His music is the most important source of information about him, but it was mostly unpublished during his lifetime. The manuscripts that preserve it leave open many basic questions, such as when he drafted his first works or the number of compositions that he actually wrote.[4]

For these reasons it is not possible to write the type of "life and works" for Bach that we expect of later composers or even of his better-documented contemporary Handel. Handel traveled across western Europe and had many accomplished, highly literate acquaintances, some of whom left discerning writings about him. Bach lived a relatively stationary life and was the subject of no lively contemporary reports. With few exceptions, it is difficult to connect biographical events to specific compositions. How he felt about the birth of a child, the loss of a wife, the taking of a new job, even the completion and performance of a major composition—none of this is available to us. Nor can we pretend to know anything specific about his training, his motives for his travels or his employment decisions, or other basic things in the life of a famous musician.

Bach therefore is a mystery. Perhaps the deepest mystery of all is how an orphan growing up in a seemingly isolated region of Europe should have become one of the continent's most cosmopolitan and proficient composers and perhaps its most virtuoso instrumentalist. It is not possible to solve that mystery in terms of individual psychology, that is, by reconstructing Bach's emotional or intellectual development. Yet careful examination of the time and place in which he lived, in connection with study of music that he knew and of his own compositions, can supply clues to how it was possible for someone of his background to accomplish what he did. Bach lived at a moment in European cultural history, in a region and within a culture, that were uniquely suited for nurturing a person of his talents. Although we cannot know Bach himself, the most interesting thing about a musician is, after all, his or her music. This we do know; how it emerged will be our central concern.

4 For a concise guide to the sources and literature on Bach, see Appendix D *(online supplement only)*.

Germany, Europe, and the Empire

For two centuries and more, the extended family into which Bach was born furnished musicians to small towns and minor courts in a rural region of central Germany. This region, roughly coterminous with the modern German state of Thüringen (Thuringia), has been neglected by historians, apart from the attention paid to notable figures who spent time within its borders. The most famous of these, other than Bach, was Martin Luther. He was a student in the cities of Eisenach and Erfurt and, after his condemnation by the emperor in 1521, took refuge at Wartburg Castle overlooking Eisenach. Yet the significance of this region for the biographies of Luther and other individuals hardly explains how a provincial, not particularly wealthy area could produce a composer such as Bach. How could a musician from this corner of Europe produce a body of work so diverse, drawing on so many up-to-date musical trends? How could one individual integrate so many innovations in musical design with new approaches to poetry, expression, and religious exegesis, in such a broad variety of compositions?

Although even now sometimes viewed as backward and provincial, during the late Renaissance and Baroque this region gave prominent places to music and education. The extended Bach family, moreover, must have had its own mini-culture that enhanced this. A period of relative stability and recovery after the Thirty Years' War (1618–1648) promoted peaceful pursuits, and the presence of numerous minor aristocratic courts in the region, although leading to political fragmentation, facilitated the development of many small local musical "scenes." The same was true of certain municipalities that lacked a resident court, notably Mühlhausen and Leipzig. By the time of Bach's maturity the region had grown more cosmopolitan as trade increased, and this too helped shape Bach, alongside an expansion of music publishing and the exchange of music and musicians between centers within and outside the region.

Bach's lifetime nevertheless was a period of significant conflicts and tensions, social and cultural as well as political: between court and city cultures; scholastic versus scientific thought and education (that is, traditional religious humanism versus rationalism); learned Baroque versus popular *galant* styles in the arts; local German versus imported French and Italian language and artistic styles; hereditary, corporate, or guild- and family-based labor versus newer forms of economy and social organization. Conflicts or cultural contradictions such as these might, under some circumstances, have prevented an artist from achieving his or her potential. For Bach and many of his contemporaries they proved stimulating, not debilitating. The lives and works of Handel, Telemann, Hasse, Quantz, and other successful German musicians of his generation and background reveal significant parallels, interweaving court and city patronage, sacred and secular music making. Such general features of Bach's environment can hardly explain his distinctiveness, which emerged very early. But they are among the conditions that made the latter possible, and before proceeding to his life and works it will be instructive to examine certain aspects of the society and culture into which Bach was born.

Bach spent his entire life within the Holy Roman Empire, a much-misunderstood entity. As is well known, thanks to Voltaire's famous aphorism, it was neither holy, nor Roman, nor a true empire.[5] Voltaire stated this in the course of describing the Golden Bull of 1356, which codified the system by which seven (later eight) hereditary "electors" selected the emperor. In Bach's time the latter, seated in Vienna, had only limited influence outside his own hereditary lands in Austria and Bohemia (and in Hungary, which lay outside the Empire). Yet the Empire was not meaningless. Especially with the resolution of the Thirty Years' War in 1648, it became a sort of republic with a citizenship comprising the higher nobility, who enjoyed legally defined privileges and powers.

Bach's career unfolded in the northern and central regions of the Empire, originally the so-called stem duchy of Saxony. By Bach's time this was no longer a coherent entity. Lower Saxony, in the northwest of Germany, was practically a foreign country, although Bach spent time there while a student at Lüneburg and visited again when he traveled to Hamburg in 1720. The name Saxony now denoted a region roughly equivalent to the modern Free State of Saxony in southeastern Germany, with its capital Dresden and, to the west, the major trade and university city Leipzig. One of the largest divisions of the Empire, Saxony was ruled by a duke who was also an imperial elector. Hence Bach spent his last twenty-six years in the realm of a duke-elector who was, additionally,

---

5 Voltaire (1764, 145): "Ce Corps qui s'apellait [*sic*], & qui s'apelle [*sic*] encore, le saint Empire Romain, n'était en aucune maniere [*sic*], ni saint, ni Romain, ni Empire."

king of Poland (outside the Empire). To the north and west of Electoral Saxony were numerous smaller domains, many of them ruled by descendants of the late-medieval Saxon dukes. Each of these retained the title "duke of Saxony," although today their designations are hyphenated to identify their much smaller realms; among them were the dukes of Saxe-Eisenach, where Bach was born (Figure 1.1).

Most of the minor Saxon duchies were located in Thuringia, the geographically diverse region west of Electoral Saxony that includes the Harz Mountains and other hill chains, as well as the fertile valleys of the rivers Saale and Werra and their tributaries. The geography of the region contributed to its political fragmentation, yet it also made Thuringia one of the more prosperous and populated areas of the Empire. During Bach's time even small Thuringian towns such as Arnstadt could boast architecturally significant churches that housed impressive organs. These organs were among the technical wonders of the age, sources of local pride constructed with wood and metal extracted from the local environment.

City, court, and family

Although Bach, like most professional musicians, was a member of the small middle class of his society, he spent most of his life at least nominally in the service of members of the aristocracy. Yet his career on the whole reveals a bifurcation between work at court and in towns or cities. This was not unusual for the elite type of musician of which his family provided so many examples. While relishing freedoms afforded by their entry into the higher levels of the urban bourgeoisie, these same musicians continuously sought honors and employment from the ruling class.

Musicians were not traditionally ranked in the higher echelons of middle-class society—the doctors, lawyers, pastors, and others who held university degrees. But this was changing in the decades before Bach's birth. Several members of the family married daughters of burgomasters, the elected chief magistrates of German towns, typically members of the merchant elite. Bach's stepmother was daughter of an Arnstadt burgomaster, and although he knew her only briefly, such a woman surely would have hoped that her sons (and stepsons) might receive some sort of higher education. Bach's older contemporaries Pachelbel, Böhm, Kuhnau, Telemann, and Heinichen, among others, all had some university training. The last three also authored writings that established their own

Figure 1.1 Eisenach today, with the Wartburg fortress overlooking the city. Although Eisenach has grown since Bach's time, the image gives an idea of the geography of the region, with steep hills rising above fertile agricultural land. Photo: Westerdam, from Wikipedia.

scholarly credentials while helping to raise the profession of music from a purely practical field to one respected by experts in other disciplines. The early deaths of his parents and consequent lack of means might have been the only things that prevented Bach from likewise gaining the university training for which his capability as a student probably qualified him.

Bach nevertheless received a good secondary education, and despite losing his parents as a child was never really poor. This was due in part to the extended Bach family, which, like other successful middle-class clans of the period, constituted a dense network of relationships and reciprocal obligations. These ensured that the boys would receive training and employment within the family specialty—music—for generation after generation. Orphaned as a child, Sebastian would be taken in by an older brother, just as his father had taken in two orphaned cousins. In addition, however, from the age of twenty-three onward, Sebastian would always hold a court title of some sort. Eventually, like his older brother Jacob, he achieved the ultimate status for a musician of the time: a royal appointment. Sebastian's royal title was largely honorary, but he performed for two kings, and two of his sons as well as a grandson also became royal musicians, one of them during his lifetime. With that the family had climbed as far as it could do within early modern German society.

CHAPTER TWO

Early Years (1685–1702)

EISENACH, OHRDRUF, LÜNEBURG, WEIMAR

JOHANN SEBASTIAN BACH WAS BORN AT EISENACH ON MARCH 21, 1685. The date is old style; the same day was designated April 1 in the Catholic regions of Europe. Until 1700, however, the small princely states of Thuringia resisted adopting the Gregorian calendar.[1] Eisenach was the capital city of one such state, the residence of the ruling Duke Johann Georg II. Among the duke's employees was Bach's father Johann Ambrosius, who had lived in Eisenach with his wife Maria Elisabeth since 1671, becoming a citizen in 1674; another was Ambrosius's cousin the organist and composer Johann Christoph Bach, who had been working in Eisenach since 1665.[2]

By this time the name Bach was shared by so many musicians in the region that it had become practically synonymous with their profession. That one family should have held a virtual monopoly on musical positions in some places was not unusual at a time when most professions were passed down from fathers to sons. By 1685 there were several distinct branches of the Bach family; Johann Sebastian belonged to the line founded by the baker Veit Bach with his move to Wechmar at the end of

---

1 In the older Julian calendar, the year 1700 would have been a leap year, like 1600, as it still was in England. But throughout Germany, February 18, 1700, was followed by March 1— barely two weeks before the teenaged Bach left his native region for Lüneburg.

2 The first name "Johann" was common within the family; individuals are and were usually called by the *last* of their given names: Sebastian, Ambrosius, and so forth.

Bach. David Schulenberg, Oxford University Press (2020). © Oxford University Press.
DOI: 10.1093/oso/9780190936303.001.0001

the sixteenth century. Close to the geographic center of modern Germany, the village of Wechmar was the site of a medieval castle that guarded the Via Regia, a major east-west route across Germany. Wechmar's significance for the Bach family lay in its proximity to the larger towns of Arnstadt, Gotha, and Erfurt, as well as to the village of Ohrdruf—none more than twenty miles away, each eventually home to various members of the family. Travel in the seventeenth and eighteenth centuries was slow, horse-drawn wagons and carriages proceeding at little more than a good walking pace (perhaps four miles an hour); twenty miles was nevertheless a single day's journey, given good weather and dry roads.

Veit Bach was not a professional musician, but his son Hans or Johannes received musical training, as did three of *his* sons, each of whom became a professional musician. Many descendants continued the tradition. One of these, Sebastian's grandfather Christoph, served as town musician in Arnstadt as well as Erfurt, as did the latter's son Ambrosius, Bach's father. So too did Ambrosius's twin brother Johann Christoph. Their older brother Georg Christoph, who briefly attended university in Leipzig before becoming an organist and cantor, was, in addition, a composer, although not the first of the Bach clan to achieve that distinction. Georg Christoph's uncles Johannes and Heinrich were composers as well, as were Heinrich's sons, Johann Michael and another Johann Christoph. The latter, whom Sebastian later described as a "profound" composer, served for almost forty years as organist at Eisenach's St. George Church and as keyboard player for the ducal court.[3] One would think that he, together with Ambrosius, would have been the strongest musical influence on Sebastian during his earliest years.

Only Bach's oldest brother, another Johann Christoph, seems to have been destined as an organist by their father, being sent in the year of Sebastian's birth to Erfurt to study with the distinguished composer and keyboard player Johann Pachelbel. Such study was not cheap, and the fourteen-year-old Johann Christoph must have shown considerable potential for his father to pay for study with the most famous organist and

---

3 "ein *profonder Componist*," according to Sebastian's entry in the Bach Genealogy, BD 1:258 (no. 184), trans. in NBR, 288 (no. 303). This Johann Christoph Bach (1642–1703), Sebastian's first cousin once removed, is not to be confused with the latter's uncle (1645–1693), his brother (1671–1721), or several more distant relatives all bearing the same name.

composer in the region. On the other hand, Ambrosius might have expected his younger sons Johann Balthasar, Johann Jacob, and Sebastian to follow in his own footsteps as all-purpose town musicians, as indeed Balthasar and Jacob did. By the time of Sebastian's birth, Ambrosius had achieved an honored position as head of the city musicians; he was also chief instrumentalist at the ducal court. As such he must have played and taught both stringed and wind instruments. That he was valued more highly than an ordinary *Stadtpfeifer* is evident from his relatively high pay and, apparently, the honor of having his portrait made by the court painter.[4] Balthasar died young in 1691, while still apprenticed to Ambrosius. Jacob, however, went on to become a military musician (*Oboist*) and then chamber musician to the king of Sweden, the first member of the family to gain the high distinction of a royal appointment (in 1713).[5]

Bach's mother, born Maria Elisabeth Lämmerhirt, was the daughter of an Erfurt businessman and city councilor; her membership within the upper bourgeoisie was a sign of Ambrosius's own high social status. Following her marriage in 1668, she bore eight children, only four of whom lived to adulthood. Sebastian was the last and lived the longest, but already as a young child he learned how frequently death could come even within a relatively well-off early modern family. His brother Balthasar, who had just begun working as his father's apprentice, died at the age of eighteen when Sebastian was six; their sister Johanna Juditha had died at age six only a few months after Sebastian was born. The following year saw the death of another apprentice, Johann Jacob Bach—not Bach's brother, but the son of Ambrosius's cousin Johann Christian. Then in 1693 Ambrosius's twin brother Christoph died at Arnstadt, and in 1694 he and his children suffered a graver loss with the death of his wife Maria Elisabeth, Bach's mother.

4 As argued plausibly by Freyse (1959), who warns that the widely reproduced but poorly preserved portrait of Ambrosius Bach was heavily overpainted in the nineteenth century, substantially altering its color and many significant features, including the figure's clothing.

5 The term "oboist" (*Hautboiste*) applied to Jacob Bach in the Genealogy (BD 1:259 [no. 184]) could signify any instrumental or military musician; at Dresden the "Bande Hautboisten" included flutes (recorders?), oboes, and bassoons in 1696, and some members played strings and trumpet as well (see Oleskiewicz 1998, 20–24).

The grim sequence of deaths cannot have been the only notable events in Sebastian's early life, but we have few other signposts and can do little more than speculate about how he might have begun his studies or his involvement in music. We may suppose that Sebastian attended the wedding of his older brother Christoph in October 1694 at Ohrdruf; Ambrosius himself remarried a month later, barely six months after the death of his first wife. Sebastian's stepmother, born Barbara Margaretha Keul, was already a relative by marriage; her first husband had been Ambrosius's cousin Johann Günther Bach, organist and instrument maker at Arnstadt. She too was from a prominent family, daughter of an Arnstadt burgomaster. Already twice widowed, she brought to Eisenach two daughters from her previous marriages. But the swift reconstitution of the family did not last; less than three months after his second marriage, Ambrosius too died, leaving Sebastian an orphan.

For the time being, Sebastian and Jacob went to Ohrdruf, where their oldest brother Christoph had been serving as organist since 1690. Ohrdruf, although little more than a village, was a secondary residence of the counts of Hohenlohe-Gleichen-Öhringen, one of whom had founded a well-regarded school (*Lyceum*) there. Here Sebastian, who had begun his formal schooling at the age of eight at Eisenach, advanced in less than three years from the third to the first class. The latter, had he completed it, would have made him eligible for a university education at the age of just fourteen or fifteen.[6] It was also here that his brother Christoph taught him "first principles at the keyboard"—the Latin word *principia* suggesting elements of music theory (harmony) beyond the rudimentary instruction that he might already have received at Eisenach.[7]

Christoph, fourteen years older than Sebastian but still fairly new in his career as a professional organist, may not have been a composer but nevertheless was extraordinary in certain ways. Like Sebastian, he was both a good student in the classroom and a musician of broad musical interests, as evidenced by the three collections of diverse keyboard music

6 Students moved up from the sixth or lowest class to the first at a rate that depended on their individual progress; classes (which typically required two years to complete) were therefore not correlated with age. As a fourteen-year-old in the second class, Sebastian had already attained a higher level of education than any of his brothers.

7 "Bach . . . hat bey seinem ältesten Bruder . . . die ersten *Principia* auf dem Clavier erlernet" (Walther 1732, 64).

he is known to have possessed. Two of these survive (see Chapter 3); a third was the basis of a famous anecdote that provides a rare glimpse into Sebastian's personal life. The story concerns

> a book full of keyboard pieces by the most famous masters of that time— Froberger, Kerll, Pachelbel—which his brother owned. [This] was, despite all his pleading, denied to him for who knows what reason. . . . The book was kept in a cupboard whose doors consisted only of grillwork. With his small hands he was able to reach through the grillwork and, while it was still in the cupboard, roll up the book, which had only a paper cover. In this way at night, when everyone was in bed, he would take the book out and, because he could not light a candle, copy it by moonlight. After six months he had this musical booty in his own hands, and with great eagerness he tried to make use of it. But his brother, to his great heartache, found out and without mercy took away the copy he had made with so much trouble. . . . He did not get the book back until after his brother's death.[8]

Evidently this was a manuscript of pieces that Christoph had obtained during his studies with Pachelbel in Erfurt ten years earlier. The story, which could have come only from Bach himself, seems to have been related unselfconsciously, as an amusing bit of evidence for the child's unusual eagerness to learn more advanced music than his brother would allow him to study. Today we might read it as documenting a rigid approach to education that could hold back a talented student. But it must also reflect the older brother's concern for safeguarding a treasure for which he had probably paid dearly in both money and hours of copying. The episode evidently made a strong impression on Sebastian, but any "heartache" (*Herzeleid*) that it produced may not have lasted. In 1708 his brother's wife would serve as godmother to his own first child, and at Weimar Sebastian would take in and teach his brother's sons Johann Bernhard and Johann Heinrich, returning the hospitality that Christoph had shown him.

At the time of Ambrosius's death in February 1695, Christoph had only just married, his wife Johanna Dorothea—another daughter of a

---

8 Obituary, BD 3:81–82 (no. 666), trans. in NBR, 299 (no. 306). Christoph died in 1721— not in 1700, as the authors of the Obituary apparently believed—and when or whether Sebastian actually recovered the book is unknown.

municipal official—bearing the first of nine children that summer. Thus it is not surprising that Jacob soon went back to Eisenach, probably in 1696, to apprentice as a town musician with their father's successor. Despite his academic promise, Sebastian, too, left Ohrdruf without completing the highest (*prima*) class. He did so "for lack of support," according to the school register.[9] That support, which took the form of a choral scholarship, consisted of free board plus payments for tutoring the younger children of the local gentry. Why this support ceased early in 1700 is unknown, but it is possible that Bach had already made the decision to leave. He might have been influenced by the Ohrdruf cantor Elias Herda, appointed in 1697 after attending St. Michael's School in Lüneburg, then the university at Jena. It would have been clear to both that a university education was becoming a requirement even for a provincial cantorship. Lacking family money, however, Sebastian would have to rely on what he could earn from his "unusually beautiful soprano voice,"[10] also no doubt from his emerging talent as a keyboard player.

Sebastian departed for Lüneburg in March 1700 with his schoolmate Georg Erdmann, who likewise had to leave the Ohrdruf Lyceum. Years later, Bach reminded Erdmann of their journey together, subsequently sending him the sole letter of a genuinely personal nature that survives.[11] Erdmann, already eighteen at the time, would have a diplomatic career. That Bach went with him to a famous school in Lüneburg, 185 miles to the northwest, suggests that both, although accomplished singers, were preparing for careers beyond that of a town musician. Unfortunately, no records survive to indicate what they studied or performed as choral scholarship students at St. Michael's School. They might have sung music from the school's fine library of choral works; they could have made contacts with the aristocratic students at the Ritter-Academie for young nobles in the same town. Certainly Bach studied, in some fashion, with Georg Böhm (1661–1733), organist of St. John's Church and perhaps the most original composer of his generation in northern Germany.

9 "*ob defectum hospitiorum*," BD 2:7 (no. 4), trans. in NBR, 34 (no. 8).

10 Obituary, BD 3:82 (no. 666), trans. in NBR, 299 (no. 306).

11 A brief letter of 1726 (BD 5:85–86 [no. A13], NBR, 125–26 [no. 121]), evidently written when Bach learned of Erdmann's whereabouts from a mutual acquaintance, was followed by the famous letter of 1730 (BD 1:67–68 [no. 23], NBR, 151–52 [no. 152]).

Bach is presumed to have completed his studies at Lüneburg by Easter 1702, then to have returned to Thuringia, perhaps to Ohrdruf. But exactly when he left Lüneburg and how he spent the following months are unknown. The two certain guideposts during 1702–1703 are his failure to gain the position of organist at St. James's Church in Sangerhausen and his subsequent appointment as a "lackey" (*Laquey*) at Weimar.[12] That the teenager was precocious is clear from the fact that the Sangerhausen town council elected him unanimously to be assistant organist at St. Jacobi, the town's principal church. But the appointment was vetoed by the ruling duke of Saxe-Weissenfels, whose choice, Johann Augustin Kobelius, would go on to become his court opera composer.

As when Harrer was appointed Bach's successor at Leipzig under pressure from the electoral Saxon prime minister, the event was a small episode in a long historical process that saw towns losing their autonomy to hereditary rulers who sought absolute power. The outcome of the Sangerhausen search might have been foreordained, the council's invitation to Bach serving as an excuse to sponsor a concert and perhaps an examination of the organ by a visiting virtuoso. Apart from receiving a lesson in the arbitrary power of hereditary rulers, Bach would have seen his reputation enhanced, if reports of the successful audition by a seventeen-year-old spread across the region. Bach would maintain a relationship not only with the town but also with the ruling Weissenfels court, eventually providing music for the latter and sending his son Johann Gottfried Bernhard as organist to Sangerhausen.

Sangerhausen might have been a suitable locale in which to gain experience as a provincial organist. But even a minor role as an actual court employee was a firmer stepping stone to higher ground for Bach, who during his brief first stay at Weimar during 1703 could have met a more impressive array of musicians. Weimar was actually the principal residence of two rulers, for in theory it and its territory were governed jointly by Duke Wilhelm Ernst and his younger brother Johann Ernst III. In practice the latter took little part in governing; both dukes, however, were interested in music. Bach, during this first period in Weimar, officially worked for Johann Ernst, although what he did is unknown. When,

---

12 The Sangerhausen application is known only from Bach's own account, in a letter of 1736 (BD 1:93 [no. 38]; NBR, 187 [no. 189]).

however, Bach was subsequently hired at Arnstadt, the authorities there described him as the Weimar "court organist," which presumably tells us more than his official title there.[13]

The fact that Bach could be offered employment in at least three places within barely a year suggests that he spent the time visiting towns and impressing locals through performances. Possibly he also carried out organ evaluations, in addition to the one known to have taken place in summer 1703, which led to his Arnstadt appointment. Word of his return to the region doubtless spread via the extended Bach family, which included not only organists and town musicians but the daughters of local officials who had married Bach's cousins and uncles. A traveling organist offered hospitality in a burgomaster's home would have been happy to provide an impromptu clavichord or harpsichord recital, also accompanying anyone in the house who sang or played an instrument.

Although brief, Bach's initial period at Weimar could have been of considerable personal significance. He must have played organ there in some capacity, perhaps substituting for the actual court organist Johann Effler, who had connections with the Bach family and could have recommended Sebastian to one of the dukes.[14] Bach's official title of "lackey" implies having to carry out unglamorous duties, but for a musician these might have included tuning harpsichords, helping to copy out parts, and playing viola or second violin in the court and chapel ensemble when needed. If the latter, he would have performed under Vice-Capellmeister Georg Christoph Strattner, a singer and composer who had probably played a prominent role in the short-lived Weimar court opera. He would also have played alongside the violinist Westhoff, who in 1696 had published six suites for unaccompanied violin, a precedent for Bach's *Six Solos*. Even if he worked officially only for the junior duke, Bach would have caught the attention of the senior Wilhelm Ernst, who would bring him back to Weimar for a longer period just five years later.

---

13 The Arnstadt church consistory believed Bach to be "princely Saxon court organist" (*Fürstliche Sächsischer HoffOrganist*; BD 2:10 [no. 7], NBR, 40 [no. 15]); court records show that he was paid as "lackey" by the junior duke Johann Ernst (BD 1:10 [no. 6], NBR, 39 [no. 13]).

14 Wolff (2000, 69) notes that Effler "became affiliated" with Johann Christian Bach (cousin of Sebastian's father) at Erfurt.

CHAPTER THREE

Bach the Student

B ACH'S FORMAL SCHOOLING WAS LESS COMPLETE THAN THAT OF HIS most important German contemporaries, and perhaps for this reason he remained, in some ways, a student throughout his career. Prodigiously skilled in music, he was reluctant to express himself in writing for much of his life. This emerges from the brevity of his letters, many of them laconic testimonials for his pupils, and from his failure to publish any significant prose, not even prefaces for his printed works. He did not respond even after Mattheson invited him, in print, to provide biographical information for what would become a sort of Who's Who of German music.[1] The excuse that he was modest or had no time for such things does not ring true, although it is understandable that he later allowed others better equipped for polemic writing to defend him in print when he and his music were criticized. Other German composers of the time, including Graun, Pisendel, Walther, Heinichen, and Telemann, who must have been just as busy as Bach, left more voluminous and more interesting writings and correspondence, preserving their views on music and accounts of other musicians. Each of these, however, received some university training, whereas Bach must have been painfully aware of this gap in his education.

Thus it came as something of a surprise that Christoph Wolff could name Bach a "learned composer" in the title of his biography published

---

1 Mattheson (1717, 222fn.).

Bach. David Schulenberg, Oxford University Press (2020). © Oxford University Press.
DOI: 10.1093/oso/9780190936303.001.0001

in 2000.[2] The idea rested in part on Bach's mastery of compositional technique, which might be equated to the mastery of his older contemporary Isaac Newton in the sciences. Bach's early promise as a schoolboy, his understanding of several European languages, and his collecting of theological books later in life also formed part of the picture. But although Bach's younger contemporaries might occasionally compare him with Newton,[3] the analogy was inapt, for Bach's learning was scientific only in the archaic sense expressed by the Latin word *scientia* (or modern German *Wissenschaft*). Newton's was the modern experimental science, represented mathematically by the newly invented calculus. The latter might have been the part of Newton's work that most intrigued Bach's contemporaries. They could grasp the significance of the new mathematics while bearing in mind the traditional relationship of numbers to music as one of the seven liberal arts. Yet the new science differed fundamentally from the humanistic learning represented by Bach's musical, linguistic, and theological knowledge.

Still, despite his lack of university training, surely Bach could draft a competent dedication or formal letter, perhaps in French or even Latin as well as in German. The dedication of the manuscript of the Brandenburg Concertos, in French, is in his own hand. Of course, any commoner addressing a member of a royal family might have had another capable person check it over. On the other hand, one might have expected a dedication in Italian for these compositions in an Italian genre; Bach's use of French might mean that he felt comfortable in that language but not Italian.[4] Unsureness in Italian might also account for the fact that we have at most only two settings by Bach of Italian texts.[5] That he was a sensitive reader of German is clear from his other vocal music. But when he does write in his native language it is in a somewhat old-fashioned manner, liberally supplemented by foreign (especially Latin) expressions.

---

2 Wolff (2000), especially the "Prologue: Bach and the Notion of 'Musical Science'," pp. 1–11.

3 As by his pupil Agricola (BD 2:485 [no. 620]; partial translation in NBR, 358 [no. 349]).

4 Emanuel Bach's "Prussian" Sonatas of 1742, representing another Italian genre and likewise dedicated to Hohenzollern royalty (King Frederick "the Great"), have a dedication in Italian.

5 BWV 203 and 209; Bach's authorship of the first has been disputed, and the existing text of the second may not have been the original (see Dürr 2005, 923).

Such writing might in Bach's youth have seemed learned, but as the eighteenth century progressed it would increasingly have been regarded as stilted and pretentious.

All this must reflect the fact that Bach's formal schooling ended before his eighteenth birthday. The earliest biographical sources, however, emphasize his self-instruction. This continued throughout his career, not only in the common form of gathering and performing music by others, but also, at least later in life, in collecting books, especially on theology. In addition, many of his compositions can be seen as exercises that he set for himself, to improve his already prodigious capabilities as composer and performer. Hence Bach's education did not end when he left school in 1702. He was in a real sense a student through most of his life.

Early School and Musical Training

Bach presumably began attending school in Eisenach at the age of five, as required by local law. In advancing to the Latin School when he was seven, he followed in the footsteps of Martin Luther, as he was no doubt often reminded. He had probably gained some basic literacy at home, for he was immediately placed in the fifth class (of six). "Class" assignments were not based on age but were literally classifications of students corresponding to their level of education. Advancement was contingent on demonstrated proficiency rather than annual promotion. Most students took two years to complete each class, few reaching the first (highest). Sebastian seems to have excelled as a student, proceeding quickly, more so than others (including his brothers), except when illness or deaths in the family impeded his progress.[6]

Today the school curriculum seems medieval, as does the teaching method, which focused on rote instruction and memorization of bible passages. In fact, Bach's school training reflected methods introduced earlier in the seventeenth century by the Moravian educational reformer Comenius. These, however, remained remote from what would be advocated by Enlightenment scholars during the next century. That the mature Bach was not sympathetic with newer approaches to education might be gleaned from his later conflicts with the reforming rector

---

6 The early academic progress (or lack thereof) of the Bach boys is summarized from school records in Helmbold (1930).

Ernesti at the St. Thomas School in Leipzig. He nevertheless would see to it that his three oldest sons attended university, where they would come into contact with broader and more enlightened views of the world than he did at Eisenach. Still, compared to that of Britain, France, or the Netherlands, even the most advanced German education during Bach's lifetime might have seemed backward, particularly in the persistence of orthodox religious indoctrination. There is no evidence that Bach was ever troubled by this. On the contrary, his resistance to Ernesti's reforms, although in the first instance likely due to their deleterious effect on students' musical preparation, could also have reflected the rector's abandonment of the traditional type of instruction that Bach had received.

Of Sebastian's musical training as a child we know nothing. His first lessons might have been in singing, followed by the rudiments of reading music. This was in preparation for a career that he would enter as a church chorister, with the potential of earning a scholarship to some higher educational institution—as Bach did twice. In none of this can we assume teaching methods or learning expectations familiar from present-day musical training. In a culture where music making included greater amounts of improvisation and unrehearsed performance than does modern "classical" practice, a child's first music lessons probably consisted of rote instruction and memorization, just like his or her classroom lessons. As son of a town music director, Sebastian probably also learned the rudiments of various instruments at an early age, while being assigned mundane tasks such as carrying and setting up equipment for performances.

Surely Ambrosius, as a highly regarded town and court musician, possessed an inventory of instruments and music (scores and parts) for use by his co-workers, apprentices, and family.[7] But not everything would necessarily have been made available to a youngest son before his tenth birthday. Nor do we know whether Sebastian sang publicly at Eisenach as a member of the *chorus musicus*, the roster of students from the Latin school who performed in church and elsewhere. Even if so, he might only have helped lead the congregational singing of unison chorales. Given his father's profession, it might be assumed that Sebastian was destined from the beginning to be an instrumentalist and trained accordingly, however

---

7 Although a list of Ambrosius's musical holdings does not survive, we have similar material for Leipzig town musicians (see Schulze 1985).

good a singing voice he possessed as a boy. Yet the musician later regarded by contemporaries as the greatest living organist was neither son nor pupil of a well-known professional on the instrument.

Scholars have wondered about Sebastian's relationship to his father's cousin Johann Christoph Bach, the Eisenach city and court organist. In the family Genealogy, a document first drawn up by Sebastian Bach in 1735, where the latter described the older Christoph Bach as "a profound composer," Emanuel Bach subsequently added "great and expressive."[8] Sebastian's comment might have been meant only to distinguish Christoph from other members of the family with the same name. But in the Obituary for his father—another early biographical document—Emanuel singled out Christoph for both his musical rhetoric and his counterpoint, mentioning two extraordinary vocal works that Emanuel could have known only through Sebastian, who might have heard or performed in them as a child.[9] Unmentioned, however, and absent from most of the musical collections associated with Sebastian or his brother Christoph, is the keyboard music now attributed to the older Christoph Bach, which includes organ chorales and other pieces.[10]

In short, whether Sebastian received any systematic training on keyboard instruments at Eisenach is unknown. Johann Ambrosius surely had some proficiency at the keyboard and expected the same of his sons, but he sent the oldest to Erfurt in 1685 to study organ with Pachelbel—rather than with the older Johann Christoph in Eisenach. The latter, suffering from a poor income and contentious relations with the local authorities,

---

8 "ein *profunder Componist*" and "Dies ist der große und ausdrückende Componist" (BD 2:258 [no. 184] and annotation to entry no. 13 in the Genealogy [BD 2:265]).

9 The first work, which Emanuel described as a motet written about seventy years earlier (i.e., ca. 1684), has not been identified, but Emanuel writes that its composer used the augmented (*übermäßiger*) sixth; this must have been a prominent element in the "expression of the words" (*Ausdruck der Worte*). The second composition is the *concertato* motet *Es erhub sich ein Streit*, which, as the Obituary notes, is for twenty-two vocal and instrumental parts (BD 3:80 [no. 666]). It is part of the Old Bach Archive; Melamed (1999, 349) notes a conflicting attribution elsewhere to Christoph's brother Johann Michael, but Emanuel surely would have mentioned that fact if he knew about it, for Michael was his own grandfather.

10 The extent of the older Christoph Bach's output is uncertain due to the possibility of confusion with others of the same name; see Melamed (1999) and Dirksen (2010). The "Neumeister" codex (see Chapter 5) includes a few chorale settings attributed to "J. C. Bach," presumably the older Johann Christoph.

probably could not accept his cousin's sons as apprentices while raising four sons of his own.[11] Nevertheless, at least two of those became organists, including Johann Friedrich, who would succeed Sebastian as organist at Mühlhausen's St. Blasius Church.

As Sebastian was growing up, his father was directing the town and court instrumental ensembles; he did so probably while playing violin, perhaps also cornetto and other wind instruments. Sebastian and his brothers surely learned at least the rudiments of violin playing, for there would always be work for string players—as Handel, like Sebastian's pupil Kirnberger, would find to his benefit early in his career.[12] Sebastian would send his first son Friedemann to study violin with the virtuoso Gottlieb Graun, but not Emanuel or the younger boys, and of all the family members only Sebastian ever composed in truly virtuoso fashion for the violin.[13] Like Mozart, Sebastian must have learned to play the instrument well enough to understand its capabilities and to write difficult solo pieces for it. Even if he could not execute his own violin compositions as well as a specialist, he would understand how to push string players beyond conventional limits without asking for the impossible.

Bach's training at Eisenach, considered more broadly, would have included hearing performances by what was, for a small city, a distinguished group of court and town musicians. He could not have attended every court function, but he would have regularly heard the older Johann Christoph playing organ at church and his father directing instrumental ensembles there and at the town hall. If he indeed attended court performances—perhaps while assisting his father in some way—he might have heard some of the lost music of Daniel Eberlin, Telemann's

---

11 The most recent biographical study of this J. C. Bach remains Freyse (1956).

12 Handel worked as a violinist in the opera orchestra after moving to Hamburg in 1703 (Burrows 2012, 21). Kirnberger served briefly as violinist in the royal Prussian chamber orchestra during 1752–1753; he was later chamber musician to the king's sister Anna Amalie (see Oleskiewicz 2011, 109–10).

13 Even Friedemann never held a position as a violinist, and neither he nor his younger brothers composed substantial amounts of music for solo violin, although Johann Christoph Friedrich and Johann Christian, the two youngest, composed many pieces with solo string parts. Friedemann's studies with the older Graun are known from a letter of 1749 (in Bitter 1868, 2:370); Falck (1913, 8) placed these in the period 1726–1727, but this was based only on Friedemann's absence from school in Leipzig.

future father-in-law, who was Capellmeister until at least 1689. Eberlin wrote German and Latin sacred works, but because he was active only during Bach's earliest years—and was forced to leave in 1692 after being involved in fiscal irregularities—his music is unlikely to have been heard much by the time Bach began his training. Sebastian is more likely to have heard or even sung in compositions by the cantor Dedekind. In any case, Ambrosius's repertory probably included the solid but conservative types of music that comprise the Old Bach Archive. This was a selection of works by older members of the family, mostly for small ensembles of voices and strings, that Sebastian eventually owned. From such compositions a young musician might have gained a sense of musical propriety and basic craftsmanship. Yet these, or the occasional flashes of originality in the extant music by the organist Christoph Bach, could not have conveyed much idea of the possibilities that were emerging from contemporary composers in France and Italy.

Studies at Ohrdruf and Lüneburg

Everything changed when Bach's father died—if not already nine months earlier, at the death of his mother. Surely the loss of Maria Elisabeth and the entry into the household of a significantly younger stepmother greatly changed life at home. Sebastian's progress at school appears to have been severely disrupted by the family events that took place during his ninth year, and we can imagine the same for his musical development as well.[14] Like other successful people, however, he evidently learned at an early age to cast off personal misfortunes and persevere, making the best of his situation. By 1700, when he left Ohrdruf, he would have understood, at least intuitively, how to turn even the most profound bereavement into an opportunity. The loss of his parents and his forced departure from home made possible study with his talented older brother and attendance at a distinguished high school. In this, and in subsequent experiences, a religiously minded youth could hardly fail to see the hand of a provident God.

The Lyceum, the school Bach attended in Ohrdruf, had a high reputation, with a curriculum that seems to have been broad for the time,

---

14 Bach's absences, recorded in student registers (in BD 2:3–4 [no. 2], trans. in NBR, 32 [no. 6]), peaked during 1695, although by then he had advanced to the fourth class.

inspired by Comenius.[15] Bach was apparently a model pupil, reaching the highest (*prima*) class at fourteen, younger than his classmates. His studies incorporated readings in theology and Latin literature, including the comedies of Terence—models for the libretto of his Coffee Cantata. Today, when few study Classical literature, it is necessary to point out that Latin poetry presents challenges even to a native speaker of another inflected language such as German. The peculiar grammar of literary Latin encouraged ancient authors to manipulate syntax in a virtuoso manner that was imitated by seventeenth-century European writers. Ancient Greek and Latin poetry, moreover, was written in a variety of complex but precisely defined poetic meters. These too were emulated by contemporary German poets, who also imitated the forms and rhyme schemes of French and Italian poetry of their own time. Today hardly anybody, not even literary historians, treats rhyme schemes or the patterns of accented and unaccented syllables as important elements of poetry. But the craft of prosody was central to poetic study and criticism when Bach was in school, and he must have learned to pay close attention to precisely how a poem is constructed. It went without saying that a musical setting of a poem must reflect the form of the latter.

Modern writers on Baroque music have focused on rhetoric, another element of literature that, like prosody, also has a parallel in musical composition. Bach surely studied rhetoric as well, through exercises that included memorizing and declaiming ancient poetry and passages from plays. He might even have done some acting as a student, demonstrating the arts of public speech and gesture on stage or at least before classmates; performances of Latin plays were a common exercise in elite education of the time. But rhythm and form are more fundamental elements of literary craftsmanship. Both were directly related to music in the ancient Mediterranean world, where Greek poetry was danced and poetic meters were therefore both rhythms and choreographies. For a composer of vocal music it was essential to grasp the structure of a poem—its meter, rhymes, and division into sentences

---

15 The few available facts about Bach's secondary education are given in his school attendance records (BD 2:6–7 [no. 4], trans. in NBR, 34–35 [no. 8]). Spitta (1873–80, 1:184–86 and 213–15) reconstructs Bach's studies at Ohrdruf and Lüneburg, based on earlier writings on education.

and stanzas, if any—before seeking ways of reflecting its meaning or its rhetoric in music. Bach would have begun to do this seriously as a student of Latin at Ohrdruf.

The fact that Bach was later reticent to express himself in writing does not mean that he lacked a sophisticated understanding of several languages. Rather he was sufficiently educated to understand the limitations of his learning. Knowledge of Latin nevertheless would have assisted him in quickly grasping French and possibly some Italian during his subsequent years in Lüneburg and at the courts of Arnstadt and Weimar. More important, reading Latin poetry would have instilled in him the attention and sensitivity to literary form and rhetoric that are evident in his settings of librettos of all sorts.

We know nothing concrete about Bach's musical instruction at Ohrdruf. But, living in the home of a capable older brother who was the town organist, and who, moreover, had recently completed a course of study with Pachelbel, Bach must have received not only fundamentals but more advanced training at the keyboard.[16] One can imagine their mother Maria Elizabeth or an older brother getting Sebastian started at the clavichord while still in Eisenach. But the Obituary also mentions "pieces his brother voluntarily gave him"—that is, written music supplied for free that he might have started to play only at Ohrdruf, as opposed to simple pieces learned by rote as a small child. Whatever his musical experiences as a child at Eisenach, they were probably overshadowed, at least in conscious memory, by those that followed, as Sebastian moved from one stimulating environment to another during his teens. He surely did learn something from the older Johann Christoph at Eisenach, perhaps even gaining some understanding of the organ by observing work ongoing there on the instrument in St. George's Church. But he probably learned

---

16 As noted in Chapter 2, Walther reported that Bach learned the "fundamentals" (*Principia*) of keyboard playing at Ohrdruf, using a word that happens to be the title of Newton's most famous book. Its root meaning is "first things" or "beginnings," and it is the sort of Latin expression that Bach might have used in an autobiographical letter to Walther that formed the basis of the biographical entry for Bach in the latter's *Lexicon* (Walther 1732, 64; ed. in BD 2:231 [no. 323], trans. in NBR, 294 [no. 304]). No such letter survives, but a 1729 letter from Telemann became the basis of Walther's entry for the latter (596–97). Bach was probably more comfortable sending such a letter to a friend, relative, and quasi-colleague than to the opinionated Mattheson.

much more about organ music, construction, and maintenance during five years living and studying with his older brother.

Prior to his departure for Lüneburg, Sebastian may also have attended one or more of the periodic gatherings of the Bach clan later described by Forkel.[17] One of these is supposed to be commemorated in the Quodlibet BWV 524, a comic medley for four voices and continuo that survives in Bach's fragmentary manuscript copy of 1707 or 1708.[18] But exactly when and where those events took place, or what they entailed musically, is not known. Perhaps as important as these gatherings—if not identical with them—were weddings and similar occasions, as when Sebastian's brother Christoph was married at Ohrdruf in 1694. This is presumed to be the event at which Ambrosius was reported to have performed alongside Pachelbel.[19] It took place less than a month before Ambrosius's own (second) marriage; either occasion might have seen a performance of a wedding cantata by the older Christoph Bach that survives in Ambrosius's manuscript copy.[20]

One product of Bach's scattered early years must have been an awareness of the transitoriness of life, including the difficulty of holding on to material possessions. As a ten-year-old orphan at Ohrdruf, a fifteen-year-old scholarship student at Lüneburg, and an eighteen-year-old "lackey" at Weimar, Bach could have brought few belongings with him. He certainly could not have traveled with valuable instruments, and even books and written music would have been hard to carry in any quantity; besides, manuscripts copied for his teachers did not necessarily become his unless paid for. Any music that he was to own personally would have been carefully selected and treasured, worth the cost and the labor of writing out and carrying. Bach nevertheless must have early acquired his habit of collecting music, an activity that he seems to have shared with, and might have been encouraged in, by his brother Christoph. As

---

17 Forkel (1802, 3f.), trans. in NBR, 424.

18 The loss of the title page and of the opening of the piece leaves its authorship uncertain, although it has been assumed to be Bach's since its discovery and first edition by Max Schneider (Leipzig: Breitkopf und Härtel, 1932).

19 According to a document by Dedekind, cited by Schulze (1985a, 70n79).

20 *Meine Freundin, du bist schön;* Ambrosius's manuscript parts for the work became part of the Old Bach Archive.

a schoolteacher, moreover—Christoph began teaching at the Ohrdruf Lyceum in 1700—his older brother must have owned at least a basic book collection on such topics as Latin grammar and theology. From him, or from the Ohrdruf cantor Herda, Sebastian would have understood that any future educational career of his own would require him to assemble a similar collection.

Bach's eventual amassing of theological books might have been a way of compensating for his lack of a university education. But it doubtless also reflected real enthusiasm for the subject, albeit one that might have remained an aspiration until he had the means and time to pursue it. The impressive number of musical instruments that he owned at his death must also have reflected a lifelong, purposeful assembly of tools needed for his profession, even though he never followed his father as a town musician. Bach's collecting activity might have begun at Lüneburg, taking the form of copying out pieces more challenging and in a greater variety of styles than those available at Eisenach and Ohrdruf. Traces of this activity can be seen in the two surviving manuscript anthologies owned by Christoph Bach; these probably included music that Sebastian brought back from Lüneburg.

Nevertheless, Bach's years there are even more of a mystery than those at Eisenach and Ohrdruf. By the age of fifteen he must have been maturing rapidly, both personally and professionally, yet we have practically no information as to how. As a choral scholar at St. Michael's School he might have sung regularly in services, had his voice not broken soon after his arrival. Yet this occurrence could hardly have been a surprise, given his age, and although officially a chorister he might have been expected from the start to work primarily as a keyboard player. Nor could Bach have come to Lüneburg without expecting to learn in some capacity from the organist Georg Böhm, who had been born near Ohrdruf and was surely known there. It is puzzling that Emanuel Bach later doubted that his father had studied with Böhm.[21] For the latter seems, more than anyone

---

21 Emanuel crossed out the words "his Lüneburg teacher Böhm" (*seinem Lüneburgischer Lehrmeistern Böhmen*) in his 1775 letter to Forkel (BD 3:288 [no. 803]; NBR, 398 [no. 395]). Also still living at Lüneburg during Bach's time there was the aged organist of the church of Saints Nicholas and Marien, Johann Jacob Löwe (known as "von Eisenach," although only his father was from that city). He had studied with Schütz, but Bach is not known to have had any contact with him.

else whom Sebastian had yet encountered, to have been a model for what he would become: a well-educated musician at an important church who had left provincial Thuringia for a more cosmopolitan environment. Böhm's keyboard music, which includes organ praeludia and chorales as well as dance suites, reflects acquaintance not only with the north-German style of Reinken and Buxtehude (see below) but also newer trends, particularly in French music. The organ at St. John's was under repair during Bach's time there, but this would hardly have prevented Bach's learning from Böhm. Sebastian also traveled to Hamburg to hear Reinken, and Böhm was not necessarily the only potential source for the music by Buxtehude and others that Bach brought back to Thuringia. In any case, Christoph Bach's manuscript collections reflect the types of music available in and around Hamburg at this time, gathered at least in part "at the home of Georg Böhm" (Figure 3.1).[22]

The Obituary suggests that, although Bach was "well received" at Lüneburg because of his soprano voice, he was unable to use his "uncommonly fine voice" there after it broke.[23] The account then turns to matters involving the organ, as if little else from these years was significant for Bach's musical development. But Lüneburg was a relatively large residence town, more populous than Eisenach. Living there, and at least occasionally visiting Hamburg—one of the largest and wealthiest cities in Europe—must have had a powerful effect on a young musician who up to this point had spent his time in the provinces. The Obituary's focus on matters relating to the organ could reflect things that seized Bach's attention at the time: the great instrument at St. Catherine's in Hamburg, the playing of its organist Reinken. Surely, too, Bach's memories were colored by his later visit to Hamburg in 1720; what he really learned from his early trips there, musical and otherwise, is unknowable.

Still, the cliché that travel is broadening is usually true. Without ever going to Italy or even Austria, as did other German musicians of the time, before he was twenty Bach had journeyed far from his native region. This greatly expanded the range of musical experiences available

22 As Bach indicated in the colophon to his recently discovered manuscript copy of pieces by Reinken and Buxtehude (Wollny and Maul 2008).

23 "wurde unser Bach, wegen seiner ungemein schönen Sopranstimme, wohl aufgenommen," BD 3:82 (no. 666), trans. in NBR, 299 (no. 306).

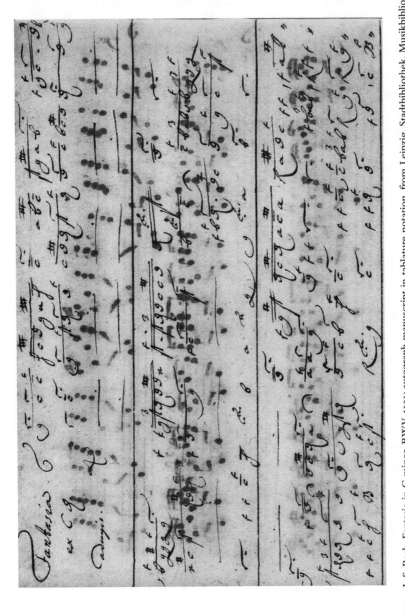

Figure 3.1 J. S. Bach, Fantasia in C minor, BWV 1121; autograph manuscript in tablature notation, from Leipzig, Stadtbibliothek, Musikbibliothek, Mus. ms. III.8.4 (the Andreas Bach Book, originally owned by Sebastian's brother Johann Christoph), from Bach-Digital.

to him through contact with various local musical styles, practices, and instruments. Not every musician would take equal advantage of such an opportunity. Bach's well-traveled contemporary Heinichen cultivated a narrow stylistic range as a composer throughout his career, merely shifting from a conservative German idiom to a fashionable Italian one after visiting Rome and Venice. Telemann, on the other hand, would travel somewhat farther than Bach over the course of his career—to Poland, later to Paris—picking up many musical ideas from his travels; like Bach, he was clearly open by nature to diverse styles and types of composition. Through visits to a major city Bach also would have learned that large numbers of people might listen enthusiastically to both sacred and secular music. Music at a court, such as that of Eisenach, was essentially for a single person, the ruler, and in a small town musicians served, in effect, a few influential officials and their families. Music in a real city, especially an independent republic like Hamburg, was for the public—not exactly the public as we understand the term, but a relatively large, diverse body of middle- and upper-class citizens. Bach would get by successfully in all these types of environment—which is not to say that he avoided conflict and disappointment in court, town, or city.

Although the Obituary mentions only Reinken in the context of Bach's Lüneburg years, one wonders whether the music of Buxtehude, surely the greatest composer then living in northern Germany, was not also heard in Hamburg. Bach already knew something of Buxtehude, whose music he had copied before leaving Ohrdruf.[24] Visits to Hamburg could have led to a desire to hear Buxtehude in person at Lübeck, as Bach would do a few years later. Böhm might have encouraged this interest, but although he must have provided Bach with exemplary keyboard pieces, he might not have been as helpful in the sphere of vocal music. Although he lived until 1733, Böhm seems never to have adopted the new type of Italianate sacred cantata that was starting to be composed in Germany at the turn of the century. Böhm's few surviving vocal works, although not as old-fashioned as those Bach would have heard at Eisenach and Ohrdruf, remain conservative—and as they are undated, whether they were even composed by the time of Bach's studies with him is unknown.

24 Wollny and Maul (2008, 70).

Also uncertain is what other vocal music Bach might have heard or performed at Lüneburg. Presumably this music was drawn from the library of St. Michael's School, whose extensive inventory constituted a cross-section of seventeenth-century German and Italian sacred music.[25] Much of this was relatively new, including works by living or recently deceased composers, such as the Leipzig cantor Johann Schelle and Joachim Gerstenbüttel, Telemann's predecessor at Hamburg. But this music remained old-fashioned, focusing on the correct presentation of texts in styles that went back to Schütz and Monteverdi, even Palestrina. Bach could have learned much about proper voice leading and text setting by singing or accompanying such compositions. But the Hamburg opera would have provided more up-to-date examples of vocal music, as well as exciting ideas about how one might write for an orchestra. Bach's first surviving vocal compositions, written a few years later, nevertheless remain close to older models. It could be that Bach, still a teenager being groomed as an organist, was not yet ready to expand his horizons. Even if he was aware that a new type of church music was being cultivated elsewhere in Germany, he might have had no access to its texts or music. To do so it was necessary to return to Thuringia and serve at one of the small courts where it was now being cultivated.

---

25 The inventory is preserved in Seiffert (1907–1908); the collection itself is lost.

CHAPTER FOUR

Arnstadt, Mühlhausen (1703–1708)

Arnstadt

IN AUGUST 1703 BACH WAS HIRED AS ONE OF THREE ORGANISTS AT Arnstadt, where he would stay for just under four years. Only twenty miles southwest of Weimar and even closer to Ohrdruf, Arnstadt was another small town, with a residence and a so-called New Church that really was relatively new—finished in 1683—as well as a brand-new organ.[1] The appointment, like the one at Sangerhausen that went to someone else, was approved by the local ruler, Count Anton Günther II of Schwarzburg-Sondershausen. It followed Bach's examination of the new instrument, by Johann Friedrich Wender, the previous month. Now, at eighteen, he was the master of a significant organ in a not insignificant town.

Bach's move from Weimar to Arnstadt was the first of several that raise a recurring question: was he more interested in a church job or a court position? The two were not necessarily distinct; during his brief stay at Weimar he probably played organ in the ducal chapel while holding a court appointment, and he surely participated in court music as organist at Arnstadt. But for someone already possessing a good sense of his own capabilities, plus a penchant for furthering the cause of true religion through music, the greater power and prestige perceived in a court job must have been irresistible. Many rulers in the region, including those of

---

1 "New" churches were common in northern Europe; the one in Arnstadt was more properly the Church of St. Boniface, now officially the "Bach Church."

Bach. David Schulenberg, Oxford University Press (2020). © Oxford University Press.
DOI: 10.1093/oso/9780190936303.001.0001

Weimar and the other Saxon duchies, viewed themselves as promoters of Christianity, even writing philosophical tracts and poetry on the subject. Yet Bach left the court of Weimar to become organist in the third-ranked church of Arnstadt, the residence of only a minor ruler who was, however, a collector and patron of the arts. The count, who had previously sought to replace one Bach with another,[2] is likely to have seen to it that Sebastian, although organist at the junior New Church, enjoyed better pay and lighter duties than the two other organists in town. Unlike them, Bach had no official duties at court. On the other hand, the New Church was the largest of the city's three, and there Bach might have played regularly for as many as several thousand congregants.

Bach's four years at Arnstadt were probably pivotal in the development of his mastery of the organ, perhaps leaving him already the greatest living performer on the instrument. That, plus a very rapid evolution of his ability to write for it, would have been his chief musical accomplishment of the period, overshadowing the possible composition of a few vocal works. Unfortunately we know little more about Bach's musical development at Arnstadt than we do about his earlier training and experience. There is not a single composition to which a specific date during the Arnstadt period can be securely attached. Therefore we cannot say how, or how far, Bach progressed musically between 1703 and 1707—despite assertions in the voluminous Bach literature about the chronology of his surviving music. Even biographical data remain sparse. These years evidently did see at least three critical events. One must have been his engagement to the woman who would bear seven children, two of them major musical figures in their own right. Another was an extended journey to Lübeck, home of Buxtehude, the leading German composer of the day. A third, less auspicious, was a protracted conflict with the Arnstadt church administration, the first

---

2 Bach's stepmother reported that Count Anton Günther had asked her if the family could supply a replacement after the death of Johann Christoph Bach (Ambrosius's brother) in 1693; at that time she wrote, strangely, that "God had caused the musical Bach family to run dry during the last few years" (*der liebe Gott das Bachische musicalische Geschlecht binnen wenig Jahren vertrocknet*, BD 2:5 [no. 3]; NBR, 33 [no. 7]). This was a play on the word *Bach*, meaning "stream." Daughter of an Arnstadt burgomaster and twice widow of members of the Bach family, Barbara Margaretha was not an unlikely source of musical advice for the count.

of several instances in which Bach found himself seriously at odds with his superiors.

Bach's appointment followed his examination the previous month of the newly finished Wender organ, a task for which he was selected over the two organists already in town. Although it may not have been unusual for youthful players to serve as organ inspectors,[3] the "examination" of the organ might have been essentially a recital that demonstrated Bach's already recognized prowess at the instrument.[4] No formal audition for the position as organist seems to have taken place, perhaps because the count had already resolved to hire him. Bach's contract includes the customary instruction that he was not to give unauthorized persons access to the instrument. It did not, however, direct him to follow the family tradition of composing, which went back at Arnstadt to his great-uncle Heinrich and the latter's sons Johann Christoph and Johann Michael. Composing might, however, have been one of several things expected of Bach that were not mentioned in the document. Another, clearly, was that he would direct performances of music for vocal and instrumental ensembles. His having to do so would have justified his high salary, which surpassed that of his predecessor Börner—who now continued as organist at one of the two other churches, with reduced pay and more extensive responsibilities. Bach's failure to fulfill everything expected of him was a probable cause of the difficulties in which he found himself two years after his arrival.

These were set off by a confrontation between Bach and an older student named Johann Heinrich Geyersbach. This led to the first in a series of complaints, recorded in the minutes of meetings of the church board (consistory). They were:

> he insulted the bassoonist Geyersbach (August 4, 1705)

> he did not perform ensemble music with the students (August 19, 1705; again February 21 and November 11, 1706)

3 Williams (2016, 59) mentions a "report on" the organ at Ohrdruf made by Sebastian's brother Christoph at the time of his appointment there at nineteen (see Schulze 1985a, 69). This, however, was apparently not a full-scale organ "test" (*Probe*).

4 The same word *Probe* was used for both organ examinations and organist auditions. The document that records Bach's payment for the inspection mentions that he was to "test and play the new organ for the first time" (*die newe Orgel probiren und zum ersten mahl schlagen*, BD 2:10 [no. 7]; NBR, 41 [no. 15]).

he stayed away at Lübeck for too long (before February 21, 1706)

he played chorales with "strange embellishments [*wunderliche variationes*]" in "odd keys [*Thone*]," confusing the congregation (February 21, 1706)

he played (chorale preludes?) either too long or too short (February 21, 1706)

he allowed a woman to perform music in the choir gallery (November 11, 1706).[5]

Individually, each of these things might seem trivial. Together they suggest significant tension on both sides. Bach nevertheless remained in his position until making his own decision to leave, in 1707. However serious his transgressions, they were insufficient to lead to more than a reprimand. With the count, the church superintendent Olearius, and perhaps the burgomaster all on his side, the consistory might have been unable to do more.

We have no information about how much time Bach spent in Lübeck itself or what he did there, although having left Arnstadt during fall 1705 he seems not to have returned until after the Christmas season. He had already had some exposure to Buxtehude's music, as we know from at least one early manuscript copy in his hand. Later copies of Buxtehude's organ music owned by Christoph Bach were not necessarily made from manuscripts that Sebastian brought back to Arnstadt in 1706—but surely some were. Buxtehude is now known chiefly for his organ compositions, but he is equally important for his vocal music. Bach's journey took place at a time of year when a visitor could have heard Buxtehude's famous Vespers concerts (*Abendmusiken*) during the Advent season.[6] In 1705 these took the form of two "extraordinary" concerts occasioned by the installation of a new emperor in Vienna. Lübeck, like Hamburg, was essentially independent, but as another free imperial city it saw splendid concerts honoring the late emperor Leopold I and his successor Joseph I. Bach is presumed to have been present for these, and it is hard to believe that he did not also take the opportunity to play for Buxtehude and make copies of as much

---

5 Extracted from BD 2:15–21 (nos. 14, 16, and 17); NBR, 43–48 (nos. 19–21).

6 These performances were widely known during Bach's time, as a contemporary guidebook to the city makes clear (Snyder 2007, 54).

of the latter's music as he could. However significant Bach's previous encounters with Böhm and Reinken might have been, that Buxtehude exerted a decisive influence—not to mention inspiration—seems clear in Bach's music of the next few years.

It is possible that Bach's interest in traveling to Lübeck went beyond merely hearing or learning from Buxtehude. Buxtehude was approaching seventy at the time of Bach's visit, and the prospect of succeeding him must have crossed the young virtuoso's mind. When Buxtehude indeed died less than two years later, however, his place was taken by a very minor figure, Johann Christian Schieferdecker, who married Buxtehude's daughter Anna Margreta. It was not uncommon for apprentices to marry masters' daughters before inheriting their businesses; Buxtehude had married the daughter of his predecessor Tunder. Whether marriage to Anna Margreta was a formal prerequisite for taking the job, and whether Bach, like Handel and Mattheson before him, lost interest in the position for this reason, is unknown.[7] At the time of his visit, Bach, unlike Handel, Mattheson, and Schieferdecker, had composed no major vocal works, so far as is known. He therefore might not have been considered qualified; he might, too, already have had his eye on Maria Barbara back in Arnstadt.

The remaining complaints that Bach had to face upon his return relate more directly to how he carried out his duties as organist. Despite the consistory's imprecise use of musical terminology, there can be no doubt that some members objected to Bach's unconventional harmonizations and lengthy improvisations on chorale melodies. Bach responded to criticism by cutting his playing short: "The organist Bach had played rather too long, but after the superintendent brought this to his attention he immediately fell into the other extreme and made it too short."[8] Who the *frembde Jungfer* was that he admitted to the choir or organ loft to "make music" (*musicieren*) is unknown, nor are the German expressions transparent. The first has been translated as both "out-of-town singer"

---

7 Mattheson (1740, 94), in a biographical sketch of Handel, reported that he and Handel had traveled to Lübeck together from Hamburg but neither "had the slightest inclination" (*die geringste Lust bezeigte*) to take the position after learning of the "marriage requirement" (*Heiraths-Bedingung*).

8 BD 2:20 (no. 16); NBR, 46 (no. 20).

and "unauthorized [maiden]";[9] the second could refer to her playing or her singing together with other musicians. The girl could have been Maria Barbara Bach,[10] who, although not known to have been a musician, was the daughter and mother of composers and doubtless had some musical training. Whether Sebastian subsequently employed any female singers in church music is not recorded, but during his lifetime women did begin to participate in church music in some German localities. His second wife certainly performed with him, possibly even in church (but not at Leipzig).[11]

The woman who would become Bach's first wife, his second cousin Maria Barbara, was five months older than he (born October 20, 1684), just as his mother had been somewhat older than his father. An orphan like Sebastian, she was the daughter of Johann Michael Bach, whom Sebastian described as "able" (*habil*) in the family genealogy. This was upgraded by Michael's grandson Emanuel to "honest" or "strong" (*braf*), a term Emanuel tended to apply to musicians as a favorite if vague term of approbation.[12] Sebastian's original adjective might have been intended to distinguish the somewhat unimaginative Michael from his "profound" brother Johann Christoph, the Eisenach organist. But Sebastian's first wife was nevertheless the daughter of a significant musician and a member of a somewhat more prestigious branch of the family than his own. Her connections through birth and marriage included not only city officials in Arnstadt but the village pastor who married them at nearby Dornheim. The wedding took place on October 17, 1707; a month earlier,

---

9 Wolff (2000, 88) and Williams (2016, 64), respectively. Williams notes that Pachelbel's contract as organist at Erfurt used the same word (*Frembder*) to mean someone not authorized to be in the organ loft.

10 As first suggested by Spitta (1873–1880, 1:325), who assumes that the woman sang for some private purpose, not a church service.

11 Anna Magdalena evidently sang in the funeral music *(Trauer Music)* for Prince Leopold of Cöthen; see BD 2:190–91 (no. 259); NBR, 139 (no. 139). This raises the possibility of earlier performances during Leopold's lifetime; as a Calvinist he would not have been expected to patronize elaborate church music such as Bach's, but on this and perhaps other matters he may have bent the rules. Wolff (2000, 88) reports that women might serve as choral *Adjuvanten*, but not in churches with Latin school choirs, which presumably included Arnstadt's New Church.

12 See, for example, Emanuel's remark that "Hamburg is no place for a *braver Musicus*" (letter of December 9, 1769, to Georg Kottowsky, in Suchalla 1994, 1:188 [no. 80]).

Bach had unexpectedly received an inheritance from Tobias Lämmerhirt, his mother's well-off brother, which amounted to more than half a year's salary at Arnstadt.[13]

Mühlhausen

By the time of his marriage, Bach had moved on to the free imperial city of Mühlhausen, where he began serving as organist of St. Blasius's Church on July 1, 1707. Mühlhausen was a major city with no fewer than thirteen churches, of which St. Blasius was the largest. Although he would spend only a single year there, it is from Mühlhausen that we finally have his first precisely dated composition—Cantata 71, written for the city council installation ceremony of February 4, 1708. Together with at least two other major vocal works that also appear to have been composed at Mühlhausen (Cantatas 131 and 150), this serves as an indispensable guidepost indicating how far Bach had come by this point as a composer. We lack similar guideposts for the far more numerous keyboard works that Bach must have been writing during these years. But by the time he left Arnstadt, still in his twenty-second year, he was surely well on the way to becoming the great composer for organ and harpsichord that we know from works composed during the next decade.

As at Arnstadt, Bach's appointment at Mühlhausen is likely to have been facilitated by family connections. Johann Herrmann Bellstedt, the town secretary who proposed Bach's name and then negotiated his appointment with him, was related by marriage to both Maria Barbara and her Arnstadt host the burgomaster Martin Feldhaus. Moreover the organ builder Wender, whose instrument Bach had approved and used daily at Arnstadt, lived in Mühlhausen and might have recommended Bach; Bach would recommend Wender's further expansion of the organ at St. Blasius to the city council before his departure.[14]

Bach's audition took place at Mühlhausen on Easter Sunday 1707—another major feast day when he was absent from Arnstadt—and he

---

13 Bach inherited 50 Taler; his salary at Arnstadt was 50 florins (43.75 Taler), to which were added 30 Taler for room and board (BD 2:12 [no. 8]; NBR, 41 [no. 16]).

14 BD 1:152–55 (no. 83, including commentary); NBR, 55–56 (nos. 30–31). Information on this and other organs with which Bach was associated is gathered in Wolff and Zepf (2012).

appeared before the Arnstadt consistory at the end of June to request his dismissal and return the organ key.[15] He was succeeded at Arnstadt by his cousin Johann Ernst, a native of that city. His appointment letter at Mühlhausen was again rather casual in enumerating his responsibilities, failing to specify, for instance, that the organist of St. Blasius's traditionally provided music for the annual installation of the city council (*Ratswechsel*)—which nevertheless took place at the other main church, St. Mary's. Taking the form of a special church service, the annual council installation was an occasion for which Bach would regularly provide music at Leipzig, producing what are known as his council election cantatas (*Ratswahlkantaten*). Only at Mühlhausen, however, was Bach's contribution for this event printed, leaving us the sole example of any of his cantatas to be published during his lifetime; the sumptuous print, proudly issued by the city council, closely mirrors Bach's meticulously notated manuscript score (4.1a–b and 4.2).

Bach's contract also failed to mention that the organist of St. Blasius participated in services on weekdays at several other churches in the city.[16] One of these, the so-called Brückenhof church, also had a new organ by Wender, albeit a small one with just one manual and a single pedal rank.[17] Bach must also have played and perhaps composed music for surrounding towns, as his letter of resignation indicates knowledge of music making outside Mühlhausen. All in all, his weekly responsibilities were greater than at Arnstadt, but his pay was considerably better. As Mühlhausen was a larger city than Arnstadt, it also offered more opportunities for private employment, chiefly weddings and funerals. Bach nevertheless would leave after barely more than a year for a second and much more substantial court appointment at Weimar.

Bach's letter of resignation from Mühlhausen is the earliest surviving document of a personal nature in his own hand. It is famous for twice referring to what the most commonly cited English translation calls his

15 BD 2:24–25 (no. 21) and 2:26–27 (no. 25), in NBR, 50–51 (nos. 23–24).

16 Thus Bach played at four smaller churches in the city on a rotating basis, in alternation with the organist of St. Mary's; details in Wolff (2000, 107).

17 Wolff and Zepf (2012, 74). This church was attached to a girls' school in the old Augustinian convent.

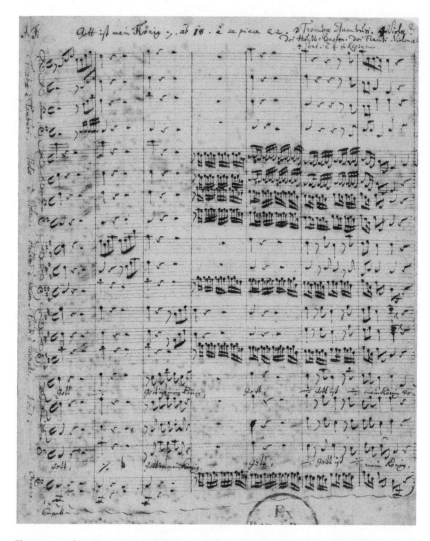

Figure 4.1 *Gott ist mein König*, BWV 71, autograph manuscript, Berlin, Staatsbibliothek, Mus. ms. Bach P 45, fascicle 1: first page of music. The pious "J. J." in the upper left corner (*Jesu juva*, Help me, Jesus) was a common indication. From Bach-Digital.

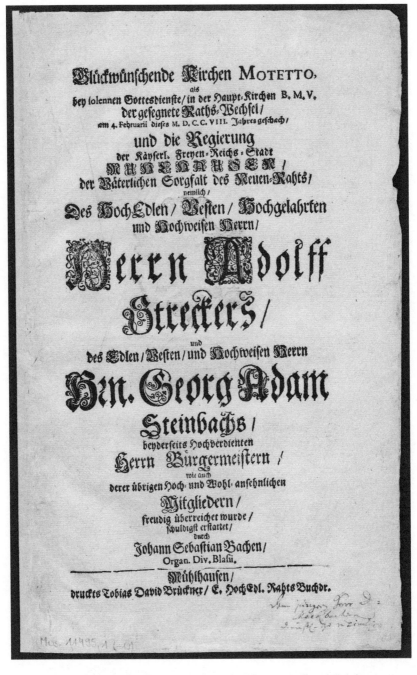

Figure 4.2 Bach's first printed work: title page of BWV 71, grandly naming the
Mühlhausen city council members whom it honored. Bach's name appears toward the
bottom; his autograph handwritten addition in the lower right corner names "the younger
Mr. Meckbach," that is, Paul Friedemann Meckbach, later godfather of W. F. Bach, who
presumably received a copy. Berlin, Staatsbibliothek, Mus. 11495, from Bach-Digital.

"goal of a well-regulated church music."[18] This makes it seem as if Bach, at twenty-three, had already adopted as his life's end the systematic creation of those cantatas and other sacred compositions for which he is now famous. But the quoted phrase does not appear in the German, which refers more mundanely to "well-ordered church music" and "the due ordering of church music."[19] Exactly what these phrases meant is unclear; one possibility is that here the word *Music* stood for something like "available musicians," that is, a roster of capable performers on which Bach could draw as needed for a given performance.[20] As further justification for his departure, Bach contrasts the prospect of higher pay at Weimar with the poor living he can afford at Mühlhausen due to rent and other costs. Those sympathetic to Bach must have understood that what he called the "unanticipated" (*unvermuthet*) summons back to Weimar, to become organist and chamber musician to the ruling Duke Wilhelm Ernst, was irresistible.

18 NBR, 57 (no. 32).

19 From the English translation of Spitta (1873–80), 1:373–74; the German reads "eine regulirte kirchen music" and "die wohlzufaßende kirchenmusic" (BD 1:19–20 [no. 1]).

20 As argued by Rifkin (2002, 16–17).

CHAPTER FIVE

Bach the Organist

EARLY KEYBOARD AND VOCAL WORKS

URING HIS LIFETIME AND FOR AT LEAST HALF A CENTURY AFTER-
ward, Bach was known primarily as an organist. He served officially
in that capacity only from 1703 to 1714, at Arnstadt and Mühlhausen and
then at Weimar during the first part of his tenure there. Yet he performed
throughout his professional career in organ recitals and examinations,
and some of his organ compositions must have been written for such
occasions. He also regularly composed pieces for teaching or private performance that arc playable on harpsichord or clavichord as well as organ.
Hence keyboard pieces are the one category of compositions that he
produced throughout his life, and it could be argued that they are the
most important part of his output, if one part must be so designated.[1]

We lack original composing manuscripts for most of this music, and
most of the surviving compositions were revised, often several times.
Bach's penchant for reworking older music seemed remarkable enough
that Forkel, his first biographer, devoted an entire chapter to it; it involved above all his keyboard works, if only because of their quantity.
They were the part of his output that Bach regularly made available to
students and fellow musicians through manuscript copies and, eventually, printed editions. By the time he left Weimar, and perhaps already

---

1 This is the view of Williams (2016, esp. ix), and it may have been Bach's during his final
decade, when he focused his attention on Part 2 of the *Well-Tempered Clavier*, the *Art of
Fugue*, and other sets of keyboard compositions.

Bach. David Schulenberg, Oxford University Press (2020). © Oxford University Press.
DOI: 10.1093/oso/9780190936303.001.0001

when he arrived there, it seems to have been his practice to make sure that any piece that he was prepared to disseminate was not only flawless from a technical point of view but also as up-to-date in style as possible. Early works were either discarded or updated, sometimes radically, so that pieces from an early period do not necessarily retain their original form or style. Unfortunately, this, together with the loss or destruction of Bach's composing scores, makes it impossible to achieve anything more than a rough idea of when individual pieces were first written or how the style of his keyboard music developed.

The same is less true of Bach's vocal music, of which we have a handful of works from his first years as a professional, especially at Mühlhausen. These compositions mark crucial points in Bach's development and are performed today with some frequency. Hence vocal music must occupy part of this chapter on Bach "the organist," even as discussion of his most important keyboard works is reserved for later chapters. Indeed, most of Bach's better-known organ compositions reached their familiar forms only after his promotion to concertmaster at Weimar in 1714. Yet his most intense involvement with the organ must have taken place before that, when he could devote himself to mastering techniques of keyboard performance and composition.

The duties of organists in Lutheran Germany during this period are enumerated in contracts such as Pachelbel's at Erfurt. There "preluding" (*praeambulandus*) on chorales is followed by maintaining and tuning the instrument, plus submission to authority and the like.[2] At Erfurt an annual recital was expected as well; Bach was never explicitly required to do this, but he might have felt bound to give public organ concerts if professionals elsewhere were doing it. Of course, in a court chapel such as Weimar's the organist would have played whenever and whatever the ruler ordered. Organists were not expected to have advanced academic training (like cantors). Yet it was understood that their profession required both musical insight, including knowledge of counterpoint and the hymn repertory, and some understanding of organ construction and tuning systems. This was, of course, in addition to a level of playing ability

---

2 The most comprehensive discussion of the duties and practices of Lutheran organists during Bach's day remains that in Williams (1980–84, 3:32–55); this matter is absent from the second edition (Williams 2003).

that had to be at least comparable to that of their fellow musicians in a given city or court.

The order of service, including how the organ was used, varied from one church to another, although all Lutheran practices ultimately went back to those formalized by Luther himself in the sixteenth century.[3] The main Sunday service at each of the four churches in Arnstadt, including the chapel of the ruling count, incorporated congregational chorales as well as the traditional Ordinary of the mass (Kyrie, Gloria, etc.). These might be sung by a *chorus musicus*, probably a small ensemble drawn from students at the local lyceum and directed by the cantor Heindorff. It was also possible to have polyphonic ("figural" or "concerted") music just before the sermon. This corresponded to what we call the cantata, and although heard regularly only at the court chapel and the so-called Upper Church, figural music might have been something Bach was expected to provide occasionally.

The repertory favored at court might have included motets and "arias" for small mixed ensembles of voices and instruments, such as were composed by older members of the Bach family and preserved in the Old Bach Archive.[4] But even these compositions, mostly rather modest in scope and in their demands on the performers, might have been beyond the resources of the city churches. Music at the latter may normally have involved nothing even as complicated as the *a cappella* motets published in 1698 by the local court composer Nicholaus Niedt.[5] Perhaps the court also heard the somewhat more sophisticated but still old-fashioned type of music found in two volumes of strophic arias by Philipp Heinrich Erlebach, published in 1697 and 1710; the first was dedicated to two members of the ruling house of Schwarzburg.

---

3 Wolff (2000, 82) gives a table summarizing practices in the Arnstadt churches; Williams (1980–84, 3:2–7) provides sample orders of service from other Lutheran cities that Bach knew, and Leaver (2010, 156–57) offers a summary of the Leipzig liturgy.

4 Once thought to have been personally collected by J. S. Bach, this collection of twenty works (or at least a portion of it) was apparently assembled by the Arnstadt cantor Heindorff (see Wollny 2002, 43–44).

5 Seen here were the five pieces attributed to Niedt in *Denkmäler deutscher Tonkunst*, Vol. 15 (1915). *A cappella* in this context indicates the absence of any instrumental accompaniment other than basso continuo, the voices being joined by organ and possibly doubled (or individual parts replaced) by string or wind instruments.

Bach's refusal to perform even simple concerted music in church could have reflected both a lack of capable singers and his understanding that he was required only to "arrange" for the singing of chorales by the congregation.[6] It suggests, moreover, that at this stage in his career he saw his unofficial work for the court as more important than that in church. Even the latter, however, would probably not have required him to train a choir of schoolboys, for the modern conflation of church organist with choir director was not yet typical. Vocal polyphony would more likely have been sung by a small body of soloists or "concertists," training of the boys as a group (for leading chorales) being the province of the cantor.[7] Still, the available soloists might have been simply inadequate for any music that Bach wished to perform. He may also have desired assistance in handling the logistical problems of assembling music and organizing rehearsals while shuttling between his responsibilities in the various churches in town. The same would later be a concern at Leipzig, but there Bach could delegate many duties to prefects (student assistants).

Rarely if ever do documents call specifically for the preludes and fugues now typically played on the organ before and after services, although these might have been considered appropriate for the "preluding" or "intonations" that took place at certain points during worship. Nor is it always clear whether organists accompanied congregational hymn singing, as in modern services. During Bach's lifetime, many localities seem to have maintained older *alternatim* practices, in which the organist might first play the chorale alone—thereby setting the pitch and reminding parishioners of the melody—followed by, or alternating with, unaccompanied congregational singing.[8] Most church hymnals during Bach's day

6 As noted by Leaver and Remeš (2018, 138), citing BD 2:17 (no. 14), trans. in NBR, 45 (no. 19c). The verb *bestellen* in this context perhaps referred to the organist's improvised setting forth of each hymn melody prior to its singing by the congregation.

7 For one-on-a-part performance of vocal parts in German Baroque "concerted" music, see Rifkin (1982), elaborated in Rifkin (2002) and affirmed by Parrott (2000) and Melamed (2005, esp. Chapter 1). Although one continues to see arguments to the contrary, there is simply no evidence that church works such as Bach's cantatas were sung during his lifetime by more than two voices to a part, usually only one. How one chooses to perform this music today is, of course, a different matter.

8 On this issue see especially Leaver (2010, 157–58), who shows that it remains uncertain whether the organ accompanied congregational singing at Leipzig, although "organ chorale

still gave only the words, not the music. Printed collections of chorale melodies with harmonizations were becoming more common, however, and Bach, like Schütz and other composers before him, contributed to these, but unlike modern hymnals they were not meant for congregational use in church. If organists owned copies of such works, these might have been manuscript copies, perhaps more for study and teaching than everyday practical use, for which memory and improvisation probably served.

The boy choristers who led the congregation in the hymns did not necessarily include the soloists who performed in any figural vocal music also heard during a service. The contract offered to Bach at Halle in 1713 required his participation in the latter type of music, which the organist had to "exhibit" and "direct."[9] But surely the organist in such a large town did not also have to provide elementary training for the boys, a responsibility rather of the cantor. Directing the ensemble of solo voices and instruments that performed polyphony would have involved not a conductor in the modern sense but a cooperative effort between a leading singer or violinist and the keyboard player. As in other types of ensembles, the latter probably communicated with fellow musicians as much by aural cues—how the basso continuo was realized, the strategic rhythmic placement of chords and the like—as visual ones.

This serves as a reminder that the organist's musical duties consisted largely of improvising elaborations of single lines: the melody in chorales, the figured basso continuo in polyphony. Hence, even more than for other Baroque musicians, an organist's daily routine comprised unwritten music making. For this reason, it cannot be assumed that Bach's surviving keyboard music corresponds with what he actually played in church. Auditions for organ jobs often required improvising on a given chorale melody or fugue subject. Many of Bach's keyboard pieces therefore may represent ideal improvisations that served as models for real ones.

accompaniments were common elsewhere." It remains debatable whether the so-called Arnstadt organ chorales (such as BWV 715) were "accompaniments for congregational singing," also whether the words *einschlagen* and *spielen* in instructions for organists with regard to chorales should be translated as "accompany" (as assumed in Leaver 2016, 28).

9 BD 2:50 (no. 63); the words are *exhibiren* and *dirigiren*, the latter anachronistically translated as "conduct" in NBR, 67 (no. 48).

Other works, especially the early ones considered in this chapter, might have been self-imposed exercises in composition and organ playing. As much is suggested by the title of the Little Organ Book (*Orgelbüchlein*), compiled at Weimar but incorporating revised versions of at least a few earlier pieces. When, around 1722, Bach added a long descriptive title to the manuscript, he might have remembered his reasons for first writing these pieces, "in which a beginning organist receives instruction in all sorts of ways of developing a chorale, as well as in gaining fluency in the study of the pedal."[10]

For Bach, "all sorts of ways" was not a figure of speech. It meant literally working out chorale melodies through all the traditional devices found in compositions by Pachelbel, Buxtehude, and other predecessors, as well as inventing new ones, including various types of canons. As for "study of the pedal"—the latter word being short for "pedalboard"—this too must have been something to which Bach devoted himself with unprecedented zeal in order to "treat the pedals in an entirely independent manner."[11] The results include some maddening exercises that train the player to free the left hand completely from its traditional role of playing the bass line—that is, to use the pedals as more than an optional complement or reinforcement of the left hand.[12] On the other hand, some early works, including certain ones printed on three staves in modern editions, are either entirely playable on manuals alone or use the pedals only intermittently. Such pieces are not necessarily any earlier than true *pedaliter* works, for throughout his life Bach also wrote purely *manualiter* pieces for organ. But the distinction between the two types is not always clear in his early organ compositions or in those of his predecessors.

---

10 "Worinne einem anfahenden Organisten Anleitung gegeben wird, auff allerhand Arth einen Choral durchzuführen, anbey auch sich im Pedal studio zu habiliteren . . ." (BD 1:214 [no. 148]; NBR, 80 [no. 69]).

11 ". . . das Pedal gantz obligat tractiret wird" (this is a continuation of the same title cited in the previous note).

12 See, for example, the use of double pedal throughout BWV 653b (the early version of BWV 653) or the systematic use of contrary motion between tenor (left hand) and bass (pedals) in the fugue of BWV 550.

Instruments and Organ "Tests"

In many German towns the organ must have been the single most expensive and technologically advanced piece of equipment owned by the municipality—hence the considerable attention paid by governing councils to its design, upkeep, and responsible personnel. To advise those entrusted with decisions about them, organs were subjects of serious scholarly publications (notably those of Andreas Werckmeister and Jacob Adlung) long before other instruments received comparable treatment. Towns competed with one another to have a prestigious player and instrument, and, in an environment unpolluted by motorized traffic noise and other sounds, the organ must—with the possible exception of church bells—have been one of the loudest things in the city, echoing beyond the city walls. Within the church building, the sound of the instrument would have been experienced physically, like the amplified music of a modern rock concert.

The organ of the New Church at Arnstadt was of moderate size (twenty-one ranks), with two keyboards and pedals. Although "plain" by one account and typical of the organs that Pachelbel and his pupils knew,[13] it evidently had a high pitch level and an up-to-date "well-tempered" tuning.[14] One might have expected the latter, as J. P. Treiber, son of the rector of the town's Lyceum, had demonstrated the harmonization of chorales in multiple keys in a manual on organ playing published the year after Bach's arrival.[15] The town's older "upper church" (*Oberkirche*) had an older organ of comparable size. Both instruments were rebuilt during the twentieth century, and only the one at the New Church incorporates any

---

13 Williams (1980, 112–13). The best critical discussion of organs known to Bach remains that of Williams (1980–84, 3:117–38), even if some of the information has become dated.

14 *Wohltemperiert* does not necessarily refer to equal temperament, but it does imply the capability of playing in all keys, as already required by early works such as BWV 729a (first cadence to C-sharp minor) and BWV 566 (in the E-major version). The pitch of the Arnstadt organ is reported to have been a′ = 465 Hz (Wolff and Zepf 2012, 10), a whole step or more above the chamber pitch of the time and substantially higher than modern concert pitch.

15 *Der accurate Organist*, published at Jena in 1704 but presumably written at Arnstadt; see Leaver and Remeš (2018, 132ff.). The focus on transposition in this and other treatises of the time suggests that organists were expected to give pitches for congregational singing of hymns at levels more comfortable than those in which the latter might have been customarily notated.

parts surviving from Bach's day. It is audible and visible through YouTube videos, although as with all such reconstructions it is difficult to judge how closely the present instrument resembles that which Bach knew. As important as the tone colors of the pipes is the touch of the keyboards as well as the wind system. Each of these originally involved materials and designs that could be quite different from those of later instruments, including twentieth-century imitations. For instance, the keys of the original pedalboard are relatively short and arranged in a straight line rather than a concave arch. The older arrangement discourages use of the heels, which became common only in the nineteenth century and facilitated the use of legato in bass lines.

The organ at St. Blasius's in Mühlhausen was larger than any of those at Arnstadt, even before its expansion by Wender. For its renovation Bach urged, among other things, the addition of an entire division (*Brustwerk*); together with individual stops added elsewhere, this expanded the range of available sonorities, including new string and reed timbres as well as a massive thirty-two-foot double-double bass. The latter was doubtless inspired by the corresponding stop on Reinken's instrument at Hamburg's Church of St. Catherine, which Bach later praised to his pupil Agricola.[16] From such evidence it seems that Bach even in his youth favored a powerful bass and colorful registrations, especially reeds—useful not only as solo stops for chorale melodies but also for a French-style reed chorus (*grand jeu*) in contrapuntal music. Nevertheless, his scores, like those of his contemporaries, rarely give clues to organ registration beyond indications for the use of multiple keyboards and occasionally of octave register $(4', 8')$.

The frequent calls on Bach to "test" organs have been taken as evidence for unusual expertise about their construction and maintenance. But how much detailed knowledge of organ building was required to write the types of recommendations authored or signed by Bach has been disputed.[17] Some "tests" (*Proben*) may have been little more than public recitals. Still, there can be no question that, having already experienced

16 As reported in one of Agricola's notes to Adlung (1768, 288); trans. in NBR, 364 (no. 358a).

17 Wolff (2000, 142) describes Bach as "an organ expert of the first rank," but Williams (2016, 96–98) is skeptical, arguing that Bach possessed little more than any good player's "basic knowledge."

many fine instruments across northern and central Germany, by the time he left Arnstadt Bach had clear ideas of how a large organ should sound. Perhaps even more important from a player's point of view, he also understand what a good instrument should be like to play in terms of touch and responsiveness. This is evident from his report to the Mühlhausen parish council and at least three further organ evaluations signed or co-signed by Bach over the course of his career.[18] Further organ examinations are documented by records of the fees, sometimes substantial, that Bach received for visits that must have been anxiously anticipated and long remembered.[19] That many more trips and organ "tests" took place than are recorded is suggested by hints of further journeys in other types of surviving documents.[20] Among these is Forkel's biography, which although very late must reflect persistent memories of Bach's "severe, but always just" appraisals of many organs—which "seldom added to the number of his friends."[21]

Forkel also gives us an idea of what Bach played on such occasions: first a prelude and fugue for the "full organ," then smaller pieces, all improvised on a given subject; after that, improvisations on a chorale that allowed him to demonstrate not only individual stops but varied combinations of the same. Forkel, relying on reminiscences of those who had been there, hinted that Bach's sometimes unconventional registrations, like his use of full-voiced harmony on the *organum plenum*, could make builders nervous.[22] This information came from Emanuel Bach, who wrote that his father would begin a test by determining "whether the organ has good lungs," then playing in a full texture on "every speaking stop," which would often cause the builder to "grow quite pale with fright."[23] Any advice that Bach would draw from such a test was obviously important for

---

18 These are gathered in BD 2:152–74 (nos. 83–90) and translated in NBR (nos. 59, 72, 235, 236). Not all of these are comprehensive reports; one is lost.

19 As when he received 50 Taler (half his base salary at Leipzig) for a *Probe* at Kassel in 1732 (BD 2:227, 228 [nos. 316, 318]; NBR, 155 [nos. 157–58]).

20 As in the "Fleckeisen" letter (see Maul 2017, esp. 47). Wolff (2000, 143) lists twenty-one "organ projects and examinations" from 1703 to 1748.

21 Forkel (1802, 22), trans. in NBR, 440.

22 Forkel (1802, 20), trans. in NBR, 438–39.

23 Letter to Forkel of 1774 (?), BD 3:284–85 (no. 801), trans. in NBR, 396 (no. 394).

advising the officials who commissioned costly instruments, but there was more to such an inspection than simply playing and evaluating the organ. A visiting player who was also a famous member of a high-ranking court or who held a senior position in another major city would have enjoyed some celebrity status. His visit would have reflected positively not only on the community that invited him but also on the prince or city that granted him leave to go. A ruler could see this as a magnanimous act of charity both to his employee, who would earn a nice fee, and to society at large—part of the program of education and social better-ment that some aristocrats seem to have taken seriously at the time. The organist would enjoy not only his honorarium but relatively luxurious accommodation for a few days (both are documented in account books), while enhancing his reputation and perhaps making contacts for future teaching or sales of music.

For the organist there were also potential risks. It went without saying that the inspector had to examine the terms of the contract carefully and guarantee that its provisions had been fulfilled by the builder (including use of specified types of wood and metal for pipes and other parts). But those who hired him were also seeking ratification of their decisions about the size and nature of the instrument, their choice of builder, and the amount they had agreed to pay for it. It could be awkward to have to inform them that they had made mistakes, especially if they were po-tential future employers—as was the case for Bach when he evaluated organs at Arnstadt, Leipzig, and Halle. The builders, meanwhile, were quasi-colleagues of the player, who needed to work with them to main-tain or improve other instruments. Organ building involved investment in valuable wood and metal, not to mention months or years of work onsite, sometimes far from home. Like other contractors, instrument makers needed to weigh their own costs against potential gains and risks when negotiating prices; a negative assessment of the product, requiring additional work for no gain, could ruin them.

When Bach wrote in 1746 that the organ by Hildebrandt at Naumburg required additional voicing and regulation of its action,[24] he probably un-derstood that these were relatively minor problems that could be solved

---

24 BD 1:170–71 (no. 90), trans. in NBR, 222 (no. 236).

without the replacement of parts or other major expense of labor or material by the builder. Some criticisms of this nature might have been expected if a report was to be credible—especially if the town council knew that Bach's co-examiner Silbermann had taught Hildebrandt, with whom Bach too had done business.[25] On the other hand, when Bach mentioned in 1717 that certain pipes on the new Leipzig organ by Scheibe were speaking "coarsely and noisily," also describing further problems of voicing and keyboard touch,[26] this probably required the maker Scheibe to do more extra work than the latter had hoped to do. Such observations might have instigated the criticism that Bach's music would later receive from Scheibe's son. In the same report, however, Bach also mentioned problems with the design of the organ. These had been forced on the builder by the location within the church stipulated for it. In mentioning this, Bach implicitly criticized the contracting authorities while excusing the builder. This was doubtless the sort of thing that led Forkel to speak of Bach's "justice to organ builders."[27]

We know less about Bach's views on harpsichords and other stringed keyboard instruments. These cost far less than the smallest organ and were never subjects of detailed court or municipal documents. Bach's brother Christoph evidently owned a special type of clavichord or harpsichord, perhaps one with a so-called short octave, and in 1719 Sebastian brought a new double-manual harpsichord by Michael Mietke to Cöthen from Berlin. It was probably similar to one on which he might have performed the Fifth Brandenburg Concerto at Berlin—but we know nothing more about either instrument.[28] Although Bach's sons, like Bach himself at Cöthen, worked as players of stringed keyboard instruments, for most of

25 One of Bach's lute-harpsichords was by Hildebrandt, according to Agricola (in Adlung 1768, 139; trans. in NBR, 366 [no. 358e]).

26 *graß und blatterend*, BD 1:164 (no. 87), trans. in NBR, 84 (no. 72). Bach also complained about the instrument's heavy touch (*Tractirung*), although he seemed unsure whether anything could be done about this, "on account of the too close construction" (*zu engen Structur*).

27 *Geregtigkeit gegen die Orgelbauer* (Forkel 1802, 23; trans. in NBR, 441).

28 Regarding Christoph's "Italian keyboard" (*Man. Italiana*, used in BWV 989), see Schulenberg (2006, 94); on the harpsichord owned by Christian Ludwig of Brandenburg, see Oleskiewicz (2011, 109). Bach's payment for a Mietke instrument was recorded at Cöthen in March 1719 (BD 2:73 [no. 95]; NBR, 87 [no. 77]).

his life he might have regarded such instruments as serving chiefly for training organists or practicing organ music. At his death Bach owned at least eight stringed keyboard instruments,[29] but how long these had been in his possession and what he owned earlier in life are impossible to say. Forkel reported that Bach "liked best to play upon the clavichord," but this could not have been true "in his younger years."[30] Then he would have had to play on the small, so-called fretted (*gebunden*) type of clavichord, which was unsuitable for music outside a narrow range of keys. Rather, Forkel probably had in mind a large "double clavichord with pedal" such as Bach apparently owned at his death, used by organists for practice at home. Forkel mentions this as well as the double harpsichord with pedals as something that Bach used for playing contrapuntal pieces.

Forkel also attests to Bach's ability to tune and maintain stringed keyboard instruments, for which he was in fact paid at Weimar.[31] Presumably he had been trained to do this as a boy, although it cannot be assumed that his father or older brother owned anything more expensive than a fretted clavichord. Even that is undocumented,[32] but until Bach had a permanent position at Arnstadt he is unlikely to have practiced regularly on anything more sophisticated. On the other hand, his experience as a court musician from 1703 onward must have given him at least occasional opportunities to play fine harpsichords. His own first harpsichord probably resembled the unpretentious single-manual example now in the Eisenach Bach Museum. This has been described as producing "a comparatively loud but rapidly decaying tone with a full, fundamental

29 His estate included five harpsichords (*clavecins*) and two lute-harpsichords (*Lautenwerke*), listed in BD 2:492 (no. 627); NBR, 251–52 (no. 279). In addition, there was a composite instrument comprising three clavichords (two manuals and pedal) that went directly to the youngest son, Johann Christian Bach, although only after some disagreement between the survivors (see BD 2:501 [no. 628], trans. in Speerstra 2004, 25).

30 "Am liebsten spielte er auf dem Clavichord" (Forkel 1802, 17 and 14; trans. in NBR, 436 and 433).

31 BD 2:41 (no. 49); NBR, 60 (no. 37). Exactly what was meant by *zurecht zumachen* and *anrichten* or on what type of *Clavicymbel* he performed those repairs or maintenance is unknown.

32 We have no records of instruments owned by Ambrosius Bach or Christoph Bach (Sebastian's brother). Only once does a *Clavier* appear in the lists given by Schulze (1985) of instruments owned by Leipzig town musicians, and it was "unusable" ("so ganz unbrauchbar," 43).

quality."[33] German harpsichords, however, varied enormously, some revealing a predilection for colorful "lute" and sixteen-foot stops. The inclusion of such ranks on harpsichords reflected the fact that most German harpsichord makers were also organ builders. Terms such as *Cornet* and *Flöte*, used for organ stops, were also applied to ranks on the harpsichord. Bach, however, never specified registrations for the latter apart from the *piano* and *forte* that appear in a few pieces, implying a two-manual harpsichord. Still, the music that Bach was writing at Weimar by 1714 or so, including such compositions as the English Suites, shows a sense of the possibilities of harpsichord sound and articulation. This in turn suggests familiarity with the sophisticated French instruments of the day.

The same cannot be said of Bach's earlier keyboard works. Forkel praised Bach for his grasp of the distinction between organ and "clavier" playing, but this could be because it was a hard-earned achievement that he stressed in his teaching.[34] Early works cannot be unequivocally assigned to one instrument or another; this is one reason for doubting that certain pieces designated in the sources as *manualiter* (for manuals only) were specifically for organ.[35] A few exceptional pieces, such as the fantasia on "Ein feste Burg" (BWV 720), have been linked to specific performances on specific organs, on the basis of keyboard compass or registrational considerations. But such claims are easily refuted.[36] Besides, even harpsichords and clavichords could be, and were, fitted with pedals, and not every organ had a pedalboard or an organist who could play it.

Early Works for Keyboard Instruments

In considering Bach's keyboard music, it is worth bearing in mind how difficult it was for most players to come by any sort of written music in the early eighteenth century. Printed scores were expensive, and with

---

33 Koster (1999, 61).

34 Forkel (1802, 18, trans. in NBR, 437) claims to have known of only two players, Bach and his son Wilhelm Friedemann, who understood this distinction; as he never actually heard Sebastian play, his information must have come from Friedemann.

35 As argued by Marshall (1986).

36 In this case by Williams (2003, 461–62), casting severe doubt on Spitta's theory that the piece was written for the organ at Mühlhausen after it was rebuilt to Bach's specifications. BWV 720 is one of the few works preserved with information about registration, but the latter (also discussed by Williams) varies from one source to another.

press runs that might have comprised no more than a hundred copies they were not widely distributed. Manuscript copies (even of printed music) were the normal means by which students and professionals gained access to scores, but these had to be made painstakingly—even staff lines were drawn by hand—and of course one needed access to an exemplar (*Vorlage*) and time to copy it. Teachers were not necessarily eager to make their own copies available to pupils even for a fee.[37] On the rare occasions when one got to listen to a visiting virtuoso or traveled to hear one, that person was not necessarily willing to share professional secrets in the form of notated music. Despite such impediments, Bach must have amassed a substantial collection of diverse pieces by an early point in his career. As we have seen, he evidently shared these with his brother, whose two surviving manuscript compilations provide a sample of the diverse repertory that a diligent provincial organist in Germany could possess during the first decade or two of the century. Containing preludes and fugues, suites, and other pieces by German and Italian composers, as well as arrangements of French instrumental music, these manuscripts also include a selection of Sebastian's early compositions, some in his own hand. Nothing comparable survives that Sebastian himself owned, but he reportedly possessed collections of similar pieces as well as keyboard chorale settings, which are largely missing from Christoph's two extant anthologies.

At Leipzig, Bach is said to have begun his performances by playing a written composition in order to "set his powers of imagination in motion," proceeding then to improvisation.[38] This suggests that, even in auditions, Bach might have used written pieces as launching pads for extemporizations. But "improvisation" is a tricky concept; formulas can be memorized, and any organist must have been prepared to play more or less ready-made elaborations of popular chorale melodies. Bach, moreover, must have realized early on that only by putting compositions

---

37 Pachelbel charged his pupil Eckelt for the right to make copies, as Eckelt himself noted in the manuscript known by his name (the "Eckelt tablature," Crakow, Biblioteka Jagiellioñska, Mus. ms. 40035); see Welter (2008, 8–9).

38 From a 1741 report by Theodor Leberecht Pitschel, who applied the following year to serve as conrector in the St. Thomas School. BD 2:397 (no. 499), trans. in NBR, 333–34 (no. 336).

into writing could he bring them to the perfection—their complete, integrated development—for which he was later famous.[39] Writing things down also challenged a player-composer to invent counterintuitive melodic lines or complex counterpoint (such as canons) that would be difficult to hold in one's head.

In the absence of datable manuscript sources for Bach's early keyboard works, commentators have labored to produce chronologies based on perceived advances in style or technique. But like similar chronologies that have been produced for ancient Greek art, these could be overturned by a single well-contextualized early source or by changes in how scholars understand stylistic evolution. Some pieces not discussed until Chapter 7, such as the seven *manualiter* toccatas and several of the great organ praeludia—now called preludes and fugues—probably originated at Arnstadt or Mühlhausen, even if they did not receive their final touches until later. Even so, Bach's keyboard music, like his vocal compositions, reveals a distinction between early works that remain close to older German models and those which incorporate newer elements of style, especially from Italy. The line between the two types is not always clear, nor can it be certain that the more cosmopolitan pieces were all composed after the move to Weimar. Nevertheless, the remainder of this chapter considers only what appear to be more old-fashioned types of composition.

This music can sound stylistically remote from Bach's better-known later works. Only occasionally do we hear pre-echos of the latter; the composer is inventive but still working in idioms close to those of his seventeenth-century predecessors. The keyboard music can be divided between chorale settings, on the one hand, and "free" pieces without pre-existing melodies, on the other. Most compositions of both types, whether *manualiter* or *pedaliter*, must have been written with the organ in mind. Many, however, are also playable on harpsichord and clavichord, although only a few suites and related works were clearly for the latter types of instrument.

---

39 "Perfection" (*Vollkommenheit*) was a favorite expression of Forkel for Bach's accomplishment, although applied more to Bach's "fine feeling and polished taste" (Forkel 1802, 64; trans. in NBR, 475) or his abilities as a performer than to individual compositions.

There is much that is audacious even in these early pieces, but before leaving Arnstadt Bach must have learned to temper his melodic and harmonic invention with a sense of what made for practical keyboard counterpoint. "Practical" does not mean easy, however, and another lesson that Bach probably taught himself at Arnstadt was how to push the limits of what he, or anyone else, could perform, while remaining true to the idiom in which he was writing. He would soon apply this principle to string instruments and the voice as well as the keyboard. If, as is likely, this led to resistance from other musicians—such as the students at Arnstadt—a few debacles involving incompetent players would have given Bach valuable experience in how to manage performers less skilled and disciplined than himself.

Keyboard Chorales

Chorales, the congregational hymns of the Lutheran church, were initially more central to Bach's work than the fugues for which he later became known. From an early age, Bach seems to have set out to explore systematically every imaginable way of working hymn tunes into settings that range from the abstruse to the virtuoso. Commentators have long sought to relate Bach's keyboard settings of chorales with their words or with the seasons of the church year to which they are appropriate. But although this may sometimes be justified, composers in the central and northern German traditions that Bach was following often seem instead to have deliberately avoided affective settings, sometimes favoring a learned approach that could produce rather dry exercises in restrained counterpoint. Bach occasionally took that approach as well, perhaps to demonstrate his ability to work the traditional melodies into archaic polyphony. But even among the early chorale settings are pieces that look like preliminary exercises for the more varied types that he would be writing before he left Weimar.

Although today called chorale preludes, Bach's smaller hymn settings were not necessarily used to introduce congregational singing of the same tunes. Nor are they always clearly distinct in style or dimensions from the larger chorale elaborations usually known as fantasias. Multiple settings of the same chorale melody could be grouped together to form a set of variations; this genre was popular in the circle of Pachelbel, who published a collection in 1693. Such a series of variations, today called a chorale "partita," might have been particularly useful for training an organist to improvise in diverse ways on a given tune during an audition. Bach, however, left only a few examples, mostly early, and these could have originated as separately composed chorale preludes or short fantasias.

When it came to assembling chorale compositions into collections, Sebastian seems to have been less interested in compiling variations on individual tunes than in creating cycles of pieces based on different melodies, for use over the course of the church year. In doing so he might been inspired by contemporary pastors and poets, such as the younger Olearius at Arnstadt, who were busy creating annual cycles, or *Jahrgänge*, of sermons, bible commentaries, and poetry. Today, when even regular churchgoers are unlikely to know many hymns, this may seem an arcane field of specialization. For a Lutheran musician in the eighteenth century, it was a vital way to express religious commitment, a worthy goal for an organist aspiring to a place among pastors and scholars.

If at Arnstadt or Mühlhausen Bach was already assembling some such cycle of keyboard chorale settings, it survives only in fragments. Among these are the chorale preludes in the so-called Neumeister manuscript, a collection of the later eighteenth century (named for its copyist) containing much older repertory, including compositions by several members of the Bach family. The rapid evolution of Bach's ideas and capabilities as a composer might have led him to abandon these early pieces, most of which survive only in peripheral and often inaccurate manuscript copies. There they occur alongside doubtful and misattributed pieces, so that many of the keyboard chorales listed as BWV 690–765 are clearly spurious; those certainly by Bach are mostly early.[40] These pieces range from straightforward harmonizations and archaic chorale motets to fughettas, embellished melodies with accompaniment, and miniature fantasias. There is also an important group that builds canons from the phrases of the melody. The canons are not always strict, and they are preserved side-by-side with other types of chorale compositions, including fugues (Example 5.1). All these types, however, reveal the young Bach

---

40 Exceptions include seven late *manualiter* chorale fughettas for Advent and Christmas, BWV 696–99, 701, and 703–4.

Example 5.1   (a) Example of canon, from "Ach, Gott und Herr," BWV 724, mm. 38–41 (dotted line marks canonic imitation); (b) example of fugue, from "Machs mit mir, Gott," BWV 957, mm. 1–3 (asterisks mark notes of the chorale melody)

grappling with formal or technical devices that would recur in more developed form in later pieces. Evidently Bach continually returned to and polished techniques for the elaboration of chorale melodies first essayed in his youth.

Fugues and Other "Free" Pieces

In view of the emphasis on fugue later in Bach's career, the number of early compositions actually called fugues is smaller than might be expected. But the modern idea of fugues as independent compositions (or as self-contained movements) comes largely from Bach's own later music. Earlier pieces headed by the Latin word *fuga*, especially the many left by Pachelbel, tend to be short and were probably understood more as "examples of imitative counterpoint" than compositions as such. Although the young Bach did leave a few independent fugues, a greater number occur as sections within larger works—vocal as well as for keyboard. His early "free" keyboard works include several praeludia, suites, toccatas, and a sonata, as well as at least one set of variations (apart from several chorale partitas) and a few hard-to-classify pieces. It is, however, the fugues that have probably received the most intense attention, beginning with Bach himself. Hardly any of these occur within compositions belonging to the traditional genres of seventeenth-century contrapuntal keyboard music: fantasias, ricercars, and the like. Only late in life, especially with the *Art of Fugue*, did Bach systematically take up the *stile antico*, the archaic style traditional for such works. Until then, Sebastian evidently preferred to employ imitative polyphony in more up-to-date types of music, using lively or expressive subjects, not the more neutral ones common in older keyboard fugues. This could be because, as Emanuel reported, his father learned composition on his own, not through any traditional mode of study.[41]

Sebastian did follow one venerable tradition, writing several fugues and other pieces based on music by other composers. Composing a fugue on a borrowed subject was, in principle, no different from composing a fugue on a chorale melody. If, however, the subject was from a recently published Italian violin sonata, then the style of the theme and therefore of the fugue based on it might be quite catchy and up-to-date. Several fugues with subjects borrowed from Italian composers nevertheless are still reminiscent of Pachelbel or Buxtehude stylistically and might have been drafted during the Arnstadt or Mühlhausen years. At least two of these, a *pedaliter* fugue supposedly on a theme by Legrenzi (BWV 574) and one for manuals only, using a chromatic subject by Albinoni (BWV 951), were later revised.[42] Evidently Bach thought highly enough of both works to refine them and make them available to students and colleagues in later years. His revisions of the Albinoni fugue—one of three based on subjects by the Venetian composer—were particularly far-reaching,

41 "It was entirely his own study that made him, already in his youth, a pure and strong fugue composer" ("Blos eigenes Nachsinnen hat ihn schon in seiner Jugend zum reinen u. starcken Fugisten gemacht"). Letter to Forkel of January 13, 1775 (BD 3:288 [no. 803]; NBR, 398–99 [no. 395]). Several late eighteenth-century manuscript copies of contrapuntal pieces by Frescobaldi and Froberger may represent the repertory that Bach studied; see Ishii (2013).

42 Zitellini (2013) identifies the subject of BWV 574 as actually deriving from a work of Giovanni Maria Bononcini, but the inexact parallelism between the two themes suggests that Bach had another source. The early version of BWV 574 is BWV 574b, copied by Walther as well as Christoph Bach of Ohrdruf; the status of another version, BWV 574a, is uncertain (see NBA, IV/6, KB, and Williams 2003, 174).

replacing the rambling, discursive writing also seen in Bach's early chorale settings with a more unified or integrated design.[43]

Of all the music that has been assigned to the youthful Bach, the most
famous—possibly the composition most closely associated with Bach in
the popular mind—is the so-called Toccata and Fugue in D minor for
organ, BWV 565. Yet the attribution of this work to Bach may reflect a
misunderstanding of the late eighteenth century, when interest in Bach
was growing but even knowledgeable musicians could be quite fuzzy
as to which pieces were his and which were by pupils, sons, or unre-
lated composers.[44] If so, BWV 565 is one of several frequently performed
compositions that "sound like Bach" only because they incorporate
elements of his style in a somewhat simplified, easy-to-grasp form.[45]

Almost as famous and more certainly Bach's is the *Capriccio sopra la
lontananza de il fratro dilettissimo* ("Capriccio on separation from a most
beloved brother"), BWV 992. Whether the title should be understood
literally, and if so to which "brother" it refers, is uncertain. It might
even refer to Sebastian's own separation from his brother Christoph
after 1700.[46] The programmatic piece was surely inspired by the famous
Biblical Sonatas of Kuhnau, published in 1700 and likewise comprising
short sections labeled with descriptive rubrics.[47] Whatever its precise date
and subject matter, BWV 992 employs an expressive language common
with Bach's early vocal works. One section also reveals a symbolic use
of counterpoint: the friends of the departing "brother" signal their

---

43 Schulenberg (2007) includes an in-depth comparison of BWV 951 and the early version
BWV 951a.

44 See Schulenberg (2011, 169–70). Doubts about Bach's authorship of BWV 565, first raised
by Williams (1981), were substantiated by Claus (1998).

45 Others of this type are the little minuet in G (BWV Anh. 114), now known to be by
the Dresden organist Christian Pezold, and the Christmas cantata BWV 142, sometimes
thought to be by Kuhnau but best regarded as anonymous.

46 Spitta (1873–1880, 1:231) assumed that the brother in question was Johann Jacob and that
the composition reflected his departure from Eisenach around 1704 into the retinue of
Charles XII of Sweden. Wolff (1992, 148–49) argued that the word could be interpreted
metaphorically, referring to any close male friend.

47 Properly titled *Musicalische Vorstellung einiger Biblischer Historien* (Leipzig, 1700); five of the
six sonatas were copied into the Andreas Bach Book, mainly by Johann Christoph of
Ohrdruf.

concern for his safety in a four-part fugue whose successive entries cycle downwards through the circle of fifths.

The Capriccio is likely to have been composed by, if not during, Bach's visit to Buxtehude in fall 1705. One also feels the impact of that journey in the organ Praeludium in E, BWV 566, the most Buxtehudian of Bach's works.[48] Strongly reminiscent of Buxtehude in both its melodic material and its overall design, this work comprises two prelude-fugue pairs, the subject of the second fugue being a triple-time version of that of the first.

The not quite fully tonal language of BWV 566 is also reminiscent of the older composer.[49] Yet the piece is just as clearly the work of an independent musical personality—one who was now an unrivaled master of pedals as well as manuals, as is clear from the virtuoso writing for both hands and feet. The second fugue brings the piece to a brilliant conclusion. But although a rhythmic motive from the subject persists almost to the end, the climax is generated through the gradual replacement of fugal counterpoint by running figuration, first in the right hand, then in the pedals. The effect is magnificent on any decent instrument, but Bach would soon learn how to conclude even a virtuoso fugue in a way that remains true to the contrapuntal character of the genre.

Bach accomplished this in the grandest of his early keyboard works, arguably his first truly great composition: the Passacaglia in C minor, BWV 582. Like BWV 566, the Passacaglia contains many echoes of Buxtehude's music, but it is substantially more accomplished and individual—which is not to say that it must be a much later work. A passacaglia is a piece built on a repeating bass line or ostinato, here apparently borrowed from a French work: the Christe eleison of an organ mass by André Raison.[50]

---

48 BWV 566 is designated "Toccata" in some older editions but not in any early manuscript sources, although some of these give the alternate title *Fantasia.* A version of the piece in C major is probably a later adaptation; details in the author's edition: *Johann Sebastian Bach: Complete Organ Works,* Vol. 1 (Wiesbaden: Breitkopf und Härtel, 2013), 13.

49 Editors have sometimes wrongly modernized accidentals in BWV 566, which reflect an archaic sense of tonality and modulation (see Schulenberg 2010b, 61).

50 An organ mass is a set of organ pieces that were meant to be played in alternation with chanted portions of the liturgy. Bach's Passacaglia borrows from the "Trio en passacaille" of the second mass ("Messe du deuziesme ton") in Raison's *Premier livre d'orgue* of 1688. In addition, the subject of Bach's much later fragmentary fugue in C minor (BWV 562/2) is almost an inversion of Raison's subject. Raison was probably one of the "old and good

Hence Bach took his inspiration from multiple sources, drawing too from Raison the idea of treating the ostinato bass like a fugue subject. Thus the Passacaglia begins with the theme alone, in the pedals (see Example 9.8a below). Halfway through the opening section, the ostinato moves from bass to soprano for variations 11–12. Then it moves to the alto for variation 13. After seven more variations, an actual fugue follows in which the ostinato (now a subject) is always combined with a countersubject—*two* countersubjects from the third subject entry onward (see Example 9.8b). The combination produces a staggering effect as the virtuosity of both composer and player reaches a climax in the fugue's concluding phrases.

Early Vocal Works

How Bach learned to compose vocal music is shrouded in even greater mystery than his early keyboard music. As a boy chorister, he must have sung and memorized much of the chorale repertory. But what he sang beyond that is unknown, and how any composer learned the craft of writing for voices is not well documented. The choral library at Lüneburg contained a famous collection, chiefly polyphony from the seventeenth century, but whether Bach sang (or accompanied) any of this music or had opportunities to study it is unknown. Virtually all this music would have been preserved only in parts, not scores, making study difficult outside of actual performances.[51] Although his manuscript copies survive from this period for a few keyboard pieces, we have almost nothing comparable for vocal music from before the Weimar years.

In a small town such as Arnstadt, Bach might have heard less varied, less up-to-date types of music than at Lüneburg and Hamburg. Still, as the ruling count maintained not only a court chapel but a theater at Neideck Castle, Bach probably had opportunities to hear and participate in music beyond the limited variety performed at the New Church. Presumably this included music for the court theater, perhaps also Italian cantatas such as were collected and performed at Weimar and Cöthen during the next

---

Frenchmen" whom Emanuel Bach neglected to identify by name when recounting for Forkel the composers whose works his father studied (BD 3:288 [no. 803], trans. in NBR, 398 [no. 395]).

51 One important exception was Schütz's *Auferstehung* (Resurrection) oratorio, which was present in score (*Partitura*) according to the list preserved by Seiffert (1907–1908).

two decades. Such music would prove more important for Bach's future work than anything by Buxtehude, Pachelbel, or other older German composers. His first vocal compositions, however, remained close to the older tradition, either because the newer type of sacred music had not yet reached the places where Bach was working or because he or his superiors as yet had no interest in it. Simple recitative (*recitativo semplice*) would have been particularly difficult to compose for one who had never heard it, or who heard it only occasionally. More than arias or choruses, the gradual infiltration of the new type of recitative into vocal music by Bach and his contemporaries (as in Example 5.2b below) may be the best measure of how far they had gone in assimilating the new style.

Such recitative is absent from Bach's earliest vocal compositions, where instead we find a sort of arioso similar to that found in music by older contemporaries (Example 5.2a). Yet these are not student works; the composer of Cantatas 4, 71, 131, 150, and especially 106 was already a master. These works include ingenious examples of the text painting (or word painting) that was expected in vocal music of the time; Bach's early

Example 5.2 (a) "Arioso" (so designated) from *Gott ist mein König*, BWV 71, mvt. 4, mm. 24–25; (b) possibly Bach's first true simple recitative, the opening of the "Hunt Cantata," BWV 208, mvt. 1, mm. 1–2 (probably from 1713):

Du machest, daß beide, Sonn und Gestirn,   You make both sun and stars,

Was mir behagt, ist nur die muntre Jagd!   What suits me is only the jaunty hunt!

Example 5.3   *Gott ist mein König*, BWV 71, mvt. 6, mm. 3–4 (without oboes, bassoon, and doubling string parts):

Du wollest dem Feinde nicht [geben
die Seele deiner Turteltauben]

You would not give to the enemy [the
soul of your turtledove]

use of this device is notable for being not only pictorial in a conventional way but also expressive and ingeniously creative. Thus, in Example 5.3, the drooping soprano melody (echoed by the recorders) combines with flowing passagework for the newfangled cello, creating a musical image of the turtledove mentioned in the psalm verse.

Among the many uncertainties surrounding these compositions is one that at first seems trivial: what to call them. The term *cantata* has been applied to most of Bach's sacred vocal works since their first printed editions in the nineteenth century. At that time the word could be used for almost any multi-movement work for voices and instruments. The expression is not entirely anachronistic when applied to the sacred and the secular compositions that Bach wrote from around 1714 and afterwards. The librettos of those works were explicitly modeled on those of the Italian secular cantata of the period, which consists primarily of alternating recitatives and arias. Bach, however, reserved the word *cantata* for the small number of comparable compositions that he wrote for a single solo voice. Larger compositions were called motets, concertos, church pieces (*Kirchenstücke*), or simply "music" for a given church service or other occasion. To avoid using the word *cantata* anachronistically, works here will often be cited by BWV numbers, which for the church pieces correspond to the familiar "Cantata" numbers. As with Bach's other works, the BWV numbers for the cantatas are not chronological, following instead the sometimes seemingly random order of these compositions in Schmeider's thematic catalogue.

One reason not to call Bach's earliest vocal compositions "cantatas" is that their texts and music differ fundamentally from those of later works. Several are essentially settings of biblical texts, especially psalms. BWV 4, on the other hand, is one of a handful of Bach's vocal works based entirely on a single chorale—both the traditional strophic poem and its melody. Only with the addition of newly written "madrigalian" poetry to the traditional bible and chorale verses would Bach or his listeners have thought of these works as having anything to do with the Italian cantata. The words were indeed paramount: following an aesthetic that went back to the beginning of the Baroque around 1600, music was the servant of the text, the composer merely preparing the words for presentation to an audience or congregation. To be sure, when the words were from the bible, translated by Martin Luther—or an original poem by him, as in the chorale used for Cantata 4—a pious idealist would have been moved to set them as vividly as possible. For Bach, the composer's duty included attention to details of counterpoint and other matters unlikely to be noticed by anyone without access to a score. Hence even these early works demonstrate the same "supererogation"—doing more than was necessary or expected—that was characteristic of Bach throughout his career.[52]

Evidently the products of one-time commissions, Bach's early vocal compositions were probably not intended for routine use in church services, as would be the sacred works composed later at Weimar and Leipzig. Each libretto follows a distinctive design; to what degree Bach

52 Thus Williams (2016, 613).

was involved in the pre-compositional planning is unknown. Yet the symmetrical arrangement of contrasting solo and choral passages in both BWV 106 and 131 suggests that here Bach collaborated in some way with the Mühlhausen pastor Eilmar, who had requested the music of the latter work. Although archaic in many respects and looking back stylistically to music by Buxtehude and other late seventeenth-century German composers, both compositions contain novel musical ideas; many listeners find them as moving as any later works.

How would Bach, faced by a psalm or a chorale text, have conceived the task of setting it to music? Older types of polyphonic vocal music could be composed according to tried-and-true methods that favored a reserved melodic and rhythmic style while following certain basic principles of musical rhetoric.[53] Any accompanying instrumental parts would have to respect certain limitations of idiom, as in trumpet and timpani parts, which were confined to the small number of available pitches.[54] Otherwise the instruments might merely double or echo the voices. The newer style, already encroaching on the old in works by Schelle, Erlebach, and other members of the previous generation, required better-trained soloists—players as well as singers. This in turn required a more precise understanding by the composer of what is possible in a soloistically conceived recitative or aria; even choral movements increasingly demanded more expert use of both instrumental and vocal idioms. By 1705 Bach was no doubt accustomed to pushing against the limits of what he himself could play in his keyboard music. Yet in his first vocal works he was writing for performers of more limited musical insight and abilities. Some things that he wrote might have been unperformable, but if this indeed happened (perhaps at Arnstadt), he must soon have learned how to challenge his colleagues without asking for the impossible.

---

53 Musical rhetoric—the effective setting of texts to music—was codified in the writings of Christoph Bernhard, one of Schütz's most distinguished students (see Hilse 1973). Similar ideas can still be seen in Walther's *Praecepta* (1708), an unpublished compositional manual written for his pupil Prince Johann Ernst of Weimar.

54 Natural (valveless) brass instruments were limited, essentially, to notes of the harmonic series—the tonic triad and, in the top register, its major scale. Timpani were almost always used in pairs, with only two notes available, usually tonic and dominant.

Today, when composition is understood as a distinct profession, student composers can be spoiled by the availability of performers specializing in new music, who can sing and play extraordinarily difficult parts. But to be a composer "was not an occupation or profession" at the time of the young Bach,[55] nor was improvisation or performance of new music unusual. Rather every performer was a new-music specialist. Today it can take years for a composition student to develop a personal style while learning to write realistically for actual performers. The process had to go faster in Bach's day, when composers were also improvisers and were expected to turn out finished pieces quickly. Trained as an organist and accustomed to extemporaneous playing, Bach could treat composition as written-down improvisation—but only up to a point. Years of practice in making up music on the spot could condition a talented composer to write scores prolifically and quickly. This facilitated the enormous output of contemporaries such as Telemann and Graupner. Bach would complete fewer individual compositions than either of them, yet the greater length of so many of his works, not to mention the greater number of independent performing parts in most of them, makes his *oeuvre* a more imposing body of music. At Leipzig he produced very substantial vocal compositions at a rate of roughly one per week, a respectable rate of production by contemporary standards. Yet he did not sustain that pace for more than a few years, and earlier in life he may have completed works with greater deliberation. As talented and precocious as he was, there is no evidence that Bach was a child prodigy; what he did was the product of enormous and sustained effort, the first distinctive fruits of his compositional labors appearing no earlier than when he was in his late teens.

On the other hand, there is no evidence that Bach's earliest surviving vocal works, which date from 1707 or 1708, were preceded by a significant number of lost efforts. Several compositions once thought to be early works in archaic style, such as BWV 15, have been shown to be by other composers.[56] The Quodlibet of around 1707 could be Bach's earliest known vocal work, but it is so unlike anything else that it tells us

---

55 As Melamed (1999, 346) observes, pointing out that Sebastian distinguished only two of the many members of the family listed in the Genealogy by the term *Componist*.

56 BWV 15 is by Johann Ludwig Bach, who probably preceded Sebastian as a composer of sacred cantatas (see Chapters 7 and 11).

little, except that he had a propensity for humor manifested also in the Capriccio BWV 992 from around the same time. A few passages in the Quodlibet resemble the arioso-like recitative of Buxtehude and other predecessors; a greater number recall the simple, song-like, arias of early German opera—hardly a surprise in what seems a mash-up of fragments from popular songs. Several references to academic life, including a few lines of Latin sung to what sounds like a psalm tone, are a reminder that some of Sebastian's older relatives had received university training. In view of Bach's later compositional interests, it is ironic that the fragment ends with an abortive fugue; could the anonymous text, which here asks "what is this that sounds so fine and fugal," have been his own?[57]

Writing even a less than serious piece such as the Quodlibet would have given a young composer valuable experience in composition for voices. Yet the (intentional) failure to sustain any musical idea for more than a few measures leaves the Quodlibet remote in style, form, and dimensions from the sort of work that would have been expected, for example, from someone auditioning for a church job. Bach's Weimar cousin Walther remembered writing two church pieces for his audition at Mühlhausen in 1707.[58] He subsequently withdrew his application, but it would be reasonable to suppose that Bach, competing for the same position, prepared in a similar manner. It has been supposed that Bach composed BWV 4 for the occasion,[59] which took place on Easter Sunday. That would have been appropriate for a work based on Luther's famous Easter hymn "Christ lag in Todesbanden."

BWV 4 opens with a sinfonia for five string instruments (and organ continuo). There follow seven movements setting the seven stanzas of Luther's chorale. The work is therefore a set of chorale variations, like

---

57 Translation by Z. Philip Ambrose, from his website (https://www.uvm.edu/~classics/faculty/bach). Kraft (1956, 152–53) suggested that the text might be by Johannes Avenarius, whom Sebastian knew at Ohrdruf before his departure for university studies at Erfurt, but could this be so if the work really celebrated some Bach family event such as a marriage?

58 As recalled in his letters (in Walther 1987, pp. 70 and 219f.).

59 For example, by Wolff (2000, 103). In fact the church council proceedings refer only to Bach's having "just played the test at Easter" ("neülich auff Ostern die probe gespielet," BD, 2:23 [no. 19]; NBR, 49 [no. 22a]). Had he in addition performed BWV 4, one might have expected some record of that, although Rathey too (2016b, 458) considers an audition at Easter its "likely purpose."

the organ "partitas" of roughly the same date. No other early vocal work of Bach does this, but the focus on a vivid and varied musical surface is a point in common with Bach's keyboard music of the period, especially the early chorale settings. Here the musical invention clearly reflects the changing imagery and subject matter of the successive stanzas of the poem. Much the same approach to text-setting prevails in the other early vocal compositions, including the council election cantata performed at Mühlhausen on February 4, 1708. We can surmise that the same was true of Bach's two subsequent works of this type, which unfortunately are lost (unless BWV 143 is one of them).[60]

The great vocal work of these early years is surely BWV 106. Its precise date and place of composition cannot be determined, and it might have been composed only after Bach's move to Weimar. Yet it remains within the tradition represented by BWV 71 and other early works. The now-familiar Latin title *Actus tragicus* is already present in the work's oldest extant source, but that is a manuscript copy from 1768. An *actus* could be any ritual with sacral associations, and the work does appear to have been composed for a funeral.[61] Eschewing the use of violins, Bach assigns the instrumental parts to two recorders and two viola da gambas—quiet instruments appropriate to an intimate funeral work.

The text, whose compiler is unknown, again consists largely of bible selections, now drawn from various books of both the Old and the New Testaments. Indeed, it juxtaposes the "old" and "new" laws, here associated with death and life, respectively. Emotionally, it presages many of Bach's later sacred works by following an arc from quiet resignation to ecstatic joy. Modern editions and performances usually divide the work

60 BWV 143, if by Bach at all, must be an anonymous adaptation with altered scoring; Glöckner has reconstructed a putative original version (in NBA, revised edition, Vol. 2, 2012). He and Rathey (2016b, 450) propose that this is the lost work for the Mühlhausen council election of 1709, yet it is odd that the printer received a little more for printing the 1709 piece than he did for BWV 71 in 1708. One would expect the opposite if the much smaller BWV 143 was indeed the composition for 1709.

61 Among those whose funerals have been suggested as possible occasions for the work are: Bach's maternal uncle Tobias Lämmerhirt, who died on August 10, 1707; Dorothea Susanna Tilesius (d. June 3, 1708), sister of Eilmar, who has been proposed as the compiler of the text; and the Mühlhausen burgomaster Adolph Strecker, who died in September 1708 (Rathey 2006, 84–88). Telemann left a similarly scored early work under the title *Trauer-Actus* ("funeral rite"), the chorale motet *Ach wie nichtig* TWV 1:38.

into two halves, but (as in BWV 131) its vocal sections are arranged symmetrically around a central quartet. This is flanked on either side by music for soloists, plus opening and closing choral movements. The solo movements, however, and even the central quartet now constitute dialogs, in which different voices enter at different times, singing verses from different textual sources. Even the instruments participate in the dialog, adding a wordless chorale to the quartet. Here Bach combines *three* musical ideas: a fugue for the three lower voices, setting a verse from Ecclesiasticus ("This is the old law"); an arioso for the soprano, singing a line from Revelation ("Yes, come, Lord Jesus"); and the chorale melody "Ich hab' mein' Sach' Gott heimgestellt" (I have left everything to God), played by the two recorders in unison. The movement concludes with the pathetic plea of the soprano, who is left unaccompanied even by the continuo for the final invocation of Jesus' name.

CHAPTER SIX

Weimar (1708–1717)

B ACH'S OFFICIAL POSITION AT WEIMAR WAS INITIALLY THAT OF COURT
organist. But in his letter of resignation at Mühlhausen he
described himself as having been appointed to the duke's "court chapel
and chamber music,"[1] which implies something rather more special. To
work as a court organist meant merely to play in the ducal chapel. But to
perform in a monarch's chamber implied a more intimate role closer to
the seat of power: playing and perhaps leading ensemble performances
within the ruler's private quarters—for the monarch and his household
as well as the occasional visiting potentate. This represented a significant step up for a former municipal organist, and as he prepared to leave
Mühlhausen Bach might have expected his employers to understand that,
as he entered the duke's personal service, he would be participating in
the "duly ordered" church music that Mühlhausen lacked. His superiors
there probably knew that Duke Wilhelm Ernst was famous, if not noto-
rious, for the strict regulation of religion in his domain. The fact that the
city of Weimar, although not the duchy as a whole, was smaller in population than Mühlhausen would have mattered little at a time when a duke
ranked above any private citizen or even an entire municipal council.
Whether or not Bach believed that going there would realize a life goal,
he knew for sure that it would improve his annual salary (as he made

1 "dero Hoffcapell und Cammermusic," BD 1:20 (no. 1); NBR, 57 (no. 32).

Bach. David Schulenberg, Oxford University Press (2020). © Oxford University Press.
DOI: 10.1093/oso/9780190936303.001.0001

clear to the Mühlhauseners). But before ten years were over, he would learn that he had also sacrificed his freedom.

Like other residence towns, Weimar, said to have housed about five thousand people during Bach's time there, revolved around the court, which reportedly employed about a third of the population, dominating the economy.[2] The Weimar court was a peculiar place. There were two dukes, in theory co-rulers; in fact the senior duke Wilhelm Ernst merely tolerated the presence of the secondary court of his nephew Ernst Augustus, who lived in a separate palace. Known as the Red Castle, this was connected by a guarded corridor to the main one, the Wilhelmsburg; relations between the two were so strained that court musicians, including Bach, were at times forbidden to serve the junior duke. Weimar itself was not yet the major cultural center that it would become during its so-called golden age a century later. But like certain other small German states, it appears to have been undergoing a renaissance during Bach's lifetime. Misrule by Wilhelm Ernst's nephew, who eventually succeeded him, would temporarily suspend that renaissance, however. It would be chiefly the enlightened regency of Duchess Anna Amalia, a niece of Frederick "the Great" who married Ernst August's son, that would make Weimar a haven for learning and the arts—the home of Goethe and Schiller—from the late eighteenth century onward.

The court chapel, completed in 1658 to a design by Johann Moritz Richter, was called the Himmelsburg, or more correctly the *Weg zur Himmelsburg* (way to heaven's castle). Its interior architecture is known from a depiction by the court painter Christian Richter (Figure 6.1).[3] Its distinctive design included a gallery some 65 feet above the floor that contained the organ and, after a renovation completed in 1714, space for perhaps as many as twenty musicians, apparently including

2 Wolff (2000, 118), apparently relying on a work by Hans-Rudolf Jung not seen here. As Williams (2016, 185n. 4) notes, whether eighteenth-century population figures represent individuals, households, or other units can be unclear or inconsistent.

3 This Christian Richter (1587–1667) was one of a family of artists and architects represented at Weimar during Bach's time there by another Christian Richter (1655–1722). Neither is known to have been related to the Leipzig architect also named Christian Richter (ca. 1625–1684). For further details of the interior, which housed paintings and gravestones of members of the ruling family, see Koch (2006, 55–57).

Figure 6.1 Interior of the Weimar court chapel, known as the Himmelsburg; oil on canvas by Christian Richter (ca. 1660), Klassik Stiftung Weimar. Photo: Jenapolis.de, from Wikipedia.

a harpsichordist. The harpsichord might have been used chiefly for rehearsals; a sliding panel could be used to close off the gallery from the rest of the chapel, helping to keep it warm during the winter but potentially making the organ unbearably loud within the enclosed space. This arrangement must have required congregational singing of hymns to be led by a separate body of choirboys "in a gallery behind the altar,"[4] but something similar was probably customary for Lutheran churches of the period.

Presumably both sides of the divided ducal family, together with courtiers, pages, and household employees, attended services here, making at least a pretense of setting aside their differences. Looking up into the music gallery, they would have seen on its ceiling a Baroque painting depicting clouds and angels—heaven itself (hence the name of the chapel). Visible, too, was the organ originally by Ludwig Compenius, rebuilt shortly before Bach's arrival. It was again under repair from summer 1712 into 1714, as part of the general remodeling of the chapel. Bach naturally was involved in the renovation, together with the court organ builder Trebs, though just how is impossible to say, given our limited information about the instrument during Bach's period there. Bach also knew and perhaps performed occasionally at Weimar's main city church of St. Peter and Paul, now called the Herder Church, after the poet who was pastor and superintendent there from 1776 to 1803. The organist there was Johann Gottfried Walther, a cousin of Bach and author of an important music dictionary (1732). A third church, St. Jacob's, was dedicated in 1713; it is the only one whose organ (also by Trebs) survives even partially. None of the Weimar organs was particularly large, and it has been claimed that they emphasized "wide-ranging colours and combinations" rather than "heavy, obtrusive organ sound."[5] If so, then Bach's Weimar organ works, which comprise the greatest part of his music for the instrument, may be better represented by clear, colorful registration than by massive or overpowering sonority.

Bach's appointment at Weimar, although occasioned in the first instance by the effective retirement of his predecessor Effler, might have

---

4 Williams (2016, 155), citing Jauernig (1950, 70–71), whose meticulous examination of the archival evidence is supplemented by the more recent research, including findings on acoustics and sight lines, summarized by Grychtolik (2013). Wolff (2000, 159) does not give a source for the statement that the choir boys "joined the capelle . . . for the cantata performance preceding the sermon."

5 Williams (1980–1984, 3:126–27), whose critical discussion supplements the summary account in Wolff and Zepf (2012, 91–95).

been part of a broader program of the senior duke to reconstitute his chapel—building, facilities, and personnel, as well as a new repertory of sacred music, as described below. As court organist, Bach must have played regularly for services and other occasions, but whether these included organ recitals for the court is not documented, nor is Bach's contribution to vocal music in the chapel before 1714. That he continued his previous activity as an organ "tester" is clear from documented evaluations at Taubach (near Weimar) in 1710 and elsewhere.[6] The Taubach instrument was again by Trebs, with whom Bach must have worked on the building of the new instrument for St. Jacob's. Bach must also have traveled occasionally to perform at nearby courts, although only a few such trips are documented, included one to Gotha in 1711.[7]

As a member of the Weimar court *Capelle* or musical ensemble, Bach joined a small group of professional musicians. This put him in a very different position from that at Arnstadt or Mühlhausen, where he might have worked alongside other professionals only occasionally. His salary was likewise of a different order, nearly double what he had received at Mühlhausen, although the additional value of various emoluments received at each place (such as bushels of grain and pails of beer) makes it difficult to evaluate Bach's earnings accurately for any given period. Moreover, the potential for earning extra money for weddings and funerals at Weimar, if permitted at all, was surely much lower. Salary raises in 1711 and 1713 further increased Bach's income, however, so that by the time of his promotion to Concertmaster his base pay was higher than that of his nominal superiors the Capellmeister and Vice-Capellmeister.

These two, Johann Samuel Drese and his son Johann Wilhelm, were apparently relatives of Adam Drese, Capellmeister at Arnstadt prior to Bach's arrival there. The Weimar Dreses remain ciphers for us, due in part to the disappearance of the numerous church pieces and other music that the father is reported to have composed.[8] That they outranked Bach

---

6 Bach's rather cursory, if positive, report on the little organ by Trebs is in BD 1:155–56 (no. 84), trans. in NBR, 64 (no. 42).

7 Ahrens (2007, 49–53) lists numerous visits by musicians to Gotha, suggesting that there, at least, guest artists were a regular feature of court life.

8 By Walther (1732, 217), who calls him Adam's "cousin" (*Vetter*); he says nothing of the son.

was stated explicitly in the court record of his promotion in 1714,[9] and as longtime servants of the court they clearly were trusted to maintain ducal traditions regardless of the level they had achieved as musicians. Samuel had been hired in 1683 and presumably was taught to compose in the old-fashioned style of Adam Drese.[10] Wilhelm was paid during 1702–1703 for musical study in Venice; this suggests that he had some acquaintance with the newer types of vocal writing that would soon be routine in German chapel music. If not a composer, the younger Drese was at least a copyist (*Notist*), likely providing the court with manuscripts containing recent Italian or Italianate compositions.[11] In 1706 he succeeded Strattner as Vice-Capellmeister, and for the next ten years he evidently stood in for his father before being named Capellmeister himself, after the latter's death in December 1716.

Also senior to Bach in the court hierarchy, although not a musician, was the court poet Salomo Franck. A skillful if not great writer, capable of imaginative diction and vivid late-Baroque rhetoric, Franck published several cycles of librettos for each Sunday and holiday of the Lutheran church year, as well as massive quantities of secular poetry. Bach set Franck's texts of both types to music, not only at Weimar but later at Leipzig. Born in 1659, Franck, like the Dreses, was clearly prized by the ruling duke, who evidently entrusted him with a substantial part of his cultural and religious program. Not only did Franck write texts heard in church almost every Sunday, but he was also the duke's librarian, curator of his coin collection, and chief secretary of the Weimar church consistory—a position that must have carried considerable authority within the theocratic statelet. Whether Bach actively collaborated with such a person in planning his church pieces, as opposed to dutifully setting texts that were set before him, is impossible to know, but Bach's Weimar church music consistently elaborates Franck's librettos in ways unlikely to have been anticipated by the poet.

---

9 BD 2:53 (no. 66); NBR, 70 (no. 51). The same document nevertheless specified that the other musicians were to appear for rehearsals of the new piece ("zu solchen proben") for which Bach was now responsible each month (see below).

10 To judge from a concertato motet by Adam Drese for four voices and five instruments, *Das Himmelreich ist gleich einem Könige* (ed. Constantin Grun in *Musik in der Residenzstadt Weimar*, ed. Klaus Hortschansky, Leipzig: Hofmeister, 2001).

11 As established by Küster (1996a, 91–92).

We know little about home life for Bach and his growing family during this period, and Maria Barbara's musical training and abilities are unrecorded. Yet she and her two older sisters, as daughters of a composer and minor town official, were surely literate, musically as well as verbally. Both Maria Barbara and her unmarried sister Friedelena Margaretha Bach, who had joined the household by 1709, would therefore have been prepared to give first lessons to her children: Catharina Dorothea, Wilhelm Friedemann, Carl Philipp Emanuel, and Johann Gottfried Bernhard, born at Weimar in 1708, 1710, 1714, and 1715, respectively. Having lived and worked up to this point only among male musicians (so far as we know), Sebastian could now learn something about the adult female voice, perhaps too of the ability of women to understand sophisticated compositions, as well as the theological concepts expressed in their texts.

To be sure, he probably already knew of the religious poetry of Countess Aemile Juliane, wife of the ruler of Schwarzburg-Rudolstadt and a relative of his former overlord at Arnstadt. Among her many texts is the chorale poem "Wer weiß, wie nahe mir mein Ende," used in the Leipzig church works BWV 166, 27, and 84. The librettos of nine other Leipzig cantatas are by Mariane von Ziegler. The Empire was nevertheless a less nurturing place than France or Britain for a talented woman, and Roman law denied women some of the few legal rights they enjoyed elsewhere, such as that of inheritance.[12] But Bach's generation saw a number of what seem to have been genuine musical partnerships involving married couples, such as the composer Hasse and his wife Faustina. At Leipzig, the wife of the critic and poet Gottsched would be a significant author in her own right—and evidently a fan of Bach.[13] Bach himself seems to have been a true professional partner of his second wife—insofar as that was possible at the time for two people of their status. Their relationship was perhaps a model of sorts for their son Johann Christian, Sebastian's

12 Except in the case of widowhood; thus the wife of Bach's music printer Balthasar Schmid carried on the family business after her husband's death in 1749, issuing compositions by Emanuel Bach, among others.

13 Luise Adelgunde Victoire Gottsched mentioned the difficulty of Bach's keyboard pieces, but also that they were beautiful (*schön*), in a letter of August 30, 1732, published in Vol. 1 of her *Briefe* (Dresden, 1771); extract in BD 2:223 (no. 309). On Ziegler, see Chapter 10.

youngest, who also married a younger singer. But of Sebastian and Maria Barbara as a couple we know essentially nothing.

It is often supposed that Sebastian made special efforts to teach his first son Friedemann, who is said to have been his favorite. The most tangible evidence for this is the little book of keyboard pieces that Sebastian created for him at Cöthen (see Chapter 9). Sebastian would later help Friedemann in writing job applications and probably other matters, providing a crutch that may have been necessary but in the long run could not have made the boy more self-reliant. It would be no surprise if the young father modeled the upbringing of his first son on his own, failing to understand how far his own capabilities—and expectations—exceeded Ambrosius's. Possibly, too, the orphaned Sebastian overcompensated by lavishing care on his first son, unintentionally creating a heavy burden for the child. Friedemann went on to become a significant composer and a famous keyboard player, yet he would live his adult life in the shadow of his more congenial and more prolific younger brother Emanuel. The elder Bach cannot be faulted for lacking a modern understanding of parenting, or of the potential conflicts of raising children in competition with one another and with their parents. Such were inevitable elements of life in a professional clan such as the Bachs, whose members might bid against one another for jobs (or spouses). That the family found ways to deal with such problems is evident from its success in producing at least six generations of capable musicians, but how they managed to do so and how happily they lived are unknown.

During the same period in which he headed a growing household at Weimar, Bach also became for the first time a really significant teacher. At least one pupil, Johann Martin Schubart, followed him from Arnstadt or Mühlhausen to Weimar, eventually succeeding his teacher as court organist there—in which position he was followed by a second Bach pupil, Johann Caspar Vogler.[14] Both are known for making manuscript copies of Bach's music, an activity they likely began in their teacher's house, whether or not they lived there as formal apprentices. Others who probably did live with the family were Sebastian's nephew Johann Bernhard and his cousin (once removed) Johann Lorenz. Both went on to become

---

14 Information about both comes from Walther (1732), whose affection for the short-lived Schubart is evident in his quotation from the latter's gravestone.

small-town organists and minor composers, Bernhard doing so as successor to his father Christoph (Sebastian's brother) at Ohrdruf. Another of Bach's Weimar pupils, Philipp David Kräuter, is remembered because of the survival of several documents in his hand that shed light on Bach's teaching (see Chapter 13). These mention music copying as an important part of his studies. None of Kräuter's copies of Bach's keyboard music survive, but another Weimar pupil, the locally born Johann Tobias Krebs, left many extant manuscripts of Sebastian's Weimar compositions. Some of these, however, were evidently obtained already during previous study with Walther, others not until after Bach left Weimar.[15]

Bach's professional activities at Weimar, including composition, are only sparsely documented during his first five years there. We know of a return visit to Mühlhausen for the city council election of 1709, and Bach was probably there as well in 1710.[16] Nine months later he and Maria Barbara saw the birth of Wilhelm Friedemann.[17] An organ report of 1710 and a testimonial that Sebastian wrote early in 1711 for the court organ builder Trebs show that Bach knew instruments made by the latter in nearby Buttstädt (Krebs's home town), as well as in Taubach and perhaps elsewhere.[18] We know also of a few payments for teaching and instrument maintenance at court. That Bach held a high place in the ruler's regard is evident from the salary increase he received in 1711, after the death of the old court organist Effler.[19] But only in 1713 do we begin to learn of more significant biographical events, and only from

---

15 Krebs owned the three composite manuscripts Berlin, Staatsbibliothek, Mus. mss. Bach P 801, 802, and 803. Each is a major source for Bach's music, made up of what were originally separate copies of many of his most important keyboard compositions.

16 The first Mühlhausen visit is documented by a payment on February 7, 1709 (BD 2:38 [no. 43]; NBR, 52 [no. 28b]). Someone, presumably Bach, was again paid for music and (apparently) also for travel expenses on February 20, 1710 (BD 2:38 [no. 43, commentary], trans. in NBR, 52 [no. 28c]).

17 The baptism took place in the city church (not the court chapel). Wilhelm Friedemann was named not for the ruler Wilhelm Ernst but for Wilhelm Ferdinand von Lyncker, a valet de chambre (*Cammer-Juncker*), and for Friedemann Meckbach, a member of the Mühlhausen city council who had been instrumental in Bach's appointment there (see Figure 4.2; Bach would have seen him earlier in 1710 if he visited the city that year).

18 See BD 2:42 (nos. 50–51) and 1:155–56 (no. 84), the latter trans. in NBR, 64 (no. 42).

19 Küster (1996, 192–93), trans. in NBR, 60 (no. 38).

that year onward can a few compositions be attached to specific dates or occasions.

First came a trip to Weissenfels, where Bach is presumed to have performed for Duke Christian's birthday. This was the younger brother of the Duke Johann Georg who had vetoed Bach's appointment as organist at Sangerhausen in 1703. Although his domain bordered on that of the Weimar dukes—members like himself of the Wettin dynasty—Christian belonged to the Albertine branch of the family that also held Electoral Saxony (and the crown of Poland). But the long borders of the two territories—neither of which comprised a single integral unit, rather a tortuous collection of little enclaves—meant that the two neighbors needed to stay on good terms with one another. Weissenfels was closer, geographically and polit-ically, to Electoral Saxony, which was far larger and wealthier than either, its capital the great city of Dresden. But the minor courts of Weimar and Weissenfels continued for the time being to assert their pretensions to ducal status. One aspect of this was their heavy spending on music—through which Christian, like Ernst August of Weimar, later expressed his "love" for Sebastian Bach (see Chapter 10), but which eventually played a role in ef-fectively bankrupting both statelets.

Christian, a few years older than Bach, had succeeded his older brother as duke in 1712. One acknowledgment of his succession was the gift of the Weissenfels Hunting Cup, a gaudily decorated gold-enameled trinket from the Elector; another was a little allegorical opera or serenata performed the following year, following an actual if ritualized hunt.[20] The serenata was the so-called Hunt Cantata by Bach, who was in Weissenfels on February 21 and 22.[21] This was just before Maria Barbara delivered the twins Maria Sophia and Johann Christoph on February 23—which also happened to be Duke Christian's thirty-first birthday. The singers for the performance, doubtless led by Bach himself, probably included his landlord Weldig, who had just moved to Weissenfels but had not yet

20 The *Weißenfelser Jagdpokal* is now in the Grünes Gewölbe (Green Vault), part of the state art collection in Dresden. Eighteenth-century "hunting" by European aristocrats could involve shooting animals that had already been driven into an enclosure.

21 The sole documentary hint of a performance of BWV 208 on this occasion is the record of Bach's payment for two days' accommodation (BD 2:45 [no. 55]; NBR, 64–65 [no. 44]), but his autograph score appears to date from this time rather than that of the work's likely reperformance in 1716.

sold his house in Weimar.[22] Bach's music is truly grand and remarkable in many ways, as the new Weissenfels duke probably appreciated. Yet the composer could not have known whether he would find his wife and infants alive when he returned to Weimar. In fact, Christoph died immediately, and, as Weimar and Weissenfels were separated by at least one long day's journey (38 miles), it is possible that Bach arrived home to find his second son already buried. Maria Sophia died three weeks later.[23] Undaunted, Sebastian and Maria Barbara would see Carl Philipp Emanuel born barely a year later, on March 8, 1714.[24] By then, moreover, Sebastian had experienced several further propitious events.

One of these, seemingly minor, was the dedication on November 6, 1713, of Weimar's new (second) city church, St. Jacob's. An ostentatious gift of the ruling duke, demonstrating his wealth, power, and piety, the church was opened with the type of sumptuous procession and ritual that was documented in obsessive detail in publications of the period—with particular attention to the rank and title of every member of the court and city hierarchy who attended. Bach marched to the church together with the rest of the *Capelle* and what seems the entire intelligentsia of the duchy. It is unknown whether he was the composer of any of the music performed on the occasion, which included a mass and a ten-movement cantata.[25] Bach did, however, write a long strophic aria—the only known example of such a work by him—for the annual celebration of the duke's birthday; this took place the day before.[26] A month later Bach was invited to Halle, where he received but eventually declined the offer of a position as organist.

22 The census record of Bach's residence in Weldig's house also indicates that his older sister-in-law was living there; see BD 2:39 (no. 45, including commentary).

23 Christoph's death is reported in the same document that records the twins' birth and emergency baptism (*Noth Taufe*) on February 23 (BC 2:45 [no. 56]). His sister died on March 15 (BD 2:46 [no. 57]).

24 BD 2:54 (no. 67).

25 Only the text of the cantata survives, given in full in Johann Christian Lünig, *Theatrum ceremoniale*, Vol. 2 (Leipzig, 1720), 354–55; its form, alternating madrigalistic choruses and arias in da capo form with bible verses, is not found in any extant works of Bach. Wollny (2015, 132–33) suggests plausibly that the mass performed on this occasion was a magnificent polychoral work in G (BWV Anh. 167) that was once attributed to Bach but clearly belongs to the late seventeenth century.

26 According to Koch (2006, 58–59); the duke's actual birthday was on the preceding October 30.

That Bach was successfully negotiating the minefields of politics at a divided court is evident from his promotion to Concertmaster in March 1714, some three weeks before his twenty-ninth birthday and less than a week before the birth of his second surviving son Carl Philipp Emanuel. Bach's salary, which had already overtaken that of Capellmeister Drese the year before,[27] now was raised to 250 florins. A year later, the ruling duke ordered that Bach was to be treated as equal to the Capellmeister in the distribution of occasional extra payments, such as the annual new year's gift.[28] In 1715, too, Bach's household grew again with the birth of Johann Gottfried Bernhard. Both younger boys, like Friedemann, would become professional musicians, although Emanuel's long, successful career would contrast markedly with the short, ultimately ignominious one of Bernhard. High hopes, not to mention Sebastian's growing circle of prominent contacts, are evident in his choice of Telemann as Emanuel's godfather and namesake. Having served as Capellmeister at Weimar's sister court of Eisenach, Telemann was now director of church music at Frankfurt, raising the question of whether he was present for the baptism.[29] But there can be little doubt that Telemann was well known to both Bach and the Weimar court. After the early death of Prince Johann Ernst, he edited a volume of latter's compositions.[30] He would exercise decisive influence on his godson Emanuel, and likely on Sebastian as well.

If, as seems likely, Bach's promotion was part of a larger ducal project to enhance church music at the court, the plan soon ran into obstacles, not least the death in August 1715 of Prince Johann Ernst, son and heir of the junior duke Ernst August.[31] This led to a three-month cessation of court musical performances, part of a

27 An effective raise from 200 to 215 florins per year had followed Bach's return from Weissenfels in February 1713; see BD 2:36 (commentary to no. 39).

28 "distribuirende Accidentien," order of March 20, 1715, in BD 2:57 (no. 73); NBA, 73 (no. 57).

29 Exner (2016, 13–14) notes that C. P. E. Bach's baptismal record (BD 2:54 [no. 67]; NBR, 72 [no. 55]) contains no indication that Telemann stood in absentia, as Bach did for Weldig's son that same month.

30 Six violin concertos (op. 1, 1718); Bach transcribed two of these, nos. 1 and 4, for keyboard as BWV 982 and 987.

31 The prince had suffered since 1713 from some sort of infection or tumor for which medical treatment proved ineffective; he died at Frankfurt. Glöckner (1985) reproduces the

longer (six-month) mourning period. The prince's death would have served as a reminder of how the well-being of the entire *Capelle* could depend on the health of a single member of the ruling family. Bach might have composed the music for a memorial service that took place the following April; by then, however, the court had seen a more hopeful event, the marriage of the junior duke in January 1716. We might expect Bach to have composed something for this occasion as well, but although Franck's texts survive for both, the music does not.[32] We might also suppose that, during the mourning period, Bach took advantage of the cessation of regular rehearsals and performances to think more deeply about his approach to the chapel music, or to polish existing compositions for potential sale or distribution. But no new strains are immediately obvious in the church pieces that Bach resumed composing in November. At least one of his keyboard transcriptions of the young Prince's concertos may have been already completed by the previous spring, when Johann Bernhard Bach of Eisenach could have obtained his copy.[33] Certainly there is no basis for the romantic idea that these arrangements for harpsichord and organ were meant as a "private salute for eternity."[34]

With the death of the heir apparent, the marriage of Ernst August to a princess of Anhalt-Cöthen had become a matter of some urgency, which may be why it took place before the end of the mourning period.[35] The ceremony was held at Nienburg Castle in Anhalt, on the Saale River near the border with Magdeburg, some seventy miles north of Weimar.

documents relevant to the prince's death, including the text that Bach (presumably) set to music for the memorial service the following April.

32 See Glöckner (1985) and BD 2:61 (no. 77, commentary). It has been proposed that Bach reworked some of the twenty-two movements of the funeral piece for a so-called Weimar passion. If he did so, it would have served as a precedent for the re-use of another memorial piece, the *Trauerode* BWV 198, in the lost St. Mark Passion.

33 BWV 982 was one of twelve concerto transcriptions copied by Johann Bernhard Bach in the manuscript Berlin, Staatsbibliothek, Mus. ms. Bach P 280. This Bernhard, Bach's second cousin, had succeeded the older Christoph Bach as organist at Eisenach in 1703; he is thought to have visited Weimar in 1715.

34 "ein verschwiegene Gruss in die Ewigkeit" (Schering 1902–1903, 241).

35 This was Eleonore Wilhelmine's second marriage, following that in 1714 to another Saxon prince, Friedrich Ehrmann of Merseburg, who died just fourteen weeks later.

In addition to composing music for this event, Bach is presumed to have done so for the birthday of the new duchess that May; it is also thought that his Hunt Cantata was repeated for Ernst August's birthday on April 19, 1716.[36] The marriage to Princess Eleonore Wilhelmine would prove significant for Bach, who a year and a half later would be appointed Capellmeister to her brother Leopold. If he did perform for Ernst August's birthday celebration, almost immediately thereafter he returned to Halle to inspect the now finished organ by Cuncius, afterward presumably partaking of a grand banquet that included fish, several types of meat, and various delicacies including asparagus (then in season).[37] Conferring there with Kuhnau, another of the organ inspectors, Bach must have learned much about Kuhnau's position as cantor and director of church music at Leipzig. Perhaps, too, Bach discussed with Kirchhoff, the Halle organist appointed in 1714, the pros and cons of taking a municipal job after serving as a ducal Capellmeister—as Kirchhoff had done previously at the court of Holstein-Glücksburg. Leaving that court was, in principle, a step down in the social hierarchy of the time. But from Kirchhoff Bach might have begun to understand, if he had not already done so through conversations with Telemann, that life as a city musician could provide greater income and security than a court appointment, however prestigious.

Such considerations grew more serious for Bach during his last twelve months at Weimar, when his position, or at least his relationship with the ruling duke, seems to have sharply deteriorated. Things may have remained normal for a few months after the Halle trip of April 1716, and in July Bach traveled to Erfurt for another organ inspection.[38] Meanwhile, however, Telemann visited Gotha, capital of another of the Thuringian Saxon duchies, whose ailing Capellmeister Christian Friedrich Witt was perhaps already unable to fulfill his duties. He would

---

36 Evidence for all these performances is largely circumstantial. In favor of an April 1716 performance of BWV 208 is Bach's alteration of "Christian" to "Ernst August" throughout the autograph score (Berlin, Staatsbibliothek, Mus. ms. Bach P 42/3) and the visit at that time of two horn players, required by the score, from Weissenfels (Dürr, in NBA, Vol. 1/35, critical commentary, 43, citing Jauernig 1950, 99 [recte 100]).

37 The menu is given by Terry (1933, 109–10), trans. in NBR, 77 (no. 60).

38 Bach's rather perfunctory report, co-signed with the Arnstadt organ builder Weise, is in BD 1:161–62 (no. 86), trans. in NBR, 77–78 (no. 62).

die in April 1717; meanwhile a number of more and less prominent musicians served as substitutes, presumably also being evaluated as potential replacements. Some merely sent music; Bach was one of several, including (probably) the Cöthen Capellmeister Stricker, who appeared in person.[39] Telemann was eventually offered the position, and it was also proposed that Telemann should be named "general Capellmeister" for all the Thuringian Saxon courts.[40] This would have required Telemann to supply occasional compositions to each of the latter, as he was already doing for Eisenach.

Telemann remained at Frankfurt, however, and Witt would eventually be succeeded by Gottfried Heinrich Stölzel. The Cöthen Capellmeister Stricker, present at Gotha in May, was soon on his way to Neuburg-on-the-Danube to join the court of the new Elector Palatine Charles III Philipp. This left open the position at Cöthen, whose music-loving ruler Prince Leopold now evidently sent for Bach; he agreed there to become his Capellmeister as of August 1.[41] Bach could not have been impressed by the town, which was smaller and less prosperous than Weimar. Moreover, the prince was a Calvinist, meaning that he would have no use for Bach's sacred vocal music or organ pieces in his chapel. But unlike his fellow Calvinist King Friedrich Wilhelm of Prussia, Leopold was an avid collector of music and musicians and a capable player himself on the viola da gamba. Following the dismissal of the Prussian royal Capelle in 1713, several of the previous king's musicians—including Stricker and his wife—had left Berlin for Cöthen, which therefore had a splendid little court band, likely surpassing that of Weimar. Hence Cöthen was not without attractions for Bach, and although the chapel organ was not used for

39 Details in Glöckner (1995); on Stricker, see Ranft (1985, 166).

40 "allgemeiner Capellmeister," from Telemann's autobiography in Mattheson (1740, 364). According to Telemann the proposal came from Ernst August; Spitta (1873–80, 1:578n. 20) suggested that Telemann actually meant Wilhelm Ernst, but subsequent correspondence between Telemann and the junior court bears out the supposition of Jung (in Telemann 1972, 168–69) that Telemann remembered accurately and had "much closer relations" with the younger Ernst Augustus than with the latter's uncle Wilhelm Ernst.

41 Evidence for the visit and the agreement is limited to a postdated entry in the Cöthen accounts for an initial payment on August 7, plus back pay received on December 29 for the period beginning August 1 (BD 2:67 [no. 86]; NBR, 82 [nos. 70b and 70a]).

court services, it would be accessible to Bach, as presumably were at least two other organs in town.

The seventy-mile journey back to Weimar must have given Bach time to consider what had just transpired. Although he must have made the trip with permission of the senior duke, the latter might not have been aware of or approved the departure of his concertmaster to an ally of his estranged co-ruler. Ernst August presumably supported Bach in this endeavor and perhaps had even arranged for the appointment. But, given the poor relations between the two dukes, Bach probably could not count on Ernst August to obtain his dismissal from Wilhelm Ernst. He apparently continued as concertmaster at Weimar for three or four months after receiving the title of Capellmeister at Cöthen. During the same period, or immediately afterwards, he also traveled to Dresden and Leipzig. In addition, he received his first known mention in a printed book: *Das beschützte Orchester* by Johann Mattheson. The precise chronology of these events is, as usual, uncertain, as are the details of the two most important ones: the visit to Dresden, which made Bach a celebrity, and his dismissal from Weimar, the nature of which has forever darkened the reputation of Duke Wilhelm Ernst.

Mattheson's brief if flattering notice suggests that samples of recent vocal as well as keyboard compositions by Bach had reached Hamburg. A composer, singer, and voluminous writer on music, Mattheson would meet Bach in person when the latter visited Hamburg a few years later. Yet Bach is not known to have replied to Mattheson's request for biographical information, included in the same notice.[42] One reason could be that it appeared in a book responding to a publication by the Erfurt organist Buttstett, who had attacked Mattheson's own previous work, *Das neu-eröffnete Orchester*.[43] Bach had family connections to Buttstett, a pupil of Pachelbel who had married Martha Lämmerhirt, a relative of Maria Barbara. Sebastian was not necessarily sympathetic to Buttstett's

---

42 Reproduced in BD 2:65 (no. 83) but not in NBR, 324 (no. 318, with an erroneous reference to BD 2, no. 200). NBR gives only the first of two sentences; the second makes it clear that Mattheson did not yet know Bach personally.

43 "The newly established orchestra" (Hamburg, 1713), essentially a treatise on modern or *galant* musical style. The title of Mattheson's 1717 publication ("The orchestra defended") alluded to its defense against criticisms laid out by Buttstett.

reactionary musical ideas, but he might have wished to avoid being seen as an adherent to either side of the controversy.

More significant for Bach's fame within the region and for eternity was his visit to Dresden, which thus became the site of one of the most famous non-events in European music history: Bach's musical duel with the French keyboardist and composer Louis Marchand. Although recounted in every biography of Bach, the incident was first recorded by writers who were not present and who failed to give crucial details, such as the date. The clearest, if not necessarily the most reliable, account is that of the Obituary, which places the event prior to Bach's departure for Cöthen.[44]

Musical contests were a storytelling trope that went back to antiquity. This made them no less real or entertaining for a society that enjoyed historical reenactment—whether onstage, as in operas about historical figures, or in court concerts. Bach's Leipzig serenata on the contest of Phoebus and Pan (BWV 201) would dramatize an ancient Greek myth; his participation in an actual competition at Dresden would have echoed an earlier one there involving Froberger and Weckmann.[45] Marchand had published two small books of harpsichord pieces in 1702, and some of his organ music was printed after his death in 1732, but little else survives to document his reputation as a virtuoso on both instruments. During 1713 he toured the Empire, playing for the emperor, among others. In fall 1717 he visited Dresden, where he was supposedly offered a court position. Bach, invited as a guest by the concertmaster Volumier, heard Marchand "secretly" (*heimlich*), then wrote him a letter inviting him to compete. Marchand agreed, and when the time came to appear at the home of the Saxon prime minister Count Jacob Heinrich von Flemming, many "of high rank and both sexes" were waiting expectantly—but Marchand had left early that morning.[46] The elector awarded Bach a large sum, but

---

44 BD 3:84 (no. 666), trans. in NBR, 302 (no. 306); see also Birnbaum's account, BD 2:348 (no. 441), trans. in NBR, 79–80 (no. 67). These and many further sources of the story are listed, and their relationships to one another analyzed in the manner of a philological *stemma*, by Breig (1998, 8–14).

45 This supposedly took place in 1649 or 1650; only Mattheson (1740, 396) gives the story, but it is likely to contain a kernel of truth.

46 The quote, which affirms the public nature of the event, is from the Obituary (BD 3:83 [no. 666], trans. in NBR, 301 [no. 306]).

it was embezzled by someone, and Bach won only the fame of having defeated a French rival, at a court where French music had until recently been preferred. Bach also presumably won the admiration of Count Flemming, whose older brother Johann Friedrich would receive at least two works from Bach during the 1720s and 1730s, while serving as governor of Leipzig.[47]

By the end of 1717 Bach may have been less concerned with composing or performing than with getting himself and his family out of Weimar. Although the Obituary (like Forkel's biography) delicately skips over it, we know that Bach was removed from office and incarcerated for close to a month, "on account of his stiffnecked declaration and

Figure 6.2 The restored Weimar Bastille, possibly where Bach spent his last month in the city. Photo: Pudelek (Marcin Szala), from Wikipedia.

47 BWV 210a and 249b, which survive in other versions, and BWV Anh. 10, whose lost music was attributed to Bach by Smend (see Dürr 2005, 880) on the basis of the extant text by Picander.

too forceful demand for his dismissal."[48] The biblical language—Luther used *halßstarig* to describe the stubborn Israelites who resisted Moses—suggests that it was more Bach's attitude than any particular action that led Wilhelm Ernst, or his appointed judge, to condemn his now "former" Concertmaster. What exactly Bach "declared" and how his demand for his dismissal could have been "too forceful" were evidently recorded in a more detailed document that does not survive. Could these events have been somehow precipitated by Bach's participation, or lack thereof, in celebrations of the two hundredth anniversary of the Reformation? This had been observed during October 31 through November 2;[49] four days later Bach was being held in the "local judge's chamber" (Figure 6.2). There he remained for nearly four weeks until December 2, when he was released with notice of his dishonorable discharge.

48 "wegen seiner Halßtarrigen Bezeügung v. zu erzwingenden *dismission*," BD 3:65 (no. 84). In NBR, 80 (no. 68), this is paraphrased as "too stubbornly forcing the issue of his dismissal."

49 Documented by a publication containing Franck's librettos for five separate church pieces, performed during the three days (see Bojanowski 1903, 47–48). No composer is named, and there is no evidence Bach had anything to do with it, yet if he was present one would expect him to have taken part in so important an event.

CHAPTER SEVEN

Bach the Concertmaster

CHORALES AND CANTATAS

BACH ARRIVED AT WEIMAR IN 1708 AS A TWENTY-THREE-YEAR-OLD virtuoso, clearly a genius but not yet the "Bach" that we know from the mature keyboard and vocal music. In the church works of 1714, however, we recognize the composer of the famous later compositions, as we do in the organ music and other instrumental works written by the time he left for Cöthen at the end of 1717. It was at Weimar that Bach became Bach as we know him, the transition being marked, symbolically at least, by his advancement first to concertmaster and then (on his departure) to Capellmeister. But it would be futile to seek a detailed reconstruction of his development as a composer during this period, for any attempt to place the music in a strict chronological sequence, even the vocal works, is fraught with fundamental uncertainties.[1] Moreover, despite its title, this chapter on Bach as concertmaster must examine not only the vocal music but the very substantial amount of keyboard music composed at Weimar.

Bach's responsibilities as chapel organist must have included the same basic duties as in his previous positions: "preluding" during services, and accompanying singers and instrumentalists. But the latter were now professionals, and Bach was expected to perform in the dukes' chambers

---

1 The precise chronology of Bach's Weimar church pieces remains uncertain, despite efforts by Glöckner (1985), Hofmann (1993), and Kobayashi (1995); in general, the dating followed here is that of Dürr (2005).

Bach. David Schulenberg, Oxford University Press (2020). © Oxford University Press.
DOI: 10.1093/oso/9780190936303.001.0001

as well as in their chapel. As at least two surviving vocal works predated his appointment as concertmaster, it is possible that before 1714 he was already leading rehearsals and performances of such compositions, perhaps also of instrumental and vocal music by others. The order promoting him, or rather the surviving abstract of the order, included the rather vague command to "perform new works monthly," adding that Bach was authorized to summon court musicians to rehearse those same works. Three weeks later another order forbade rehearsals at home, requiring these to be held in the chapel.[2] The first order echoed one that had been issued when Georg Christoph Strattner was named Vice-Capellmeister in 1695, a position he held until his death in 1704. That document specified that Strattner was to compose a new work for at least every fourth Sunday and was also to substitute for the Capellmeister Drese whenever that became necessary.[3] A similar rotational or alternating pattern applied to the court pastors as well.[4] Rehearsals were nevertheless to take place in Drese's house, an arrangement that finally ended with the new order of 1714.

The stipulation that rehearsals were to be held in the chapel eliminated any need for compensating the owner of another rehearsal space. The renovated Himmelsburg included a sliding partition that made it possible to close off the gallery from the rest of the chapel, conserving heat in the winter. As noted in Chapter 6, however, this might also have made the organ unbearably loud within the confined quarters, necessitating use for rehearsals of the harpsichord that was also kept there. The harpsichord was presumably also used when repairs to the organ left the latter unusable, as it was during the second half of 1712.[5] The new rule moved rehearsals to a place where Bach's authority might have been clearer. But it also held the musicians, above all their director, more accountable

---

2 Both orders were abstracted in the same document (in BD 2:53 [no. 66]); the first order was dated March 2, 1714, the second March 23. Trans. in NBR, 70–71 (nos. 51–52).

3 Even at that time, the elder Drese evidently suffered from poor health or "weakness" (*Leibesbeschwerung*); from the court order quoted by Spitta (1873–80, 1:391).

4 Koch (2006, 48) reports that the chief court cleric (*Oberhofprediger* and *Generalsuperintendent*) Lairitz and his successor preached every three or four weeks; the sermon otherwise was given by the *Hofprediger*, a position held during Bach's time by Johann Klessen.

5 Jauernig (1950, 73–74) describes the frantic efforts to make the organ usable for Wilhelm Ernst's birthday celebration that October, but it was not playable until Christmas.

to the ruling duke, who could have listened in on rehearsals, perhaps without the knowledge of the musicians high up in the gallery. By the time of these orders, Bach might already have begun taking on additional responsibilities, perhaps reflecting the salary increase granted him after the death of the former organist Effler in 1711.[6]

Bach's musical activities at the Weimar court can hardly have been confined to the chapel. Although the Himmelsburg was the most famous part of the palace complex, the residences of the two dukes contained other spaces where music could be performed. This might have involved anything from solo keyboard to the substantial chamber ensembles required by the Brandenburg Concertos and similar compositions. Such music might have been heard in the large ballroom (*Festsaal*) or in a music room (*Schall-Saal*) that has been described as an architectural masterpiece.[7] Modern focus on the chapel, and on Bach's works for voices and for organ that were performed there, has probably led to a discounting of other types of music making in which he must have participated at Weimar, both before and after his promotion to concertmaster.

Bach as Concertmaster

What did it mean to be named concertmaster? Today the term refers to the principal first violinist of an orchestra ("leader" in British terminology). Most of those who held the title during Bach's lifetime, such as Pisendel at Dresden and Johann Gottlieb Graun at Berlin, were indeed violinists, responsible for training and leading the instrumental forces of a court opera or chapel.[8] Emanuel Bach later credited his father with being able to play the violin "cleanly and penetratingly," implying that this was how he led an ensemble.[9] But a keyboardist

---

6 The document recording this, given by Küster (1996, 192–93), is translated in NBR, 60 (no. 38).

7 Performances of chamber music have been reported erroneously as occurring in the Himmelsburg; see Grychtolik (2013, 315).

8 This was also the meaning assumed by Mattheson (1739, 483).

9 Emanuel adds—probably having in mind what he knew from Leipzig (but not necessarily Weimar)—that from the violin his father "kept the orchestra in better order than he could have done with the harpsichord" ("spielte er die Violine rein u. durchdringend u. hielt dadurch das Orchester in einer größeren Ordnung, als er mit dem Flügel hätte ausrichten können," BD 3:284 [no. 801], trans. in NBR, 397 [no. 394]). *Orchestra* could have meant an

could also send aural signals to the rest of the ensemble while playing continuo at either harpsichord or organ, and by the early eighteenth century it was customary for composers of theater music to lead from the harpsichord. This could be placed at the front of the orchestra, so that the player, facing toward the stage, could see both players and singers. In churches the organist was not usually seated in a position that facilitated this, and performances probably did have to be led by the principal first violinist or a singer, sometimes working together.[10] Rehearsals, however, are another story, and the harpsichords kept at Weimar and in both principal Leipzig churches must have been used for the same.[11] Their use during performances cannot be entirely ruled out either, for, although the evidence in favor of "dual accompaniment" is slim, Bach always had pupils who might have played organ continuo while he presided from the harpsichord.[12]

Whatever his exact role as concertmaster, it is possible that Bach, already a veteran of diverse types of music making, was expected, like Pisendel and Graun, to raise the general level of the court ensemble, in part by introducing repertory in new styles that required greater virtuosity and unanimity in performance than older works. In reporting his father's ability on the violin, Emanuel Bach also mentioned Sebastian's

ensemble comprising singers as well as players, and it was not necessarily of any particular size (see Oleskiewicz 2007).

10 As shown in the famous frontispiece of Walther's *Lexicon* (1732), which depicts a singer conducting a fairly large instrumental ensemble in an organ loft with a rolled-up sheet of paper. Some of Bach's Weimar works require a comparable ensemble; the list of official court musicians given, for example, by Wolff (2000, Table 6.2 on p. 158) cannot have sufficed for every performance, and town musicians must have provided some of the instrumental parts, such as the two solo cellists required by BWV 163.

11 The available space in the musicians' loft of the Himmelsburg was probably somewhat tighter than previously imagined (see Grychtolik 2013, 311–12), throwing into doubt the hypothetical floor plan shown by Wolff (2000, 150). The harpsichord, if indeed placed there, must have been quite small, and most of the singers and players must have performed standing.

12 Dreyfus (1987) assembled evidence that seemed to point to Bach's use of organ and harpsichord together, but in most cases the separate harpsichord and organ parts that survive for certain works appear to have been prepared for different performances, sometimes for ones that took place when the organ was not usable. Wolff (2000, 158) assumes that Bach directed at least his first regular Weimar vocal work (BWV 182) as principal violinist, with a student assisting as continuo player, but no archival document mentions his violin playing.

ability to discern every part in an ensemble, an essential skill for anyone directing complex or challenging compositions. The thin two- and three-part textures of many Italianate compositions might not have required great perspicuity, but with Sebastian even a viola or third oboe part could incorporate voice leading essential to the harmony or the contrapuntal structure. Such parts, moreover, could be as technically challenging as any other, making it necessary for the leader to detect and correct any impre-cision even in the inner voices of a polyphonic texture.

Sebastian was not the only composer of new types of music that were making increased demands on performers after 1700. Lully's ballet pieces, introduced into Germany during the previous generation, had already required greater precision and uniformity of rhythm and articulation than had previously been customary. Now the virtuoso music of Vivaldi and other Italian composers was making its way to German courts, in manuscript copies as well as printed editions. Many such works were printed in Amsterdam, and Prince Johann Ernst could have brought examples back from the Netherlands in 1713; others were obtained through the exchange of manuscript copies with other courts.[13] Bach must have been involved in performances of these as well as his own instrumental works.

He must also have performed in and perhaps directed sacred vocal music by other composers. The ruler's 1714 order promoting Bach did not, as we have it, state explicitly that every new piece that Bach performed had to be his own, or that it had to be for the chapel. Also unstated is what was performed on days when Bach did not provide music. If Bach indeed composed one church work every four weeks during his three-plus years as concertmaster, then the twenty surviving compositions can represent only about half of what he wrote. While serving as concert-master Bach received regular allotments of paper. These would have pro-vided many times the number of pages required for writing out scores and performing parts for his surviving works.[14] But we do not know

13 See Schulze (1984, 146ff. and 165–67). Górny (2019) raises the possibility of further acquisitions through a Halle bookseller.

14 Wolff (2000, 166–67) calculates that up to 80 percent of Bach's Weimar output has been lost, based on the paper supplied to him during 1714–1717, but how much of this comprised unique original compositions is unknown.

whether this same paper served for copies of music by other composers, for extra parts, or even for purposes other than music, including copies of librettos, accounts, and correspondence.

One of the many questions that arise in this regard is who actually owned the scores and parts that Bach or any court musician copied onto this paper. Bach clearly brought scores and some parts with him from Weimar to Cöthen and eventually Leipzig. But he might have been expected to leave many things in the ducal archive, especially the valuable performing parts for his and others' compositions. As the library went up in smoke in 1774, together with most of the castle itself, the musical documents that may have belonged to it are long gone. Other losses could have been the results of deliberate decisions by Bach himself. It would have been a waste of effort to carry un-needed old scores or parts from one place to another. Even if there was space to store them, a composer ran the risk that someone might find an early work (or an early version of a revised one) and damage his reputation by disseminating it. Emanuel Bach might have been merely following his father's example when he burned "a ream or more" of older compositions late in life;[15] he considered it laughable (*possierlich*) that the king of England preserved youthful works by Handel. Traces of lost material have nevertheless been detected in later compositions that Sebastian is thought to have adapted from Weimar works that no longer survive.

Among Bach's Weimar works are keyboard arrangements of concertos by Vivaldi, Prince Johann Ernst, and others. Their survival, as well as that of a few manuscript parts and scores for compositions by others, points potentially to his having prepared many more such copies, for study as well as performance. One wonders in particular how much of Telemann's music was heard at Weimar. Telemann would exert a pro-found stylistic influence on Emanuel Bach, whose instrumental and vocal compositions would be more like those of his godfather than his father. There are also indications that Telemann was an important influ-ence on Sebastian himself during these Weimar years. Bach arranged one of Telemann's concertos for solo keyboard and copied out performing

---

15 "ein Ries u. mehr alte Arbeiten," letter of January 21, 1786, to J. J. Eschenburg (Suchalla 1994, 1133 [no. 529]), trans. in Clark (1997, 244 [no. 287]).

parts for another.[16] Moreover, the new type of church music that Bach began to compose regularly in 1714 had seen its first really intensive and systematic cultivation by Telemann. At Eisenach, Telemann had already composed his first annual cycle of church pieces during 1710–1711. This must have been known at Weimar, and the cantatas that Bach wrote there could, to some degree, have been modeled on those of Telemann even while being intended to surpass them. In 1714 Bach's pupil and assistant Schubart was paid for copying music after returning from a trip to Frankfurt; he had gone there to visit the ailing Prince Johann Ernst, but might he also have picked up music from Capellmeister Telemann?[17]

Telemann himself reported studying "models" (*Müster*) of sacred and instrumental music by older Italian and German composers.[18] Bach knew works by at least two of these, Corelli and Caldara. Other composers from Italy and France are represented in surviving remnants of Bach's music library, which included keyboard works by Frescobaldi, Grigny, and Dieupart; concertos by Albinoni and Vivaldi; Latin polyphonic compositions going back to the late Renaissance; and a cantata and a solo motet, respectively, by Antonio Biffi and Francesco Bartolomeo Conti.[19] Today these last two composers are obscure and seemingly insignificant, but for Bach they were older contemporaries to be taken seriously. Some of this music, such as the organ works by Frescobaldi and Grigny (printed long previously), might have been accessible to Bach before his arrival at Weimar. But once there, Bach had many more opportunities to study such music, not least by sharing his holdings with those of Walther, likewise an inveterate collector. Not all this music was up-to-date, but Bach's interests went beyond the currently fashionable. Although he might already have had access to important works of the past at Lüneburg and Mühlhausen, he would have gained a different perspective by exchanging music with the university-trained Walther. Old polyphonic compositions by Palestrina and others, which he previously

---

16 Bach arranged the violin concerto TWV 51:g21 for keyboard as BWV 985; his manuscript parts for TWV 52:G2 survive in Dresden, Landesbibliothek, Mus. ms. 2392-O35a, to which Pisendel added extra ripieno violin parts around 1720.

17 Schubart's payments are recorded in the Weimar archives; details in Jauernig (1950, 99).

18 In Mattheson (1740, 357).

19 Details about most of these in Beißwenger (1992).

might have seen only in individual performing parts, now took their place in a collection of scores that also included more recent models of composition by such living composers as Albinoni and Vivaldi.[20]

Today we tend to see the latter as writers of virtuoso showpieces such as the *Four Seasons*; modern teaching of Baroque performance emphasizes the impulsive *bizzarria* of the Italian Baroque. Bach, however, is more likely to have viewed even contemporary Italian composers as learned successors of Palestrina, for he seems particularly to have valued the fugues or fugal movements in their sonatas and concertos. These were not concert pieces in the modern sense, rather chamber music, played by and for small gatherings of connoisseurs—academies (*accademie*), to use the historical term. A work such as Corelli's "trio" sonata in B minor, op. 3, no. 4, involved only one or two fewer players than a violin concerto by Vivaldi, and Bach made adaptations of music by both: a *pedaliter* fugue based on subjects from the Corelli work (BWV 579), and the series of keyboard arrangements of concertos by Vivaldi and others, mostly *manualiter* (BWV 972–86) but including five examples with pedals (BWV 592–96). The "Corelli" fugue, like the *manualiter* fugues on subjects by Albinoni (see Chapter 5), retains enough traces of earlier German organ style to suggest that it dates from no later than Bach's first years at Weimar. The concerto transcriptions must have been carried out over a period that probably extended into the later part of Bach's Weimar period. In any case they document his knowledge not only of Vivaldi's printed Opus 3 (twelve concertos of various types) but also of individual concertos that appeared in later publications.[21]

His acquaintance with these and diverse other compositions doubtless fired the still young Bach to all sorts of efforts. Unfortunately, the five-year gap in precisely datable works between BWV 71 (February 1708) and BWV 208 (February 1713) leaves us in the dark as to how Bach was evolving as a composer. Plenty of Bach's organ music is likely to date from this period—many organ chorales, including the more old-fashioned

---

20 The list of compositions by Palestrina available to Bach (and emulated by him and Walther) was expanded by Wiermann (2002); further discussion in Melamed (2012).

21 Bach's transcriptions of two concertos later printed in Vivaldi's op. 4 appear to have been made from early versions transmitted in single manuscript copies (see Schulenberg 2006, 125, 127).

of the "Great 18," as well as the more retrospective preludes and fugues. Such could well constitute the bulk of Bach's work from these years. On the other hand, the refinement and assuredness of his vocal works from 1713 onwards, which are in a style entirely different from his earlier ones, suggest that we have lost many transitional compositions from the previous four or five years. If so, however, these have left no traces. We should not discount the possibility that a genius could have produced works such as BWV 21 and 208 with no prior exercises other than the vocal compositions that survive from an earlier time.

Crucial for Bach's development during this period must have been the availability of free time in which to work out his ideas both on paper and at the keyboard. As chapel organist—a role he might have continued to play after his promotion to concertmaster, although possibly assisted by students—Bach was probably required to be present for various weekly services, in addition to regular Sunday and holiday worship. But even after his promotion, the requirement to perform a new work only once every four weeks would have given him a far more leisurely composition schedule than that of Telemann or Drese. Bach fulfilled this duty with compositions that are larger than those of his contemporaries, if not always in absolute length then in the number of independent vocal and instrumental parts. To write in this manner was evidently his choice, and although he would do the same during his first few years at Leipzig, at Weimar he must have had more time than later. This would have allowed him to reflect on the libretto he was to set, then to draw up plans and write out his score, possibly in multiple successive drafts.

The failure of Bach's working papers to survive from Weimar—unlike some of those from Leipzig—has probably influenced scholars to assume that the hectic pace of Bach's first years at Leipzig, which saw the production of roughly one cantata every week, was typical throughout his career. But within his career as a whole the rate of activity during 1723–1726 seems to have been exceptional, and Bach was able to maintain it for only those few years. During that period he did produce what seems by later standards a large body of music. Yet Telemann was not the only contemporary who produced far more, composing at a prodigious rate with little let-up even in his last few years. Evidently Bach differed from many contemporaries in his tendency to revise previously written compositions—a habit that he was already indulging at Weimar—and in his apparent withdrawal from active composing for substantial periods of his life, perhaps even the majority of his working years.[22]

Whatever his working routines, one likely product of Bach's Weimar years, especially as concertmaster, was the crystallization of what have been called his "music-writing" habits. Although his manner of composing never became routine, in the sense of repeating formulas, the requirement to prepare new works for the *Capelle* on a regular basis would have led to, if it did not merely confirm, systematic practices in everything from the ruling of music paper to details of notation. It was, for example, around the time of his promotion that Bach switched to the modern usage of natural signs to cancel accidentals. This replaced an older way of notating such things with sharps and flats alone, so that a flat on F might cancel a previous F-sharp. The shift is meaningless from the point of view of sound, but it helps scholars attach dates to Bach's manuscripts. It also points in a small way toward a more modern way of understanding tonality, a gradual process that led to the Well-Tempered Clavier (see Chapter 9).

Bach's Weimar Compositions

Table 7.1 provides an overview of the music that Bach is thought to have composed during his Weimar years. There are many uncertainties, particularly with regard to the chronological placement of the "free" keyboard pieces (those not based on chorales), as well as the few works for instrumental ensemble. Nevertheless the table conveys the main categories of compositions in which Bach produced many masterpieces at Weimar, most of them in forms and styles that were still new.

Because the individual compositions vary so greatly in size—both in length and in number of performing parts—it is difficult to judge the relative "weight" of one group of compositions as compared to another. But three categories dominate: organ chorales, preludes and fugues for solo keyboard (including related compositions, especially toccatas), and

22 During 1717–1718 Telemann did return to his Eisenach *Jahrgang* of 1710–1711, revising or replacing certain of his earlier settings of Neumeister's cantata texts, but only seventeen works from what might have been his fifth annual cycle have been identified (see Poetzsch-Seban 2006, 107–18, as well as the overview on 280–87). The reworking seems to have been prompted more by the availability of a larger body of musicians at Frankfurt than by an impulse to perfect the original compositions.

Table 7.1   Works Probably Completed at Weimar

Keyboard

Suites: BWV 806–11 (the English Suites), 818, 823, 996

Preludes and fugues (and related pieces) without pedal: BWV 894–95, 899–904, 944

Praeludia (preludes and fugues) with pedal: BWV 538, 540–43, 545–46, 572

Forty-six chorale preludes with pedal, later called the *Orgelbüchlein*: BWV 599–644

Sixteen larger organ chorales later revised at Leipzig: BWV 651–66 (early versions)

Other chorale settings, mostly with pedal, including: BWV 694–95, 709–13, 717, 721, 727, 730–31, 733, 734a, 735a, 736, and 740

Pieces possibly drafted before mid-1708 but completed or revised afterward: praeludia BWV 532, 550, 922; toccatas BWV 564, 910–16; passacaglia BWV 582; fugues BWV 574, 951; chorale partita BWV 768; "Arnstadt" chorales BWV 715, 722, 726, 729, 732, and 738

Other instrumental

Six cello suites: BWV 1007–12

Violin sonata BWV 1023 and fugue BWV 1026

Violin concerto BWV 1052 (original version)

Sinfonia BWV 1046a (early version of Brandenburg Concerto no. 1)

Vocal

Kyrie BWV 233a

Motets BWV 228, Anh. 159 (?)

Aria BWV 1127

Serenata (Hunt Cantata) BWV 208

Twenty-two church pieces (listed in possible chronological order): BWV 21, 199, 182, 12, 172, 61, 152, 18, 54, 31, 165, 185, 163, 132, 63, 155, 80a, 161, 162, 70a, 186a, 147a

church pieces (sacred cantatas). Others are of secondary importance from the point of view of Bach's overall development, with the possible exception of keyboard suites. Of the latter, however, not all those listed were necessarily composed or completed at Weimar, and as they are allied with works that are clearly later, their discussion is postponed until Chapter 9.

Viewed from the broadest perspective, the great achievement in these Weimar compositions was the merging of elements of music in the current Italian style with older principles that Bach had already mastered in his early works. Among these principles are an insistence on rigorous counterpoint, constant searching for inventive harmony and modulation, and the obsessive development of a limited number of motivic patterns in any one piece (as opposed to continuous free invention). New elements from Italian—especially Venetian—vocal and instrumental music include certain large-scale formal patterns or designs, as well as specific types of melodic writing that proved useful for filling out and articulating the new musical forms. What these abstract formulations meant in practice will become clear through the examination of specific compositions.

Another consistent principle in these works, although harder to discuss objectively, is Bach's constant striving for a challenging type of expressivity, evident especially in the intense chromaticism of many works, instrumental as well as vocal. Allied to that is a type of musical rhetoric in the sacred works that often leads to departures from any formal plan implied by the text, as in the irregular musical setting of an aria whose poem is in standard da capo form. Composers of the time normally followed poets with respect to the forms of arias, which could be signaled by the forms of their texts. Ternary (ABA) or da capo form was most common, but there were also bipartite (AB) and other designs. Bach often disregarded the clear implications of his librettos for expressive or rhetorical purposes, not least in his Weimar works.

The transition from Bach's early style to an up-to-date Italianate one is evident in the so-called Little G-minor organ fugue BWV 578, which is actually not so little: sixty-eight measures based on a long subject, which is presented in three expository passages separated by episodes.[23] The date of this work is far from certain, but it was most likely written early in Bach's Weimar period, and in any case it already follows new compositional principles typical of larger and probably later pieces. One of these principles is *tonal design*, the purposeful tracing of a series of modulations away from and then back to the tonic; the most remote keys are reached in the central parts of the piece. A second principle will be described as *recapitulation*: the transposed restatement of a previously heard passage.[24]

---

23 This analysis regards the parallel passages at mm. 22 and 45b as episodes; other "free" passages as at m. 29b are considered "bridges" that join entries of the subject but are not articulated as distinct sections.

24 "Recapitulation" in this sense is distinct from the customary understanding of the term as applied to Classical sonata form. In the latter, the recapitulation is a distinct section—the third one in a sonata-allegro movement. With Bach, recapitulation, that is, the transposed restatement of a passage, can occur anywhere within a movement, often more than once.

Of course the subject of a fugue recurs repeatedly in the expositions, but always in new contrapuntal contexts. The same is true of the ritornello in a movement from a concerto. By "recapitulation" is meant here the restatement of matter *other* than the subject or ritornello theme, that is, passages from the episodes. Older composers, including Bach at an earlier date, might have regarded the restatement of such a passage as a failure of the imagination—even if the music was transposed or individual melodic lines redistributed between the various parts, as is typical with Bach. But symmetry and patterned restatement were now seen as positive features, rendering a complex design audible. In the "Little" G-minor fugue, the resulting clarity has helped make this piece a favorite for introducing students to the analysis of fugues.

"Free" Keyboard Works

The adoption of new Italianate features remains incipient in what are probably Bach's earliest keyboard works of the Weimar years. His move there took place rather suddenly, and at first he must have continued to write and play much as he had been doing previously. Some seemingly transitional compositions combine elements of older German and newer Italian music, the latter coming to the fore in what are ostensibly later works. Accompanying this is an increase in virtuosity as well as a trend toward greater monumentality; both elements reach a climax in several organ works of enormous length that nevertheless hold the attention of an alert listener to the very end. This is due partly to stunning effects of harmony and counterpoint, as well as pure technical display, as in the so-called Dorian toccata and fugue BWV 538. Equally important is the use of modulating designs that are articulated not only by restatements of an easily recognized theme or subject, but also by the selective recapitulation of entire passages. These features, which Bach could have heard in instrumental music by Albinoni or the Marcello brothers (but not that of Reinken or Buxtehude), made it possible to construct an unbroken musical argument lasting ten minutes or longer from a limited number of motivic ideas, as in the shattering F-major toccata and fugue (BWV 540).

Toccatas

The most important of the "transitional" works—the quotation marks are warranted because we do not know whether they were actually

Example 7.1   (a) Toccata in C, BWV 564/1, mm. 20–21 (b) Toccata in D minor (*manualiter*), BWV 913, mm. 1–3

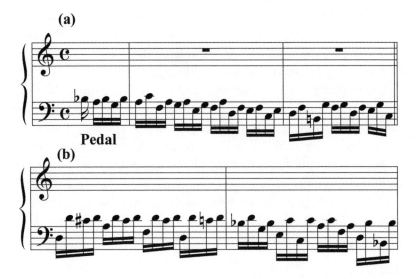

completed during a specific transition period—are eight toccatas, one with pedals, seven without. The *pedaliter* work (BWV 564) has always been understood as an organ piece, whereas the manuals-only toccatas are usually regarded as having been written for harpsichord. At least some of the *manualiter* toccatas (BWV 910–16) were probably drafted before Bach reached Weimar, but if meant specifically for the harpsichord they raise the question of where they might have been heard. Public recitals on stringed keyboard instruments were unknown, yet these toccatas are clearly display pieces, intended for more than private study. Performances at court or for wealthy private patrons, on harpsichord or clavichord, are possible but undocumented. These pieces certainly imitate organ idioms, as in the left-hand (bass) solos heard in several of them (Example 7.1). Yet unlike the pedal solos of real organ pieces, such passages in the *manualiter* toccatas—usually part of an opening improvisatory section—can migrate into higher tessituras. Together with the presence of idiomatic features of harpsichord music, they reduce the likelihood that Bach intended his *manualiter* music for the organ.[25]

25 As hypothesized by Marshall (1986), who suggested that the term *manualiter* in original titles pointed to performance specifically on organ, without pedals.

The toccata had been an important early-Baroque genre, as in the music of Frescobaldi. Bach, probably following a few examples by Reinken and Buxtehude, seems to have understood any toccata as alternating between free figuration and fugue, sections of the latter type serving as the goal or culmination of the former. Each of his toccatas includes a grand final fugue, although there may also be a brief concluding passage in a distinct style and tempo. Apart from the latter, or brief bridge passages elsewhere, the individual sections are longer than in early-Baroque toccatas. The fugues, in particular, are sufficiently substantial that they could stand as self-contained movements and might have done so at early stages in these pieces' compositional histories. Yet each of these toccatas as we have them comprises a series of contrasting sections with a unique overall shape, recalling older Baroque keyboard music even as it evokes more recent Italianate instrumental types, including the Venetian solo concerto.

Concerto Transcriptions

It is possible that Bach's later evocations of Italian instrumental music, in works like the *pedaliter* toccatas in D minor (BWV 538/1) and F major (BWV 540/1), really were prompted (as has been suggested) by the return of Prince Johann Ernst in 1713 from studies in Utrecht, laden with performing parts for Italian concertos. But Bach's concerto transcriptions—including the twelve copied by Bernhard Bach—show different degrees of finish, suggesting that work on them took place over more than a single brief period. Walther, who like Bach made both *manualiter* and *pedaliter* transcriptions of Italian concertos, seems to have arranged only somewhat earlier pieces, composed or published a few years before his arrival at Weimar—hence among the very first such compositions to be disseminated in Germany.[26] Bach also arranged a few examples of this early type, but in Bernhard Bach's set of twelve pride of place is given to more recent works by Vivaldi.[27] Forkel was wrong to state that Bach made keyboard versions of "all" Vivaldi's concertos (which number in the

---

26 Walther's transcriptions were included in the edition of his collected keyboard works by Max Seiffert (*Denkmäler deutscher Tonkunst*, Vol. 26/27, Leipzig: Breitkopf und Härtel, 1906).

27 The earliest piece arranged by Bach may have been the concerto in D minor, which has been regarded as either a work by Torelli or an early composition of Vivaldi, transcribed as BWV 979; see Sardelli (2005, 75–77).

hundreds). But it is not impossible that Bach did arrange all twelve works that made up Vivaldi's ground-breaking Opus 3. Issued at Amsterdam in 1711, Vivaldi's *L'estro armonico* comprised four solo, four double, and four quadruple concertos (all for strings), published in the form of eight part-books. Bach's keyboard versions, which might have been the most convenient form in which to study such pieces, survive for three of the solo concertos and two of the double concertos.

The modern terms are anachronistic and a little misleading: a "solo" concerto was a piece for three violins, viola, and continuo, with one of the violins more prominent than the others.[28] The "double" concertos have four distinct violin parts, two of which are soloistic, but one of the two cello parts may also have occasional solos, as in the D-minor concerto transcribed by Bach (as BWV 596). A solo concerto was more easily arranged for a single-manual instrument; the two known transcriptions of Vivaldi's double concertos are for organ, with pedals.[29] The four quadruple concertos, in which all four violins have soloistic material, could not be convincingly arranged for a single keyboard player, but Bach eventually made a version of at least one of these for four harpsichords and strings.[30]

Praeludia (Preludes and Fugues) and Other Pieces

Bach is known to have composed roughly a dozen large *pedaliter* preludes and fugues for organ—known simply as praeludia in the seventeenth and probably still in the early eighteenth century. A few early examples, like the toccatas, remain relatively close to German seventeenth-century pieces. Other works were not necessarily all later in origin, yet their stylistic affinities to the newer Italian types of instrumental music are evident in their textures, motivic ideas, and allusions to the alternation

28 As published, the "solo" violin concertos of Vivaldi's Opus 3 include the same eight parts as the others, but the third and fourth violin parts are identical, as are the two violas. This effectively reduces the number of real parts to five—often fewer, as all four violins may be in unison in the ritornellos.

29 Bach also made organ arrangements of Vivaldi's solo concerto R. 208 (BWV 594) and two of Johann Ernst's solo concertos, although we have only a single movement for one of the latter (BWV 595); all three movements of the same concerto appear in the *manualiter* arrangement BWV 984.

30 BWV 1065 (based on Vivaldi's op. 3, no. 10) is thought to date from Bach's Leipzig years, which is when the surviving manuscript parts were copied.

between ritornellos for the "tutti" and episodes for one or more soloists. The Praeludium in D (BWV 532) still has much in common with the D-major *manualiter* toccata (BWV 912), of which it is sometimes considered a *pedaliter* companion. Each piece opens with straightforward scales—placed in the pedals in BWV 532, a jab at any organist who could not yet execute such a thing (Example 7.2). Both pieces also reveal an obsession with remote modulations, implying that Bach wrote them for instruments whose up-to-date tuning allowed each piece to wander to keys such as F-sharp and even C-sharp minor without producing intolerably sour triads.

In addition to preludes and fugues, Bach wrote other types of "free" keyboard pieces at Weimar, two of the most extraordinary being examples of the fantasia. This genre could encompass strict contrapuntal writing, but it could also take the form of a written-out improvisation, incorporating modulations even more striking than those in BWV 532 and 912. Bach left two famous examples, one for organ, one for harpsichord; neither assuredly originated at Weimar, but the Chromatic Fantasia (BWV 903/1) for harpsichord contains apparent echoes of Vivaldi's "Grosso Mogul" concerto, arranged there for organ as BWV 594. The

Example 7.2   (a) Praeludium in D, BWV 532, mvt. 1, mm. 1–2; (b) Toccata in D, BWV 912, mm. 1–2

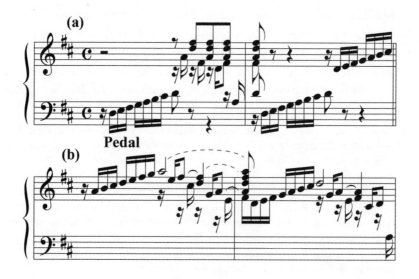

echoes of the latter involve not virtuoso display music but instrumental recitative—that is, imitation of the vocal idiom, which Vivaldi used as the basis of the second movement and which Bach, in turn, imitates in the second half of the fantasia (Example 7.3). Neither composer imitated recitative in a literal manner—unless singers habitually added flourishes and little cadenzas of the type seen in both pieces, which seems unlikely. Rather Bach, like Vivaldi, treated instrumental recitative as a free, chameleon-like type of music that modulates frequently and dramatically. The recitative passage in the Chromatic Fantasia is preceded by an equally remarkable preludial section in the tradition of his organ praeludia. A fugue on a chromatic subject follows, but although resembling other Italianate fugues of the Weimar period, it is less compelling than the fantasia and may not have originally been paired with it.

The *pedaliter* fantasia in G minor (BWV 542/1) is a very different composition, deliberately avoiding—or so it seems—many features of the traditional organ prelude. This might mean that it is a significantly later work, yet it still consists—like the prelude of BWV 532—of free

Example 7.3   (a) Concerto in C, BWV 594 (after Vivaldi, R. 208), mvt. 2, m. 5; (b) Chromatic Fantasia in D minor, BWV 542/1, mm. 50–51

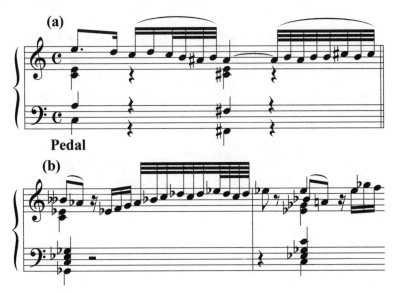

outer sections that frame a more "composed" central section (here in a highly attenuated binary form). In place of the ostentatious pedal solos of several earlier organ preludes, the outer sections incorporate a type of written-out melodic embellishment that Bach would have learned from Italian violinists, or from the decorated adagios in the Amsterdam reprint of Corelli's Opus 5 (Example 7.4). This style, which Bach also imitates in instrumental parts from some of the Weimar vocal works, had antecedents in embellished keyboard chorales by Buxtehude and other seventeenth-century composers. But by the time of BWV 542 Bach had developed his own vocabulary of decorative figures, adapted to the keyboard and subsequently deployed in his music for violin and other solo instruments.

The really remarkable aspect of both fantasias is their modulations, which take them to tonal regions far removed from their home keys. The organ fantasia is in some ways even more extraordinary than BWV 903/1, for its harmonic adventures take place not in the free outer passages but within the more strictly composed middle section of the piece. These

Example 7.4   (a) Corelli, Sonata in G minor for violin and continuo, op. 5, no. 5 (as published in embellished form by Roger of Amsterdam, ca. 1712), mvt. 1, mm. 1–2; (b) Fantasia in G minor, BWV 542/1, mm. 1–2

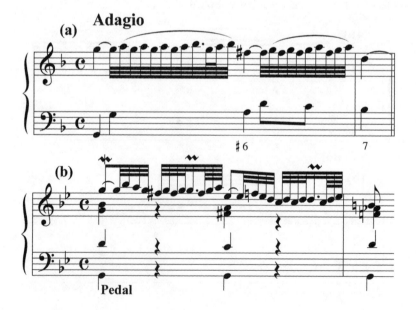

modulations are even more jarring, many of the individual sonorities more dissonant, than those in the Chromatic Fantasia. Yet they are handled with complete authority, demonstrating a mastery of harmony that is as astonishing as Bach's counterpoint in other works. As with the Chromatic Fantasia, a fugue follows that probably originated separately. In this case the fugue—its subject apparently based on a Dutch folk song[31]—has nothing to do with the style of its prelude, although it is another impressive recital piece in concerto style.

Even more overwhelming in performance are Bach's two biggest organ praeludia, each of which is designated a toccata and fugue in certain manuscript copies (no autograph material survives for either). BWV 538, in D minor, was notated in what was becoming an archaic fashion, without a flat as key signature; it therefore is known today as the "Dorian" Toccata and Fugue. It is, however, entirely tonal and has none of the modal character of which Bach, Walther, and their contemporaries were well aware in chorale melodies and other older music. Its first movement seems inspired as much by concertos as by older toccatas; the first movement of BWV 540, in F major, is more justifiably described as a toccata on account of its long pedal points. These were a traditional feature of a type of toccata that went back to the time of Frescobaldi; Bach would have known more recent examples by Pachelbel.[32] Needless to say, Bach surpasses those pieces in every conceivable way, including sheer length. Yet as he wrote both toccatas, he must have realized that he was pushing the limits of what was possible even for him.

Of the two fugues, the "Dorian" (BWV 538/2) is one of Bach's most austere, uncompromising instrumental compositions. Its particular concern is canon: precise imitation, as opposed to the relatively free type of imitation typical of ordinary fugues. There are no fewer than fifteen canonic passages over the course of the fugue; these increase in complexity and level of dissonance as the piece progresses. The F-major toccata and

---

31 Mattheson (1731, 1:34–35) gives a version of the subject, which he says was the basis of an unnamed player's organ audition at the Hamburg Cathedral on October 24, 1725. This was almost three years after Bach had been heard in Hamburg, but as Mattheson also gives Bach's countersubject, he apparently knew BWV 542, which had surely already been composed well before Bach's visit (as suggested by Wolff 2000, 213).

32 No fewer than four toccatas constructed over pedal points occur in the Möller and Andreas Bach manuscripts, all edited by Hill (1991).

fugue is easier to enjoy, although it too is not exactly likable, if only be-cause of its intimidating grandeur. One recurring passage in the toccata is of particular interest, as it is constructed over a bass line that quotes the letters of Bach's name: B-flat (called B in German terminology), A, C, and B-natural (German H). Those pitches never occur literally; instead the line is transposed, beginning on A-flat (m. 204), D-flat (m. 318), and finally C-flat (m. 424). In each case the chord built over the first note is a stunning harmonic surprise, making each statement of Bach's name a dramatic event, particularly the last time. That the Bach name could be the basis of a musical "idea" would soon be well known, if it was not al-ready.[33] Its most famous appearance in Sebastian's music is from near the end of his career, in the *Art of Fugue*, where it is used as a secondary fugue subject (see Chapter 13).

Keyboard Chorales

Exactly how the surviving keyboard chorales were used in the chapel, in teaching, or otherwise in Bach's work during the Weimar period—including recitals and organ "tests" elsewhere—is unknown. As in earlier periods, these make up the single largest group of his works, in terms of sheer numbers. They also include the two earliest sets of organ compositions that Bach is known to have gathered into formal collections, although neither set was finalized until after Bach left Weimar. Pieces from the two sets—the *Orgelbüchlein* and the misnamed "Leipzig" or "Great Eighteen" Chorales—are much studied by organists. For others, however, these are the least well known of Bach's major works, despite occasional efforts to bring them to wider audiences through transcriptions (such as Busoni's for piano). Today their liturgical character may make them seem remote to many listeners, but they are no more or less "sacred" than other repertories, being religious only in their use of hymn tunes as a source of melodic ideas. Whether they express anything more specific than "affects" or emotions associated with their melodies (such as joy or sorrow) is controversial. Certainly they are as brilliant compositionally and as rich in opportunities for virtuoso display as any other category of works by Bach.

---

33 Walther (1732, 64) mentions it in his entry for J. S. Bach.

The collection of shorter chorale settings, which Bach copied into a manuscript while at Weimar, was later designated the *Orgelbüchlein* or Little Organ Book. The title, added at Cöthen, explained that here an "inquiring organist" would receive "guidance . . . in how to implement a chorale in all kinds of ways, and at the same time to become practised in the study of pedalling."[34] The manuscript was planned as a collection of hymn settings, starting with a selection ordered according to the church year, then continuing with hymns appropriate to any season (*de omne tempore*). Bach entered the titles of 164 chorales on 182 pages, but at Weimar he wrote only 45 pieces into the book, probably during the period 1713–1716. He added a single complete setting and one additional brief fragment around 1740 at Leipzig.[35]

We call these pieces chorale preludes on the assumption that they were used to introduce congregational singing. But whether that was the practice at Weimar is unknown, and Bach never used the expression "prelude" as a title for such pieces. By the same token, the word *fantasia* is part of the original title of only a few of some two dozen larger chorale settings that Bach also composed at Weimar. Seventeen of these were later revised and copied into a manuscript collection now known, confusingly, as the "Leipzig chorales." To these was added one more piece, so that the same collection is also called the "Great Eighteen." The collection lacks an original title, however, and its intended extent is uncertain; Bach copied only the first thirteen pieces as a unit, and the last three are not even in his hand.[36] Hence the status of this set and the basis of its organization have been controversial, although there is little question that the early versions of its contents were all or mostly composed during the

34 Berlin, Staatsbibliothek, Mus. ms. Bach P 283, as translated by Williams (2003, 227).

35 The exact dating and sequence of the entries have been a matter of controversy; see, for example, Stinson (1996, especially 12–25) and Williams (2003, 231–33). Some pieces are fair copies, presumably copied from lost older scores, whereas others appear to have been composed directly into the surviving manuscript.

36 The manuscript is part of a composite or convolute that also contains the six organ sonatas BWV 525–30 (Berlin, Staatsbibliothek, Mus. ms. Bach 271); in addition, the Canonic Variations BWV 769a are interposed before BWV 668, the last of the "Eighteen." BWV 668 is in the hand of an anonymous copyist, and BWV 666–67 were copied by Bach's son-in-law Altnickol.

Weimar years. It is likely that Bach planned a revised set of fifteen pieces around 1740, at a time when he was assembling other sets of keyboard music as well (see Chapter 13). But when first written, over a period roughly spanning his Weimar years, these may have been conceived, like the praeludia, as separate pieces for concerts or study. Both sets are diverse in style and expressive character, ranging from strict canons among the chorale preludes and austere chorale "motets" in the "Great Eighteen" to exuberant free settings inspired by the latest Italian concertos and trio sonatas.

Vocal Works

The vocal music that Bach began to compose on a regular basis in March 1714 consisted of church pieces of the type that we call cantatas. He wrote these through December 1716; a handful may also have been composed during the previous year or two alongside several other vocal works. Most but not all of their texts were by the court poet Franck, who eventually published many of them as parts of two yearly cycles (*Jahrgänge*) of such librettos. It is possible that, when Franck embarked on the second such project toward the end of 1716, Bach anticipated writing an entire annual series of compositions based on Franck's poetry during the following months. Telemann had done as much at Eisenach during 1710–1711, using texts by his former and future colleague Neumeister. If so, this was not to be; Bach failed to receive the appointment as successor to the late Capellmeister Drese, and more than six years would pass before he began to incorporate some of these Weimar compositions into his first *Jahrgang* of church cantatas at Leipzig.

The type of Italian opera that provided models for both the texts and music of these works was not a mere pastime. Cultivation of serious opera (*opera seria*) was a way for an aristocratic patron of the time to demonstrate devotion to the arts and education while disseminating pleasant myths about the beneficence of an enlightened ruling class. In Baroque opera, plots from ancient history provided models of moral behavior, and poetry and music exemplified learning and reason. But a small Thuringian court could not maintain an operatic theater on the same scale as a major power like Electoral Saxony or Prussia. There the eighteenth century saw opera established under royal support or sponsorship, on the models of Paris and London. Nevertheless, it was the realization of the Lutheran pastor Erdmann Neumeister at the end of the seventeenth century, shared with his aristocratic patrons, that forms of poetry and music originating in the theater could further religious instruction and fervor even in small court chapels or municipal churches. During a career that lasted more than half a century, Neumeister wrote hundreds of cantata texts, some consisting solely of recitatives and arias, others interpolating verses from chorales and the bible. The underlying design of each work, however, was that of an Italian secular cantata, which corresponded in essence to a scene or two from an opera.

For much of the eighteenth century, therefore, German Lutheran chapels propounded sacred doctrine in the same terms used by secular courts across Europe to propagate the ideologies of the *ancien régime*. Operas and church cantatas both continually declared the fundamental goodness of the monarchical system and the divine election of aristocratic rulers. Poetry and music expressed the thoughts and feelings of believers, sometimes even of Jesus, Mary, and other biblical figures, through the same means used to represent Julius Caesar and other idealized heroes from ancient history. The plots and staging of serious opera encouraged contemporaries to identify with those historical figures, and, as the new sacred librettos used the first person to express the doubts, fears, and religious convictions of believers, Bach and his listeners participated vicariously in the little sacred dramas that were enacted every Sunday and holiday in church. Religious conversion and belief became theatricalized, and by shaping a listener's emotional experience, a poet or a musician also structured each listener's religious experience. The latter thus followed the conventions of eighteenth-century staging, narration or dialogue given concisely in recitative leading to an emotional response expressed at length in an aria. Inasmuch as the upper bourgeoisie accepted the same type of poetry and music into their worship services in cities such as Frankfurt and Leipzig, what was initially a type of religious music confined to a few Saxon courts became the norm across Protestant Germany.

After abandoning a short-lived court opera during the 1690s, Duke Wilhelm Ernst enlisted Franck, the Dreses, and Bach to cultivate this new form of liturgical drama at Weimar. Meanwhile his second cousin Ernst Ludwig I of Saxe-Meiningen was apparently writing sacred texts of the composite type championed by Neumeister; these were set to music by Johann Ludwig Bach, a distant cousin of Sebastian.[37] During the same period, Telemann was composing like works at Eisenach, using librettos by Neumeister himself. Meanwhile the nearby court of Weissenfels heard hundreds of comparable compositions, some of them on Neumeister's texts, by its Capellmeister Johann Philipp Krieger. Bach might not have known any of Krieger's Neumeister settings; the sole surviving example is a relatively early work from 1699, still close in style musically to older German sacred music. But he certainly came to know some of the more up-to-date compositions of Telemann and J. L. Bach.[38]

It could be that, just as the neighboring court of Gotha heard church music by various composers during a period when its Capellmeister was incapacitated, Weimar did the same during the second decade of the century. If so, Telemann's Neumeister settings could have been prominent among them, serving as models for Bach's church pieces. Today Telemann's sonatas and other instrumental compositions are his best-known works, but sacred vocal music makes up the great preponderance of his immense output. Although simpler in many respects than Bach's, Telemann's vocal works reflect their poetic texts with a wealth of musical ideas.

This is most obvious in the arias, which, already in Telemann's Eisenach cycle, employ distinctive instrumentation as well as certain types of ritornellos also found in Bach's music.[39] The recitative in these works is the true *recitativo semplice* ("secco" recitative) of eighteenth-century Italian opera—not the more measured arioso of older settings—adopted expertly to Neumeister's German poetry. Old-fashioned polyphonic settings of chorales and biblical texts also occur, but even these often incorporate atmospheric ritornellos or instrumental accompaniments.

37 Ernst Ludwig's librettos, printed anonymously, seem to have been first set to music by his Capellmeister Georg Caspar Schürmann. His compositions, to judge from the few that are available, remained in late seventeenth-century style (three works are edited in Feld and Leisinger 2003). He was succeeded in 1711 by Johann Ludwig Bach, claimed in the Genealogy to be descended from the brother of Sebastian's great-grandfather Hans Bach. Bund (1984, 118) assumes that his settings of the same librettos date from after this appointment.

38 Eighteen of J. L. Bach's cantatas were copied by Sebastian for performance during 1726 at Leipzig, where at least a few of Telemann's were also heard (see Chapter 11).

39 For instance, trumpets and drums accompany the aria "Jesu dir sei Dank gesungen" from TWV 1:1451, foreshadowing "Heiligste Dreieinigkeit" in BWV 172.

Example 7.5
Possibly the first "simple" four-part chorale harmonization in one of Bach's cantatas, from
Gleichwie der Regen und Schnee, BWV 18, mvt. 5, mm. 1–2:

Ich bitt, o Herr, aus Herzens Grund,   I pray, oh Lord, from the bottom of my heart

Throughout, the musical rhetoric is less hectoring and ponderous than it can be in older compositions by Krieger or Kuhnau, if only because Telemann never works an idea longer than necessary. Even the "simple" four-part chorale settings included in most of these cantatas are by no means as bland as those in later compositions by Telemann that were probably meant to be joined by the congregation.[40] At least with respect to chorales, however, Bach evidently demurred from emulating Telemann too closely; only with Cantata 18 of (probably) 1715 does he seem to have closed a work, as Telemann was already doing routinely, with the type of four-part harmonization now often wrongly described as a "Bach chorale" (Example 7.5).[41]

That Telemann was not only a musical influence but also an inspiration, mentor, and rival of Bach during the latter's Weimar years could all be deduced from what we know about their careers during the second decade of the century. By 1714, Telemann had probably composed well over a hundred sacred works for the Lutheran liturgy, the great majority of them of the new type. Indeed, Telemann's cycle of 1710–1711,

40 At Hamburg, where Telemann spent the last forty-six years of his career, it was apparently the practice for the congregation to sing along in the homophonic chorale movements of a cantata or passion; there is no evidence for this in any of the places where Bach worked.

41 At least two probably earlier chorale harmonizations of the simple or "cantional" type, in Cantatas 12 and 172, go beyond Telemann and older composers of such settings in adding a fifth, obbligato instrumental, part.

composed in Bach's home town, may have been the first annual cycle of such pieces to be written within a single year, an accomplishment that could hardly have escaped the notice of Bach. That Bach's first efforts in the new type of composition immediately surpassed those of his most distinguished contemporary in the region—in length, richness of ideas, and complexity—would have been a prime instance of his striving to follow and then "swerve away from" contemporaries, something he would continue to do to the end of his career.[42]

Yet Telemann would continue to be one of those whom Sebastian esteemed "in his last years," according to C. P. E. Bach.[43] The context makes it clear that Emanuel had primarily Telemann's vocal works in mind when he wrote this, but Sebastian must also have studied and emulated the latter's instrumental music. Bach is known to have arranged only one of Telemann's concertos for keyboard, as BWV 985. But he would have found models for vocal as well as instrumental compositions in works like Telemann's G-major concerto TWV 52:G2, for which Bach's manuscript parts include an unfigured cello and a figured "Organo" part.[44] This composition is *not* a Corellian concerto grosso, which was essentially a trio sonata expanded by ripieno parts. Rather it is a true double violin concerto, its second movement a double fugue with episodes for the two soloists, the finale a substantial ternary form—both prefiguring movements in Bach's Brandenburg Concertos.[45] The slow movement of Bach's own "double" violin concerto echoes that of Telemann's concerto in G for four violins—not precisely, yet too closely, in view of the common melodic skeleton, the imitation at the fifth, and the staccato accompaniment, to constitute merely the use of the same generic formulas (Examples 7.6, 7.7).[46]

42 As argued by Williams (2003a, 141) for Bach's later keyboard music.

43 According to his letter of January 13, 1775, to Forkel, in BD 3:289 (no. 803); NBR, 400 (no. 395).

44 In D Dl Mus. 2392-O-35a. These parts survive only because Pisendel took them to Dresden. Perhaps he gained them in exchange for copies of his own music that were destroyed when the Weimar castle and chapel burned in 1774.

45 Especially the third and first movements of Concerto 4 (BWV 1049), respectively.

46 Zohn (2008, 542n. 69) dates a Frankfurt copy of Telemann's concerto to "ca. 1715–1716," but it could have been composed several years before then.

Example 7.6   Telemann, Concerto in G for four violins, TWV 40:201, mvt. 1, mm. 1–6

Example 7.7   Bach, "Double" Concerto in D minor, BWV 1043, mvt. 2, mm. 1–3

Another work, Telemann's seven-part concerto TWV 44:43, might have inspired a sound heard in many of Bach's works, that of a double-reed ensemble of three oboes and bassoon. Although ultimately reflecting court military bands—at the time comprising double reeds, not brass—the scoring of the Telemann work seems to echo not only in Bach's Hunt Cantata but in his First and Third Brandenburg Concertos (Examples 7.8, 7.9, 7.10). Both of the latter emulate Telemann's scoring while adding further soloists to his trios of oboes and violins. There are also more specific parallels, such as the

Example 7.8　(a) Telemann, Concerto in B-flat, TWV 44:43, mvt. I, (a) mm. 1–3 (compare Ex. 7.10), (b) mm. 25–28 (compare Ex. 7.9)

Example 7.9   Brandenburg Concerto no. 3 in G, BWV 1048, mvt. 1, (a) mm. 1–2, (b) 125–26

Example 7.10   Hunt Cantata, BWV 208, mvt. 7, mm. 1–2

use of a unison passage to mark a particularly dramatic formal articulation (as in Example 7.9b).[47]

Such colorful scoring is rare in earlier music, in which the vocal
writing is also more restrained. Older composers, including Krieger and
Kuhnau, had already incorporated recitatives and arias into sacred works.
Yet their conception of church music remained close to seventeenth-
century ideals: recitatives are more arioso than the eighteenth-century
"speaking" type; most arias resemble lieder, lacking substantial melismas,
text painting, and obbligato instrumental parts. Although Kuhnau, who
was now a city cantor working for the high bourgeoisie, held the theatrical style in disdain, it is easy to see why the popularity of the new
type of church piece soon spread beyond court chapels.[48] Kuhnau seems
to have aimed at grandeur and monumentality, composing music that
develops a small number of motivic ideas at considerable length; his
compositions achieve a measure of variety by modulating to various
keys and alternating between solos, vocal ensembles, and instrumental
interludes. But his conventional melodic ideas grow wearying, at least
to anyone who knows the new approaches that younger composers less
prejudiced against the theatrical style were already cultivating by the
second decade of the eighteenth century. The new church pieces not
only of Telemann but of lesser composers such as J. L. Bach at Meiningen
and Christian Ludwig Boxberg at Görlitz must have struck those who
paid attention as a breath of fresh air. Not only Telemann but Boxberg
turned to the new genre only after short careers writing for the opera
at Leipzig. Christoph Graupner, who must have met Telemann during

47 The Third Brandenburg Concerto was probably a septet, like TWV 44:43, before Bach
    added a few notes in the first movement for second and third cellos. Zohn (2008,
    262) considers TWV 44:43 an early work, composed by 1710–1711. Quantz, who started as
    an oboist, may also have known it; the last movement of his third flute quartet, mm. 72–73,
    echoes mm. 50–51 of the final movement of TWV 44:43 (Quantz made manuscript copies
    of other early Telemann works, listed in Oleskiewicz 1998, 673–74).

48 Kuhnau drew on the customary distinction between sacred and theatrical music, regarding
    the latter as inferior to the former; see the preface to his *Texte zur Leipziger Kirchen-
    Music* for 1709–1710, reproduced by Richter (1902) and discussed by Schering (1918, xlii).
    Kuhnau's views were probably colored by the competition he had experienced from
    Telemann during the latter's early years as an organist and opera composer at Leipzig.

studies at Leipzig, similarly composed operas at Hamburg before taking up a career as a prolific composer of church cantatas, rivaled in the extent of his output only by Telemann.

Bach, too, may have made his first effort in the new style with an operatic composition, the Hunt Cantata, which is really a quasi-dramatic serenata. Even more than his organ music, this and other Weimar vocal works reveal a complete turn in style from his earlier compositions. The change must have reflected not only the tastes of the ruling family but also the types of music that now became available to him at Weimar. The astonishing facility demonstrated in the Hunt Cantata could only have been the product of careful attention to compositions in the current Italian style. The virtuoso character of the music must reflect the experience of collaborating in performances of similar music with other professional musicians—as opposed to the students with whom he previously had had to work. Some of the German and Italian composers from whom Bach learned this new style now seem insignificant, but Bach did not necessarily view them as such. One of the largest surviving manuscripts from his Weimar years is his copy of a German passion oratorio that has been attributed to the Hamburg composer Reinhard Keiser, with additions by Bach.[49] We also have Bach's somewhat earlier copy of an Italian cantata by Biffi, as well as one of a Latin motet by Conti that Bach himself dated 1716.[50] But these could hardly have been the sole models for the music that Bach now set out to write. It could be that he learned most of what he knew of this style aurally or by playing continuo parts that belonged to the court, to one of the Dreses, or to Telemann himself—perhaps visiting from Eisenach with music in hand.

49 Was it on the basis of this work that Emanuel Bach included "Kayser" among the composers admired by Sebastian (in his letter of January 13, 1775)? Sebastian copied out parts for this work together with his pupil Schubart (in Berlin, Staatsbibliothek, Mus. ms. 1147/1); he later adapted it for performance at Leipzig. At times the work has also been thought to have been written by Keiser's father Gottfried or by Friedrich Nicolaus Brauns.

50 Bach's copy of *Amante moribondo* by Biffi (Berlin, Staatsbibliothek, Mus. ms. 1812, identified by Wollny 1997, 8–20) includes unusually detailed basso continuo figures, amounting to a written-out realization that must be Bach's own. The Conti copy (in Mus. ms 4081) is item I/C/2 in Beißwenger (1992).

Church Pieces (Cantatas)

As incredible as it might be for a work as polished and original as the Hunt Cantata to emerge out of thin air—Bach is not known to have previously written anything remotely like it—we should not assume that this was impossible. It would not have taken long for someone as perceptive and open to new ideas as Bach to grasp the style of the Italianate works on which it was modeled. Franck left many other poems for birthdays and similar occasions, and even if these were all set to music by others—presumably the Dreses—Bach is likely to have heard or performed in them during his first five years at Weimar. If so, he surely would have considered how better to set the same texts to his own music. Writing a piece for a neighboring duke would have been a way to demonstrate his capabilities; one could imagine a similar origin for a few sacred works that cannot be placed with complete certainty in the period after his promotion to concertmaster. Two solo cantatas, one for soprano and one for alto, stand out not only for their scoring but for being based on texts by the Darmstadt court poet Lehms. Earlier dates have been posited for both,[51] and in any case they might have been written for performance elsewhere than the Weimar chapel—for a private hearing in one of the palaces, or at Weissenfels or another regional court.

One of these works, BWV 199 (*Mein Herze schwimmt im Blut*), is a tour de force for a soprano soloist; evidently a favorite, it received repeat performances at Weimar, Cöthen, and Leipzig in revised versions.[52] Like the Hunt Cantata, it is a completely assured exercise in the Italian style. Indeed, it is a more genuinely dramatic work than the serenata, as it traces an emotional arc from torment in the opening accompanied recitative ("My heart swims in blood") to an almost excessively exuberant concluding aria in gigue rhythm ("Wie freudig ist mein Herz": how joyful is my heart). Notable features include an adagio aria whose embellished oboe ritornello recurs repeatedly in *Einbau*—a type of

---

51 For example, by Kobayashi (1995, 304), who offered a chronology based on the development of Bach's handwriting during the period, refining that previously given by Hofmann (1993). Hofmann (2013, 210–11) subsequently summarized the problems with respect to BWV 199 without reaching a conclusion as to its precise date of origin.

52 Anna Magdalena Bach naturally comes under consideration as soloist in later performances, presumably outside of church; whether Maria Barbara Bach could have sung it is unknown.

Example 7.11

Mein Herze schwimmt im Blut, BWV 199, mvt. 2, (a) mm. 5–6; (b) mm. 35–36 (asterisks mark the BACH motive):

Wie mein sündlich Herz gebüßt   How my sinful heart repents

scoring repeated in further Weimar arias, combining the ritornello with the voice in counterpoint. The bass line of this aria happens to incorporate the shifting chromatic motive formed from the letters of Bach's name; the latter occurs transposed several times, once accompanying the words *mein sündlich Herz* ("my sinful heart," Example 7.11).[53] Graupner, who had set the same text shortly beforehand at Darmstadt, treated these words in a simpler manner, although not without a pictorial element: short notes in the accompanying strings represent heartbeats (Example 7.12). The idea recalls Bach's own imitation during the same

53 Example 7.11 is from the original Weimar version of the cantata, in C minor. The BACH motive appeared "untransposed" only when Bach revised the work at Cöthen and again at Leipzig, in D-minor versions.

Example 7.12 Christoph Graupner, *Mein Herze schwimmt im Blut*, mvt. 2, mm. 14–15:
Wie mein sündlich Herz gebüßt.   How my sinful heart repents.

period of Jesus knocking at the door (in BWV 61) and of funeral bells in other works.[54]

Another work, BWV 21 (*Ich hatte viel Bekümmerniss*), has a complicated history that probably began prior to its first documented performance at Weimar on June 17, 1714. In its familiar form, it comprises eleven movements of varying style and scoring. Four choral movements look back to older music in the absence of ritornello design; the line-by-line construction of three of them recalls choruses in BWV 71 and other early works. The old-fashioned treatment of the text in the first of these choruses came under criticism from Mattheson, who objected to the rhetorical stuttering on the opening word ("I—I—I—I suffered much affliction," Example 7.13). Mattheson also objected to the repetitious declamation of other movements.[55] Yet Cantata 21 also includes an up-to-date da capo

---

54 As in the first aria of Cantata 127. Cortens (2015) argues, based on parallels in other movements, that Bach knew Graupner's setting of *Mein Herze schwimmt im Blut*, dated 1712 by the composer (autograph score in Darmstadt, Universitäts- und Landesbibliothek, Mus. ms. 420). In the accompanied recitative "Siehe! ich stehe vor dem Thür' und klopfe an" from BWV 61, Bach represents the words "See! I stand before the door and knock" through staccato string chords exactly like those in Example 7.12.

55 Mattheson (1725, 368), extract in BD 2:153 (no. 200), trans. in NBR, 325 (no. 319). The fault, if it is one, was not wholly Bach's, as Mattheson also implicitly criticized the series of nouns that opens the text of the first aria ("Seufzer, Thränen, Kummer, Noth": sighs, tears,

Example 7.13
Ich hatte viel Bekümmerniss, BWV 21, mvt. 2, mm. 1–3:

Ich hatte viel Bekümmerniss,   I had much affliction,

aria with a virtuoso cello part (no. 10, "Erfreue dich, Seele"); this recalls a similarly scored aria in the Hunt Cantata (no. 13, "Weil die wollenreichen Herden"), in the same key of F major. BWV 21 just might have been a favorite of Prince Johann Ernst, who in spring 1714 was preparing to leave Weimar, in a fruitless search for a cure for the ailment that would kill him. It has been proposed that the dialog movements at the center of the work, comprising an accompanied recitative and another duet in through-composed da capo form, were recast for tenor and bass to better represent the prince himself in conversation with Jesus.[56]

sorrow, anguish). This was a typical feature of Franck's poetry, recurring in the opening chorus of BWV 12.

56 In support of this idea, Hofmann (2015) points out that the lost memorial music for the prince, performed on April 2, 1716, included a part representing the departed Johann Ernst himself (Glöckner 1985 gives the text).

If BWV 21 represents a transitional stage between earlier and later types of sacred works, Bach had largely moved on by the time he began composing cantatas on a regular basis in March 1714. A small element of uncertainty could be seen in Bach's calling for five rather than the now customary four string parts, but this ended after Easter 1715. The work for that day, BWV 31, uniquely included five vocal and five double-reed parts. For later reperformances of his Weimar works Bach revised the instrumentation, perhaps also eliminating the second soprano part of BWV 31.[57]

It is apparent from the distinctive crafting of almost every movement in these Weimar compositions that Bach was striving urgently to demonstrate both originality and zeal in projecting the rhetoric of their texts. Simple recitatives and conventional da capo arias are relatively infrequent in the compositions from the first twelve months or so, up to and including BWV 31. Even the opening instrumental movements of these works seem designed to demonstrate mastery of different types of writing: decorated adagios in BWV 12 and 21, fugue in BWV 152, Venetian-style concerto allegros in BWV 18 and 31. Presumably Bach believed that instrumental movements of these types could serve sacred as well as secular ends; there was a long tradition of opening German sacred works with an instrumental movement, but few older compositions had such up-to-date virtuoso sinfonias, which now resembled the sonatas and other instrumental pieces that could be heard during services in Catholic countries. Perhaps Bach also was moved to include such movements in sacred works because he lacked regular opportunities to perform his own instrumental pieces with the *Capelle*.

Most of the Weimar vocal compositions after BWV 31 are relatively small in scale, as if Bach lowered his ambitions (or was told to tone down his writing). Yet these works continue to display remarkable invention, and there was a brief burst of exceptional writing again at the end of 1716; after that, however, Bach evidently stopped writing music for the Weimar chapel. Today the most famous of the Weimar vocal works are two that do not survive in the forms in which they were first drafted there. These are BWV 80, based on Luther's iconic chorale "Ein feste

---

57 Dürr (2005, 269) cites the autograph title page that survives (without the corresponding score or parts) for a performance possibly in 1735.

Burg," and BWV 147, famous for its setting of another chorale known in English as "Jesus, joy of man's desiring."[58] BWV 147 originated as the very last of Bach's Weimar vocal works, probably composed for but not performed on December 20, 1716 (the fourth Sunday in Advent). BWV 80, known today as a grandly scored chorale cantata for Reformation Day, was originally a small-scale composition, most likely written for Oculi 1716, a Sunday during Lent. Both works were thus originally written for penitential seasons during which many other localities dispensed with elaborate church music. Leipzig was one of those places, and when Bach repeated these compositions there, he gave them in substantially revised versions that repurposed them for other days in the church year. In the process he apparently obliterated portions of the original works, adding, however, the chorale choruses that have made these two compositions famous.[59]

58 The English lines are actually Robert Bridges's paraphrase of a seventeenth-century poem by Martin Jahn, "Jesu, meine Seelen Wonne." The latter was originally sung to the earlier chorale melody "Werde munter, mein Gemüthe" (by Johann Schop).

59 One of the most distinctive features of BWV 80, the brass choir of three trumpets and timpani, was an even later addition. This was made by Friedemann Bach when he arranged two movements from his father's composition for a special event at Halle, probably in the 1750s (as demonstrated by Melamed 2008; see Schulenberg 2010, 237–39).

CHAPTER EIGHT

Cöthen (1717–1723)

The exact date and manner of Bach's arrival at Cöthen are unknown, but within four weeks after his release from prison in Weimar (on December 2, 1717) he had not only acknowledged the receipt of back pay as Capellmeister in his new home but traveled to Leipzig to inspect the organ at the university church there.[1] A Cöthen court account from the end of the month describes him as "newly arrived,"[2] but a later document suggests that he could already have held a rehearsal in his lodging at Cöthen on December 10.[3] The day was the prince's birthday,

---

1   The organ report, in BD 1:163–65 (no. 87), trans. in NBR, 83–85 (no. 72), is dated December 17, and the following day he signed a receipt for a payment of 20 Taler from the rector of the university (BD 1:189 [no. 109]; NBR, 86 [no. 73]).

2   Bach apparently was appointed as of August 1, for he received a payment on December 29 for the last five months of 1717 (BD 1:190 [no. 110] and 2:67 [no. 86], trans. in NBR, 82 [no. 70]). In the first entry for that date he is described as *neüangenommen*, and his monthly salary is set at 33 Taler and change, yielding an annual income of 400 Taler. An entry immediately below, recording an additional 50 Taler bonus on signing (*Capitulation*), must have been added subsequently although it is dated August 7.

3   An entry dated October 1, 1718, records that Bach was paid 12 Taler as rent (*Hauß-Zinß*) for a period that began the previous December 10; a similar entry for October 13, 1719, is more explicit, recording a payment in the same amount for "holding rehearsals in his house and keeping up the harpsichord" ("habender Probe in Seinem Hause und die *Clavecin* im stande zu erhalten"), BD 2:70 (no. 91); NBR, 86 (no. 74). One imagines that, after his experience at Weimar, Bach had been careful to request this additional annual payment, together with permission to hold rehearsals at home.

Bach. David Schulenberg, Oxford University Press (2020). © Oxford University Press.
DOI: 10.1093/oso/9780190936303.001.0001

when in subsequent years (at least) Bach would provide an annual serenade or cantata. Yet Bach must have been in Leipzig immediately after
that date, for on December 17 he signed a relatively lengthy report on a
renovation of the organ at St. Paul's church.[4]

Bach's new employer, Prince Leopold of Cöthen-Anhalt, belonged
to a family whose domains as a whole coincided roughly with the
modern state of Sachsen-Anhalt in eastern Germany. The title borne
by the men of the family, *Fürst*, is rendered in English as "prince," but
it is not the same word as *Prinz*—also translated "prince"—which
refers to the son of a ruler (such as Johann Ernst of Weimar). Rather it
designated a sovereign ruler holding a distinct rank above a count and
below a duke.[5] Anhalt-Cöthen, like Saxe-Weimar, was one of several
adjoining territories whose rulers, all cousins, competed and bickered
with one another but tended to share interests in music and literature,
among other things. The principality of Cöthen may have been somewhat larger in area than the duchy of Weimar, but it was distinctly less
wealthy and less populous, its princely palace and capital city—little
more than a village—smaller and less distinguished architecturally.[6]
Moreover, Anhalt as a whole, like the modern state, lay off the most
important lines of trade and communication and was not particularly
prosperous. A rural region, it lacked the lively competition between
localities in building and maintaining schools, churches (with their
organs), and other aspects of cultural life that characterized Saxony
and Thuringia. Nevertheless, in moving there Bach gained the higher
and more prestigious title of Capellmeister while taking on greater

---

4 BD 1:163–65 (no. 87), trans. in NBR, 83–85 (no. 72); complete text and translation also in
   Williams (1980–1984, 3:149–51). The unusual length of the report was perhaps reflected in
   a chronicler's observation that Bach examined everything "with diligence" (*mit Fleiß*, BD
   1:166, quoting Sicul).

5 The princes of Anhalt in fact claimed ducal rank, reflecting the family's rule over Saxony
   during the Middle Ages; this presumably made possible the marriage alliance between
   Weimar and Cöthen, which in turn facilitated Bach's move.

6 Czok (1982, 26) gives population figures of 50,000 and 4,669 for the duchy and city, respectively, of Weimar during the 1690s, as opposed to 4,000 for Cöthen in the mid-eighteenth
   century, noting that whereas the duchy of Weimar included five other towns, Anhalt-
   Cöthen contained none. Wolff (2000, 188) gives the population of the entire principality of
   Anhalt-Cöthen as 10,000.

formal responsibilities and a higher salary, probably also enjoying greater personal freedom.

The prince not only was a generous patron but was genuinely knowledgeable about music, playing violin and viola da gamba in a tradition of European sovereigns who attained near-professional capability as musicians (Figure 8.1).[7] King Louis XIII of France and Emperor Leopold I were good enough composers for their music to be performed in court ballets and in the Habsburg chapel, respectively; Louis XIV in his youth was a fine dancer. The short-lived Prince Johann Ernst of Weimar had emulated such rulers, the greatest of whom would be King Frederick the Great of Prussia. Frederick's performances of his own flute sonatas and concertos would be accompanied by Emanuel Bach; Sebastian would use the king's theme as the basis of the Musical Offering. King Frederick's performances took place in private,[8] and the same can be assumed of those in which Sebastian and other favored musicians joined Leopold, who would not normally have entertained his court or even visiting dignitaries with his own playing. Concerts for visitors and members of the ruling family would probably have taken place in the largest room of the Cöthen palace, now known as the Hall of Mirrors. Built by 1602, it predated the better-known hall of the same name at Versailles.[9] It was ideal for musical performances by relatively large ensembles, such as took place for important dynastic events: above all the prince's birthday (observed on December 10) and New Year's celebrations, for both of which Bach wrote an annual cantata, perhaps beginning as early as the end of 1717. Only two of these works survive intact, but several others are partially extant in the form of later sacred parodies.[10] The text of one

---

7 Bunge (1905) gathered documents for the musical instruments collected by Leopold and later sold by his successor (see esp. 19–21). According to Gerber (1812–1814, Vol. 2, col. 616) the prince also sang bass "very well" (*recht gut*).

8 The fact is not made clear in famous accounts such as that of Burney (1775, 152ff.), who must have heard the king and his musicians from outside the royal music room, as shown by Oleskiewicz (2007a, 255).

9 Daw (annotations to Smend 1985, 175) notes that the modern restoration of this room may include some decoration postdating Bach's time there, but it probably preserves its original "comfortably spacious proportions, and its warm but responsive acoustics."

10 On Bach's use of parody (the word in this context has no satirical implications) see Chapter 13.

Figure 8.1 Prince Leopold of Cöthen–Anhalt, anonymous portrait, oil on canvas, Historisches Museum und Bachgedenkstätte, Köthen. From Wikipedia.

opened with a psalm verse, indicating that these works could blur the boundary between liturgical and secular music.[11]

Cöthen itself (spelled Köthen in present-day German) could not have been a very exciting place. Yet Leopold's band must have been one of the better ensembles of its type in Germany, and adding Bach to it would have been a crowning achievement from the point of view of many an aristocratic collector of musicians. The latter already included, among others, the violinist and gambist Christian Ferdinand Abel, whose son Carl Friedrich would partner with Bach's son Johann Christian in the famous Bach-Abel concerts at London. Abel himself had previously served the king of Sweden and in that capacity might have known Sebastian's brother Jacob. At its height in 1720, the permanent, salaried members of the ensemble comprised about sixteen musicians.[12] These included at least two further violinists as well as players of flute, oboe, and bassoon, two trumpeters and a timpanist, and several singers, plus several more musicians who probably played varying roles. Inasmuch as every player could probably double on several instruments, such an ensemble was capable of performing almost anything Bach had written to date, especially if amplified when necessary by visitors or town musicians, as was standard practice. Singers might have been in short supply, but as the ensemble did not regularly perform church music there was no need for anything resembling a chorus in the modern sense. Indeed, Bach's few surviving vocal works from Cöthen seem, even more than those for Weimar, to treat the singers as soloists, rarely calling for a full four-part ensemble.

Bach's Cöthen period began and ended with trips to Leipzig: the organ examination at the end of 1717 and his return there early in 1723, when he was under consideration for the position he would enter that

---

11 This was the lost BWV Anh. 5, *Lobet den Herrn, alle seinen Heerscharen*, performed during the service (*Gottes-Dienst*) on the prince's birthday in 1718, according to the reprint of the text in Hunold's *Auserlesene . . . Gedichte, 13. Stück* (Halle, 1719), 194. Paczkowski (2017, 146) suggests that the psalm chorus survives in parodied form as the opening movement of BWV 69a. The same day saw the performance of a *serenata* honoring the prince, *Das frolockende Anhalt* (in Hunold's *Auserlesene . . . Gedichte, 12. Stück*, p. 84).

12 Wolff (2000, 193–94) provides a list, gathering together information from a number of sources.

spring. In between came trips to a remarkable variety of destinations, including a royal capital and an upper-class resort. He also visited other rural centers resembling Cöthen, as well as the great international trading city of Hamburg. Bach might have regretted never traveling to Venice, Rome, Paris, or London, but he was as well traveled within Germany as anyone, and his trips brought him into contact with an extraordinary variety of music and musicians, not to mention patrons and performing environments. Traveling as a princely Capellmeister and organ virtuoso, he may not have enjoyed the popular celebrity of the greatest Italian singers. But he was certainly one of the most highly respected German musicians of his day, eliciting admiration and curiosity from knowledge-able professionals and amateurs alike.

The most famous journey of Bach's Cöthen period, undertaken in spring 1719, is documented by his dedication of the Brandenburg Concertos to a member of the Prussian royal family. The dedica-tion, which heads Bach's manuscript score of the six works, is dated March 24, 1721, and is addressed to Margrave Christian Ludwig.[13] It was customary to refer to compositions after their dedicatees; Emanuel Bach's six keyboard sonatas W. 48, dedicated two decades later to King Frederick II, are known as the "Prussian" Sonatas, and Sebastian him-self would refer to a movement from his *Musical Offering*, also ded-icated to Frederick, as the "Prussian fugue."[14] A minor figure in the Hohenzollern hierarchy, Margrave Christian Ludwig was one of sev-eral holders of the title who had no power of their own but faithfully served the king as state and military officers, receiving in exchange estates, incomes, and suites in the huge royal palace at Berlin (Figure 8.2). Bach might have been brought to his attention through the cel-list Christian Bernhard Linicke, who had served the margrave before coming to Cöthen in 1716.[15]

---

13 The dedication, like the original title of the work, is in French (the preferred language of court diplomacy), given in BD 1:216–17 (no. 150) and translated in NBR, 92–93 (no. 84) from the autograph score in Berlin, Staatsbibliothek, Amalenbibliothek ms. 78.

14 In a letter of 1748, in BD 1:117 (no. 49), trans. in NBR, 234 (no. 257); see Butler (2002, 325).

15 Oleskiewicz (2011, 81).

Figure 8.2 The likely site of an early performance of the Brandenburg Concertos: the Royal Palace, Berlin (as it appeared in an early twentieth-century postcard photo; the dome was added in 1845). Margrave Christian Ludwig's apartment was on the ground floor to the right of the entry that leads to the crossing. From Wikipedia.

Christian Ludwig today is sometimes described as margrave of Brandenburg-Schwedt, but he was not so designated at the time, and he never administered the provincial domain of Schwedt, which was assigned to his oldest brother, afterward his nephew. But he was apparently Bach's host at Berlin in March 1719, when the composer "had . . . the pleasure of appearing before Your Royal Highness . . . by virtue of Your Highness's commands." This most likely took place in a music room on the second floor of the Berlin palace.[16] Another of those commands was

16 The exact location within the *Stadtschloss*, demolished after World War II, is uncertain, but Oleskiewicz (2017, 43–44) shows that this was probably the same room used for music after 1786 by King Frederick William II, directly above Christian Ludwig's apartment (see the palace floor plan online at https://www.press.uillinois.edu/books/oleskiewicz/bp11/06.html).

that Bach should "send Your Highness some pieces of [his] composition," and thus two years later the margrave received the "Six Concertos with Various Instruments." Whether Bach drafted the dedication himself is unknown,[17] but, although obsequious to modern eyes, it is far from a conventional dedication of the time, and the personal information in it could have come only from Bach.

A court official such as a Capellmeister probably could not have made such an offering without knowledge and permission of his prince. Surely, too, Leopold had heard these astonishing compositions prior to Bach's sending them to another official at the court of a friendly and far more powerful neighbor. One aim of Bach's visit in 1719 was apparently the acquisition of a fine harpsichord for the Cöthen court—perhaps the double-manual example by Michael Mietke, instrument maker to the first Prussian king, that was still listed in a court inventory of 1784. By then the instrument was somehow defective.[18] When new it might have resembled the blue- and silver-lacquered harpsichord by the same maker, also with two manuals, that was listed in the estate of Christian Ludwig after his death in 1734.[19]

Bach could have used either instrument for the solo part in what we know as the Fifth Brandenburg Concerto, in performances at Berlin and Cöthen respectively. His dedication gives no indication that the music was exclusive to the margrave, as might have been the case for a

17 Wolff (2000, 488n. 50) suggests that it was "provided" by Prince Leopold's former French tutor.

18 As indicated in the court inventory; see BD 2:74 (note to no. 95); NBR, 87 (no. 77). Hübner (2006, 101) suggests that this harpsichord might have replaced an instrument that the prince had brought to Carlsbad the previous spring, which required repairs on its return. Bach's dedication states only that he had visited Berlin "a couple of years" (*une couple d'années*) earlier, but the date is confirmed by the sum of 130 Taler with which he was entrusted on March 1, for the instrument and travel expenses (as indicated by court records, BD 2:73 [no. 95]; NBR, 87 [no. 77]).

19 As reported by Oleskiewicz (2011, 109). The presence of eleven music stands in the same estate suggests that the margrave had the resources to present performances of any of Bach's concertos, at a time when the king had no band (*Capelle*) of his own. Two other Mietke instruments, known from their decoration as the "white" and the "black" harpsichords, still survive at Berlin (see Kottick 2003, 323–25). These are sometimes associated with Bach, who is not, however, known to have played them.

commissioned composition. Whether Bach returned to Berlin in 1721 to hand-deliver his manuscript score is not known, nor is there any record of his receiving payment for it, although he might have hoped for as much, if not also for some future commission, even an appointment. The manuscript eventually became part of the collection of Princess Anna Amalie, sister of Frederick the Great and a grand-niece of Christian Ludwig. As such it came under the care of Johann Philipp Kirnberger, her librarian and a pupil of Bach at Leipzig. No copies of individual performing parts survive from Berlin, but it is not impossible that such were prepared for use in private concerts sponsored by Christian Ludwig or another member of the royal family.

Bach is supposed to have made another trip in summer 1719 to another Prussian dominion: Halle, where he hoped to meet Handel, then visiting his home town en route from London to Dresden. Bach's visit, however, is documented only by an account of uncertain origin; according to this, Handel left for Dresden earlier on the very day that Bach arrived in haste to see him.[20] There is no reason to doubt that Bach lamented his failure to meet a "really great man whom he particularly respected."[21] One wonders, however, why Bach did not continue to Dresden either then or a few weeks later, when the diplomatic and cultural event of the decade took place there. The marriage of the Saxon prince Friedrich August (the future Augustus III) to the imperial princess Maria Josepha was marked by public celebrations of extraordinary sumptuousness. Handel might still have been there—he had gone to recruit singers for his Royal Academy in London—and Prince Leopold also is supposed to have attended.[22] It has been suggested that illness in the

---

20 The so-called Comparison of Bach and Handel is traditionally attributed to C. P. E. Bach, as in NBR, 401 (no. 396); the original is in BD 3:437–44 (no. 927). This document dates from 1788; how accurately it describes an event that took place when C. P. E. Bach was just five years old is impossible to know. Handel's visit to Halle in 1719 is well documented, as is his return in 1729; he may also have been there in 1750 (see Burrows 2012, 133, 166, and 455–56). The claim that Handel avoided "all opportunities" (*alle Gelegenheiten*) to meet with Bach was already made during his lifetime by Marpurg in his *Historisch-kritische Beyträge zur Aufnahme der Musik*, Vol. 1, Part 5 (Berlin, 1755), 450; the "Comparison" fleshes out this insinuation, which perhaps was common knowledge among Bach's admirers.

21 As stated in the "Comparison," BD 3:443 (no. 927), trans. in NBR, 408 (no. 396).

22 Geck (2006, 103) asserts that Leopold went to Dresden for the wedding in September 1719, but he provides no documentation.

Bach family could have prevented Sebastian from traveling;[23] his little son Leopold August, born the previous December, died on September 28. This was just two weeks after the royal marriage celebrations in Dresden reached their climax with the performance of the opera *Teofane* by the Venetian composer Antonio Lotti.

Although Bach evidently did not reach the Saxon capital on that occasion, he had previously traveled through Saxony and would do so again in 1718 and 1720 in the entourage of Prince Leopold, en route to the resort town of Carlsbad (Carlovy Vary) in what is now the northern Czech Republic. Journeys to Carlsbad might have taken several routes, passing through either Halle or Leipzig—university cities in which a visiting prince might have allowed his Capellmeister and other musicians to perform for the locals. Carlsbad itself, still known for its mineral springs, had been a resort for the aristocracy since the time of the fourteenth-century Emperor Charles IV, for whom it is named. It was no ordinary spa, rather a place where members of the ruling class could enjoy the hot springs while engaging in conspicuous consumption, impressing one another with the quality and number of their retainers. Contemporaries took note of who traveled there; guidebooks listed each year's noble visitors, implying that one attraction was the opportunity for lesser aristocrats to rub shoulders with greater ones. The highest-ranking visitor during the two years when Bach came was Christiane Eberhardine, Saxon Electress and Queen of Poland, in whose memory Bach would later write the Funeral Ode BWV 198. Such a person would not have come without a substantial train of noble attendants and servants, musicians probably among them.[24]

For Leopold, who suffered from frequent unidentified illnesses, these visits, each lasting some five weeks, may have been ostensibly for the supposed medical benefits of the springs. He had already been there in 1717, just prior to his appointment of Bach as Capellmeister.[25] His costs

---

23 Schröder (2012, electronic edition).

24 She is listed first among the visitors of 1719 and 1720, with her "attending high court personnel" (*beyhabend hohe Hofstaat*), in *Neu- verbessert- und vermehrtes denckwürdiges Kayser Carls-Baad* (Nuremberg, 1736), 91–92. Prince Leopold is also listed as visiting in both 1718 and 1720 with his *Hofstatt*.

25 In May–July 1717. Court officials visited Weimar several times in subsequent months, perhaps contacting Bach but more likely following up diplomatically the marriage of Duke

doubled for his visit in 1718, which he used to display his musical patronage, bringing along Bach and six other musicians as well as a harpsichord (not yet the Mietke instrument). Although the medicinal value of
the waters is doubtful, rulers might have justified the expense of traveling
there by undertaking diplomatic or dynastic business. Their musicians
might have taken the opportunity to exchange music and news from
grander and more distant realms than they could visit themselves, as well
as to meet potential patrons. It could have been here that Bach first
encountered two Bohemian nobles with whom he later corresponded
about the sale or rental of music: Johann Adam and Franz Anton, counts
of Questenberg and Sporck, respectively.[26] The town's facilities included at least one hall suitable for concerts, and in bringing a harpsichord Leopold doubtless intended to show off the capabilities of his
Capellmeister as well as his own musical taste and largesse.

It was while Bach was on the second of these trips, in July 1720, that
his wife Maria Barbara suffered some sudden fatal illness. According
to the Obituary, she was well when Sebastian left for Carlsbad, but
on returning he found his wife already buried, learning of her death
only "when he entered his house." The entire choir of the Lutheran
St. Agnes school was present for her funeral; whether the latter took
place before or after Sebastian's return is unclear, although a court record shows that a payment was made to Sebastian three days earlier.[27]

Ernst August to Prince Leopold's sister in 1716. Details on all three of Leopold's trips are
in Hübner (2006).

26 Neither is listed in the guidebook cited above, but they would have been among the unnamed "spiritual as well as secular high nobles, knights and persons of quality" from the
Empire "and other places and lands," mentioned just after Prince Leopold in the list for
1720. Sporck would borrow Bach's performing parts for the Sanctus in D, which was later
incorporated into the B-Minor Mass (see BD 3:638); he was also dedicatee of a passion
oratorio by Bach's Leipzig librettist Picander (Wolff 2000, 296). Questenberg seems to
have sought compositions from Bach late in the latter's life (see Plichta 1981, 26). This has
given rise to the hypothesis that Questenberg might have overseen a performance of the
B-Minor Mass in Vienna (most recently in Maul 2013a), although this is doubted by Rifkin
(2011, 77n. 1).

27 BD 2:68 (item 86, commentary) and 76 (item 100), the latter trans. in NBR, 88 (no. 80).
Possibly someone from the household picked up Bach's payment in his absence, or perhaps actual payment took place after the date for which it was recorded. The presence of
the entire choir on the occasion—rather than a "half school" (Halbe Schule), as at Leopold

Whatever the precise circumstances, the shock of returning from a holiday adventure to a family in mourning must have been dreadful, leaving its mark not only on Sebastian but on Emanuel, who at six years of age would have been just old enough to be deeply affected by the loss of his mother.[28] Of course, deaths in the family were hardly rare. Less than a year had passed since the death of Leopold August, Maria Barbara's last child and the only one born at Cöthen. The infant, who was godson not only of Prince Leopold but of the latter's sister and brother, had been baptized in the court church on November 17, 1718, in what must have been a splendid occasion for both parents.[29] The unexpected loss of a wife must have been utterly confounding, and it has been suggested that "life at Cöthen . . . must now have become distasteful" for Bach.[30]

During the following months Bach traveled to Hamburg, where he gave a famous organ recital but refused to make the payment necessary for receiving an appointment as organist. He remarried twelve months after his return from Hamburg, on December 3, 1721, less than a year and a half after the death of his first wife. He was not unusual in making his second marriage when he did or to a much younger woman.[31] Just as Bach almost certainly had known Maria Barbara for some time prior to their engagement, he probably was acquainted with Anna Magdalena and her family long before either contemplated marriage to the other.

August's funeral—might merely have reflected Sebastian's high rank at court, as it is unclear how the Prince could have commanded it if he too was still traveling (as noted by Williams 2016, 206).

28 In his account in the Obituary (BD 3:87 [no. 666]; trans. in NBR, 304–5 [no. 306]), Emanuel steps out of his objective role as reporter to mention his father's heartfelt distress (*empfindliche Schmerz*) at the sudden and unexpected end of his "happy marriage" (*vergnügte Ehe*).

29 BD 2:73 (no. 94); NBR, 87 (no. 78). The inclusion of Leopold's younger brother August Ludwig among the godparents is of some interest, as the two would soon afterward engage in disputes that saw troops of the reigning prince occupying territory assigned to August Ludwig (their mother Gisela Agnes taking the side of her younger son); a settlement would not be reached for another three years.

30 Boyd (2006, 74).

31 Kevorkian (2017, 103) summarizes typical rates and ages of remarriage for women as well as men of Bach's background.

Descended like Bach from musicians on both her parents' sides, Anna Magdalena was born in 1701 at Zeitz, where her father Johann Caspar Wilcke was a trumpeter for the ruling duke Moritz Wilhelm (a cousin of the Saxon elector in Dresden).[32] Wilcke was "court and field trumpeter," indicating that he served in both a military capacity and as a player for the chamber and the church.[33]

Sebastian first might have gotten to know Wilcke's son, also named Johann Caspar, who joined the neighboring court of Zerbst as a trumpeter in 1717.[34] Not only Johann Caspar Jr. but at least two of his sisters, including Anna Magdalena (the youngest), received musical training, the latter surely for a time from Pauline Kellner, one of the first professional female singers in Germany. Kellner's career had taken her from Württemberg and London to Weissenfels, where she worked for Duke Christian from 1716 onward. The Wilcke family moved there as well after the dissolution of the court at Zeitz, following the death of Duke Moritz Wilhelm in 1718. Bach had been known to Duke Christian since his Weimar years and would later receive an honorary title from him; he therefore is unlikely to have passed through Christian's territory in August 1721 (while on a journey to Schleiz, further south) without paying his respects to the duke and meeting some of his musicians.

Bach was not the only member of the court to marry during this time. Prince Leopold's marriage to a cousin from the neighboring principality of Anhalt-Bernburg took place the day after his twenty-seventh birthday celebration in December 1721. Princess Friedrica Henrietta died a little more than a year later, aged just twenty-one, yet Bach in 1730 described her as *amusa*, uninterested in the arts, implicitly blaming her for a cutback

---

32 Reliable information about Anna Magdalena and her family was first gathered by Schubart (1953) and more recently summarized by Schulze (2013); information given below is from both sources. Anna Magdalena's family name is spelled in various ways, including Wülcke, but the Saxon "ü" was essentially indistinguishable from the letter *i* in pronunciation.

33 Schubart (1953, 39n. 2) suggests that the more prestigious title of *Feldtrompeter* was earned by real military service, possibly during warfare against Louis XIV or the Turks in the years between 1688 and 1691.

34 Also at Zeitz was Magdalena's oldest sister Anna Katharina, married since 1710 to another court trumpeter and mother of Bach's future pupil C. F. Meißner.

in court spending on music that took place after the wedding.[35] This suggests that she lacked Leopold's unusual knowledge of and enthusiasm for music, even though she did own at least a few music books.[36] During her time at Cöthen, however, court expenses on music did see a small reduction from their height in 1719–1720, although Bach continued to receive his full salary (as did Anna Magdalena).[37]

The decisive event in Bach's life following his second marriage was his application for the double position of cantor in the St. Thomas School and city music director at Leipzig, which he would gain in 1723 and hold until his death. The protracted process of applying and then deciding to move to Leipzig, abandoning the role of courtly Capellmeister for that of educator and city musician, must have preoccupied Bach for much of his last year at Cöthen. Johann Kuhnau had held the position from 1701 until dying in June 1722; having tested organs alongside Kuhnau in 1716 and 1717, Bach would have known of the older musician's age and any infirmities, and the possibility of succeeding him must have been present in both men's minds. Indeed, Bach may have received a "pre-audition" of some sort at Leipzig in 1721, when his cantata BWV 172 was apparently performed there, at a time when Kuhnau is thought to have been ill.[38] Yet Leipzig, a university city famed for both the scale of its triannual book fair and the orthodoxy of its clergy and professoriate, might have seemed unlikely to hire a successor to Kuhnau who lacked university training, no matter how talented musically. Not only Kuhnau but four of his five predecessors—Calvisius, Schein, Tobias Michael, and Schelle— had attended the Leipzig University. Michael and Schelle had also attended the St. Thomas School, where the cantor gave lessons not only in music but in Latin. Bach's education nevertheless would be deemed sufficient for a position that was unusual (for one in a large city) in combining oversight of music in the municipal churches with instructional

---

35 In the letter of 1730 to Erdmann, BD 1:7 (no. 23); NBR, 151 (no. 152).

36 Geck (2000, 113, citing Günther Hoppe).

37 See Table 7.4 in Wolff (2000, 203), who cites Günther Hoppe.

38 Glöckner (2008, 176), citing Schabalina (2008, 57–58), who raised the possibility that Bach sent the so-called Cöthen parts for this work to Leipzig; the performance is documented by a printed libretto for Pentecost 1721.

responsibilities in the St. Thomas School: hence the double title of cantor and music director.[39] Only two of the four city churches, St. Thomas and St. Nicholas, regularly heard new polyphonic compositions. But that did not relieve the music director of responsibility for the singing of hymns and motets in the two other churches, and he was also expected to provide music on certain occasions for a fifth church, that of the university.

There were differing opinions among the Leipzig elite about the desired level of complexity and sophistication of the music in the two main churches. Some members of the city's ruling council may have wished the cantor to be more a schoolteacher and less a Capellmeister, that is, a virtuoso musician.[40] Certainly the council was divided over more general concerns about municipal finances and the city's ability to maintain an institution that was both a charitable educational establishment and a provider of music for the churches. But for over a century the cantors of the St. Thomas School had been distinguished and prolific composers of sacred music, and it is unlikely that anyone around 1720 foresaw a time when the position would be exclusively or even primarily an educational one. Less than six weeks after Kuhnau's death on June 5, 1722, the Leipzig city council selected Telemann to succeed him ahead of five other candidates. Telemann, who had moved to Hamburg only the previous summer, must nevertheless have seriously considered returning to the city whose university he had attended while beginning his career as a professional musician. He came promptly for an audition in August, turning down the offer only in November, after getting the Hamburg authorities to improve his salary and other aspects of his position there. A remark in the Leipzig council minutes suggests that this behavior, which perhaps should have been anticipated, led to lasting resentment.[41]

---

39 Smaller towns might have been more likely to combine the two positions, as in Salzwedel, where Bach visited in 1744 (see Langusch 2007, 11).

40 But it is not certain that there were clearly drawn lines between "cantor" and "Capellmeister" "parties" on the Leipzig council, as argued by Siegele (1983, 8–11). Maul (2018, 185–86) describes the council as divided into three factions that nevertheless agreed on Bach's appointment.

41 During the meeting of the city's Three Councils five months later at which Bach was elected, the presiding burgomaster Lange noted that Telemann "had promised to do

Bach, who must have followed these events with interest, might have learned details from Telemann himself, who could have passed through Cöthen on his way to and from Hamburg. That Bach did not initially throw his hat into the ring was, he later claimed, due to uncertainty as to whether he could tolerate the step down from courtly Capellmeister to municipal cantor. His eventual decision was swayed by the presence of the famous St. Thomas School as well as the university, for his sons "seemed inclined toward studies."[42] Friedemann, just turning thirteen, as well as Emanuel would indeed study not only at St. Thomas (where they were joined by Bernhard) but at the university, although neither earned a degree there. Sebastian, however, entered into the competition only after Advent Sunday (November 29), when music by three other candidates was heard in the Leipzig churches, apparently without eliciting enthusiasm.

By the time Bach came under consideration, at the council meeting of December 21, another Capellmeister had also applied. Christoph Graupner, a graduate of the St. Thomas School, had attended the Leipzig university before becoming a composer and harpsichordist for the Hamburg opera. He was now serving Landgrave Ernst Ludwig of Hesse-Darmstadt. Graupner thus outranked Bach in several respects, and on the day set for his audition, January 17, 1723, he was favored with the opportunity of presenting not only two cantatas during the main Sunday service but also a Magnificat at Vespers that afternoon. When Bach auditioned three weeks later with just two cantatas, it was as the backup candidate for the so-called Capellmeister faction, ahead of two or three musically less distinguished candidates also in the running.[43] The council had already

everything, but had not kept his promise" ("er hätte auch vesprochen alles zuthun, jedoch sein Versprechen nicht gehalten"), BD 2:94 (no. 129), trans. in NBR, 102 (no. 98).

42 "denen *studiis incliniren* schienen," letter to Erdmann of October 10, 1730 (BD 1:67 [no. 23]; NBR, 152 [no. 152]). Earlier in the letter Bach wrote that he "postponed his decision for a quarter of a year," even though someone had described the position to him in "favorable terms" ("jedoch wurde mir diese station dermaßen favorable beschrieben"). Could that "someone" have been Telemann? And by *resolution* did Bach mean the decision to apply or the decision to accept the job?

43 The sources give ambiguous information; still in contention appear to have been Georg Friedrich Kauffmann, organist and music director at nearby Merseburg and a gifted composer; Georg Balthasar Schott, organist at Leipzig's New Church; and possibly Andreas Christoph Duve, a cantor from Braunschweig (Brunswick).

sent Graupner back to Darmstadt as the chosen candidate, with a letter to the landgrave requesting his release. But this was not forthcoming, despite several further entreaties from the Leipzig authorities (Graupner, did, however, secure himself a raise, like Telemann). Finally, on April 9, the governing council voted to hire Bach, but only after hearing the oft-quoted observation of one council member: "Since the best could not be obtained, mediocre ones would have to be accepted."[44] The argument seems to have been that it would be better to hire someone who could both teach and perform, even if only at a middling level, than to select an accomplished composer such as Telemann, who would be allowed to assign some of his teaching duties to an assistant. The same dispensation was, however, granted to Bach, whose musical capabilities were not in question; his audition, according to a newspaper report, had been "highly praised by everyone who could judge it."[45]

Supporting Bach and evidently facilitating the council's approval of his appointment was Gottfried Lange, who presided over the governing council for the year as well as the larger body known as the Three Councils. A member of the supposed Capellmeister party, he was both a former law professor and a poet, and it has been proposed that he wrote the librettos set by Graupner and Bach for their auditions, as well as for some future works by Bach.[46] If so, Leipzig saw Bach repeating his Mühlhausen experience of collaborating with an important municipal official in the production of public vocal compositions. Lange might have smoothed over any opposition to Bach in the council, but a more challenging task that Bach still had to face was the examination of his theological learning that would qualify him for teaching as the third-ranking faculty member in the St. Thomas School. Bach could never have had any doubts about his musical abilities, but he might have had

---

44 "da man nun die besten nicht bekommen könne, müße man mittlere nehmen" (BD 2:92 [no. 127]; trans. in NBR, 101 [no. 94c]). The speaker was Abraham Christoph Platz, one of Lange's colleagues as burgomaster.

45 "von allen, welche dergleichen ästimiren, sehr gelobet" (BD 2:91 [no. 124]; NBR, 101 [no. 95]); this report appeared in a Hamburg newspaper with the dateline Leipzig, February 9. Williams (2016, 260) wonders whether it was Bach himself who acted as correspondent on this and other occasions; if so, his spinning of the media would be emulated later by Emanuel in the same city (cf. Schulenberg 2014, 304).

46 Wolff (2000, 221), following a suggestion of Hans-Joachim Schulze.

some concerns about his mastery of Latin and theology. The aural examination by two members of the university's theological faculty was a substantive part of the vetting process. A candidate already approved by the council was interrogated on matters ranging from mechanical understanding of the bible (such as knowing the number of chapters in each book) to real theological comprehension. Bach undoubtedly knew that a cantor could be disqualified for not being able to answer questions adequately; lacking university training, he might have faced this part of the process with greater trepidation than any other.[47]

On the other hand, Bach could long have anticipated being tested for some such position. He would have known what to expect, from personal acquaintance with family members who had passed such examinations. His answers would need to follow orthodox Lutheran doctrine; this could explain three anti-Calvinist book titles copied onto the title page of Anna Madaglena's 1722 "clavier" manuscript. As an employee of a Calvinist court, Bach could have expected to be tested with particular rigor about the errors of the Reformed church.[48] Yet merely by working at Cöthen, Bach revealed the same pragmatism that later made it possible for him to seek and accept a court title from the Roman Catholic elector of Saxony. However strong his orthodox Lutheran convictions, he set a precedent for even greater religious pragmatism among his sons.

Bach passed the tests, arriving with his family at Leipzig on May 22, 1723. The event was significant enough to be noted in far-off Hamburg, where he had visited two and a half years earlier.[49] Sophisticated readers might have understood it as a victory for the "Capellmeister" side of the teacher/musician controversy, and perhaps it persuaded some students to attend university at Leipzig, as Bach's supporter Lange claimed it would.[50] Bach, like Telemann, would retain an honorary court title of some type to the end of his life, but for the rest of his career he would be a resident

---

47 Petzold (1998) describes the process in detail, showing that a year previously Bach's principal examiner, Johann Schmid, had prevented a candidate from becoming cantor in nearby Zwickau without three months of additional study, after failing his initial examination.

48 As suggested by Chafe (2014, 40–41), who argues that Bach probably did not yet own the three listed publications by August Pfeiffer, a prolific polemicist against Calvinism.

49 In a newspaper issue published there on June 4, 1723 (BD 2:104 [no. 138]; trans. in NBR, 106 [no. 102]).

50 "die Herren Studiosi animiret werden möchten" (BD 2:95 [no. 129]; NBR, 103 [no. 98]).

official of a city if not an independent "republic." This would have fundamental implications for him, personally and professionally. Before considering those, however, we must turn to the music that Bach produced during what he would later come to view, in retrospect, as the happiest period of his career.

CHAPTER NINE

Bach the Capellmeister

SUITES, SERENADES, AND RELATED WORKS

I N MOVING FROM WEIMAR TO CÖTHEN, BACH ALSO MOVED UP FROM THE new and somewhat uncertain status of concertmaster to the traditional and highly respected position of Capellmeister. The German word *Capelle* (*Kapelle* in modern spelling) today means "band," including the type that plays polka music at weddings. But it originally meant "chapel," and *Capellmeister* was a direct translation of the old Italian title *maestro di cappella*, which Monteverdi had held at Venice, Schütz more recently at Dresden. A Capellmeister might serve in either a municipal church or an aristocratic household, but the latter was the more prestigious position, as it involved direction of music for a ruler's private worship services. That was not in fact Bach's function at Cöthen, but to be a court Capellmeister was to be the highest-ranking musician of the realm, or at least in the ruler's household.[1] Just a few months before Bach's arrival in Cöthen, Mattheson had dedicated his *Beschütztes Orchestre* to thirteen "world- and wide-renowned" German Capellmeisters and music directors. It must have galled Bach that his name could not be included alongside that of Handel, Telemann, or his predecessor Stricker on the book's opening pages.[2] He would nevertheless continue to hold

---

1 In 1741, when Carl Heinrich Graun was appointed Capellmeister at another Calvinist court, that of Frederick the Great in Berlin, it was to compose and direct operas, not church music.

2 Mattheson (1717, f. 2v): "den . . . Herrn Capell-Meistern, directoribus musices, welt- und weit-berühmten, teutschen melothetis." Mattheson dated his dedication February 21, 1717,

Bach. David Schulenberg, Oxford University Press (2020). © Oxford University Press.
DOI: 10.1093/oso/9780190936303.001.0001

an honorary Capellmeistership, like Telemann, after leaving Cöthen; he remained Capellmeister of Cöthen *von Haus aus*, that is, in absentia, until 1729, when he received a similar title from the duke of Weissenfels.[3] As such he was probably expected to visit or send compositions periodically, as Telemann did to Eisenach, and when present he probably had full command of the court's musical forces.[4]

Working at Cöthen for a youthful prince, Bach might have been inspired both to delight and to instruct or shape him, much as a court preacher did—always from a properly subordinate position, of course. Bach was called Capellmeister, but the prince may have referred to his ensemble as a collegium musicum and Bach as "director of our chamber music," that is, of music performed in his personal quarters—a high honor.[5] Bach continued to identify himself as Capellmeister throughout his Leipzig years, giving that court title ahead of his municipal ones of cantor and director of church music. The prince's view of his chamber music as a sort of "collegium" hints at its being conceived like a learned academy, albeit one that saw private performances in which the prince himself participated. Leopold's capabilities as a player of violin and viola da gamba are often mentioned in connection with the Brandenburg Concertos, which are likely to have been played in his presence, possibly with his participation. But he was also a singer, as was Bach's predecessor Stricker, who, after leaving Cöthen, rejoined his former Berlin colleague Finger to collaborate on operas and ballets at Neuburg on the Danube. Sebastian (and Anna Magdalena) surely knew Stricker's Opus 1, a set of six

but the book was not published until the end of September (Michaelis). Bach's friend Mizler did include Bach in the similarly worded dedication of his Leipzig dissertation in 1734 (BD 2:245 [no. 349]; NBR, 163 [no. 168]).

3 Bach took care to mention this at the end of his own entry in the Genealogy, BD 1:259 (no. 184); NBR, 290 (no 303).

4 Emanuel Bach would similarly hold an honorary title as Capellmeister to Princess Anna Amalia, sister of Frederick the Great, after moving from Berlin to Hamburg, sending her music on request of her librarian Kirnberger (see Schulenberg 2014, 297–99); his nephew Wilhelm Friedrich Ernst, Sebastian's grandson, would be Capellmeister to Frederick's widow.

5 Leopold described Bach as "Capellmeister und Director unserer Cammer Music" in his formal notice of dismissal (BD 2:93 [no. 128]); Bach used a similar phrase to describe himself in the Genealogy (BD 1:259 [no. 184]; NBR, 290 [no 303]). The phrase *collegium musicum*, today used in association with concert-giving organizations, occurs in the first court record of a payment to Bach for holding rehearsals at home (BD 2:70 [no. 91]).

Italian cantatas published at Cöthen in 1715 by the court printer Löffler.[6] Surely, too, this publication hints at the type of music that Stricker provided for the court—and of what Bach was expected to perform if not also compose. Although chiefly for soprano and continuo, Stricker's publication, in the popular "Neapolitan" style of the time, concludes with a cantata that adds an obbligato oboe in its first aria and a chalumeau—an early form of the clarinet—in the second, concluding aria. The latter is in the style of a minuet, a French dance. It opens with an instrumental ritornello in binary form (two repeated halves), which is then followed by a texted vocal version of the same music. Can it be a coincidence that this design, which can be traced to Lully's operas, recurs in Bach's vocal music of a few years later?[7]

The few available instrumental compositions by Stricker include a trio sonata that likewise combines Italianate and French movements.[8] It resembles pieces that Heinichen, Telemann, and other Germans were producing during the second decade of the century: tuneful and with a lightly contrapuntal texture, mixing easy-to-play Italianate figuration with French dance rhythms. Scored (in one copy) for flute and violin, alongside one or two sonatas for flute, it suggests that the latter instrument, then new to chamber music, was already being cultivated at Cöthen before Bach's arrival.[9] Fascination in new instruments such as the chalumeau was also manifest at the same time in Telemann's music for

6 This was Löffler's only musical issue, apart from librettos for court serenatas (including those by Bach); other publications during Bach's time there included Calvinist sermons and theological tracts.

7 As in the closing movement of the Cöthen cantata BWV 173a and the undated wedding cantata BWV 202 (which might, however, stem from the Weimar years). A minuet aria also closes Stricker's fourth cantata, with continuo only; the third cantata, a dialog for Cupid and an unnamed devotee, has an obbligato violin.

8 Preserved in two Dresden copies, Dresden, Landesbibliothek, Mus. mss. 2139-Q-1a and 2139-Q-1b; edition by Thomas A. Schneider on imslp.org.

9 One of the solo sonatas (in D) is preserved elsewhere with attributions to Handel and Quantz (as QV 1:Anh. 15a; see Oleskiewicz 1998, 693). The latter, together with Stricker's sonata in A, is included in a manuscript anthology of pieces for solo flute, oboe, and violin with continuo (Brussels, Bibliothèque Royale, ms. XY 15115). Bach's first known use of the flute, as opposed to the recorder, is in BWV 173a (see below). A likely player in these works was Johann Heinrich Freitag, one of three members of that family who worked in Cöthen and who composed at least six sonatas preserved in the same anthology.

Eisenach. Bach's Weimar cantatas reveal fewer signs of the same interest, but at Leipzig in 1717 he was impressed by the local builder Scheibe's crafting of colorful organ ranks, and after moving there he would take up innovations by other instrument makers in the city.[10]

In his Cöthen compositions Bach now wrote with a lighter touch than in his major Weimar works. He also turned sharply toward writing music for stringed keyboard instruments and for instrumental ensembles—or at least this has been the assumption of scholars, based in part on the fact that at Cöthen Bach had no official responsibility for writing vocal music. In addition, the autograph fair-copy manuscripts for three important sets of instrumental compositions bear dates from the Cöthen years: the violin solos (1720), the Brandenburg Concertos (1721), and the first part of the Well-Tempered Clavier (1722). It was also at Cöthen that Bach put together the little keyboard book for Wilhelm Friedemann (1720) and the first of two such books for Anna Magdalena (1722), as well as the collection of inventions and sinfonias (1723). Yet Bach is supposed to have composed at least a portion of the Well-Tempered Clavier at Weimar. Other instrumental compositions probably also existed in some form before Bach revised them and assembled them into sets at Cöthen. That he was deliberately consolidating some of his existing music is clear from the fact that he also prepared a new title page for the *Orgelbüchlein*, begun at Weimar. The latter nevertheless remains incomplete, lacking the majority of the chorale melodies for which he left blank pages in the manuscript.[11]

This chapter therefore considers not only music that Bach is known to have written at Cöthen, but also the collections of pieces that either originated or were completed there. These remained in manuscript during Bach's lifetime; his publications will be taken up in Chapter 13. The list of works produced during some five and a half years at Cöthen looks very different from the one given previously for the nine and a half years at Weimar (compare Tables 7.1 and 9.1). The focus is now on works for stringed keyboard instruments and instrumental chamber music. A few of the items listed in Table 7.1, notably the cello suites, are

---

10 Such as the woodwind maker Eichentopf, whose oboe d'amore was used in at least one of the Leipzig audition pieces (see Ahrens 2014).

11 The new title page is dated to 1722 or 1723 (Dadelsen 1963, 77).

Table 9.1   Works Partly or Completely Composed, Revised, or Compiled into Sets
at Cöthen

Vocal

Birthday and New Year's works for the court: BWV 66a, 134a, 173a, 184a; BWV Anh. 5–8 and 197

Other secular cantatas: BWV 202 (earlier?), 203 (if by Bach)

Church pieces for the Leipzig audition: BWV 22, 23

Keyboard

Preludes, fugues, and other smaller pieces in the two Cöthen *Clavierbüchlein*

Fifteen inventions and fifteen sinfonias (three-part inventions)

Forty-eight preludes and fugues in all keys (the Well-Tempered Clavier, Part 1)

Six English Suites

Six French Suites

Other Instrumental

Six cello suites

Six violin "solos" (three sonatas and three partitas)

Other pieces for solo instruments, with and without continuo: BWV 996, 1013, 1034 (?)

Trio sonatas and related works (or their prototypes?): six organ sonatas; six violin-and-keyboard sonatas; flute and gamba sonatas BWV 1030, 1032, 1027–29

Six Brandenburg Concertos and other works for larger ensembles: BWV 1041–43; BWV 1066; early versions of other concertos and "orchestral" suites?

repeated here, as they may have been finished and gathered into a set only at Cöthen. Other collections—the French Suites, organ sonatas, violin sonatas with keyboard, and the second part of the Well-Tempered Clavier—definitely were not completed until after the move to Leipzig, but a substantial portion of their contents was composed at Cöthen if not at Weimar. A few organ works have been traced to the Cöthen years, and one imagines that Bach would have prepared something new for an event like the Hamburg audition, possibly for Leipzig as well. Yet there is no unequivocal evidence for that.[12]

---

12 The organ work most likely to date from the Cöthen years is the big concerto-style fugue in G minor BWV 542/2, apparently described by Mattheson (1731, 1:34–35). This fugue was eventually paired—not necessarily by Bach—with the fantasia in the same key (BWV 542/1, discussed in Chapter 7).

This seems like a lot of music, and the seven sets containing six pieces each, together with the forty-eight preludes and fugues—eight further half-dozens—make up nearly a hundred works (several times that many individual movements). Yet by comparison with Vivaldi, Telemann, and other contemporaries, Bach was not a prolific composer of music for instrumental ensembles. Nor is the output for stringed keyboard instruments particularly large for a member of his generation. The popularity of a small number of works in modern concert programming can make such compositions seem more important within Bach's output than they really were, although it is possible that much has been lost. Indeed the court paid significant amounts for copying and binding music during Bach's time there—far more than could be accounted for by his surviving ensemble works.[13] But how much of this music was of Bach's own composition is unknown, and it could be that this activity was meant to build a diverse music library. No information survives about the repertory of the Cöthen Capelle, but an inventory from the neighboring court of Zerbst lists vocal and instrumental works by many German and Italian composers, evidently collected there from 1722 onward by the Capellmeister Johann Friedrich Fasch, for Prince Leopold August.[14] At Dresden, Pisendel assembled a similar repertory for the electoral Saxon court, and it would be surprising if Bach did not do the same for his own ensemble.[15]

Bach's Collections of Instrumental Works

Unlike his vocal works and his organ music, the compositions on which Bach apparently focused at Cöthen are mostly gathered into collections

---

13 Wolff (2000, 200) concludes that over 350 works, "mainly chamber and orchestral music," were added to the court library from 1718 through May 1723. He estimates that two thirds of this "stemmed from the capellmeister's pen," implying the loss of some two hundred original compositions.

14 The inventory of the so-called Zerbster Concert-Stube, transcribed by Engelke (1908, 54–75), is heavy on compositions by Fasch himself but also includes numerous works by Telemann, Vivaldi, and many others—but not Bach.

15 The collection of Pisendel, who served as concertmaster from 1730 to his death in 1755, and before that was responsible for the repertory of the *Cammer Musici* (see Oleskiewicz 1998, 53–54), passed eventually to the court, as did that of his predecessor Volumier; both are now part of the Sächsisches Landesbibliothek (ibid., 163n. 13). Pisendel's own compositions make up only a small portion of this repertory alongside greater quantities of music by such contemporaries as Telemann, Handel, Heinichen, and Fasch.

organized by dozens and half-dozens. There was long precedent for this in printed music. Corelli's six sets of sonatas and concertos, the last issued in 1714 and all frequently reprinted, each consisted of twelve works, and numerous Italian and German composers followed suit. Although Bach would not publish his music in print until after moving to Leipzig, already at Weimar he may have begun organizing certain pieces into sets. He might have done this for his pupils, for dissemination in manuscript copies, or for purely personal reasons. Organization of like pieces into sets could have been a form of self-realization, a way of demonstrating to himself that he had mastered a particular genre of composition. It was also a way of going beyond the perfection of individual compositions. Creating a larger work, an *opus* comprising multiple examples of the same basic type, demonstrated greater achievement, signifying that, as a mature musician now in his thirties, he was producing an oeuvre comparable to that of his most illustrious predecessors and contemporaries.

Bach assembled these collections with care. Similar features in different pieces within the same collection can suggest that Bach wrote them during the same period. Sometimes, however, as in the case of the First English Suite or the sixth sonata for keyboard and violin, one piece stands out from the others for its style or sequence of movements, suggesting that it was composed at a different time. We know, too, that Bach changed his mind about the make-up of some of these sets; this suggests that the neat half-dozens in which they are now preserved may not reflect the forms in which they were first conceived. Bach is unlikely to have set out to write any collection exactly as we have it, or to have proceeded methodically from one piece in a set to the next. Nor does the order of pieces within a set necessarily reflect that in which they were written. Yet in most cases the individual compositions are ordered in some logical way, systematically traversing different keys or incorporating particular types of movements.

The organization of the Well-Tempered Clavier is the grandest instance of this, although the idea of setting forth preludes and fugues for keyboard instrument in all twenty-four keys was not as obvious then as it seems to us. The number of usable tonalities could be debated; are E-flat minor and D-sharp minor the same? Students needed to learn to cope with pieces written either way. The arrangement of preludes and fugues by ascending half-step (C, C-sharp, D, etc.), with the minor mode following the major, was not necessarily the original one. Earlier collections of keyboard music had employed fewer keys and different orderings; even the decision to start with C was not a given at a time when key signatures were not standardized. D minor, descended from the old mode 1, could still be written without a flat, as in the "Dorian" Toccata and Fugue for organ. The WTC (as it will be abbreviated), like other collections, must have been compiled partly from existing older compositions. That could mean that some worthy pieces had to be left out or transposed to avoid repeating a key within a set. On the other hand, it might be necessary to write new compositions to fill out the plan of a given collection. Early manuscript copies by Bach's pupils provide clues about the evolution of the WTC and other sets. But in every case the first version is lost, although this has not prevented scholars from reconstructing hypothetical originals.

Keyboard Pieces, Including the Inventions and the Well-Tempered Clavier

Today the first exposure of many pupils to Bach's music is through the little pieces in the keyboard books for Wilhelm Friedemann and Anna Magdalena. Some of these, notably the famous Minuet in G, are actually by other composers, examples of what Bach's children probably learned before proceeding to his own music. The inclusion of such compositions within these two manuscripts suggests that Bach kept a larger collection of pedagogic pieces in copies acquired by sale or exchange. These would have been useful not only for teaching but for keeping himself informed about current trends. The greatest number of these little pieces take the form of dances—chiefly minuets and polonaises, which were musically similar, the latter not yet the virtuoso showpiece of Chopin. Many are by Dresden composers, including Hasse and Christian Pezold (composer of the G-major minuet); Bach was by no means too proud to offer his family and pupils fashionable music by younger contemporaries. There are also a few marches and chorale settings, and the second (1725) book for Anna Magdalena eventually included several songs as well as an arrangement of a favorite aria from one of the Leipzig cantatas (BWV 82).

Another type of keyboard piece was the prelude, which could take many forms but whose name at the time implied something improvised and therefore following no set form. Friedemann's little

Example 9.1   (a) Invention in C, BWV 772, mm. 1–2; (b) Sinfonia in C, BWV 787, mm. 1–3

keyboard book contains many examples of various sorts. Several look like small versions of the preludes in concerto style that Bach composed for organ and as opening movements in the English Suites.[16] Others, including two examples in C in Friedemann's book, are written-out versions of a traditional type of prelude based on broken chords (arpeggios).[17] The most important are early versions of some of the preludes included in the WTC, plus fifteen little preludes that Sebastian recopied a few months later into another manuscript.[18] The latter group provided Friedemann with lessons in two-part imitative counterpoint at the keyboard. They were joined in both sources by fifteen further pieces, originally called fantasias, then sinfonias (Example 9.1). Today the two sets are known as the two- and three-part inventions, respectively.

16 These are BWV 925 in D and BWV 928 in F, perhaps also the fragmentary BWV 932 in E minor.

17 BWV 924, the second piece in Friedemann's book, perhaps provided a model for a second composition of the same type in the same key added several years later, BWV 924a.

18 Berlin, Staatsbibliothek, Mus. ms. Bach P 610.

Bach's revised copy of the inventions is headed by a long title setting out their purpose: the thirty pieces are to teach the discovery of
musical ideas (*inventiones*) as well as their development or working out
(*Durchführung*), providing a "foretaste" (*Vorschmack*) of *Composition*. The
latter word probably meant counterpoint, consistent with the later testimony of E. L. Gerber that Bach's pupils studied these pieces before
proceeding to the WTC.[19] Bach does not distinguish what we would call
theory from practice, and while providing models of composition the
pieces also constitute exercises in "singing" at the keyboard. Today *canta-*
bile (literally, "singingly") is often taken to mean legato, but it is impossible, if only for reasons of fingering, to play many passages in these pieces
in the smooth, unarticulated manner taken for granted today by many
pianists. The word must rather have meant that Bach expected each voice
in the two- and three-part pieces to have the same beauty and coherence
as if sung as a solo line (or played on a solo melody instrument like the
flute). Clear articulation, not legato, was expected in both singing and
playing, and the lessons learned here would have extended to the WTC
and other more advanced pieces.

The fifteen two-part inventions are in as many of the most commonly
used keys. All are contrapuntally conceived, the parts for the two hands
absolutely equal, but they vary in form and in the specific ways their
"ideas" are "developed." The same holds for the three-part pieces, which,
although published in modern editions alongside the two-part inventions,
are less often studied. Despite their equally compact dimensions and pedagogic intent, they are considerably more difficult to play, some passages
as challenging as anything in the WTC. Indeed, Bach drafted them in the
little keyboard book for Wilhelm Friedemann during the same period
that saw the completion of Part 1 of the latter work.

The WTC has become so familiar that its innovatory character is no
longer readily obvious. For more than a century, European composers had
been producing collections of exemplary keyboard pieces arranged by
key or mode. None, however, approached Bach's in size, variety, or thor-
oughness. The work most often cited as a predecessor, Fischer's *Ariadne*

---

19 Gerber (1790–92, Vol. 1, col. 492; trans. in NBR, 322 [no. 315]); this Gerber was son of
Bach's pupil Heinrich Nicolaus Gerber, whose manuscript copies of many keyboard works
(but not the inventions) survive.

musica (1702), remains relatively small in both scale and the demands that it places on the performer. Nevertheless, at least three of Bach's fugue subjects also occur in the collection by the south-German Fischer, whose published volumes of suites for keyboard and for ensemble provided further models for Bach.[20] Additional precedents for the WTC could be seen in toccatas by Frescobaldi and Buxtehude, versets by Muffat and Kerll, and short fugues by Pachelbel.[21] Yet it is thanks to Bach that we understand a "prelude and fugue" as two complementary movements, usually of similar dimensions and always in the same key, but otherwise self-contained. In fact the prelude-fugue pairs of the WTC, like the inventions and sinfonias, constituted a new genre; no two of them repeat the same forms, movement types, and expressive characters.

Book I of the WTC was, if one believes the customary interpretation of the account by E. L. Gerber, composed during Bach's imprisonment at Weimar. As we know it, however, it is a product of the Cöthen years, as is clear from its inclusion of preludes that Friedemann copied into his Little Keyboard Book, sometimes with help from his father. Only subsequently were they revised for inclusion in the autograph manuscript of the WTC. The revisions lengthened certain movements, notably the prelude in E minor. This was originally a harmonically inspired prelude of the broken-chord type, working out a single recurring motivic idea, like two of the simpler little preludes entered previously into Friedemann's manuscript (BWV 924 and 926). In its revised form, the E-minor prelude practically doubled in length, the original portion being transformed by the addition of an ornately embellished melody (Example 9.2). For any student (such as Friedemann Bach) who had access as well to the original, the revised version would have served as a lesson in how to spin a melody out of a harmonic progression.

---

20 The common subjects are those for the fugues in F major and G minor from Bach's Book I and the E-major fugue from Book 2; at least in the F-major fugue, the parallelism extends beyond the subject (see Schulenberg 2006, 224). Whether Bach knew Fischer's complete *Ariadne musica* is uncertain; he is not known to have owned a copy, and although Walther (1732, 246) mentioned a 1702 edition, apparently no copy dated earlier than 1713 survives.

21. Two preludes and fugues attributed to Pachelbel in the "Eckelt" tablature, copied by a fellow pupil of J. C. Bach of Ohrdruf, are probably by other composers; these are the "Prelude and Fugue" in E minor and the "Toccata and Fugue" in B-flat in the old Pachelbel complete works edition by Max Seiffert (*Denkmäler der Tonkunst in Bayern*, Vol. 4/1, 1903).

Example 9.2 Prelude in E minor, mm. 1–3: (a) early version, BWV 855a; (b) revised
version, BWV 855

The familiar title of the WTC is first documented on the first page
of the 1722 autograph. It is just a part of a long heading—practically a
preface—in which Bach announced his intentions for the volume, following the model of printed works such as Mattheson's recently published
Organisten-Probe.[22] The implication is that Bach regarded his collection of
contrapuntal pieces as the equivalent of a serious printed work. Like
Mattheson, Bach provided exercises in all keys, something possible on
a keyboard instrument only if the latter is tuned in suitable fashion.
Keyboard tuning was on the mind of German musicians of Bach's generation, to judge from theoretical as well as practical publications of the
time. Their concern was more precisely with temperament: the practice
of slightly mistuning thirds, fifths, and other intervals to allow organs,

22 Mattheson (1719), an early version of his *Grosse General-Bass-Schule* (1731). Both contain
exercises in improvisation over a figured bass.

harpsichords, and clavichords, with their fixed pitches, to participate with other instruments and voices in the expanded tonal idiom of the early eighteenth century. We do not know Bach's preferred keyboard temperament, although after his death his son Emanuel evidently favored equal temperament.[23] The latter had been known since the early seventeenth century, but it was only one of any number of tuning systems that made a keyboard instrument "well tempered."

That Bach had been thinking since his youth about the possibilities of tuning and modulation, or of what "all keys" might mean, is evident from early or experimental pieces that make startling excursions through remote tonalities. The overture BWV 822, the praeludium BWV 922, even the toccata BWV 910—each of which contains at least one long ramble through multiple remote keys—might have been composed at Arnstadt in the same year (1704) that J. P. Treiber published his *Accurater Organist* there, showing how to accompany two chorale melodies in twenty different keys. Two years previously his *Sonderbare Invention* had shown how to harmonize an "aria" in "all" keys.[24] That one could construct a major or a minor scale on each of the twelve notes of a chromatic keyboard was not obvious prior to the eighteenth century, thanks to the use of older tuning systems that made it impossible to play triads on certain notes.[25] The same tuning systems discouraged the idea that one could modulate continuously by fifths, returning eventually to the original key. Nevertheless, sophisticated musicians and instrument makers were assuredly aware of the possibility of doing precisely that. By 1700, moreover, composers of opera and cantata were frequently calling for remote modulations, at least in recitative. Professional players could no longer avoid tonalities that had previously been regarded merely as theoretical possibilities.

23 Direct evidence comes only from a treatise by the instrument maker Barthold Fritz (1757); Emanuel himself wrote only that his father favored a "new type" (*neue Art*) of tuning, just as Sebastian also employed a "new fingering" (*neue Finger-Setzung*) for scales and other keyboard figuration (1753–1762, Vol. 1, introduction, para. 14, and chap. 1, para. 8).

24 In 1702 Treiber also published an anti-Judaic tract; his musical writings were a mere sideline, but authors such as Werckmeister revealed similar concerns.

25 For instance, in the quarter-comma meantone temperament advocated by many seventeenth-century writers, playing a triad on what looked like the note A-flat would result in the very dissonant sonority G-sharp–C–E-flat. In this temperament, G-sharp was an audibly lower pitch than A-flat, as could be demonstrated on the occasional keyboard instrument that had separate keys for the two notes, or on any properly played violin or flute.

Example 9.3 Praeludium in G minor, BWV 535/1, mm. 19–20 (notes with downward stems are played by the left hand, those with upward stems by the right; the pattern continues for a total of twelve bars, through m. 30)

It was now a teacher's job to prepare keyboard students for playing in all keys, and a virtuoso could impress knowledgeable auditioners by making swift passages between distantly related tonalities (such as C major and C-sharp minor)—even if Bach's doing so confused certain listeners at Arnstadt.[26] A passage from one of his earlier organ preludes, perhaps composed during the first years at Weimar, suggests that he might often have improvised his way around the circle of fifths, using arpeggiated diminished-seventh chords to modulate by half-step (Example 9.3).[27] An organist, in any case, had to be prepared to play in more "difficult" or "remote" keys than those of the voices and instruments that he accompanied, thanks to changing pitch standards during the long life of an organ. As a result, the organist might have to play in B-flat minor or C-sharp major while the rest of the ensemble read parts written in C minor or E-flat. We do not know the pitch of the organs at Weimar and Cöthen during Bach's time there, but at Leipzig Kuhnau treated the organ as a transposing instrument. Bach would retain this convention, and his Leipzig organ parts are therefore often in odd keys. His pupils would have gained

26 If Bach continued in this vein later in life, it could explain a reference to his leading a congregation to successively higher-pitched stanzas in a chorale. The document, edited in BD 5:259 (no. C1005a), is cited by Wolff and Zepf (2012, 5) in relation to Bach's probable visit to Altenburg in 1739.

27 Another instance of such modulation occurs in the somewhat doubtful BWV 948, which, if not by Bach, was probably composed by a student inspired by his example.

practice in these by learning the Well-Tempered Clavier, and Scheibe and other organ makers must have tuned their instruments in appropriate temperaments.

Bach would compile a second volume of twenty-four preludes and fugues (WTC2) by around 1740; the exact date and even the title of this volume are uncertain, as he never prepared a conclusive integral manuscript for it as he did for Part 1. Whether his views on temperament changed during the intervening two decades is unknown, but if so the practical effect is likely to have been negligible. Already at Arnstadt or Mühlhausen he must have favored organs and harpsichords so tuned that he could play the E-major praeludium BWV 566, or modulating passages in other pieces, without producing the impossibly sour chords that arose in older "non-circulating" temperaments. Nor could he have wished the sonorous F-major fugue BWV 901/2— from a group of preludes and fugues that preceded the WTC—to have sounded appreciably less sonorous when he transposed it to A-flat and doubled it in length for inclusion in Part 2.[28] Keyboard temperament and the provision of music in all keys were hardly Bach's only concerns in the WTC. If the work did originate as a series of little preludes in only the most common keys—as the selections in Friedemann's book suggest—another purpose might have been to demonstrate to students the working out of simple patterns. Some of these compositional demonstrations could also serve as technical exercises, providing a workout for, say, the weaker outer fingers of the right hand (Example 9.4). Others consist almost entirely of extended sequences of broken chords, often beginning with a variation on one particular formula (tonic–subdominant–dominant–tonic) before diverging in wide-ranging modulations (Example 9.5). Comparable streams of regularly patterned notes—*perfidia*, as they may sometimes have been called—occur also in Italian violin music, as middle movements in the first six of Corelli's op. 5 sonatas and later as solo episodes in concertos. Bach's preludes of this type also contain echoes of the unmeasured preludes of the French tradition, notated without bar lines. Bach never leaves the rhythm up to the player, as in those pieces. Yet even in Book 2, whose preludes on

---

28 The revised version of the fugue, nearly double the length of the original, was one of the last movements recopied for inclusion in WTC2 around 1740.

Example 9.4   Well-Tempered Clavier, Part 1, Prelude in D, BWV 850/1, mm. 1–2

Example 9.5   Well-Tempered Clavier, (a) Part 1, Prelude in C, BWV 846/1, mm. 1–4;
(b) Part 2, Prelude in C-sharp major, BWV 872/1, mm. 1–2

the whole are more strictly structured, a few continue to reveal their
ancestry in improvised preludes based on broken chords (Example 9.6).
Other preludes are entirely distinct in type; among these are dances
such as the siciliana (C-sharp minor in both books) and allegros
in an early version of sonata form (ten examples in Book 2 alone).
The latter resemble movements in the keyboard sonatas that Bach's

Example 9.6   Well-Tempered Clavier, Part 2, Prelude in F, BWV 880/1, mm. 1-3

younger contemporaries, including his first two sons, were writing by that time.[29]

The fugues are, if anything, even more varied. They include several rigorous examples of "demonstration counterpoint," systematically illustrating traditional fugal devices such as thematic inversion, stretto, and multiple subjects (D-sharp minor in Book 1, B-flat minor and F-sharp minor in Book 2). A few are archaic in style and notation, evoking the ricercars of Froberer and other seventeenth-century predecessors (C-sharp minor in WTC1, E major in WTC2). Most, however, have up-to-date subjects and styles and could entertain or move a listener unaware of the contrapuntal craft and the tricky keyboard technique that they entail.

The greater number of binary-form preludes in WTC2 is perhaps the clearest stylistic development between the two volumes. Although this might make Book 2 more modern than Book 1, the latter already contains at least one *fugue* in a close approximation to early sonata form.[30] And even the most archaic movements in the WTC incorporate expressive dissonances and chromatic modulations that are foreign to the old-fashioned style they ostensibly represent. Examples include the two five-voice fugues of Book 1 (in C-sharp minor and B-flat minor) and the E-major fugue of Book 2, whose subject, shared with Fischer and

29 Wilhelm Friedemann's earliest sonatas are not precisely datable, but Emanuel had composed many such pieces by 1742, when he published six of them in his first printed set (the "Prussian" Sonatas, W. 48).

30 This is the fugue in C-sharp; further discussion in Schulenberg (2008a).

Froberger, is drawn from an ecclesiastical chant motive.[31] In such pieces Bach nods to tradition while finding his own path.

Many movements are brilliant display pieces, such as the B-flat-major prelude of Book 2, with its symmetrically distributed hand-crossings (resembling those of the Goldberg Variations), or the dashing A-minor fugue of the same volume. We might imagine the occasional performance of these and other solo keyboard compositions in private "academies," including those at court. Yet their main use, as Bach's titles indicate, must have been for private practice and recreation. Although not published until after the turn of the nineteenth century, the WTC is preserved in greater numbers of manuscript copies than any other Bach work. Many of these were probably prepared by or for the use of students. E. L. Gerber, whose father studied with Bach, reported that the latter played the entire WTC "three times through for him . . . when Bach, under the pretext of not feeling in the mood to teach, sat himself at one of his fine instruments and thus turned these hours into minutes."[32]

The English and French Suites

In addition to studying his contrapuntal pieces, Bach's pupils at Cöthen and Leipzig made manuscript copies of his suites. Each of these comprises four or more dance movements, sometimes preceded by a prelude. Bach himself made copies of suites by the French composer Dieupart and doubtless others.[33] But like the "prelude and fugue," the "suite" as we know it is largely a product of Bach, who effectively codified a genre that previously had been more loosely understood. Bach's idea of the suite depended on that found in publications by Kuhnau and Fischer, perhaps also in the posthumously printed keyboard works of Froberger. But the French composers from whom these German musicians took the individual dances rarely arranged the latter in such neat, regular successions. Only in Germany did these so frequently comprise one each of allemande,

---

31 Haydn and Mozart used the same four-note theme in the fugal finales of two symphonies (Hob. I:13 and the "Jupiter," K. 551).

32 From the entry for Bach in Gerber's first music encyclopedia (1790–1792); trans. in NBR, 322 (no. 315).

33 Bach's manuscript copy of Dieupart's *Six suites de clavecin* (Amsterdam, 1701) dates from 1709–1716 (Beißwenger 1992, 282).

courante, sarabande, and gigue, in that order. Bach, following Kuhnau, usually added one or more further dances after the sarabande, such as the minuet, gavotte, or bourrée. Any of these movements might incorporate features of Italian as well as French style, and with Bach this is sometimes reflected in the use of Italian as opposed to French forms of the dance titles (such as *corrente* for *courante*).

French composers such as François Couperin and Rameau never treated the suite as systematically as their German contemporaries, and their harpsichord pieces increasingly bore descriptive titles, not merely the names of dances, even when they were examples of the latter. Even the French title *suite* is somewhat uncommon in manuscripts and printed editions from before Bach's time; Dieupart (or his Dutch publisher Roger) used it, but Kuhnau called his dance sets *Partien,* as did Graupner in a collection published in 1718. Bach surely knew these works as well as Mattheson's sumptuously engraved publication of 1714, which retained the traditional overall title *Pièces de clavecin* ("Harpsichord Pieces"), although the individual works are called suites.[34]

Today the word *clavecin* in these titles is understood as "harpsichord." Yet most German purchasers probably played music of this sort on the more affordable clavichord. Few could have owned the large two-manual French-style harpsichord that is now customary for concert use. Bach called for the latter explicitly only in two of his Leipzig publications, and even then he must have expected most purchasers to own simpler instruments. Whether he also expected buyers to play all the individual movements of each suite, in order, is less obvious. Earlier collections, especially in France, contain such unsystematic selections and groupings of pieces that players must have felt free to pick and choose individual movements, even improvising a prelude for a series of pieces that lacked a written one.

Bach evidently gave serious consideration to the order and number of movements in each suite. During the 1720s he would add, delete, and revise movements in his dance sets, eventually arriving at the three collections known as the English Suites, the French Suites, and the Partitas. The popular names of the first two sets, already in use by the end of the eighteenth century, are of unknown origin. They do not reflect any distinction

---

34 The simultaneously published German edition is entitled *Matthesons Harmonisches Denckmahl, aus zwölff erwählten Clavier-Suiten.*

in national style; indeed the dances of the "English" suites are some-what closer to traditional French types than those of the "French" suites. Each collection contains six suites, and although all follow the same basic organizing principles, the Partitas introduce greater variety in the choice of individual movements, also revealing a more exuberant approach to the keyboard.[35] Already in the last two or three French Suites, however, Bach has left the seventeenth-century models of the suite far behind, just as Rameau and other French composers were doing at the time.

Chamber Music: Works for Solo Strings

The Cöthen years saw Bach also making new ventures in the realm of chamber music. "Chamber music," for Bach and his contemporaries, was literally music performed in a room (chamber) of a private home, whether a palace or a more modest residence. Here the term is used to describe Bach's works for any number of bowed string or wind instruments, without voices. Even the compositions now described as "orchestral" suites were, with one exception, designed to be playable by ensembles of just five or six musicians. The most lavishly scored of all this music, the First Brandenburg Concerto and the fourth "orchestral" suite, required no more than thirteen players.

To be sure, the violin parts might be doubled, and Quantz—doubtless reflecting his experience in the royal capitals of Dresden, Warsaw, and Berlin—described ensembles with as many as thirty-four woodwinds and strings. With the addition of horns, trumpets, and drums, the resulting orchestra might comprise forty instrumentalists. A vocal work might add eight singers, encompassing some fifty musicians in all. Bach, however, may never have directed an ensemble of quite this size, which might have been considered desirable for only a handful of his grandest compositions. The most common ensemble for a concerto involved a single player on a part, and the extant sets of manuscript parts for Bach's works rarely include duplicates. Hence even a pair of extra violins, or the addition of a "medium-sized" double bass,[36] must have been regarded as an optional expansion of music conceived for a band of soloists.

---

35 The Partitas are considered together with other published works in Chapter 13. Bach ev-idently contemplated including two further works, BWV 818 and 819, among the French Suites, which they resemble; more on these in Schulenberg (2006, 302–8).

36 As recommended by Quantz (1752, Chapter 17, section 1, para. 16).

Bach's smallest scores, in terms of number of parts, are the suites and sonatas for flute, violin, and cello without accompaniment. He surely knew of earlier solo music for the first two instruments. The French flutist and flute maker Hotteterre had included unaccompanied flute pieces in collections published in 1708 and 1719, and the Weimar violinist Westhoff had issued a set of six suites for his own instrument as early as 1696. Bach might have known the latter through either the original publication or personal acquaintance with the composer at Weimar (where Westhoff was court secretary and chamber musician until his death in 1705). Westhoff's suites resemble certain older German examples for keyboard in consisting uniformly of allemande, courante, sarabande, and gigue. The gigues are fugal, but the counterpoint is of limited interest, with long passages in parallel thirds. Nevertheless the writing is completely idiomatic for the violin, and Bach might have learned from Westhoff to notate the lower voices as if they could be sustained— although a violin cannot in fact hold more than two tones simultaneously, on adjacent strings.

What Bach could not have gotten from Westhoff or any other predecessor was the inspiration to expand vastly on his models. His compositions for solo wind and string instruments are as grandly proportioned as his great organ works, as one sees above all in the famous chaconne for violin (Example 9.7). The final movement of the second violin partita, this series of variations on a repeating bass line is as gigantic as the earlier organ Passacaglia. Yet it is completely distinct in style and overall form, mirroring a Lullian chaconne (with a contrasting central

Example 9.7 Violin Partita no. 2 in D minor, BWV 1003, chaconne, (a) mm. 1–4 and (b) mm. 133–36

Example 9.8 Organ Passacaglia in C minor, BWV 582, (a) mm. 9–12 and (b) mm. 181–84

section in the major mode), as opposed to a Buxtehudian prelude and fugue (Example 9.8).

Earlier German-speaking composers, including the Bohemian violinist Biber and Thomas Baltzar from Lübeck (who worked in England), had also written unaccompanied violin pieces. Other antecedents for Bach's works were furnished by French compositions for solo lute and solo viola da gamba, some of the latter with optional continuo accompaniment.[37] Lute music can resemble keyboard music, but it remains relatively thin in texture. Harmonies are often suggested by broken chords

37 Marais's first book of gamba pieces appeared originally (1686) for gamba alone; a continuo part was published in 1689.

and other figuration rather than being fully spelled out, just as in music for solo violin or cello. The same was a necessity on the flute, and Bach avoids writing chords (multiple stops) in the first four cello suites as well. Even where writing just a single line, however, Bach clearly outlines specific chords, and these imply precise voice leading and harmonic progressions (to use a modern concept).

Bach was not alone at the time in understanding that a single melodic line could embody a complete polyphonic composition. His older contemporary Niedt showed how an entire keyboard suite could be spun out of a figured bass line; Mattheson, who edited Niedt's writings, might have been inspired by them to produce his *Organisten-Probe*. Quantz later demonstrated how notes in a melodic line could suggest chords, which could then be elaborated in the form of arpeggios, scales, and other figuration.[38] Telemann, like Bach, wrote pieces for unaccompanied melody instruments, even a fugue for solo flute—a tour de force never attempted by J. S. Bach (or by C. P. E. Bach, who published a solo flute sonata).

Still, to write dance movements and even preludes and fugues for solo strings, on the same ambitious scale found in Bach's keyboard music, was a challenge without precedent. The famous autograph manuscript of the violin pieces bears the title *Sei solo* (Six Solos), which Bach designated *Libro primo* (Book 1). Autographs do not survive for the cello suites, which, even if mostly composed first, might have constituted Book 2 in their final or revised form. Yet despite their less complicated texture, the cello suites are more methodical, as is evident in their organization, which resembles that of the English Suites. Each comprises a prelude, then the four "standard" dances, plus two each of another dance type inserted before the concluding gigue. This consistency suggests a relatively early origin, as does the occasional family resemblance between passages in the cello suites and the basso continuo parts of the Weimar cantatas (Example 9.9). This points in turn to another antecedent for the cello suites: pedal solos in Bach's organ works. These likewise consist chiefly of unaccompanied bass lines, suggesting harmonies by leaping between chord tones

---

38 Niedt's *Musicalische Handleitung* came out in three volumes (1700, 1706, 1717), the last posthumously; Mattheson published an expanded edition of the second volume in 1721. Quantz (1752) illustrates his Chapter 14 on embellishments with examples that show the chords implied by notes in a simple melodic line, together with variations on the same.

Example 9.9 (a) *Nun komm der Heiden Heiland*, BWV 61, aria "Öffne dich," mm. 1–5;
(b) Cello Suite no. 3 in C, BWV 1009, courante, mm. 1–4

(cf. Example 7.1). Composing solo cello music would therefore not have seemed entirely new to Bach, perhaps easier than (and preliminary to?) writing for unaccompanied violin.

The cello suites progress from relatively simple to relatively complex; even the "optional" dances evolve from modest minuets in Suites 1 and 2 to dashing bourrées and sophisticated gavottes in the subsequent suites. Less accomplished players might have started with the simpler of these "optional" movements, which can adopt a deliberately plain texture, almost a sort of minimalism, as in the second bourrée of Suite 4. Even the four main dance movements seem to have been written rather cautiously in Suite 1, one reason one so often hears that work, in the easily negotiated key of G major.

The sixth suite stands apart from the others, and not only because it was written for an instrument with an extra string. It also seems distinctly later, more mature in style, than Suites 1–5. The five-string cello called for in BWV 1012 was probably identical with the violoncello piccolo required in a number of Bach's Leipzig cantatas and built by the Leipzig instrument maker Hoffmann.[39] The fifth, higher, string (e′) facilitates

---

39 Scholars have debated how this instrument relates to *da spalla* (on the shoulder) playing and to the *viola pomposa*, an instrument not mentioned until after Bach's lifetime. Mark Smith (1998, 75) argued that the sixth suite was for a small instrument of "viola size" (*Bratschengröße*), but Vanscheeuwijk (2010, 189) argues convincingly against "trying to find *the one and only* ideal instrument," bow grip, or playing position for any of Bach's cello music (original emphasis).

playing in the upper register. The other suites call for a conventional cello, but in Suite 5 the top string is tuned a whole tone lower than usual. This permits chords and counterpoint that would otherwise be unplayable, and, not surprisingly, the fifth suite is the one that requires the greatest amount of chordal playing. Yet although it is the culmination of the five works for the conventional cello, it is also closest to traditional French Baroque style, with a French overture as prelude.

The Sixth Cello Suite is the great work of the set, comparable in this respect to the Sixth Harpsichord Partita. It is distinguished not only by its prelude—which calls uniquely for echo effects and *bariolage* (string-crossing technique)—but by its profoundly touching allemande. The latter, already distinctive for its adagio tempo (unusual in an allemande), includes florid written-out embellishment comparable only to that of the corresponding movement in the Fourth Harpsichord Partita (published in 1728).

Bach must already have had a good understanding of the capabilities and limitations of the violin before composing the six solos for that instrument. Unlike the cello suites, these do not seem to have undergone significant revision after he wrote out their autograph fair copy at Cöthen in 1720. Any reticence that he might have had in making demands on the player in the cello suites is set aside here. Although the set as a whole is titled "Six Solos," the individual pieces alternate between sonatas and what Bach called "partias," using an Italian form of a word that Kuhnau had Graupner had attached to their published keyboard suites. Bach's title is now usually adjusted to *partita*, but the latter word had the distinct meaning in the earlier Baroque of "variation," as in some of Bach's early chorale settings. By 1726, however, Bach was using the expression *partita* for the keyboard suites printed as the first part of his *Clavierübung* (see Chapter 13). Whatever shades of meaning the different forms of the word might once have conveyed were probably by then forgotten.

The sonatas of the set are of the type known as the *sonata da chiesa* (church sonata), although the four-movement scheme had no actual connection to ecclesiastical usage in Lutheran Germany. Bach's idea of what a sonata should be came from Corelli, whose twelve sonatas for violin and continuo, initially published in 1700, saw numerous reprints. Among these was the famous one by Roger of Amsterdam, who provided the slow movements of the first six sonatas with written-out embellishments (see Example 7.4a above).[40] Whether or not Bach knew that edition, he knew the type of playing it represented, which he imitated in the opening movements of the first two sonatas. Each of these preludial movements is followed by a fugue, which again clearly follows Corelli, alternating between polyphonic expository passages and more lightly textured soloistic passagework.

The first two partitas, like the first two sonatas, are relatively traditional, opening with the conventional succession of allemande, courante, and sarabande. For this reason, the unique addition of a *double* (variation) after each movement of the first partita—including the final bourrée[41]— is a little surprising, given Bach's apparent lack of sympathy for variations. Variation is also the basis of the great chaconne that concludes the second partita in D minor. The four preceding movements alone would have made Partita 2 an imposing composition. The violin chaconne from Cöthen complements the organ Passacaglia of the Weimar years, demonstrating in a grand, if not slightly terrifying, way what sort of variations Bach could invent over an ostinato bass line. The organ work is decidedly German and contrapuntal in orientation, despite its apparent derivation from a French theme. The violin chaconne is more clearly French in conception. This is especially evident in the rhythm of its opening phrases (with a two-beat pickup) and the change to the major mode for the middle section (see Example 9.7 above). Yet Bach's chaconne exceeds most earlier examples not only in absolute length but in the variety of its figuration and in the way it nevertheless coheres as a unified composition. The latter is achieved above all by restatements of the opening phrase just before the exact center and at the end.

The flute partita (BWV 1013), which is entitled "Solo" in its sole source, contains just four movements, ending (like the first violin partita) with a bourrée. Flute players today regard the opening allemande as a tour de force, thanks to its arpeggios in unbroken sixteenths—a borrowing from keyboard style. Like similar passagework in the violin and cello

---

40 According to Roger's title page (Amsterdam, ca. 1712), these embellishments were "as the composer plays them" (*Troisieme Edition ou l'on a joint les agréemens des Adagio de cet ouvrage, composez par Mr. A. Corelli comme il les joue*), a claim that has not been disproved.

41 Bach calls it *Tempo di Borea*, which might be a pun on the name Boreas (the north or winter wind). The piece does not seem unusually fast or "windy," however.

suites, however, these need not be played as fast as possible, or without pauses for breathing—which can be incorporated into the expression or "rhetoric" of a good performance. The *corrente* takes advantage of the flute's abilty to leap rapidly between registers, thereby implying distinct soprano and bass parts; the sarabande, on the other hand, focuses more on presenting a single, modestly ornate, melodic line. What makes the closing movement a specifically "English" bourrée (*bourrée anglaise*) is not entirely clear, but despite its country-dance (*contredanse*) rhythm it also alludes to Bach's distinctive brand of chromatic harmony.

Ensemble Sonatas and Others

It is striking that Bach, despite assembling two sets of unaccompanied "solos," never produced similar collections of sonatas with basso continuo. While his contemporaries, including Telemann, published numerous sets of such works, we have only four or five undisputed compositions by Bach for solo instrument with continuo. The most important of these are two sonatas for flute. One of these, BWV 1035 in E, is demonstrably a late work, possibly composed in relation to a trip to Berlin in 1741.[42] Bach's cautious treatment of the flute in his Cöthen vocal works has raised doubts that he composed anything more challenging there for the instrument. Yet the flute sonata in E minor (BWV 1034) might be plausible stylistically as a Cöthen composition, even if, like the unaccompanied "partita" (BWV 1013), it makes greater demands on the player than the flute parts in the serenatas BWV 173a and 184a.[43]

Although the two flute sonatas are deservedly popular today, Bach evidently had little interest in a genre that neither invited elaborate counterpoint nor posed the challenges of an unaccompanied "solo." His pupils followed him in this; before leaving Leipzig, Emanuel would write at least seven "trios" of various sorts, but his first solo sonata may date only

---

42 Two manuscript copies (Berlin, Staatsbibliothek, Mus. mss. Bach P 621 and 622) contain inscriptions claiming that the work was written for Fredersdorf, personal assistant (*Kämmerer*) of King Frederick "the Great."

43 There is also a flute sonata in C, BWV 1033, but despite a seemingly reliable provenance (a manuscript copy by Emanuel Bach in Berlin, Staatsbibliothek, Mus. ms. Bach St 460 attributes it to his father), its weak, inconsistent style is hard to associate with Sebastian at any time during his career.

from his university years at Frankfurt (Oder). In fact, solo sonatas with continuo had until recently been less common than trio sonatas, that is, works for two melody instruments and continuo. Corelli published twelve sonatas for violin and continuo only after issuing forty-eight trio sonatas. Telemann began his prolific publishing career in 1715 with six sonatas for violin and continuo, but six trio sonatas followed in 1718, and among his early chamber compositions those with multiple melody instruments outnumber those with just one.[44]

From Bach we have only two trio sonatas as the term is understood today. But there are at least seventeen further "trios," the term used by his German contemporaries for any instrumental piece with three obbligato lines. For Bach these included six sonatas for organ with pedals, as well as another half-dozen for violin with obbligato keyboard.[45] Another of Bach's sonatas with obbligato keyboard is his own arrangement of a conventional trio sonata, and there is evidence of several others having originated in a similar way. Yet Sebastian also wrote "trios" that were probably conceived from the outset for obbligato keyboard with violin or flute; indeed, his compositions of this type probably constituted a majority of his work in the genre.[46] Just as he plunged into the challenging field of the unaccompanied solo after writing only a few conventional sonatas with continuo, his two sets of "trios" evidently followed at most a handful of ordinary trio sonatas.

Neither the organ sonatas nor the sonatas for violin and keyboard were finalized until well after the move to Leipzig. The organ sonatas can be divided between newly composed works (nos. 2, 5, and 6) and apparent arrangements of earlier trio sonatas (nos. 1, 3, and 4). No such division emerges among the violin-and-keyboard sonatas, although the last sonata stands out from the rest and was probably added only around

44 Zohn (2008, 220) mentions just six solos and seventeen trio sonatas "transmitted mostly in Dresden manuscripts dating from the 1710s or early 1720s"; Telemann himself regarded trios as his "greatest strength" (best Stärcke, from his 1731 autobiography).

45 That is, with a fully written-out keyboard part as opposed to a partially improvised continuo part.

46 Sebastian may have allowed the option of doubling the bass with a string instrument, to judge from the title page of a manuscript copy of BWV 1014–19 (Berlin, Staatsbibliothek, Mus. ms. Bach St 162, copied in Bach's Leipzig home). But no separate bass parts survive, and only one subsequent copy repeats the option.

1725, when the set was first assembled. Both sets of "trios" differ substantially from typical trio sonatas of the time, above all in their pervasively contrapuntal texture, in which the bass is an equal partner of the two upper parts. The sonatas with violin are significantly larger than the organ sonatas, most of them comprising four movements of the church sonata type, with a fugue in second place. The organ sonatas, which are limited to three movements, are more *galant* and lighter in style, although equally contrapuntal. As with other Bach collections, there is an odd final member in both sets, the Sixth Organ Sonata standing apart for its initial movement in concerto style.

The organ sonatas may not have been finalized until around 1731, toward the end of a period during which Bach seems to have turned his attention back toward keyboard music, after focusing for several years on the vocal music needed for the Leipzig churches.[47] They may, like the concertos, have been written or revised for public performance—organ recitals, in this case—but it is also possible that Bach viewed them primarily as teaching material. Like his smaller set of keyboard trios—the three-part inventions or sinfonias—Bach's organ sonatas constitute a collection of three-part compositions exemplifying a variety of styles and forms. Here the three parts are for the two hands, playing on separate keyboards, plus the feet, playing on the pedals. The stylistic orientation of each sonata is evident from the start. Sonatas 1, 3, and 4 open with fugues, or rather imitative duos, the bass entering into the mix only sparingly, as in many contemporary trio sonatas for instrumental ensemble.[48] The three other sonatas open in ways that more clearly declare their independence from fugue.

The organ sonatas are closely related to the sonatas with obbligato keyboard, especially those with violin. Less strictly confined to three contrapuntal parts than the organ sonatas, the violin-and-harpsichord sonatas are more varied in texture. They include extensive fugal movements, most of them incorporating soloistic episodes in concerto style. But the most distinctive type of movement in these sonatas might be the aria-like

---

47 The date is based on the watermark of the paper used for the autograph manuscript (Berlin, Staatsbibliothek, Mus. ms. Bach P 271).

48 In the opening movement of Sonata 1 the bass has only two statements of the subject (mm. 29, 51), and there it is simplified to allow performance on the pedals.

adagios and andantes represented by all six slow movements in Sonatas 1, 3, and 4. In these the violin has a singing melodic line, the harpsichord an idiomatic accompaniment that is unlikely to have originated in some lost earlier trio-sonata version.

Bach wrote at least five further obbligato-keyboard sonatas, two with flute and three with viola da gamba.[49] To what degree each stems from an earlier trio sonata is uncertain, although one of the gamba sonatas also exists as a work for two flutes and continuo (BWV 1039). The idea of writing keyboard sonatas with viola da gamba might have occurred to Bach at Cöthen, where Prince Leopold played the instrument, and where the Sixth Brandenburg Concerto, with its two gamba parts, was finished and probably performed. Details in the G-minor gamba sonata (BWV 1029) seem to place it in this period if not earlier. It opens with a theme close to that of the Third Brandenburg Concerto, and it ends with the same flourish that concludes an early concerto by Telemann, transcribed by Bach as BWV 985.

Other features of the G-minor work make it, alongside the flute sonatas in A and B minor, among the clearest examples of a sonata by Bach "in concerto style."[50] This is so despite the great difference in sound and style between the vehement G-minor sonata and the subtle inter-play of keyboard and flute at the outset of the B-minor work.[51] The slow movements of those two sonatas also bear comparison. Both are in binary form, with an ornately embellished melodic line joined to an almost equally ornate accompaniment. It is clear in the slow movement of the B-minor sonata that the flute has the main line throughout, while the keyboard has a florid written-out accompaniment. In the gamba sonata, however, the two melodic lines are of equal importance and are exchanged between the players after the double bar. The point is not

---

49 Two further sonatas, BWV 1031 in E-flat for flute and keyboard, and BWV 1020 in G minor for (probably) the same instruments, might have been composed by pupils during studies with Bach; see Schulenberg (2014, 23).

50 Williams (1984) provides a speculative reconstruction of BWV 1029 as a "Seventh Brandenburg Concerto."

51 Thematic parallels between the opening of the B-minor sonata and works by other composers have been noted; Rifkin (2007, 28) follows Spitta in attaching special signifi-cance to a G-minor *ouverture* by Bernhard Bach.

always grasped by the modern cellists who have appropriated this sonata, sometimes playing this movement without noticing the equally *cantabile* part for the keyboard instrument.

Concertos and Suites for Instrumental Ensemble

Bach and his contemporaries did not make a clear distinction between chamber music and compositions for larger ensembles. A trio sonata could be turned into orchestral music simply by making extra copies of the parts, as Pisendel did at Dresden. On the other hand, when parts were copied for a concerto, extras were rarely made. This suggests that such a work was typically played one-to-a-part, just as we expect for solo and trio sonatas today (except for the continuo). Still, in pieces for which Bach includes *ripieno* parts that are essentially optional, as he does in some of his concertos, or when he adds trumpets and oboes to a suite originally for strings alone, the music is grander and a little bolder by comparison with the sonatas and suites considered thus far. Therefore it is not entirely inappropriate to speak of his "orchestral" compositions, so long as it is clear that the orchestra in question remained a large chamber ensemble by modern standards, without a conductor and with limited doublings, if any, of the string parts.

Like the word *sonata*, the term *concerto* had been in use since the beginning of the Baroque, around 1600. But sonatas were almost always purely instrumental pieces; the word literally means "played." Until around 1700 a concerto was most often a sacred work combining voices and instruments, and Bach still sometimes used the expression in that sense. By the second decade of the eighteenth century, however, the word *concerto* had become associated with a new type of purely instrumental music. The ways in which a concerto differed from a sonata were not always distinct, and some works might be copied or published under both titles. But by the 1730s a concerto usually gave soloistic parts to one or perhaps a few players out of a larger group. Hence when Bach designated one of the violins in an ensemble as *concertato*, that was a solo part, as contrasted to a *ripieno* part. Still, the *ripieno* parts were not necessarily doubled, and the Second Brandenburg Concerto might have originated as a sonata for four instruments and continuo, lacking the four *ripieno* string parts (two violins, viola, and double bass) of the work as we know it.

The earliest instrumental concertos followed no set guidelines about form or number of movements. By the time Bach began writing such compositions, however, they usually comprised three movements, in the order fast–slow–fast, and he hardly ever deviated from that model. Nearly every one of his concertos, moreover, includes at least one movement in ritornello form, alternating between a recurring passage for the whole ensemble and episodes in which the soloists predominate. Yet just as an aria with ritornellos can be of the ternary, bipartite, or some other type, the ritornellos of a concerto movement can alternate with the two or three main sections of a binary or ternary design; indeed, this is how concerto form came to be understood in the later eighteenth century.[52] Even a sonata movement for a single instrument could alternate between recurring statements of a fully scored theme and contrasting passages, as in the outer movements of Bach's Sixth Organ Sonata. It is unclear whether Bach and his contemporaries regarded such movements as resembling concertos; for a later generation they were sonatas "with two themes."[53] When the younger Scheibe described certain sonatas by Telemann as being in "concerto style," he was not focusing on their use of ritornello form. Rather he had in mind a combination of features that had originated in Italian music for virtuoso string ensembles, with a focus on soloistic figuration as opposed to counterpoint (which characterized "sonata style").[54]

Vivaldi is now the best-known composer of actual Baroque concertos, which he wrote by the hundred, including those arranged by Bach for harpsichord and organ. Bach also knew concertos by Albinoni and other Italians, as well as German imitators such as Telemann. By the time he left Cöthen, Bach might also have had the opportunity to hear similar music by the Dresden composers Pisendel and Heinichen, but the occasional resemblances between their concertos and Bach's probably reflect common influence from Vivaldi and Telemann. Also cultivated during

---

52 Thus Mozart created concertos by inserting ritornellos into sonata-form movements by C. P. E. and J. C. Bach; on the underlying theory as formulated by the late eighteenth-century writer H. C. Koch, see Stevens (1971).

53 The subtitle *Sonate con 2. Themata* occurs in manuscript copies of sonatas of this type attributed to J. G. Graun (see Schulenberg 2014, 65).

54 See Schulenberg (2008) on the *Sonate auf Concertenart*.

the first few decades of the century, alongside the brilliant Venetian concerto, was a more contrapuntal Roman or Bolognese type exemplified by Corelli's twelve examples. Today called concerti grossi, these resemble less a solo concerto than an expanded trio sonata, and they are often playable without the *ripieno* parts—as is also true of many other concertos, including some of Bach's.

The only precisely datable source for any of Bach's concertos is the famous autograph score of the six works that he dedicated to Margrave Christian Ludwig of Brandenburg in 1721. This is also the only collection of concertos clearly assembled as such by Bach, although six of the concertos for one harpsichord and strings may represent a comparable gathering.[55] Like the organ sonatas and the obbligato-keyboard sonatas, most of the harpsichord concertos show signs of having originated earlier, with other solo instruments. Indeed it is striking that, outside the Brandenburg set, all but three of Bach's concertos as we now have them involve solo harpsichord. This implies that at some point, perhaps after coming to Leipzig, he discarded the original versions, reworking them for himself to play as soloist, in some cases alongside sons or other pupils. Only three of these concertos appear to survive in their original versions, with one or two solo violins. The only surviving traces of concertos for other instruments are a few instrumental movements (sinfonias) in the cantatas.

The popularity of these works since the 1950s, together with the intellectual challenge of reconstructing their compositional history, helps explain the enthusiasm of musicians and scholars in positing early versions. Oboists have been happy to be able to play "Bach" concertos for their instrument; these, as well as further concertos for violin and other instruments, have been produced from Bach's surviving compositions with solo keyboard. How closely these reconstructions resemble what Bach originally wrote is uncertain, but the nature of the surviving solo parts implies that Bach did initially compose most of his concertos for players other than himself. He must have led first performances of many

---

55 Bach's autograph score of the concertos for one harpsichord and strings (Berlin, Staatsbibliothek, Mus. ms. Bach P 234) is a composite manuscript, prepared at Leipzig in the late 1730s; within it the first six works (BWV 1052–57) form a distinct group. Further discussion in Tatlow (2015, 364–66).

such works at Cöthen, with different members of the ensemble serving as soloists.

Already at Weimar, Bach, if not composing actual concertos, had written works that served as preliminary exercises for them. Among these were the preludes of the last five English Suites as well as the sinfonias for two cantatas from early 1715 (BWV 18 and 31). The latter would have been heard just before the likely visit by Johann Bernhard Bach from Eisenach. His interest in concertos is evident in the copy of twelve of Sebastian's concerto transcriptions that he made about then.[56] Works by Vivaldi were by no means the sole inspiration for Bach's concertos, in which "Vivaldian" moments occur alongside suggestions of other models: Corelli for the design of the fugue in Concerto 4, with its episodes of solo violin passagework; Benedetto Marcello for the highly symmetrical form of the final movement of Concerto 3; and Albinoni for the basic idea of writing the allegro of a concerto in a prevailingly contrapuntal texture.[57] Telemann, who was also writing concertos during these same years, must have provided further models for Bach, whose transcription of one of Telemann's concertos (TWV 51:g21) is of a work that Pisendel probably played.[58]

The Brandenburg Concertos were completed by 1721, when Bach sent (or perhaps delivered) their beautifully written autograph score to Margrave Christian Ludwig in Berlin. In modern times they have probably been the most frequently recorded of all Bach's works, but there is little evidence for performances of them during his lifetime and for at least a century afterward.[59] Manuscript parts survive in greater numbers for most of his eighteen other known concertos (see Table 9.2). Six of

---

56 In Berlin, Staatsbibliothek, Mus. ms. Bach P 280. Bernhard Bach also was responsible for the earliest copy of the prelude and fugue BWV 894, a keyboard work in concerto style that furnished the material for the outer movements of an actual concerto, BWV 1044.

57 Butler (1995) argues for the pervasive influence of Albinoni's oboe concertos on Bach; on concertos by the Marcello brothers, see Schulenberg (2006, 129–32).

58 See Chapter 7. Bach transcribed the shorter and presumably earlier version preserved in Dresden, Landesbibliothek, Mus. ms. 2392-O-17a; a longer version copied by Quantz (presumably during his study with Pisendel, who added the attribution) is in ms. 2392-O-17b.

59 A few tantalizing echoes of the Fifth Brandenburg Concerto can be heard in one or two concertos by Johann Gotthilf Jänichen, apparently an amateur harpsichordist who as secretary to Margrave Christian Ludwig could have had access to Bach's work (as suggested by Henze-Döhring 2009, 50).

Table 9.2 Bach's Concertos

BWV	Key	Solo Instruments	Comment
1041	a	vn	Lost early version re-used in BWV 1058 (see below)
1042	E	vn	Lost early version re-used in BWV 1054 (see below)
1043	d	2 vn	"Double" concerto, re-used in BWV 1062 (see below)
1044	a	vn, fl, hpd	"Triple" concerto, from BWV 894 (mvts. 1, 3) and 527 (mvt. 2), adaptation not by Bach?
1046	F	vn, 2 ob, 2 hn	First Brandenburg; mvt. 1 from Sinfonia BWV 1046a; mvt. 3 from a lost aria (?), re-used in BWV 207/1
1047	F	vn, rec, ob, tr	Second Brandenburg; originally a quintet sonata without *ripieno* parts?
1048	G	3 vn, 3 va, 3 vc	Third Brandenburg; mvt. 1 re-used in BWV 174
1049	G	vn, 2 rec	Fourth Brandenburg; cf. BWV 1057 below
1050	D	vn, fl, hpd	Fifth Brandenburg; early version BWV 1050a
1051	Bb	2 va	Sixth Brandenburg, with 2 viola da gambas (no violins)
1052	d	hpd	From lost violin concerto? re-used in BWV 146, 188
1053	E	hpd	From lost oboe concerto? mvts. 1–2 re-used in BWV 169
1054	D	hpd	From early version of BWV 1042 (see above)
1055	A	hpd	From lost concerto for oboe d'amore?
1056	f	hpd	From lost concerto in g for violin? mvt. 2 also used in BWV 156
1057	F	hpd, 2 rec	From the Fourth Brandenburg (BWV 1049)
1058	g	hpd	From an early version of BWV 1041 (see above)
1059	d	hpd	Fragment, presumably from lost oboe concerto re-used in BWV 35
1060	c	2 hpd	From lost concerto for violin and oboe?
1061	C	2 hpd	Originally without strings (the latter not by J. S. Bach?)
1062	c	2 hpd	From early version of BWV 1043 (see above)
1063	d	3 hpd	From lost concerto for violin and two woodwinds?
1064	C	3 hpd	From lost concerto for 3 violins?
1065	a	4 hpd	From Vivaldi, op. 3, no. 10 (1711)

tr = trumpet fl = flute rec = recorder ob = oboe
vn = violin va = viola vc = cello hpd = harpsichord

these are arrangements of other extant works, leaving a dozen original compositions of this type outside the Brandenburg set.[60] The lost early versions are thought to have included at least five solo concertos for violin or oboe, a double concerto for violin and oboe, and two concertos for three soloists.[61] A single work with four soloists was arranged from one of four quadruple concertos in Vivaldi's *Estro armonico* (published in 1711). This once led to suspicions that some of Bach's other concertos were also based on works by his contemporaries. But no such models have been found, and the modern consensus is that the original versions of the remaining concertos were his own, although there is some reason to think that Bach might have collaborated with a pupil in two other works.[62]

The Brandenburg Concertos

The dedicatee of the Brandenburg Concertos was one of those members of the Hohenzollern dynasty whose love of music could not be extinguished during the austere reign of King Friedrich Wilhelm I. Margrave Christian Ludwig might have taken a special interest in organ music, and therefore in Bach, to judge by the dedication to him of Werckmeister's *Orgelprobe*—a manual on the testing of church organs.[63] At his death the margrave employed at least six musicians, which together

---

60 In addition to those listed in Table 9.2, Bach left at least three other concerto movements as sinfonias in the Leipzig cantatas: BWV 42/1, which Rifkin (1997, 65–67) traces to BWV 66a of December 1718; BWV 209/1, like other flute works relatively late and perhaps original in this form; and BWV 1045, apparently copied for use in a church cantata of the mid-1740s that was never completed.

61 With respect to BWV 1056, Dirksen (2008, 39–47) supposes that the lost slow movement of the original violin concerto might have been the basis of a sinfonia or ritornello in siciliana style that Bach began writing for a cantata in 1729 (BWV Anh. 2). This breaks off after just six measures; whether those measures in fact represent a siciliana is open to question.

62 These are BWV 1044 and 1061. On the string parts in BWV 1061, see Schulenberg (2010, 87–88). The harpsichord part in the "Triple" Concerto BWV 1044, which survives only in posthumous sources, ascends higher than any other Bach work in the slow movement; the varied reprises of the latter recall another likely collaboration, the trio sonata BWV 1038.

63 Second edition (1698), published at Quedlinburg and Halberstadt (where Werckmeister was organist), both in Prussian territory.

with Bach (or the margrave's secretary Jänichen) would have been sufficient to perform at least the Fifth Brandenburg.[64] Christian Ludwig also owned a substantial and varied collection of instrumental and vocal music, including hundreds of concertos, sonatas, and overtures ("orchestral" suites). Eleven music stands suggest patronage of concerts involving substantial ensembles, and a double-manual harpsichord by Mietke implies an interest in solo music for the instrument.[65] Christian Ludwig's salaried musicians might on occasion have joined with those of the other minor Brandenburg courts (all based in Berlin), especially in the absence of a royal Capelle under the rule of the "Soldier King."

It is often supposed that Bach's dedication of the concertos went unrewarded, the music unplayed; indeed, there is no documentary evidence of a payment, nor any manuscript parts known to have been copied from Bach's score. Yet the latter was written with unusual precision, doubtless for the purpose of making the instrumentation clear to a copyist or music director unfamiliar with Bach's intentions. It is also by no means out of the question that when Bach visited the city in 1719, he brought with him performing parts for an early version of the concertos. These could have been heard by Christian Ludwig and any number of other potential patrons; payment for some such performance out of a noble's private purse would not necessarily have been recorded in any extant document.

At least one of the concertos had already gone through two stages of revision by the time the margrave received Bach's score. For the Fifth Brandenburg Concerto (the one with solo harpsichord) we have the composer's Cöthen performing parts. These reveal that Bach made small refinements when he subsequently recopied the score for Christian Ludwig. We also have another set of manuscript parts preserving an even earlier version, with shorter solo passages for the harpsichord in the two

---

64 If the bassoonist Kottowsky also played flute. Another musician with the same last name, Georg Wilhelm Kottowsky, played flute for Friedrich II until the Seven Years' War; see Oleskiewicz (2011, 88n. 37). On Jänichen, see note 59 above.

65 Oleskiewicz (2011, 109). The inventory of his music collection is in Besseler (1956, 33–35); it includes operas and oratorios by composers from Lully to Handel, including Stricker, but nothing by Bach.

quick movements.[66] These parts, although probably copied only after Bach's death, confirm what we would have guessed in any case: that Bach devoted special attention to this work, the first concerto by anyone with a substantial solo keyboard part.

The special use of the harpsichord in Concerto 5 is only one instance of these works' extraordinary variety of instrumentation, employed in diverse movement types. The first concerto, which probably derives from a sinfonia originally composed for the Hunt Cantata, ends in a little suite that consists of a minuet and trio, a *polacca* or polonaise, and a second trio for two horns and unison oboes that is really a march. Whereas the first concerto opens the set with its largest ensemble and greatest number of movements, the sixth closes it with a work in the customary three movements, written for an unusually quiet ensemble of just two violas, two viola da gambas, and continuo.

Concerto 2 is, in terms of scoring, the work closest to a Corellian concerto grosso. Its style, however, is that of a vivacious Vivaldian work, and it has a solo ensemble of five rather than three parts. A convincing argument makes it originally a quintet sonata, to which Bach added *ripieno* string parts.[67] The third concerto may also have undergone expansion, as the solo string parts—three each of violin, viola, and cello—could originally have included only one cello. In the familiar version, the three cellists have distinct parts for only brief passages in the first movement. Still, the work reflects an interest in contrasting "choirs" of instruments that went back to the early Baroque and continued in recent works of Telemann (cf. Example 7.8). This concerto lacks a slow movement; in its place stand just two chords, for which modern players often substitute a movement from a violin sonata or a newly composed cadenza. There is, however, no good reason for doing so, and inserting anything more than the briefest embellishment distorts the unique plan of this concerto, which is as distinctive as that of the first.

---

66 Berlin, Staatsbibliothek, Mus. ms. Bach St 132/1, previously assigned to Bach's pupil and son-in-law Altnickol but actually in the hand of Farlau, who might have been a pupil of the latter. It must remain speculative whether this version, or a movement from it, served as sinfonia in a Cöthen *serenata* (as suggested by the title of a lost work from a lost source; see the entry for BWV 1150 = Anh. 197 in Bach-Digital).

67 As reconstructed by Klaus Hofmann (Kassel: Bärenreiter, 1998).

The fourth concerto, in G, includes a prominent solo violin part along-side two somewhat less pre-eminent recorders. Bach later transposed the work down to F (as BWV 1057) and rewrote the violin part for harpsichord. The new solo part includes flamboyant realizations of several passages in which the harpsichord originally provided only the continuo accompaniment. Perhaps this reflected Bach's improvisation of an unusually elaborate continuo realization, turning an accompaniment into a solo part, in performances of the original version. But the true solo keyboard part in the Brandenburg set is, of course, that of the fifth concerto. Yet here the keyboard player emerges as soloist while again providing an elaborate accompaniment to the two other soloists (flute and violin), during the earlier stages of the first movement. Charles Rosen noted that it is only through a gradual but completely logical process that the harpsichord gains the lead role by the end of the movement. This culminates in a famous solo passage lasting over three minutes; often described as a cadenza, this might better be termed a *capriccio*, as it is a sort of free fantasia, not the elaboration of a cadence.[68]

Other Concertos

Bach's further concertos, which mostly survive only in late or revised forms, are to some unknown degree the products of his mixing and matching movements of various origins. The general consensus that these works were originally composed for solo instruments other than the harpsichord has not been shaken by a recent proposal that some might have originated as organ concertos.[69] At least for the two double concertos in C minor, we can be reasonably sure of the earlier form of each. In one case (BWV 1062) this is because the version with two solo violins actually survives; in the other (BWV 1060), the two solo keyboard parts differ in ways that clearly point to violin and oboe as the original instruments. The quick movements of this concerto, moreover, lack the exchange of material between soloists that is so basic to Bach's style elsewhere. For other works the evidence is less easy to interpret but still points away from any original versions for keyboard instruments—with

68 See Rosen (1997, 196–97). The word *cadenza* does appear in comparable contexts, including C. P. E. Bach's copy of BWV 1052a (Berlin, Staatsbibliothek, Mus. ms. Bach St 350, at mvt. 3, m. 250) and Müthel's copy of BWV 1044 (St 134, at mvt. 3, m. 218).

69 Wolff (2016).

the exception of the C-major concerto BWV 1061, which Bach composed as a harpsichord duet (without strings).

That Bach wrote solo concertos for favored colleagues at Weimar
or Cöthen, before proceeding to more ambitious works with multiple
soloists, cannot be assumed. Corelli wrote no solo concertos at all, and
the greater opportunities for counterpoint in a double or triple concerto
might have made such a work seem more worthy of Bach's attention than
one that showed off a single virtuoso soloist. The more concise works
among the solo concertos are now thought to be relatively late, in part
because of their inclusion of *galant* melodic features (such as triplets). Yet
Telemann and others were writing highly *galant* music by 1720, and it is
hard to know whether the style or form of a particular Bach work is that
of, say, 1722 as opposed to 1727.[70] In short, the precise history of Bach's
concertos must, like that of so many other works, remain a mystery.

Bach never completed the harpsichord version of one concerto in D
minor, whose outer movements became the sinfonias (with solo organ)
that open the two halves of the Leipzig cantata BWV 35.[71] The cantata is
from 1726; that the concerto was significantly earlier, perhaps one of Bach's
first efforts in the genre, is suggested above all by the rounded binary form
of the second quick movement. Binary form is rare in concertos after 1720;
Bach otherwise used it only in the first and third Brandenburgs, but he
knew it from several relatively early Venetian works that he transcribed for
keyboard.[72] If Bach did begin his activity as a concerto composer with a
work for a single solo instrument, it would not be surprising if the latter
was an oboe. His Weimar cantatas contain idiomatic solo parts for the instrument, as does the First Brandenburg. The "D-minor oboe concerto" is

---

70 Wolff (2008, 102) points to suggestive parallels with movements in the Leipzig cantatas,
which can be precisely dated. But even if Bach did begin writing siciliana-style arias only
during the mid-1720s, the siciliana of the G-minor violin sonata BWV 1001 was composed
before he reached Leipzig.

71 Bach did start arranging this concerto as a work for harpsichord, oboe, and strings (BWV
1059), but he abandoned the effort after writing just eight and a half measures into the
composite autograph manuscript of the harpsichord concertos. The slow movement of
this concerto, not incorporated into Cantata 35, instead became the opening sinfonia of
Cantata 156 according to Rifkin (1978)—it is also the Largo of BWV 1056—although this
has been disputed (Dirksen 2008, 22).

72 BWV 974 and 981, based on works by Alessandro and Benedetto Marcello, respectively, and
also BWV 975 and 980, setting early versions of concertos later published in Vivaldi's op. 4.

a lively and attractive work; if it seems simple by comparison with Bach's other concertos, this could reflect its having originated at a time when the relatively restrained works of Albinoni and Marcello provided models as plausible as the now better-known concertos of Vivaldi.

As we have them, however, the concertos for one harpsichord and strings date from the late 1730s, when Bach extended his project of revising and collecting earlier compositions to include concertos.[73] As in his other adaptations, Bach's revisions involved three main elements, the change of instrumentation usually leading to a change of key as well as the variation and embellishment of the solo part. A fourth element, the addition of new contrapuntal lines, is readily detected in a few instances where Bach superimposed further instrumental and even vocal parts on existing concerto movements. This probably also occurred in places like the opening ritornello of the A-major concerto, where the harpsichord plays a solo flourish against the violins right from the start.[74]

Change of key could bring an original solo part into a lower, more idiomatic tessitura for the keyboard instrument. It could also force adjustments of the *ripieno* string parts, but these were otherwise left largely unchanged. Even the original solo lines initially may have been left intact except where figuration idiomatic to the original instrument had to be rewritten to suit the keyboard. Melodic embellishment, which Bach might easily have improvised at an early stage of each adaptation, could have been added after the initial entry of the notes, as is documented in several slow movements (Example 9.10).[75] Quick movements saw relatively limited, often formulaic, embellishment, as in the filling out of broken chords with passing tones, although even this could prove exciting when combined with a newly elaborated bass line (Example 9.11).

73 A theory that Bach first drafted the harpsichord concertos as *solo* (unaccompanied) works (Stevens 2001) is not supported by any evidence in the sources. The keyboard parts of several concertos are almost self-sufficient, as they incorporate the main melodic lines of the ritornellos, but there are always a few gaps in the latter (as in BWV 1055, mvt. 2, mm. 1–2, and mvt. 3, mm. 57–59).

74 One clue that the harpsichord part at the opening of BWV 1055 (mvt. 1, mm. 1–2) was an addition—in effect, a highly elaborate continuo realization—is that it is really an embellished doubling of the violins, forming momentary parallel octaves with the second violin in m. 2; a verbatim doubling begins in m. 3.

75 The editors of the BG (Vol. 17) and the NBA (Vol. 7/4) gave the original and embellished versions separately, extracting both from Bach's autograph scores.

Example 9.10 Concerto in F minor for harpsichord and strings, BWV 1056, mvt. 2, mm. 1–2 and 8–9 (without strings): (a) final reading of autograph score; (b) earlier version of autograph score; (c) oboe version (from BWV 156, transposed)

The "Orchestral" Suites

Four "orchestral" suites, each starting with a so-called French overture, complement the Italianate sonatas and concertos. For Bach and his contemporaries the word *ouverture* could either refer to the opening movement alone or include as well the following movements, usually much shorter dances in binary form. In their extant forms, the suites are elaborately scored Leipzig works. But although each would

Example 9.11 Concerto in D minor for harpsichord and strings, mvt. 1, mm. 7a, 8b–9: (a) final version, BWV 1052; (b) early version, BWV 1052a

have made a splendid opening number for a concert by the Collegium Musicum, with one possible exception they went back to more simply scored versions composed at Weimar or Cöthen. Like the concertos, they are traditionally numbered according to their sequence in the nineteenth-century collected edition, but the ordering of the suites is essentially arbitrary.

All four suites begins with the grand, ceremonial type of overture famous from its use in Lully's operas, with an initial section in "dotted"

Example 9.12 An early example of a French overture by Bach, from the opening movement of his *Ouverture* in F, BWV 820, (a) mm. 1–2; (b) mm. 14–19

rhythm followed by a lively fugal section. Telemann claimed to have written two hundred such pieces during his early years. Bach included several examples in his early keyboard suites, imitating transcriptions of French opera overtures that he probably knew even before his arrival at Weimar (Example 9.12). There he incorporated movements in the form of overtures into at least one cantata (BWV 61) and, probably, the Fifth Cello Suite. Cöthen, however, might have seen his first actual overture for instrumental ensemble. The first three of these suites (as ordered in modern editions) were probably originally for strings alone, with continuo.[76] This would have been in keeping with the tradition of the famous royal ensemble at Paris, the Twenty-Four Violins of the King. The royal string band, which played for the opera and court ballets, was imitated across Germany. By 1700, Lully's ensemble of a single heavily doubled violin part, accompanied by three viola parts and bass, was being replaced by the familiar four-part scoring adopted by Bach in his later Weimar

76 See Rifkin (1997a and 2007). His assumption (2007, 10) that a flute would have been too weak to play a solo part in an original A-minor version of BWV 1067 is open to debate (see Oleskiewicz 2000, 208–10, on the "strong fundamental register" of Quantz's instruments), but it is true that this part would be at least equally idiomatic to violin.

cantatas and all his extant orchestral works.[77] If Bach indeed wrote the first three suites for a string ensemble, they obviously underwent subsequent revision, like the sonatas and concertos, but there is no evidence that he ever assembled them into an "official" collection.

The earliest sources for three of the suites are sets of performing parts, two of them for Bach's own use, presumably with the Leipzig Collegium Musicum.[78] These make it clear that Suite 1 was in existence by early 1725. Suite 4 had been written by the end of that year, when Bach re-used its first movement on Christmas Day for the opening chorus of Cantata 110. Both works are likely to go further back, as probably does Suite 3, in which the parts for winds (three trumpets, two oboes) and timpani are essentially optional—as is often the case in eighteenth-century scores. Even in Suite 1, solo passages for a trio of two oboes and bassoon could originally have been for violins and continuo, like the solo parts in Corelli's concerti grossi. Only Suite 4 calls for independent brass, double-reed, and string choirs that are all indispensable, as they echo one another from the opening measure.

Suite 2 stands apart due to its virtuoso flute part, which has long been central to the repertoire of that instrument. This suite is also a more subtle, more *galant* work than the others, and not only on account of its scoring and B-minor tonality. Yet like the sonata in the same key for flute and harpsichord, it probably originated as a violin piece—or rather, like Suite 3, a work for strings and continuo with an occasionally soloistic first violin part.[79] Still, even the lost original version of Suite 2 might have been relatively late in date; it includes movements reminiscent of those in the harpsichord partitas, published after 1725. The familiar version with flute might have been created for the Collegium Musicum during a period that also saw Bach preparing performing parts around 1730 for a work by his Eisenach cousin Johann Bernhard Bach.[80]

---

77 That is, two violin parts, one viola part, and a basso continuo part, of which all but the viola is often doubled. Traces of an original three-part scoring (with a single "orchestral" violin part) remain in the ritornellos of BWV 1052; see Breig (1976, 28–30).

78 These are parts for BWV 1067 and 1068; see Rifkin (2007, 2, and 1997a, 171).

79 As argued by Rifkin (2007).

80 As pointed out by Rifkin (2007, 12–28). This was the same Bernhard Bach who copied most of Sebastian's concerto transcriptions and had succeeded the older Christoph Bach as organist at Eisenach in 1703. That his "beautiful" (*schön*) overtures, that is, suites, had special significance for Sebastian is suggested by their receiving special mention in the latter's obituary (BD 3:81 [no. 666]; NBR, 298 [no. 306]).

CHAPTER TEN

Leipzig

FIRST YEARS (1723–1730)

A T TWO IN THE AFTERNOON ON MAY 22, 1723—THE DAY BEFORE Trinity Sunday—two carriages arrived in Leipzig bearing Sebastian and Magdalena Bach together with five children, including the newborn Christiana Sophia Henrietta.[1] Doubtless traveling with them was Bach's sister-in-law Friedelena, and possibly an apprentice or two as well. The family had been preceded by four wagons bearing their belongings, which must now have been unpacked and moved into their new lodgings within the St. Thomas School. The building, which stood next to the Church of St. Thomas, dated from 1553, but the cantor's apartment had been recently renovated, and the entire building would undergo a substantial expansion during Bach's time there. Torn down in the first years of the twentieth century, the building can be seen (in its expanded form) in old photographs, as well as in engravings that illustrated editions of the school regulations published during Bach's time there (Figure 10.1).[2] The building housed the school's dormitory and classrooms as well as the dwellings of the cantor and the school rector at either end. Bach and his family lived on the south end of the building, on three floors that included an office that served for both composing and storing music. Bach himself had made the thirty-five-mile trip from Cöthen at

---

1 BD 2:104 (no. 138); trans. in NBR, 106 (no. 102).

2 Stauffer (1996, 191–96) examines the renovation of 1731–1732, showing before-and-after illustrations as well as a nineteenth-century drawing.

Bach. David Schulenberg, Oxford University Press (2020). © Oxford University Press.
DOI: 10.1093/oso/9780190936303.001.0001

E. E. Hochw. Raths der Stadt Leipzig Ordnung Der Schule zu S. THOMÆ.

Gedruckt bey Immanuel Tietzen, 1723.

1. Die S. Thomas Kirche. 2. Die Thomas Schule. 3. Der Steinerne Wasser=Kasten.

Krügner fe. Lipsia.

Figure 10.1 The St. Thomas Church and School building, engraving by Johann Gottfried Krügner, facing title page in *Ordnung der Schule zu S. Thomae* (Leipzig: Immanuel Tietzen, 1723).

least four times during the previous few months, but for the rest of the family this was likely their first arrival in a major city, doubtless an experience of considerable excitement and not a little trepidation.

Leipzig, then as now, was a commercial center as well as a university city. Although not as large as Hamburg, nor politically independent like that city or Frankfurt, for several decades it had enjoyed an expanding economy that powered a building boom, as the city's elite of merchants and bankers vied with one another to construct fashionable grand homes.[3] The city's opera theater, which Telemann had directed during the first years of the century, had closed in 1720. But gardens, coffeehouses, and private art galleries (open to visitors) remained among the city's attractions. In these things Leipzig was not unusual among the emerging cities of northern Europe. It probably lagged behind the greatest of these, including Hamburg and Paris, in such matters as the opening of fashionable establishments where coffee and chocolate were served to a growing middle class. What set Leipzig apart were the thrice-annual trade fairs, taking place during the weeks following New Year's, Easter, and St. Michael's Day (September 29). These fairs reportedly could attract up to ten thousand visitors, potentially almost doubling the city's population.[4] They made Leipzig the leading trade center for the Empire and provided opportunities for cultural as well as commercial contacts. Books were a particularly important object of trade during the fairs, Leipzig itself being a center for printing and publishing. The most important German publisher of the period, Bernhard Christoph Breitkopf, located there in 1718. During Bach's years in Leipzig the firm, under the direction of Breitkopf's son Johann Gottlob Immanuel, expanded to encompass an extensive music publishing business, dealing in manuscript copies as well as printed music.[5] Other musical businesses in the city included the workshops of the woodwind instrument maker Johann Heinrich

---

3 Stauffer (1996, 183–91) also summarizes the "Baroque transformation" of Leipzig, listing some three dozen "important architectural projects."

4 The city's online almanac gives the population in 1699 as 15,653 (http://statistik.leipzig. de/statpubl/content/12_statistik-und-wahlen/jahrbuecher/Kapitel02.pdf). The figure of 10,000 visitors is from Wolff (2000, 38, citing Karl Czok).

5 Trade in musical manuscripts is already documented by a letter of 1735 in which Walther mentions acquiring an unpublished mass by Gasparini during the New Year fair; this work was later performed by Bach (Wollny 2013, 134).

Eichentopf and the string instrument maker Johann Christian Hoffmann (with whom Bach would establish a particularly close relationship), as well as the organ builder Scheibe—whose son would become famous as Bach's critic (see Chapter 12).

By the time he came to Leipzig, Bach had long experience dealing both socially and professionally with the ruling classes of Germany's Lutheran cities. Leipzig, however, was larger and wealthier than municipalities like Arnstadt and Mühlhausen. Gottfried Lange and other local luminaries, some of whom bore court titles, carried grander pretensions and wielded greater real power than the burgomaster or town councilors of a minor residence or free imperial city. In a university city, moreover, Bach would regularly encounter men, and occasionally women, of learning and distinction. These included not only local clergy but also university students, some of whom were to publish sermons, poetry, and learned tracts on theology, philosophy, even scientific subjects. Beside such persons an ordinary musician might not rank very high—but as a cantor and director Bach was not an ordinary musician, as he would protest vehemently when labeled a *Musikant* during the following decade.

Bach nevertheless must have been reminded frequently of his lack of a university education. He seems to have compensated through the old-fashioned use of Latinisms in his notes and letters, perhaps also imagining himself a successor to King David and other biblical musicians, although this too might have struck his younger, more enlightened acquaintances as an outmoded pretension.[6] If so, it did not prevent him from achieving some measure of popularity among the university students and others who participated in the local collegia musica. In this connection it is worth remembering that, at a time when only members of the elite attended university, and many students belonged to the minor nobility, a university student outranked a common musician. University students, distinguished by their academic regalia, would have been respected visitors in the community. Lange had expected that Bach would attract good students to Leipzig, and he appears to have done so while gaining commissions and substantial lesson fees from some of them.

Students were probably among those at Leipzig who furnished librettos for Bach's cantatas. Although the majority of his Leipzig librettos

---

6 Greer (2008) considers one instance of Bach's self-identification with biblical musicians.

remain anonymous, some have been traced to figures who attended the university. We know also of two members of the ruling elite who provided poetry. One was Lange; another was Mariane von Ziegler, daughter of a past burgomaster, Franz Conrad Romanus. Later author of several published volumes of poetry, she became a member of Gottsched's German Society and was even named imperial poet laureate, despite her father's disgrace and imprisonment, apparently for embezzling government funds. Whether Bach knew her personally is not documented. But there were family connections, suggesting that Bach, perhaps through Lange, ingratiated himself into the city's ruling class.[7] His cantatas also include harmonizations of a handful of chorales whose verses were written by women. But the nine Ziegler cantatas of 1725 were his only complete works, indeed the only eighteenth-century Lutheran church cantatas, with poetry by a female author.[8]

The fact that Ziegler was as yet unpublished, with no credentials as a theologian, obviously did not dissuade Bach from setting her texts. As a younger woman from a prominent family, her social status vis-à-vis Bach might have been somewhat uncertain by the standards of the day. This, however, could have been a positive feature of collaborating with her, from Bach's point of view. For at Leipzig he seems to have avoided working with writers who, like Franck at Weimar, were clearly his social or intellectual superiors. He collaborated only a few times with the most famous Leipzig author of his time. Johann Christoph Gottsched arrived there shortly after Bach, becoming a university lecturer and eventually professor, famed especially for his Essay on Poetic Criticism (*Versuch einer critischen Dichtkunst*). First published in 1730 (by Breitkopf), this went through multiple editions, serving as a handbook on the literary genres of the day. These Gottsched analyzed through the lens of the Enlightenment, the new French-influenced style of rationalist thought. Although Bach

---

7 Peters (2008, 3) points out that a mutual friend, Maria Elisabeth Taubert, was godmother of Bach's short-lived son Christian Gottlieb, born little more than a week before the performance of the first Ziegler cantata on April 22, 1722. Less than a year later, Ziegler's aunt was godmother for Bach's next child, Elisabeth Juliana Friederica (born April 5, 1726).

8 According to Peters (2008, 1) Bach's son Emanuel—who published a setting of one of Ziegler's lieder, the "Schäferlied" W. 199/2 of 1741—would compose a passion (H. 782 of 1769) on a libretto largely by Anna Luise Karsch, perhaps the leading female poet in Germany after Ziegler.

set several of Gottsched's texts to music—and Luisa Adelgunda Victoria Gottsched, the poet's wife and an important writer herself, admired his compositions—the two seem never to have seen eye to eye. This might have been because Gottsched viewed poetry as inherently superior to music. He certainly viewed his own high-minded version of literature as superior to that of another local author with whom Bach had a much closer relationship.

This was Christian Friedrich Henrici, known as Picander. Arriving in Leipzig a few years before Bach, he was collaborating with the latter by winter 1725, in a birthday serenata for the duke of Weissenfels.[9] The two would work together on sacred as well as secular music, original projects as well as others consisting largely of parody (which required coordinating new poetry with existing music). Although his librettos for Bach are now Picander's only familiar works, during his lifetime he was best known as a satirist. Despite a year of university training, he never received the respect of an academic like Gottsched, whom he satirized in a publication of 1729.[10] That was probably also the year of the secular cantata known as "The Contest of Apollo and Pan" (BWV 201), on which Bach and Picander collaborated.[11]

It is sometimes supposed that BWV 201 received another performance in connection with the Scheibe controversy (see Chapter 12), and Bach certainly repeated it near the end of his life, apparently to criticize the selection of his successor. But the original object of its satire might be sought not among Bach's but among Picander's enemies, with whom Gottsched surely ranks. That Bach would continue to set important librettos by both poets is therefore somewhat surprising. But we know of only two subsequent Gottsched settings, both lost, and it may be that Bach collaborated with the latter only in specially commissioned pieces. He worked by choice with Picander, not only on sacred compositions but on cantatas honoring the Saxon ruling family. Bach surely knew that

---

9 BWV 249a, performed February 23, 1725; the music is lost, but much of it was re-used in the cantata that became the Easter Oratorio, BWV 249. A possible earlier collaboration is Cantata 148, whose text resembles one published by Picander during 1724–1725, but whether Bach's composition dates from September 19, 1723 or a later year is uncertain.

10 See Otto (2007).

11 The date is from Glöckner (2008, 58).

Picander had already made a name for himself as poet of obsequious encomia for the court. This eventually won him lucrative administrative appointments, a path Bach must have hoped to follow, and by 1727 he was setting Picander's shameless flattery of the ruler for royal birthdays and name days.[12]

School and Church

Bach's colleagues at the St. Thomas School included two superiors, the rector and conrector, as well as a fourth-ranking teacher, confusingly called the *tertius*. It was the latter, Carl Friedrich Pezold, whom Bach was allowed to pay as his substitute to teach Latin and religious catechism to the boys of the third and fourth classes. Bach seems to have got along well with Johann Heinrich Ernesti, rector until his death in 1729. Subsequent changes in the school personnel and curriculum would eventually poison the working environment for Bach. At the start of his time in Leipzig, however, he appears to have found the school and his colleagues there congenial.

Less can be said about Bach's relationships with individual students and fellow musicians. Regarding this we have mostly later reports, plus his own laconic letters of recommendation and a few other not very illuminating documents. A complaint about teaching seems to have focused chiefly on Pezold's inadequacy, but it might not have arisen if Bach's own instruction had been what the council thought it should be. It is hard to know what to make of the accusation, recorded in the same document, that he had sent a choir student "into the country" without permission of the burgomaster.[13] Could this mean that Bach was requiring scholarship students to perform outside Leipzig, and one of them objected?

Today we are most concerned with the creative musical aspects of Bach's new position. Yet this was probably the least significant part of it from the point of view of his employers. Even for Bach himself,

---

12 The lost BWV 193a, subsequently parodied for the city council election of August 1727, was the first of these, which continued into the 1730s.

13 "einen Chor Schüler aufs Land geschicket," from the council minutes of August 2, 1730 (BD 2:205 [no. 280]; NBR, 144 [no. 150a]). By this point Bach was apparently on the verge of a major break with the council.

organizing his new life might at first have taken precedence over the task of creating new music for Sunday services. But within weeks of his arrival he must have established routines that would prevail for the next few years. There would be continual developments in the compositions themselves and probably in how they were performed, but the rhythm of his professional life was now set by that of the school and church calendars. Although he was not explicitly required to provide his own, new compositions for church services, this was to be Bach's usual practice for at least the next few years—but only in the two chief churches of St. Thomas's and St. Nicholas's, and only for the main "music," not for other parts of the liturgy that also required music. The latter, which included hymns and simple motets, was also under Bach's purview, and not just at the main churches but also at St. Peter's and the so-called New Church. He was not, in general, responsible for music at St. Paul's (the university church) or at St. John's, outside the city gates. But cantors had traditionally directed performances at the university church for four holiday services each year (this was known as the "Old Service"), as well as for certain academic ceremonies held there. Bach was, additionally, expected to oversee the Leipzig town musicians, auditioning them and admitting them to *Stadtpfeifer* (city piper) and *Kunstgeiger* (art fiddler) status as necessary.

All this was on top of Bach's duties as cantor in the school. In addition to private teaching in music, the cantor was expected to provide twelve hours' weekly classroom instruction. For Bach this was reduced to seven, as he paid Pezold to take up some of his non-musical responsibilities.[14] Exactly what Bach taught, musically or otherwise, is unknown, nor do we have information on the nature of his instruction, although unlike the other faculty he taught a mix of students from the four top classes (*quarta* up to *prima*). He alternated with the rector and other faculty in serving as school *inspector* on a weekly basis, ensuring discipline and leading daily

14 The cantor's teaching duties were spelled out in the published regulations of the St. Thomas School, newly reissued in November 1723 and naming Bach alongside his fellow faculty members (11–12; facsimile in Schulze 1985c). The rules cover everything from which classes are to be taught to proper behavior during church services and payments due for performances at funerals and the like. How closely Bach, or anyone, adhered to them is hard to say.

prayers.[15] Bach was also responsible for evaluating the musical abilities of applicants to the school, with special attention to the scholarship students from outside Leipzig. Known as *alumni* or *interni*, these lived in the school building and were expected to earn their education by singing in the churches—and occasionally in other venues, including on the streets after Christmas, as so-called *currendi*. We have Bach's notes for only a single class of applicants (from 1729), but these show him to have evaluated some two dozen boys, most of them thirteen or fourteen years of age. Bach found about half of them usable "in music," most probably of modest capabilities, insufficient for performing Bach's compositions.[16]

Such matters might seem peripheral to Bach's music. Yet the fact that he now lived and worked in a distinguished academic institution could not have discouraged him from incorporating learned elements into church pieces as well as other compositions. The many non-musical or non-creative duties that now fell to him were not atypical of what was expected of other artists of the time in similar positions. Bach had further mundane responsibilities, including oversight of the harpsichords in the two main churches, but like any professional of the period he could call on family members and pupils to serve as unpaid assistants. There were also student prefects chosen from among the older *alumni*, who could lead performances when Bach himself was not present (as in services at the minor churches).

Life and Work

Bach's participation in all these varied activities would seem to have left little time or energy for his own composing and practicing, or for family. Yet during the next nine years Anna Magdalena would bear as many children. Only three would survive infancy, but her three stepsons were now at various stages in their development as musicians (which they were all to become). Friedemann, Emanuel, and Bernhard would enter

---

15 The *inspector* essentially served *in loco parentis*; after 1730 Bach refused to carry out this duty (see Kevorkian 2017, 113–14).

16 Several of those "usable for music" ("Zur Music zu gebrauchende") were nevertheless of "mediocre" or "weak" proficiency (e.g., "die prefectus sind mediocre"); BD 1:131–34 (nos. 63–66); NBR, 140–42 (nos. 142–45). It is probably no accident that this is the year for which Bach's notes survive; see Maul (2018, 191ff.).

the St. Thomas School as *externi*—non-scholarship students living at home, albeit within the school building itself. Friedemann and Emanuel would also attend the Leipzig university, although neither earned a degree there. Doubtless Sebastian taught all three, but he is unlikely to have provided instruction for the younger children with the same intensity as for Friedemann at Cöthen. Most of the direct, face-to-face teaching, whether of singing, playing, or reading and writing music, might have come from Anna Magdalena or an older brother. Perhaps, too, Sebastian intentionally kept a certain distance from his children, who, like those of the aristocracy, might have grown up at some emotional and even physical remove from their parents.

The children's complex family environment included their older aunt Friedelena, often also one or two more distant relatives as apprentices or boarders. Anna Magdalena herself was only eight years older than Friedemann. Each family member must have played some role in fulfilling domestic responsibilities, the essential aim being to ensure that Sebastian could fulfill his duties without interference or impedance from family life. The risks inherent in being brought up in such a household can be seen in how two of the sons turned out. Friedemann, despite his prodigious talent, evidently remained more dependent on his father's support than the others, never achieving the worldly success and savoir-faire achieved by his next younger brother. Bernhard, the third son, did worse, dying young and bankrupt, with no lasting accomplishments to his name. Emanuel, on the other hand, became a royal chamber musician and eventually an honorary Capellmeister, like his father, not to mention cantor and music director in the greatest independent city of the Empire. Their half-brother Christian would also become a royal musician, while their brother-in-law Altnikol went on to a respectable career as organist in the cathedral town of Naumburg. At least three fellow pupils, Nichelmann, Kirnberger, and Agricola, would join Emanuel in royal appointments at Berlin.

Bach's busy schedule at Leipzig must temporarily have prevented him from continuing the organ tests and performances away from home that had occupied him since before the Weimar years. Now these journeys had to be planned around his responsibilities at Leipzig. The first trips, taken during 1724 and 1725, included several to Weissenfels, Cöthen, and Dresden, all relatively close or familiar. There was also a journey during summer 1725 to Gera, forty miles to the south. Bach had likely visited Gera once before in 1721; he now returned, probably with Magdalena and Friedemann, at a time when he would otherwise have begun work on his third annual cycle of cantatas for Leipzig.[17] The Cöthen journey of 1725 took place during the Advent season, when no cantatas were performed at Leipzig. But if Bach obtained permission for the other trips (as he had agreed to do), this would have presupposed official sanction to have a substitute direct the "music" in the two main Leipzig churches, and indeed several cantatas heard during summer 1725 were by other composers.[18]

Trips to Cöthen, which included at least one more in 1728, must always have seen performances for Prince Leopold; those in 1724 and 1725 were with Anna Magdalena.[19] During a visit to Dresden in September 1725, an anonymous newspaper report indicates that Bach played "preludes and diverse concertos" on the organ of the main Protestant church, St. Sophia (where Friedemann would become organist in 1733). Exactly what the "soft instrumental interludes in all keys" were is unknown, but the writer, who evidently knew little about musical terminology, did not necessarily mean that Bach played actual concertos with orchestral accompaniment.[20] The main purpose of Bach's Dresden trip seems to have been to present the first of many complaints to the ruling elector, petitioning that the salary for the "New Service" at the Leipzig university church should be assigned to Bach. Whether his two concert performances were

---

17 As shown by Maul (2004, 106–7). The visit was previously thought to have taken place in 1724, due to the misinterpretation of an undated court payment record (BD 2:144 [no. 183a]).

18. Maul (2006) showed that at least one work from that summer, with text by Maria Aurora, countess of Königsmarck, was not Bach's. Hobohm (1973) had previously demonstrated that several settings from Neumeister's cycle of 1711–12, probably by Telemann, were performed during the same period, with Schott, music director at the New Church, probably substituting for Bach.

19 Payment records are dated July 18, 1724 (BD 2:144 [no. 184]), December 15, 1725 (BD 2:153 [no. 199]), and May 1, 1728 (BD 2:179 [no. 241]); all in NBR, 117 (nos. 117a–c).

20 Wolff (2016) re-asserts the hypothesis first presented in Wolff (2008, 106–7), based on the report of Bach's playing "in Praeludiis und diversen Concerten mit unterlauffender Doucen Instrumental-Music in allen Tonis" (BD 2:150 [no. 193]; NBR, 117 [no. 118]). Published in a Hamburg newspaper, the reference to "all keys" (if that is what is meant) seems more apt for solo organ playing than music for instrumental ensemble.

related to this appeal is not recorded. Presumably Bach hoped to gain the elector's attention by playing in public, reportedly to the great admiration of the "virtuosos" of both court and city (*hiesigen Hoff- und Stadt-Virtuosen*). But two subsequent letters failed to produce the desired result, even though one of them, dated December 31, 1725, may be the longest, most detailed surviving document of any sort from Bach's hand. Early in 1726, the elector found—perhaps rightly—that Bach was not entitled to payments for the recently instituted regular services, but only for the so-called Old Service.[21]

If Bach was chastened by this, we have no evidence for that. And although we also have no evidence for further travel beyond Cöthen and Dresden until 1732, this does not mean that Bach did not continue to perform organ tests or concerts in the region. Yet he might now have focused on new types of work in the city that had become his home. During 1726 he planned his first publication, announcing on November 1 the printing of the First Harpsichord Partita (BWV 825).[22] Almost two decades earlier, the city of Mühlhausen had published the grand council election cantata BWV 71 and probably at least one other such work. Now Bach issued a composition under his own auspices, possibly with support from Prince Leopold, to whom Bach sent a special dedication copy in honor of the latter's newborn son, Emanuel Ludwig. This copy was accompanied by an anonymous poem, handwritten by the composer and expressing a wish to serve the little prince, though this was not to be.[23]

This work, together with five further keyboard partitas printed separately during the next four years, constituted Part 1 of Bach's *Clavierübung* ("Keyboard Practice"); a collected edition of all six partitas followed, and then three more Parts and several further engraved publications. These

---

21 The original petition, dated September 14, was followed by a short letter on November 3 and then the long New Year's Eve memo. The elector's reply followed quickly on January 21, 1725, apparently ignoring the obsessively detailed missive of December 31. See BD 1:30–40 (nos. 10–12) and 2:155 (no. 202); NBR, 118–25 (nos. 119–20).

22 In an *Extract* or supplement of the local Leipzig *Post-Zeitungen* (BD 2:160–61 [no. 214]).

23 Emanuel Ludwig lived only two years, dying of smallpox in 1728 alongside his little sister Leopoldine Charlotte. The poem is somewhat longer than convention might have required, expressing what seems genuine affection for the princely family, although it is assumed not to be by Bach himself (BD 1:223 [no. 155], trans. in NBR 129–30 [no. 128]).

printed works must have occasioned some excitement and perhaps not a little anxiety in the household, as the cost of buying copper plates and having them engraved and printed could not have been negligible for the growing family. Yet the absence of a named dedicatee on the title page indicates that Bach bore most of the costs himself. Unlike later typeset music, such a publication resembled a portfolio of fine art prints; no more than a few hundred copies could be produced before the soft copper plates began to wear. The expenses involved were such that a publication of this sort might not have brought many tangible benefits to Bach. But it would have raised his stature, perhaps compensating for any loss of dignity (or income) occasioned by his unsuccessful petition to the elector.

Another sign of Bach's prestige and of the high regard in which some, at least, held him locally, was a commission in fall 1727 for music honoring the late Electress Christiane Eberhardine, who died on September 5. She had refused to convert to Roman Catholicism when her husband Friedrich August was elected king of Poland. This made her popular with her Lutheran subjects, and after her death a group of aristocratic students at the university led by one Kirchbach commissioned an ode from Gottsched, with music by Bach, for a memorial service. The resulting work, known as the *Trauerode* (Funeral Ode, BWV 198), was performed on October 17, Bach leading the performance from the harpsichord.[24] As it took place at the university church, the event was not without controversy, for the organist of the church, Johann Gottlieb Görner, believed he had the right to the commission. Görner, a pupil of Kuhnau, had been assigned to direct the church's New Service just before Bach's arrival at Leipzig in 1723; Bach, doubtless still unhappy about losing payments for those services, refused to acknowledge Görner's prerogative.[25] Kirchbach apparently paid Görner anyway, and as the latter would serve after Sebastian's death as joint legal guardian (*contutor*) for the four youngest Bach children,[26] there appears to have been no lasting enmity between the two.

---

24 As described by a local chronicler, Christoph Ernst Sicul (BD 2:175–76 [nos. 232–33]; NBR, 136–37 [no. 136]).

25 Bach failed to sign a document stating that his payment for the *Trauerode* was "strictly a special privilege" (*eine bloße Vergünstigung*, BD 2:172 [no. 227]; NBR, 136 [no. 135]).

26 As recorded in the specification of Bach's estate (BD 2:497 [no. 627]; NBR, 255 [no. 279]) and confirmed in a later document (BD 5:180 [no. B626c]).

The memorial for the electress, who had been estranged from her husband, must have been regarded with some suspicion by the court, even as it ostensibly honored the latter. The ode was neither Bach's first nor his last work of homage for the ruling family. The other compositions, written for celebrations rather than memorials, took the form of serenatas or *drammi per musica*—the Italianate type of mini-opera with allegorical characters that Bach had been writing since the Hunt Cantata of 1713. Earlier in 1727 Bach had performed two such works, for the elector's birthday on May 12 and his name day on August 3. The music for both is lost, but more such compositions would follow in the 1730s.[27] Three weeks after their initial performance, portions of the name day work were parodied in Cantata 193. Performed for the installation of a new city council, BWV 193 was the second example that Bach is known to have composed at Leipzig for this annual civic event.[28] Like the council election cantatas for Mühlhausen, these were political works, but they were performed in the city's principal church (St. Nicholas) and were identical in style and form to a sacred cantata. The fact that in this case Bach re-used music previously performed for the elector might, if noticed, have been taken positively, signifying that Bach's immediate superiors rated the same grand poetry and music as their common ruler. The original text, by Picander, had been placed in the mouths of a "Council of the Gods" (*Rath der Götter*); members of the city council would have been pleased to hear his new verses praising God in place of the elector.

The Collegium Musicum

The performers in such works must have included members of the Collegium Musicum. There were actually two organizations of this type in Leipzig when Bach arrived. One, founded by Telemann during his university years (1701–1705), was now directed by Schott, of the New Church. The other, subsequently founded by Fasch during *his* university years, was led by Görner at the university church. Early accounts describe the group founded by Telemann

---

27 Some music for the birthday work, BWV Anh. 9, may survive in the "Et resurrexit" of the B-Minor Mass, a possibility allowed by Dürr (1992, 133).

28 The first was BWV 119 of August 30, 1723.

Figure 10.2 Gottfried Zimmermann's mansion at Katharinenstrasse 14–16, Leipzig; his coffeehouse was on the ground floor. Engraving by Johann Georg Schreiber (1720), from Wikimedia.

as having from forty to sixty members and giving concerts twice weekly; by Bach's time the two groups were each performing once a week—twice during the Leipzig fairs.[29] The older group performed at the coffeehouse established in 1717 by Gottfried Zimmermann, on the ground floor of a grand building on the city's most fashionable street or, during the summer, in his outdoor coffee garden (Figure 10.2).[30]

29 The most detailed accounts date from the 1730s (these include a report by Bach's friend Mizler, in BD 2:277–78 [no. 387], trans. in NBR, 185–86 [no. 187]; another is in BD 2:234–35 [no. 326]). Telemann's own earlier report, in his autobiography of 1718 (published by Mattheson 1731, 173), mentions "up to forty students pressed together" ("aus lauter studiosis bestehet, deren öffters biß 40 beysammen sind").

30 The date is from BD 2:235 (commentary to no. 326); the engraving of the building by Johann Georg Schreiber (destroyed in a 1943 air raid) is dated ca. 1720 in *Schicksale*

Precisely how the groups were organized, what they performed, and how many actually sang or played on any given occasion are unknown. When a report claims that forty "musicians" took part in the elector's birthday celebration in 1727, it is impossible to know whether the biblical number—which appears in many such accounts—is to be understood literally or how many of these participated specifically in Bach's composition.[31] Large numbers of choristers would not necessarily have been preferred in a type of work based on opera seria. The elector and other sophisticated listeners knew the latter as a genre involving skilled solo singers, not massed amateurs; even the occasional choral numbers in opera were typically sung only by the handful of cast members.

Bach took over the older collegium officially in March 1729, as Schott left Leipzig to become cantor in Gotha. This occurred during the same month that saw Bach's participation in funeral music for Prince Leopold at Cöthen, whose death the previous November, before his thirty-fourth birthday, must have been a blow to Bach. The timing of the two events might have been a coincidence, but together they marked the closing of one chapter of his life and the beginning of another.[32] Almost two years earlier, however, Bach had already "directed in person" (*persönlich dirigirte*) the Collegium's performance for the birthday of the elector. Augustus II was present on that occasion—the first known instance of Bach's performing for a king, who, however, is reported only to have made a generically favorable response to the homage by his Leipzig subjects.[33] A performance

deutscher Baudenkmale im zweiten Weltkrieg, Vol. 1 (Munich: Beck, 1978), 359. Stauffer (2008, 135) gives the performance schedule, which was expanded during the Leipzig fairs. Further on Zimmermann in Hübner (2018).

31 The report of forty *Musiker* comes from an account published nearly two decades later in Dresden (BD 2:167, commentary to no. 220).

32 Bach mentions assuming the direction of the Collegium in a letter to his former student Wecker dated March 20, 1729 (BD 1:57 [no. 20]). The printed libretto of the Cöthen funeral music (BWV 244a), which explicitly names the "former Capellmeister" Bach, is dated four days later (BD 2:189–90 [no. 258]).

33 According to Sicul (BD 2:165–66 [no. 220]; NBR, 133–34 [no. 132]), who, as in so many such reports, paid less attention to Bach's music than to the poem (by Christian Friedrich Haupt) and to enumerating the dignitaries who were present.

of this type, part of a grand civic ceremony that also included a procession of torchbearers and a march played by trumpets and drums,
might not have encompassed the proverbial forty musicians. But it
nevertheless must have required substantial preparation, including the
copying of well over a dozen individual performing parts and more
than the usual amount of rehearsal.[34] Ordinary weekly performances
by the Collegium, on the other hand, might not have involved any rehearsal at all, and they might have been more like community readings
of music than a modern concert series.

At the time of Bach's takeover of the Collegium, he had lost his honorary title of Capellmeister with the death of Prince Leopold. Now Bach,
who had last seen Leopold the preceding January,[35] made a final journey
to Cöthen at the end of March 1729. Together with Anna Magdalena
and, probably, Wilhelm Friedemann, he performed funeral music that included movements parodied from two great works of 1727, the *Trauerode*
for the electress and the St. Matthew Passion.[36] By this point, however,
Bach had already received a promotion of sorts. A month earlier he had
traveled to Weissenfels, twenty miles southwest of Leipzig, for an observ-
ance of Duke Christian's birthday.[37] Nothing more is known of this visit,
but it followed that of the duke himself to Leipzig during the January
fair; on that occasion Magdalena probably sang for him Sebastian's cantata BWV 210a.[38] The exact date of Bach's new appointment is unknown,
but by September he could call himself "princely Saxe-Weissenfels court

---

34 Although the scoring of BWV Anh. 9 (performed for Augustus on May 12, 1727) is un-
    known, the fragmentarily preserved BWV 193 from the following summer must have
    involved at least three trumpets and timpani, in addition to the surviving parts for oboes,
    strings, and four voices.

35 Bach received 24 Taler for his visit on January 5, 1728 (BD 2:179 [no. 241]), presumably
    performing a New Year's work that does not survive.

36 The court record of the payment (BD 2:190–91 [no. 259]; NBR, 139 [no. 139]) does not
    specify which son accompanied Sebastian and his wife.

37 BD 2:187 (no. 254).

38 The music is mostly lost but can be reconstructed from the later parody BWV 210 and
    from the printed libretto, reproduced by Tiggemann (1994, 11–14). The performance fell
    during a period when Magdalena was not pregnant; Regina Johanna had been born two
    months earlier, and Christiana Benedicta would follow in January 1730. The Cöthen and

Capellmeister" in a letter of recommendation for a student.[39] He now could boast again of being servant of a duke, moreover one belonging to the same family as the ruling Elector.

Changes at the School

Within a month came another death that affected Bach: that in October 1729, at the age of seventy-seven, of Johann Heinrich Ernesti, rector of the St. Thomas School and Bach's immediate superior. Not much is known about their relationship, but his replacement, Johann Matthias Gesner, seems to have been an old acquaintance of Bach's.[40] Gesner, however, would leave after just four years, in part because the city council refused to allow him to hold a joint appointment as professor in the university, as Ernesti had done. This stipulation, made when Gesner was appointed the following summer, echoed one in Bach's own employment agreement. It was just one sign of ongoing changes in the relationships between Bach, the school, and his superiors. These changes reduced his autonomy, at least insofar as his official work was concerned. Already in 1728, one of the pastors at St. Nicholas had complained to the local church consistory that Bach was not respecting his selection of hymns for services. Bach responded by informing the city council that the cantor had always chosen hymns, and a year and a half later the electoral Saxon consistory in Dresden seems to have overruled the Leipzig church authorities.[41] But the incident reveals a tension between Bach and certain clergy that now appears to have begun to involve members of the city council

Gera trips of 1724 and 1725 likewise took place at times when Magdalena is not known to have been carrying a child.

39 Johann Gottlieb Grahl, a student of theology who was "highly proficient in music" (BD 3:629 [no. 66a], trans. in NBR, 142 [no. 147]).

40 Gesner had been a teacher and court librarian at Weimar during Bach's time there; in 1733 his wife was godmother of Bach's short-lived son Johann August Abraham.

41 The controversy is recorded in Pastor Gottlieb Gaudlitz's letter dated September 7, 1728 to the Leipzig council (BD 1:56 [no. 19]); an order made the following day by the Leipzig church consistory, which was headed by Deyling (BD 2:182–83 [no. 246], trans. in NBR, 137 [no. 137]); Bach's letter of Sept. 20 to the Leipzig council (BD 1:54–56 [no. 19]; and a subsequent order addressed to Deyling by the electoral Saxon consistory in Dresden (given in NBR, 143–44 [no. 149] from Bitter's nineteenth-century biography of Bach).

as well. Thus when Gesner was hired in June 1730, one councilor went on record as hoping that he would "do better than the cantor."[42] Two months later the council agreed that Bach was not performing his teaching duties, one member describing him as "incorrigible."[43] Even Lange, who had previously supported Bach, concurred with the accusations, and the council voted to reduce Bach's pay, denying him his amount due for acting as *inspector*, that is, assisting in the administration of the dormitory.[44]

These developments reflected long-standing contradictions arising from the St. Thomas School's double role as both an educational institution and a provider of musical services for the city.[45] How deeply they truly affected Bach is uncertain, nor can we know how the conflicts and frustrations that he experienced at Leipzig compared with those that were inherent generally in court and institutional life of the time, just as they are now in academia and other modern institutions. They loom large in Bach's biography because of the paucity of more significant events, and because they happen to have been recorded in surviving documents. Some of the latter, including the critic Scheibe's published attack on Bach, look like an extension of private complaints into the new print journalism of the time. If Bach indeed experienced a genuine personal crisis around 1730, as has been supposed, it came only after his new court appointment and the expansion of his activity with the Collegium. It might have been more effect than cause of a drastic reduction in his output of sacred music for the churches, which had already been reduced to a trickle. He would never return to the composition of sacred music on the regular basis that characterized his first few years at Leipzig—if only because by now he had a sufficient repertory of existing compositions on which to draw.

42 "daß es beßer seyn möchte, als mit dem Cantor," from council minutes of June 8, 1730 (BD 2:203 [no. 178]).

43 *incorrigibel*, BD 2:204–5 (no. 280); NBR, 144–45 (no. 150a). Maul (2018, 199) glosses this last adjective as "an exceptionally severe legal term for someone who cannot be taught or improved."

44 Bach presumably had refused to do this alongside his three colleagues, who did receive pay for acting as *inspectores* (BD 2:206 [no. 282]).

45 Maul (2018, Chapters 3–4) traces the history of this conflict in detail, going back to before the time of Bach's predecessor Kuhnau.

On the other hand, Bach's involvement with instrumental and secular vocal music would continue, perhaps at a somewhat higher rate, during the next decade. It is possible that another death was affecting his thoughts during this period: that of the Dresden Capellmeister Heinichen in July 1729. This took place just three months after Bach had advertised sale of the latter's magnum opus, a book on continuo realization.[46] Possibly Bach, now honorary Capellmeister to Duke Christian, imagined that he might be considered for Heinichen's position at Dresden. There, as he suggested a year later in a famous document, a musician of his talents would receive better pay under less onerous working conditions.[47] This was not to be, however, and instead the following decade would see further clashes between Bach and his superiors at Leipzig.

Bach nevertheless would continue his creative work, turning back, to some degree, toward the keyboard music that had occupied him earlier in his career, occasionally also producing new masterpieces of vocal composition. With some exceptions, these followed outlines that he had drawn for his sacred music during his first three or four years at Leipzig. Those works, considered as a group, constituted the single greatest sustained creative effort of his life, and as such they constitute the chief subject of our next chapter.

---

46 The advertisement for Heinichen's *General-Bass in der Composition* (1728) appeared in the Leipzig *Post-Zeitungen* (BD 2:191 [no. 260]; NBR, 139 [no 142]) on April 18, 1729.

47 The so-called *Entwurff* is discussed in Chapter 12.

CHAPTER ELEVEN

Bach the Music Director

CHURCH AND CONCERT PIECES

B ACH'S BILINGUAL TITLE OF *director musices*—DIRECTOR OF MUSIC—AT Leipzig seems not to have been official. Still, the hybrid Latin-Greek term was an accurate description of his role in the community. It recalls his request at Arnstadt for a "director" of church music, the term then implying training and discipline of unruly students, not an interpreter or conductor as it does today. At Leipzig he had a broader variety of potential musicians with whom to work, ranging from boys in the St. Thomas School to university students and professional town musicians. The "music" that he was charged with directing included his own church cantatas, which comprise roughly half his surviving output. But Bach also bore responsibility for all the other music used in the Leipzig church services, and for much of his time at Leipzig he directed as well the Collegium Musicum, which not only gave public concerts but also participated in certain civic events.

Bach's chief model for how a city music director might function must have been his father at Eisenach, but that was both a smaller city and a princely residence. Still, the position in either place entailed much of what a modern church or concert music director must do, plus copying if not composing music, as well as some degree of professional oversight over other musicians in the city. A peculiarity of Bach's Leipzig position was that the city music director was also cantor, responsible for musical instruction of the boys in the St. Thomas School, preparing them for participation in services at the four city churches.

Bach. David Schulenberg, Oxford University Press (2020). © Oxford University Press.
DOI: 10.1093/oso/9780190936303.001.0001

Music in the City Churches

Expectations for the type of music that Bach was to provide varied according to venue and occasion. For religious services, only the two main churches of St. Nicholas and St. Thomas required cantatas on a regular basis, the others being mainly limited to motets and hymns or chorales.[1] Congregational hymns were led not by the organist (as in modern church services) but by boys under the direction of a prefect, an older student trained by Bach. Bach nevertheless held ultimate responsibility for the hymn singing; this was an essential task for the cantor and one that he took seriously.[2] His creative work consisted primarily of preparing the elaborate music heard on Sundays and holidays in the two chief churches. It seems to have been understood that Bach, like Kuhnau before him, would provide new compositions for this purpose; whether these were expected to be all or mostly his own is less certain. Selecting the repertory and assuring that it was performed adequately appear to have been entirely in Bach's hands, which, however, were tied with respect to funding.

Bach's bitter complaint to the city council in 1730—the famous "Sketch of a Well-Established Church Music"[3]—shows how conscious he had become by that date of the gulf between the city's financial backing for music as compared to that of the ruling court at Dresden. His appeal is too long to quote in full; the gist comes after Bach has given a detailed enumeration of his musical responsibilities and the personnel (both students and professionals) available for fulfilling them. He then writes:

> it cannot go unmentioned that, through the admission of so many boys who are poorly trained and not at all musically talented, the music [in the churches] has necessarily declined . . . It is well known that my predecessors, Messrs. Schelle and Kuhnau, had to rely on the participation of

---

1 The motets, heard regularly in church services at St. Nicholas, St. Thomas, and the New Church, were relatively simple compositions by older composers—not the elaborate motets composed by Bach for special occasions.

2 As shown by his complaint when his right to select hymns was infringed (see Chapter 10).

3 The title is Bach's: "Kurtzer, iedoch höchstnöthiger Entwurff einer wohlbestallten Kirchen Music," BD 1:60–64 (no. 22); NBR, 145–51 (no. 151). This document has been the subject of countless interpretations; the most critical appraisal remains Rifkin's (2002).

university students [*studiosi*] . . . for which not only certain singers . . . but also instrumentalists . . . were favored with special stipends. . . . Now, however, the state of music is entirely different from what it was, as artistic demands [*Kunst*] have increased and style [*gusto*] has changed, so that the old type of music no longer pleases our ears. Considerable assistance is therefore necessary . . . to satisfy present musical taste and provide for the new types of music, in order to give satisfaction to the composer and his labor.

Bach's "sketch," dated August 23, 1730, was hardly the first complaint to the authorities by a Leipzig cantor who was also a prominent composer.[4] Could he have been unaware of this? He submitted it less than two months after a three-day Jubilee celebrating the two hundredth anniversary of the Augsburg Confession. For this Bach prepared three special cantatas, and on August 28 he was scheduled to perform the annual council election cantata. Unfortunately, none of this music survives intact, but it is unlikely to have been any less demanding than usual; did it not go well?[5] Or was Bach's memorandum timed to follow the appointment just two months earlier of his friend Gesner as School rector, in the hope that the latter might support him?[6] Some of Bach's remarks pertain chiefly to the motets and hymns that were sung in three or in all four churches, not to his own compositions. Others were evidently addressed to those council members who expected him to modernize the repertory in the two main churches, bringing the cantatas and other music performed there to a level comparable to that of Dresden. Bach must have understood, upon taking the job at Leipzig, that he could hardly count on the type of funding available in one of Europe's most sumptuous court cities. Yet he complains of diminishing support, and he tries to explain how the music at Leipzig can never be as good as in a city where the musicians are paid as specialists:

4 Maul (2018, 55f.) quotes a comparable complaint filed almost exactly a century earlier by Bach's most distinguished predecessor, Johann Hermann Schein, and Kuhnau had offered one as well in 1720 (ibid., 206).

5 The works were BWV 190a and 120b, which survive only in parodies, and the lost BWV Anh. 4a and 3. Picander's texts survive (they can be read on Bach-Digital), as does the council's order for the election music (see BD 2:194, commentary to no. 264).

6 As suggested by Wolff (2000, 346).

one only has to go to Dresden to see how the musicians there are given salaries by his royal majesty. . . . As each is relieved of having to worry about his livelihood and required to master only one instrument, it must be a splendid and excellent thing to hear.

Evidently, then, between 1723 and 1730 Bach had experienced growing frustration. His creative efforts in the area of sacred vocal music were mainly confined to those first few years at Leipzig, afterward trailing off or being diverted toward revision and codification of an existing repertory. From the start, however, he must have known that he would need to rely on students as well as the handful of salaried city musicians, for he would now direct and compose for ensembles very different from the courtly *Capellen* at Weimar and Cöthen. Contrary to popular belief, most of the boys in the St. Thomas School rarely if ever performed in Bach's compositions. Only some were "usable" even for singing simple older polyphony, although for several of these boys we have Bach's comment that they might "in time" (*fernerhin*) and with further training be suitable for what Bach called simply "music," meaning church cantatas.[7] The students heard in cantatas therefore were probably not usually "alumni"—scholarship students in the St. Thomas School—but university students. Students were also needed to furnish instrumental parts, due to the insufficiency of the town musicians. The latter might have brought assistants or apprentices when called to perform Bach's music, but in 1730 Bach listed only a single journeyman (*Geselle*) among those "appointed to the church music."[8]

Directing the Collegium Musicum

The two collegia musica were private organizations, but upon his arrival Bach, as city music director, might have expected to exercise some degree of oversight over the older and better-known one, founded by Telemann. That group was now under the direction of Schott, organist at the New Church. Bach probably had little to do with the other organization, which met at the university church (St. Paul's), led by its organist

---

7 The *Entwurff* divides the students into three "classes," of which only the seventeen boys in the first were "usable" (*brauchbar*) in *Music* (BD 1:64 [no. 22]; NBR, 147–48 [no. 151]). Wollny (2016, esp. 75) gives biographical details on some of these student musicians.

8 "derer zur Kirchen Music bestellten Persohnen," BD 1:61 (no. 22), NBR, 147 (no. 151).

Görner. But even before the "Schottisch" Collegium came under Bach's direct leadership, he might have regarded its membership as part of the roster of musicians available for his cantatas and other works, and there must have been considerable overlap in personnel. Today the Collegium is usually associated with instrumental music, and this—including some of Bach's best-known compositions[9]—may indeed have comprised the main repertory of its regular weekly performances. More important, however, were the so-called extraordinary (*außerordentlich*) performances of vocal music, marking civic occasions such as royal name days. If the ruler or a member of his family appeared in person, the Collegium, bolstered by city musicians, might participate in a procession marking the event. This could be followed by the open-air evening performance of a vocal work—described in accounts as a "serenade"—beneath the window of the royal residence in the city. Such an event might have been attended by hundreds, even thousands, although not every listener could have heard the music or made out the words equally well.[10]

Reconstructions of the repertory of both collegia have focused on surviving music manuscripts and printed librettos. The latter shed light on the vocal repertory, which under Schott included at least two substantial vocal works.[11] There does seem to have been an uptick in Bach's copying of instrumental music around the time he officially took over directorship of the group from Schott in 1729. The copies include scores and parts not only for Bach's own concertos and orchestral suites but for similar works by such composers as Fasch and Telemann. The players must have included Bach's sons and pupils; among the works performed were two orchestral suites by Sebastian's older Eisenach

---

9 Maul (2007, 67–68) makes a good case for performances of the Brandenburg Concertos. Manuscript copies made at Leipzig of works by other composers provide hints about the broader repertory (listed by Wolff 2000, 355, and supplemented by Stauffer 2008, 151–52).

10 Accounts of such events include that of the chronicler Riemer for the royal visit on October 5, 1734, for which Bach wrote and performed the *serenata* BWV 215. Riemer, who mentions Bach by name, reports that the king was presented with a copy of the libretto and that he listened to the entire performance "most graciously" from his window, "liking it well" ("haben solche gnädigst angehöret, und Ihr. Majestät hertzlich wohlgefallen," BD 2:250 [no. 352]; NBR, 167 [no. 173]).

11 One of these was a biblical oratorio performed in two parts; see Maul (2007, 71–72), who also reports evidence for comparable works performed by the university collegium under Görner.

cousin Johann Bernhard, whose *Ouverture* in D evidently provided suggestions to Wilhelm Friedemann or another student.[12] Vocal music may have been equally important in the group's repertory. Most of the works of this type associated with the Collegium are now described as secular cantatas, but they range from true cantatas as understood at the time—contemplative or narrative works for a single voice—to *serenate* (serenades) and *drammi per musica* (musical dramas) with named characters and quasi-dramatic plots.

Bach's repertory for church as well as Collegium may have been broader than the surviving documentation indicates. It was once assumed that, after composing the majority of his sacred vocal music during the first few years at Leipzig, Bach repeated the same works for the remainder of his career, perhaps according to a regular cycle. Yet evidence for performances of a more diverse range of compositions has proliferated in recent years, as have clues that Bach exchanged sacred as well as secular pieces with other ensemble directors. For instance, during the 1730s Bach was lending cantatas to a cantor in Ronneburg, near Frankfurt.[13] During the same period he appears to have used an annual cycle of cantatas by Stölzel as the basis for his own church performances.[14] These instances are known only by chance; if they reflect general practice, they suggest that Bach's vocal compositions were not quite as unknown outside Leipzig as has been supposed, and that Leipzig heard much music besides Bach's even in church. Emanuel Bach, who would eventually occupy a position at Hamburg similar to his father's, would usually perform the music of other composers, reserving his own efforts chiefly for special occasions. It could be that Emanuel knew and followed Sebastian's model

12 BWV 1070, a suite for strings possibly by W. F. Bach (see Schulenberg 2010a, 45–54), ends with a contrapuntal Capriccio comparable to two similarly titled movements in the work by J. B. Bach. Friedemann was a student in Leipzig until his appointment as organist at Dresden in 1731; the sole source of the work by J. B. Bach is a set of parts copied by J. S. Bach and others around 1730 (Berlin, Staatsbibliothek, Mus. ms. Bach St 318).

13 Maul and Wollny (2003, 100–10). Possible performances of several of Bach's Weimar cantatas at Zerbst are discussed by Wollny (2001), who also points to later performances of further works at Weissenfels (citing Schulze; a related discussion is in Pfau 2015).

14 As demonstrated by Pfau (2008) for performances during 1735–1736.

of the 1730s, preferring this to the hectic production of new works that characterized his father's first years at Leipzig.[15]

At the time Sebastian became its director in 1729, the Collegium was giving more than sixty two-hour performances each year, prompting the observation that Bach spent more time with them than performing church cantatas.[16] The proportion of time that Bach devoted to secular compositions increases further when special performances for weddings and civic occasions are added. This supports a view that biographers might have seen greater significance in Bach's secular vocal works had more of them survived in their original forms.[17] As it is, the ease with which Bach could turn a secular cantata into a sacred parody must reflect the fact that members of an ensemble that performed in a coffeehouse until 10 P.M. on a Friday evening might be warming up their voices and tuning their instruments before sunrise on the following Sunday. Vocal works performed by the Collegium typically comprised moralizing poetry and homage to rulers and patrons. Hence the ostensive purpose of these performances was not very different from that of a church piece: to instruct and edify, and to praise an overlord, even if also imparting delight in the process.

Such activity was by no means confined to Leipzig. The musical academies and salons of seventeenth-century Italy and France were emulated throughout fashionable Europe, in institutions that were evolving toward the choral societies and concert-presenting organizations of today. During Bach's lifetime, collegia musica were established in many German towns. By the time of his death the collegium founded at Leipzig by Telemann had been succeeded by the Grosses Konzert, a forerunner of today's Gewandhaus Orchestra. In Berlin and Dresden, members of the respective royal families sponsored free concerts for the public, as tokens of aristocratic largesse—but admission to Bach's

---

15 Emanuel succeeded Telemann in 1768 as cantor and music director at Hamburg; further on his approach to sacred music in Schulenberg (2014, 249–57).

16 As suggested by Stauffer (2008, 135); this assumes that the Collegium spent all its time performing in a modern sense, not giving something like an open reading or rehearsal (see below).

17 "If their sources had been preserved as systematically as those of the church cantatas were, or if the church cantatas had survived less well than they did, common perceptions of the Bach oeuvre ever since might have been very different" (Williams 2016, 331).

Collegium concerts had to be paid for.[18] The amount of money taken in and how it was divided are not known. Even if he received only applause and beer, however, Bach would also have benefited from these performances as a form of marketing, not just for his music but for his services as a teacher and a provider of private concerts. This was especially true during the Leipzig book fairs, when extra performances were scheduled and well-heeled music-loving visitors might have sought out Bach specifically.

Bach's Musicians

Bach's complaint of 1730 suggests that it was a constant struggle to find capable singers and players willing to perform for free, whether in church or with the Collegium. Yet some were paid for their work in church, and this may have taken place more frequently than can now be demonstrated.[19] In any case, those participating had to be multi-talented, capable of playing several different instruments as well as singing. Thus Johann Christoph Altnickol, later Bach's son-in-law, served as violist and cellist "but principally as bass singer."[20] Altnickol came to Leipzig in 1744 to study theology at the university, but he had previously worked as a musician and would continue to do so afterward; he must have come expecting to sing and play for Bach on a regular basis. Such was the sort of pupil that Lange presumably had in mind when he told the council that Bach would "inspire" students.[21] Indeed, Bach's Leipzig pupils included

---

18 The price was three groschen, equivalent to perhaps ten or twenty dollars today, according to a contemporary report cited by Schulze (2008, 82), who also describes collegia at Delitzsch (north of Leipzig) and Göttingen. It is possible that admission was charged only for "extraordinary" concerts.

19 Schulze (1984a, 46–47) reproduces documents from the period 1724–1745 that list payments to seven young men for serving the Leipzig churches as musicians, sometimes more specifically as bass (singer) or violinist. Most are identified as students (that is, at the university). Rifkin (2012, 132) points out that Altnickol served similarly (see below), indicating that payment records provide only incomplete information about who actually performed.

20 "als Violiste, bald als Violoncelliste, meistens aber als Vocal-Bassiste," as Bach wrote on May 25, 1747, in support of Altnickol's request for compensation (BD 1:148 [no. 81]; NBR, 224 [no. 240]).

21 BD 2:95 (no. 129); the translation of *animiret* is from NBR, 103 (no. 98). Lange's point was that the participation of *die Herren Studiosi* (university students) would not cost the council anything if they were sufficiently "animated" by Bach.

some of the most distinguished German musicians of the next two generations: not only Altnickol but also Agricola, Kirnberger, and Johann Ludwig Krebs, son of Bach's Weimar pupil Johan Tobias Krebs—not to mention Sebastian's own sons. The presence of musicians of such caliber, attracted to Leipzig by Bach as well as by its prestigious university, meant that reliance on students was not necessarily a problem.

Nevertheless, by 1730 Bach was complaining that even the professional town musicians were aging and "not at all as well practiced as they should be."[22] This might not have been entirely fair if Bach was judging them on the basis of how they handled his own extraordinary parts—which, if he followed the norms of the time, they were not allowed to take home to practice. One hopes, too, that Bach's remark was not meant to include the trumpet player and senior city musician Gottfried Reiche. He would perform with Bach until his death in 1734 at the age of sixty-seven, shortly after performing in Bach's *dramma per musica* BWV 215.[23] Reiche's death, from a stroke, was attributed to his inhaling smoke from the torches used for illumination on the occasion—one of those grand ceremonial performances for the elector. He was also a composer, and in his portrait by Haussmann he holds music for a fanfare that is almost as difficult as anything by Bach—whom Haussmann also painted.[24] Surely Reiche in his prime could handle any part given to him, including most of Bach's first trumpet and horn parts.

Recorder, oboe, and bassoon parts, like those for brass instruments, may have been the realm chiefly of professional specialists. But the transverse flute was popular with amateurs and might often have been played by students. Among the participants in the Collegium was the future diplomat and historian Jacob von Stählin, who reported playing flute duets with Bernhard Bach.[25] String parts, especially *ripieno* ones, might also have been taken by students, including Friedemann, who (probably)

22 "Sie theils emeriti, theils auch in keinem solchen exercitio sind, wie es wohl seyn solte," BD 1:61 (no. 22), trans. in NBR, 147 (no. 151).

23 See BD 2:251 (commentary to no. 352).

24 This is the well-known portrait of Bach reproduced in Figure 12.2. Reiche presumably wrote the fanfare himself; there is no reason to think that Bach was the composer, as argued by Altschuler (2001) on the basis of a few melodic formulas found also in Bach's works.

25 Stählin confused Bernhard, whom he called "the windy one" (*der Windige*), with his much younger brother Christian (BD 5:235 [no. C895b])

during 1726 and 1727 studied violin with Gottlieb Graun at nearby Merseburg.[26] Sebastian himself may also have played violin, even directing the ensemble in that way.[27] Of course Bach is also likely to have played keyboard parts, especially in concerts by the Collegium and in a dozen or so vocal works that include obbligato organ or harpsichord parts. But the appointed church organists might have been the usual players in Bach's cantatas, especially if they followed the same rules restricting access to the instruments that had governed Bach himself during his days as an organist.

There is only limited evidence for doubling of vocal parts in Bach's cantatas, and then only in the form of a single extra copy of each for a *ripieno* singer in several works. Images of Bach conducting a large chorus or presiding over the same from the organ of St. Thomas's or St. Nicholas's convey misconceptions of the nineteenth and twentieth centuries.[28] Bach wrote in the "Entwurff" of dividing the students of the St. Thomas School into four choirs, one for each of the city churches. He also described an ideal "musical choir" of at least twelve members. By choirs, however, he probably meant not the actual vocal complements used in particular compositions but rosters of performers that needed to be available in the respective churches for hymns, motets, and "music."[29] This last category included Bach's cantatas, performed under the composer's direction with members of the first choir. But these were not necessarily all singers; one of the prefects only played violin. The second choir also performed "musical church pieces" (*musicalische Kirchen Stücke*), but only simple ones that could be led by a prefect rather than Bach himself, and only on feast days.[30] Only original manuscript parts that survive

---

26 As documented by Falck (1913, 8).

27 That is, if Emanuel's recollection of his father's leading from a string part was in connection with church or collegium performances (BD 3:285 [no. 801]; NBR, 397 [no. 394]).

28 As argued by Parrott (2000) and Rifkin (2002), in part from a close reading of the "Entwurff." Rifkin (2012, 122–25) provides a close reading of the other principal verbal source, the 1723 Leipzig school regulations (facsimile in Schulze 1985c).

29 "sie theils musiciren, theils motetten und theils Chorale singen müßen," BD 1:60 (no. 22); NBR, 146 (no. 151).

30 Details about the direction and repertories of the first two choirs emerge from documents relating to the so-called Battle of the Prefects, discussed in Chapter 12; see especially BD 1:88 and 2:275 (nos. 34 and 383), trans. in NBR, 176 and 184 (nos. 183 and 186).

Figure 11.1   Page 1 from the bass voice part for Cantata 82, 1746 or 1747, copy begun by J. S. Bach and continued by his pupil and future son-in-law J. C. Altnickol (who likely sang the part himself). Bach's singers read from manuscript parts such as this, not printed vocal scores as in modern performances. Berlin, Staatsbibliothek, Mus. ms. Bach St 54, fascicle 4, from Bach-Digital.

for certain compositions provide evidence for the constitution of the ensembles used in actual performances of specific works (Figure 11.1).

It is from these sources that we know that Bach's ensembles at Leipzig were, on the whole, only slightly larger than those at Weimar and Cöthen. Performers may occasionally have shared parts, and some original performing parts have certainly been lost. Yet there is simply no evidence for the large ensembles, with multiple doubling singers and players, that became common in performances of Bach's vocal music during the nineteenth century. This applies to music in general from Bach's Germany, not only his own works. Indeed, it makes more sense and is eminently more practical even today to perform his challenging cantatas, concertos, and other works for public performance with as small an ensemble as can cover all the parts. This assures capable performance of every part and reduces the need for rehearsal. One must abandon the romantic effects that can be achieved by a massed chorus and orchestra, but one gains clarity and transparency, and the choir becomes an ensemble of soloists such as composers and listeners must have expected in Baroque Germany.

That this is how Bach understood his church music is clear from the not infrequent choral movements in which one or more of the four vocal parts have actual solos, sometimes in arioso or recitative style. Typical is the opening movement of Cantata 109, an unjustly neglected work from the composer's first autumn at Leipzig. Here each singer pleads both individually and as part of the group for strength in the face of unbelief (Example 11.1). The sources provide no evidence that the so-called concertists in such a movement were joined by ripienists in selected passages. Modern editions sometimes add markings to that effect, and one cannot prove that it was never done. But even in less dramatically conceived choruses, soloistic performance of each part allows Bach's musical rhetoric to emerge through singers' individual attention to such details as the precise articulation of high notes and melismas. Breathing, when worked out intelligently, divides each line into meaningful phrases.

Unfortunately it is impossible to reconstruct the precise dimensions and layouts of Bach's performing spaces within the Leipzig churches or the coffeehouses (where the collegia performed). We know that Bach's compositions were heard from lofts on the west (rear) wall of each of the two main churches, but modern accounts of seating arrangements for the musicians are largely hypothetical. What is clear is that the distinct architecture of the two main churches required performers to arrange themselves differently in each. Hence there could be no standard setup usable in every venue. Zimmermann's coffeehouse, although lacking the dimensions of a church, was sufficient for recurring performances involving at least four singers and an instrumental complement including trumpets and drums. Much grander than an ordinary tavern, it seems to have comprised a spacious double room with more than 130 square meters of floor space.[31]

---

31 That is, over 1,400 square feet, as reconstructed by Neumann (1960, 23n. 38a). The building that housed Zimmermann's coffeehouse no longer exists, but Hübner (2018) provides a color facsimile of the late nineteenth-century architectural plan. Over the years, the

Example 11.1   *Ich glaube, lieber Herr*, BWV 109, mvt. 1, mm. 58–64 (without horn, oboes, and strings):

Ich glaube, lieber Herr,   I believe, dear Lord,
hilf meinem Unglauben,   help my unbelief,

We lack information about what each musician—even Bach himself—did in the ensemble or how it was led, although Bach's sons and other pupils assisted in ways that may often have gone beyond copying and performing individual parts.[32] Rehearsals, if any, and even performances were probably informal by modern standards; concerts lacked printed programs and might have included improvisations by Bach and others. Emanuel Bach's later church and concert performances at Hamburg are somewhat better documented. If these followed the patterns of his father's practice, some performances might have been preceded by a single rehearsal that was open to interested spectators, but routine performances of church music might have had no rehearsal at all.[33] Yet it is difficult to understand how compositions of such unprecedented difficulty and complexity as Bach's could have been successfully presented without some sort of preliminary reading. Even a small ensemble of virtuosos, accustomed to his peculiar style and its demands, must have struggled. Some of the Collegium's performances might have been, in effect, open rehearsals of forthcoming church pieces. On high feast days, when Bach gave each cantata twice—first during the main morning service at St. Nicholas or St. Thomas, then at the afternoon Vespers service at the other church—the earlier performance might have served as a dress rehearsal for the later one.

The maintenance of harpsichords in both main churches has been taken as an indication that these were used in rehearsals if not performances of Bach's cantatas.[34] If so, Bach could have led at least the rehearsals from the

churches have been extensively remodeled; for architectural reconstructions, see Wolff (2000, 266–67), based in part on Stiehl (1984). Braatz (2009) gives a diagram that purports to show the dimensions of the organ and choir lofts at St. Nicholas's in 1750 (sources not identified).

32 Stählin mentioned Emanuel Bach's assistance in running the Collegium (BD 5:235 [no. C895b]).

33 For single rehearsals of Emanuel's major sacred works at Hamburg, see Schulenberg (2014, 257 and 303); for a public reading of his symphonies of 1776 prior to a concert performance, ibid. (184).

34 Bach certainly played harpsichord in the first performance of the *Trauerode* (BWV 198), as reported by the chronicler Sicul in 1727 (BD 2:175 [no. 232]; NBR, 136 [no. 136]), but that was a special performance of a commissioned work in the university church. The harpsichords at the two main city churches are documented by, for example, council minutes approving Bach's request for repairs to the harpsichord at St. Nicholas's (BD 2:140 [no. 180]; NBR, 116 [no. 115]).

keyboard, as he perhaps did at Weimar and Cöthen. Today one sometimes hears harpsichord as well as organ, not to mention one or more lutes, performing the continuo in Bach's vocal works, but there is little evidence that this was his own practice.[35] Yet someone as incurably creative as Bach is unlikely to have followed the same routine for more than a quarter of a century. Especially during the early years at Leipzig, he might have tried different approaches to the conduct of rehearsals and performances. Present-day harpsichordists attempting to direct ensembles as in eighteenth-century practice usually employ modern conducting technique, at least to begin and end movements. Bach is more likely to have led as a modern jazz musician would do, chiefly through aural cues—which would be clear to members of a small ensemble, particularly if played on the violin with what Emanuel described as a "penetrating" tone. When leading from the keyboard, Sebastian might have shared the direction of the ensemble with a solo singer or the principal violinist. Even recitatives could be managed without a conductor by attentive players immersed in the style (and following a copy of the vocal line included in their part), as is demonstrated today by modern specialist ensembles.

On the other hand, as a music director and Capellmeister in a hierarchic society, Bach probably enjoyed more absolute authority than most conductors today, particularly with respect to appointing and dismissing ensemble members and selecting repertory and soloists. He would not have expected his decisions to be questioned—whether by other musicians or a church consistory—even if the music proved unpopular or performers chafed under its demands. Yet decisions about personnel that Bach did not have to explain to anyone could have led to the perception that he played favorites. According to a posthumous report, he came to "hate" those students who tended toward the humanities over music—that is, the ones who were increasingly favored as the St. Thomas School evolved from its traditional role as a choir school into

---

35 The argument (in Dreyfus 1987) that the harpsichords were played frequently alongside the organ founders on the fact that in the rare instances where manuscript performing parts exist for both instruments in a single work, these cannot be shown to have been copied at the same time for the same occasion—as demonstrated by Melamed (1995, 195–96) for Bach's performances of the motet "Erforsche mich, Gott" by his predecessor Sebastian Knüpfer. Figured lute parts (for playing continuo) do not exist for any Bach works.

a more "enlightened" liberal-arts institution.[36] When, inevitably, Bach encountered resistance from his superiors on the city council or in the church hierarchy, he might not have understood its sources, maintaining an aristocratic disregard for the feelings of anyone who could not comprehend the music with which he inspired and edified the community.

Bach's Leipzig Vocal Music

The extent and chronology of Bach's Leipzig vocal music are better understood than for any other part of his output. Gaps remain in our knowledge; Table 11.1 provides an overview. The cantatas and motets are discussed in the remaining part of this chapter, other works in Chapter 13.

What the four main groups of vocal works—cantatas, passions, oratorios, and motets—have in common is that each composition was written for a specific occasion: a church service or some civic or private event. In many cases those attending these events could purchase printed librettos, usually provided by Bach himself—who therefore was responsible for selecting librettos and making the necessary arrangements with poets and printer well in advance, financing the publication himself and then recouping his costs through sales. This was probably a reliable source of income, as the number of congregants who purchased texts for church services is likely to have remained fairly stable. Many might have paid in advance through subscription, as was the case elsewhere.[37] Bach, however, may have needed to pay musicians from the proceeds of these sales, which therefore could have been one way to finance the larger ensembles needed during the Christmas season and other holiday periods. Then the meager funds provided by the city would have been insufficient.[38] Only a few libretto booklets for regular church services survive, but from these it appears that they were issued on a periodic basis, each containing texts for a number of weeks.[39]

36 "Bach fieng nun [ca. 1736–1737] an die Schüler zu hassen, die sich ganz auf Hunamiora legten," as Johann Friedrich Köhler later wrote (BD 3:214 [no. 820]), quoted by Rifkin (2012, 139).

37 This is how Telemann operated at Hamburg, as Bach must have known; see Zohn (2008, 345).

38 That subsidy amounted to just 12 Taler annually, according to Wolff (2000, 260).

39 Printed by Breitkopf, extant examples were listed by May (1996, 12), supplemented by Schabalina (2008) and others. Neumann (1974) provided editions of the church music texts known at the time, with facsimiles of the original libretto booklets.

Table 11.1   Bach's Leipzig Vocal Works

Church pieces (cantatas)

Some 150 works for Sundays and holidays, including a few known only from librettos

A dozen or so additional works for council election ceremonies and other special services

Serenatas, *drammi*, and the like (secular cantatas)

Over 40 documented works, many known only from librettos or sacred parodies

Passions and oratorios

St. John Passion, BWV 245

St. Matthew Passion, BWV 244

St. Mark Passion, BWV 247 (lost except for parodied movements)

Christmas Oratorio, BWV 248 (in six parts, each resembling a cantata)

Easter Oratorio, BWV 249 (originally a cantata, parody of a birthday *dramma*)

Ascension Oratorio, BWV 11

Motets

5 certain works, BWV 118, 225–27, and 229, possibly also BWV 230 and 231 (the latter partly an arrangement of music by Telemann)

Latin church music

B-Minor Mass, BWV 232

4 *missae* (Lutheran masses), BWV 233–36

5 Sanctus settings, BWV 237–41 (BWV 239–241 are Bach's arrangements of music by other composers; a third original Sanctus incorporated into BWV 232)

Magnificat, BWV 243

Several further works, some of them parodies or arrangements of music by other composers

Songs (lieder and chorales)

7 selections in the second Little Keyboard Book for Anna Magdalena Bach (1725), BWV 452 and 511–16

69 selections from Schemelli's "Musical Songbook" (1736), BWV 439–507 (mostly arrangements of songs by other composers)

200 or more four-part chorale harmonizations (in addition to those incorporated into cantatas and other works), including BWV 250–438

The printed librettos have proved valuable for dating individual works. But as a rule they do not even name the authors of the poems, leaving a huge gap in our understanding of Bach's vocal compositions. A few of these, particularly a series of church cantatas for the Christmas season of 1725–1726, used texts published a decade or more earlier by Franck, Lehms, and Neumeister. Some for the years 1724–1727 appear to be by Christoph Birkmann, a theology student at the Leipzig university during that period.[40]

Having settled on a libretto, Bach might have begun composing at once into a full score; there is little evidence of the type of sketching or preliminary drafts that later composers would take for granted.[41] It is possible that, in earlier stages of his career, Bach did first draft vocal works in some sort of short score, as his sons later did. Yet by the time he came to Leipzig, he was capable of composing a complex church piece directly into an ink full score. Once finished, the notes of the score had to be promptly copied into performing parts for the individual singers and players. Students and family members assisted in this, and individual parts reveal signs of Bach's proofreading or adding performance markings, including signs for dynamics, ornaments, and figured bass (rarely included in composing scores). But the parts also reveal occasional errors that went uncorrected; how these were dealt with in rehearsal and performance can only be conjectured.

The Church Cantatas

The Leipzig church cantatas make up the lion's share of Bach's surviving vocal works. They have received intense study since their publication during the nineteenth century in the old collected edition of Bach's works (the *Bachgesamtausgabe* or BG). There they appear in essentially random order, yet their numbering in that edition became the basis of Schmieder's twentieth-century list, so that Cantata 1 is also BWV 1. This particular work was actually the last of the chorale

---

40 Blanken (2015) showed that Birkmann later published an annual cycle of texts of which at least twenty-four were set by Bach, including that for the St. John Passion.

41 The standard study of Bach's compositional process in the cantatas remains Marshall (1972).

cantatas composed during Bach's second year at Leipzig (see below). It happens to be not only one of the most sumptuously scored but also one of the most beautiful of those works. Hence, although arbitrarily chosen, it served as a splendid opening number in the series of Bach's cantatas. When these compositions were first recorded with historical instruments in the early 1970s, Cantata 1 initiated the project with what seemed at the time a ravishingly beautiful reinterpretation of Bach's vocal music, even if the massed choral forces (and the horn playing) left something to be desired.

A more scientific approach to the cantatas had already been essayed by the nineteenth-century scholar Spitta, who endeavored to put them in chronological order by studying the watermarks in the paper on which Bach had written their composing manuscripts. Alas, a disastrous error led Spitta to place many of these works during the last decade of Bach's life. It was only in the 1950s that two German scholars, Dadelsen and Dürr, showed that, far from creating sacred vocal music at a fairly steady pace throughout his Leipzig period, Bach wrote most of the surviving compositions during his first few years there.[42] The implications of their "new" chronology have yet to be fully grasped by those who cling to a view of Bach as a church-bound pastor in tones, tirelessly composing music for services. The reality of his Leipzig activity was, as we have already seen, far more diverse.

Still, the main accomplishment of Bach's first Leipzig years was the series of masterpieces that he produced on an almost weekly basis for services at St. Nicholas and St. Thomas: at least 150 sacred works, most composed between mid-1723 and the end of 1726. The Leipzig church year included about sixty days on which "music," meaning a cantata, was required in the two principal churches. The majority of these cantatas were for regular Sunday services, but some were for holidays and saints' days, and a passion oratorio was required on Good Friday. Two penitential periods, Advent and Lent, saw a halt to elaborate church music for several weeks. But both were followed by holiday seasons that made particularly intense demands on Bach and his musicians, requiring

---

42 Spitta explained the basis for his dating of the crucial groups of cantatas in the appendix to his Bach biography (1873–1880, 2:830–38). This was corrected by Dadelsen (1958) and Dürr (1957, rev. 1976).

cantatas on the three consecutive days of Christmas and Easter (also at Pentecost). The Sundays after those holidays also required cantatas, as did New Year's Day. Thus, during Bach's first year at Leipzig, five works had to be prepared for the nine-day period December 25–January 2, as well as for Epiphany and the Sunday after *that* (January 6 and 9). Bach repeated an earlier cantata for Christmas Day itself, as he had done on the first Sunday in Advent, but he also composed a new Sanctus and revised his Magnificat for performance during Christmas Vespers. The following Christmas season again required seven cantatas, all but one of which was new.

In light of such demands—on both himself and the musicians—it is not surprising that Bach did not always perform new compositions. Some works, especially during his first twelve months at Leipzig, were revisions of compositions previously written for Weimar or Cöthen. Gaps in the known sequence of new works might have been filled by lost compositions or by the music of other composers. Thus, during his third year, Bach made manuscript copies of cantatas by his Meiningen cousin Johann Ludwig Bach, using them for no fewer than seventeen Sundays and other occasions.[43] Doing so spared Bach the creative effort of new composition, but even a reperformance might require the preparation of new performing parts. Some Weimar works had to be entirely rewritten and their parts recopied due to differences in performing pitch. Adaptations of secular compositions required the creation of parody texts, which had to be precisely fitted to the existing music. The term does not imply any satiric intention; rather it refers to an accepted practice that went back at least to the Renaissance. A typical instance occurs in Cantata 173, originally a birthday serenade for Prince Leopold; the reworking included the expansion of a duet into a chorus, with new sacred words (Example 11.2).

Creating a parody text required some ingenuity on the part of the anonymous librettist, as well as careful editing of the existing score and the creation of new performing parts. Bach's adaptations of earlier music therefore were not necessarily undertaken to save time. Rather they could have been inspired by the desire not to see existing compositions

43 One of these, the Easter cantata *Denn du wirst meine Seele*, was mistakenly included in the BG and therefore is listed as BWV 15.

Example 11.2   (a) *Durchlauchster Leopold,* BWV 173a, mvt. 8, mm. 17–20, with (b) *Erhöhtes Fleisch und Blut,* BWV 173, mvt. 6, mm. 17–20, both: voices only (without flute and strings):

Nimm auch, grosser Fürst, uns auf   Elevate us as well, great prince,

Rühre, Höchster, unsern Geist,   Move, Almighty One, our spirit,

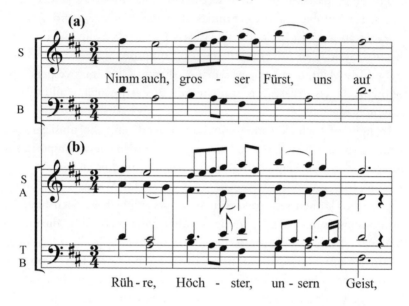

go to waste. Original texts honoring princely birthdays and the like had no use at Leipzig, but Bach evidently valued his settings of such poetry sufficiently to want to use them again. He may also have wished to honor the work of J. L. Bach and other older composers, even if their music seems pale by comparison with his own. It may even be, as was true of Emanuel Bach later at Hamburg, that his father wished to give his listeners an opportunity to hear rare compositions from what seemed distant places or the remote past. This was a novel aim at a time when few traveled outside their native region, and music history extended back in time no further than the personal memories and experiences of living musicians.[44]

---

44 During the 1780s Emanuel led a series of concerts that offered listeners the "opportunity to hear the various styles in the works of the famous composers in question," including J. S. Bach himself (from a contemporaneous review; see Schulenberg 1992, 15).

Scholars have sorted the extant sacred cantatas into as many as five annual cycles, following a claim in Bach's Obituary.[45] If he really composed
five complete cycles, many works are lost. But it has never been clear
how thoroughly or consistently Bach assigned individual cantatas to a
particular annual cycle (*Jahrgang*).[46] The second cycle is the best-defined,
comprising only chorale cantatas. The fourth cycle would have been
based on texts by Picander,[47] but the first and third cycles cannot be so
readily characterized. Only the first two cycles were composed (largely)
within single twelve-month spans. Work on the third cycle was spread
out over a two-year period, as seems to have been the case with the few
extant cantatas belonging to the fourth cycle (their dates are less certain).
If there was a fifth cycle, it has left few traces, although Bach continued
to compose individual cantatas almost until the end of his life, sometimes
to fill gaps in the existing cycles, sometimes perhaps for other reasons.

Bach's creative work at Leipzig, and therefore on each cycle, began
with the Sunday after Trinity. This, depending on the date of Easter, fell
somewhere between May 17 and June 20. Officially, however, the church
year began with the first Sunday in Advent, four weeks before Christmas.
Thus Bach commenced work close to the midpoint of the liturgical year,
and whether he initially intended his first Leipzig cantatas to constitute
parts of an annual cycle is unknown. There are indications that, as he
entered his new position, Bach intended to perform the equivalent of *two*
cantatas at each service, one before the sermon, another afterward, during
communion. Sometimes the same purpose was fulfilled by a single long
work divided into two halves, like those for his first two Sundays at
Leipzig (BWV 75 and 76). On a few subsequent occasions he performed

45 The Obituary reported that Bach wrote five annual cycles of cantatas "for all Sundays and
holidays" (*auf alle Sonn- und Festtage*), as well as five passions (BD 3:86 [no. 666]; NBR, 304
[no. 306]), but we have clear evidence for only three examples of each.

46 The main documentary evidence for the organization of these works into annual cycles is
the way in which their manuscript scores and parts were divided after Bach's death, items
belonging to a given cycle being inherited by one or another of the surviving family
members. Thus Friedemann Bach received the scores of the chorale cantatas, whereas Anna
Magdalena received their performing parts, later selling them to the St. Thomas School.
Wolff (2000, 458–59) summarizes the findings of Kobayashi (1989).

47 Hofmann (2002, 74) proposed further that the "Picander-Jahrgang" consisted chiefly of
parodies, but the conjecture cannot be confirmed or refuted based on what is known.

a shorter new work together with a revised version of an old one.[48] But Bach soon abandoned this plan, and it is unknown whether he performed two pieces of "music" on every occasion, although there would continue to be days when more than one cantata or other piece was performed as part of a single service. Thus July 2, 1723, saw both the first version of the Magnificat as well as a revised version of the Weimar cantata BWV 147. Christmas that year saw new versions of the Magnificat and of the early cantata BWV 63, as well as a new Sanctus (BWV 238).

By 1723, when Bach started work at Leipzig, Telemann had already created at least five complete annual cycles of cantatas, each united by a common librettist or some other thematic idea. If Bach ever compared himself wistfully to Telemann, he must have recognized that the latter's sacred works, however attractive and even usable for the occasional performance at Leipzig, embodied more limited aspirations than his own.[49] It is possible that, apart from the series of chorale cantatas, Bach never saw a *Jahrgang* as anything more than a pragmatic selection of compositions that could be performed over the course of a year. If so, a series of such works did not need to follow any particular organizing scheme and might even incorporate music by other composers, just as it might include poetry by various authors. On the other hand, it is also possible that Bach, upon his arrival at Leipzig, meant to incorporate his existing vocal music into a complete annual cycle, which would have been rounded out over the next twelve months. In fact, during that time he repeated the majority of his known vocal compositions from Weimar and Cöthen— at least twenty-six cantatas—while composing some thirty new works. But the diverse character of these compositions meant that the resulting cycle, if such it was, followed no particular design, nor was it made up of any particular type of cantata.

Bach clearly emulated Telemann only once, when, during his second year at Leipzig, he set out to produce an entire year's worth of cantatas on

---

48 Thus on June 20, 1723, he performed the relatively unpretentious BWV 24 as well as a lightly revised version of the Weimar cantata BWV 185. The dates given here and below for individual cantatas are from Dürr (2005), occasionally updated by subsequent research.

49 Bach performed at least several of Telemann's sacred works at Leipzig, some in his own adaptations; among these were BWV 160 and movements from BWV 145, both erroneously included in the BG alongside other spurious cantatas (BWV 53, 141, 142, 189, and 217–20).

a consistent basis, basing text and music of each work on a single chorale. Although possibly inspired by the annual cycles of sermons produced by some pastors, this was a novel way of organizing a musical *Jahrgang*. The forty-odd such works that Bach produced during 1724–1725 are often regarded as the pinnacle of his output. Each is unique, yet as a group they reflect a design that must have been decided ahead of time in conjunction with a sympathetic librettist. Each work opens with an elaborate choral setting of the first stanza of a particular chorale, employing both traditional words and melody. Subsequent recitatives and arias may quote or paraphrase further stanzas, but usually it is only at the end of the cantata that an entire chorale stanza is again presented integrally, now in a "simple" four-part harmonization.

If Bach subsequently set out to write a further cycle of cantatas according to some other plan, as by setting an entire year's worth of Picander's poetry, he did not get very far, to judge from the eleven works based on the latter that survive.[50] It is possible, however, to speculate further. Recurring patterns among the cantatas of the first and third cycles suggest that some of these could have been envisioned as parts of a *Jahrgang* of works that each open with a grand choral setting of a bible verse. Others might have been meant for a series of compositions comprising music for soloists, like the cantatas in Telemann's *Harmonischer Gottesdienst* (published serially during the same period that saw the beginning of Bach's third cycle). When composing a new work for a day of the church year for which he had previously written a cantata, Bach sometimes did so in a way that would assure variety from one year to the next. But this was not always the case,[51] and any plans to produce a coherent cycle other than the one containing

---

50 Two of these (BWV 197a and Anh. 190) are fragmentary. The idea of a "Picander *Jahrgang*" is based on the poet's praise for "the sweetness of the incomparable Capellmeister Bach" in setting his poetry ("die Lieblichkeit des unvergleichlichen Herrn Capell-Meisters, Bachs," from the preface to his *Cantaten auf die Sonn- und Fest-Tage durch das gantze Jahr*, published in 1728; extract in BD 2:180 [no. 243]). That Bach had actually made musical settings of the entire volume is not clearly stated, and it is more likely that Picander was merely expressing a hope that this might be so.

51 For instance, both works for Cantate Sunday (BWV 166 and 108) open with solo settings of bible verses in aria style. All the cantatas for the Sundays after New Year's and Epiphany are "solo" cantatas, although this could reflect a desire to reduce the need to write and rehearse more elaborately scored works immediately after major feast days.

the chorale cantatas fell by the wayside. Even the series of chorale cantatas included, in the end, no more than fifty-three of the fifty-nine or sixty works needed for an annual cycle at Leipzig.[52] Why Bach broke off work on the series in spring 1725 is unknown; the death or departure from Leipzig of his anonymous librettist is the most commonly suggested reason.

What we have is nevertheless an astonishing sequence of ambitious vocal works that Bach produced on average once every two weeks over a period of six years—one every eight days during 1723–1725. During those first twenty-four months, through some combination of heated creative inspiration and unflagging physical energy, Bach created about seventy-seven new works while also repeating at least twenty-eight older ones, sometimes in substantially revised forms. After a hiatus of about two months, he then produced at least fifty further works from July 1725 through August 1729.[53] Although in principle modeled on earlier cantatas such as Telemann's, Bach's were unprecedented in the complexity of their counterpoint and scoring. The sheer number of notes written on sheets of paper must have vastly exceeded that of any earlier cantata cycle, to say nothing of the creative labor that these required from both Bach and his singers and players.

Taken as a whole, the vocal works of 1723–1729 present a unique opportunity within Bach's output to view his progress from week to week in the development of a series of precisely dated compositions. Within the first annual cycle it is probably the choral movements that stand out, as in the expressive opening chorus of Cantata 46. Like many opening movements in this series, it sets two successive clauses of a psalm verse in a form somewhat resembling a prelude and fugue (Example 11.3a–b). The initial chorale choruses of the second cycle are, if anything, even more impressive and ingenious, as in the adoption of French chaconne style to set the chorale melody "Jesu, der du meine Seele" in the popular BWV 78 (Example 11.4). The third cycle includes a number of works

---

52 The total number of chorale cantatas includes twelve subsequently composed works as well as the early Cantata 4. Telemann's published collections, which include works for Advent and Lent, comprise over seventy compositions for each year.

53 These totals are for church cantatas only, including council election cantatas but not passions and secular works.

Example 11.3a   *Schauet doch und sehet*, BWV 46, mvt. 1, mm. 17–23:

Schauet doch und sehet, ob irgend
ein Schmerz sei wie mein Schmerz,

Look and see if there be any
sorrow like my sorrow,

Example 11.3b *Schauet doch und sehet,* BWV 46, mvt. 1, mm. 67–78:

Denn der Herr hat mich voll Jammers
gemacht am Tage seines grimmigen

For the lord has made me full of anguish
on the day of his fierce anger,

Example 11.4 *Jesu, der du meine Seele,* BWV 78, mvt. 1, (a) opening of ritornello (mm. 1–5); (b) first vocal phrase (mm. 17–20):

Jesu, der du meine Seele, Jesus, you who [have rescued] my soul,

for just one or two solo voices, including two complementary cantatas for bass, BWV 56 and 82. The first of these opens with a harsh fugal aria; the second includes a "sleep" aria modeled on slumber scenes from French opera (Example 11.5).[54] Other works from the third cycle, such

54 A version of this aria arranged for soprano and continuo appears in Anna Magdalena's second music book.

Example 11.5 (a) *Ich will den Kreuzstab gerne tragen*, BWV 56, mvt. 1, mm. 17–20 (the subject, sung here by the bass, is subsequently imitated by viola and second violin); (b) *Ich habe genung*, BWV 82, mvt. 3, mm. 10–11, without later cello part:

Ich will den Kreuzstab gerne tragen   I wish to bear the cross-staff gladly

Schlummert ein, ihr matten Augen,   Fall asleep, you tired eyes,

as Cantata 49, incorporate obbligato organ as a solo instrumental part alongside the solo voices.

Looking more closely at individual works within the first *Jahrgang*, one finds, in addition to works opening with grand or expressive *dictum* choruses based on bible verses (BWV 69a, 40; 105, 48), several remarkably dramatic "solo" or dialog cantatas (BWV 60, 90). Toward the end of his first twelve-year period, Bach relied on parodies of earlier works from Weimar and Cöthen, as he had done at the beginning.[55] But these were interspersed with the first version of the St. John Passion, performed on Good Friday, as well as BWV 67, which has been called "one of [Bach's] greatest and most original cantatas."[56] Bach must have remembered with particular fondness its unusual penultimate movement, a dialog between solo bass and the three other voices ("Friede sei mit euch"), for he later reworked it as the Gloria of the A-Major Mass (BWV 234).

Expressive designs leading from "negative" to "positive" feeling probably occur in the majority of these works, but not every cantata traces an emotional transformation. At the end of July 1723 Bach composed Cantata 105, arguably the first truly great work among these Leipzig compositions. Its text opens with the foreboding psalm verse "Do not bring your servant into judgment" (Ps. 143:2); Bach sets this in a manner that anticipates the opening movement of the St. John Passion. A plaintive soprano aria follows, then a confident bass aria, with solo horn. Yet the work ends in a dark chorale setting, fading away at the end.

Bach must have selected the text and planned his compositional work for each cantata well ahead of time, even if the actual writing out of score and parts took place only in a burst of activity a few days before they were needed. There is nevertheless a certain ad hoc appearance to Bach's output of vocal music during the first twelve months at Leipzig. At some point, however, he must have begun contemplating the creation of a truly integrated collection of church pieces for a full year's worth of

---

55 Bach used parodies or revised versions of BWV 21, 147, and 186 during June and July 1723, and of BWV 173, 184, and 165 a year later, just before commencing the second annual cycle. Palm Sunday and Easter saw the Weimar cantatas BWV 182 and 31, with Cantata 12 following three weeks later. Bach also repeated BWV 59, probably composed the previous year for performance in the university church, at Pentecost.

56 Dürr (2005, 293).

cantatas. This would have required hitting upon some general organizing principle and finding a sympathetic librettist. Discussions toward this end might have occupied Bach for some time before he commenced work on the first in the new cycle of chorale cantatas, performed on the Sunday after Trinity 1724 (June 11).

In the chorale cantatas, the entire libretto is derived from the text of a single hymn. Typically, the opening and closing movements use verbatim statements of the first and last stanzas. In addition, the intervening recitatives and arias often quote or paraphrase lines from other stanzas of the poem. The melody traditionally associated with the poem also recurs in the outer movements. The first movement takes the form of a large chorale fantasia, with ritornellos framing choral statements of the successive phrases of the hymn. The work closes with a "simple" four-part harmonization of the same melody. Internal movements may also incorporate quotations or paraphrases of phrases from the melody. Bach and his librettist (or librettists) followed this plan for some thirty-four weeks, producing at least forty chorale cantatas.[57]

These constituted Bach's most ambitious sustained project—for many, his greatest collective work. As insignificant as congregational song may seem to present-day secular listeners, it was a vital element in the musical and spiritual culture of the time and an important part of Bach's job as cantor. To compose a cycle of chorale cantatas was not only a logical extension of Bach's compilations of keyboard chorale settings; it also reflected the practice of pastors in writing commentaries and sermon cycles on hymns.[58] Certain movements composed during Bach's first year at Leipzig proved to be prototypes for what became regular elements in works of the second. In the large opening choruses, comparable to the big organ chorale fantasias, one voice, usually the soprano, sings a hymn tune as a cantus firmus in long notes. The three other voices may provide a simple harmonization, but usually they have more animated lines, developing the phrases of the chorale melody in imitative counterpoint.

---

57 The total includes BWV 1, which was not performed until Palm Sunday (toward the end of Lent), almost six weeks after the last regularly scheduled cantata, BWV 127.

58 As suggested by Rathey (2012), who points to a series of chorale compositions by Schelle, one of Bach's predecessors as Thomaskantor; these were meant to recall a series of sermons on the chorales by the Leipzig pastor Carpzov.

Meanwhile the instruments provide ritornellos and a contrapuntal accompaniment for the voices.

In the first four works of the cycle, these opening choruses reveal a deliberate pattern. The first one initiates the series by taking the form of a French overture in which the chorale melody appears in the soprano part; a week later, the alto had the tune. The tenor did so in the cantata for St. John's Day, then the bass on the third Sunday after Trinity, which in 1724 came just one day later. Thereafter Bach followed no such pattern; even within this initial group of four works, his chief aim, as in other sets, seems to have been diversity. Thus, whereas the first work (BWV 20) began with an overture, the next cantata, BWV 2, opened with a chorale motet. The first movement of Cantata 7 is a more typical chorale fantasia, but with ritornellos in the style of a violin concerto.[59]

Despite its restriction to chorale cantatas, the second *Jahrgang* probably outdoes the works of the first year in the diversity of its textures. This is true especially of the opening movements, which routinely involve counterpoint in seven or more parts, often developing three or more distinct thematic ideas simultaneously. For instance, the opening ritornello of Cantata 127, composed at the end of the series, combines the first phrase of the chorale melody with a motive in "dotted" rhythm— the rhythm of a French overture, which here might reflect one of the cantata's theological themes, that of rulership or majesty. There is also a third motive which, exceptionally, is taken from another chorale melody, the Lutheran Agnus Dei ("O Lamm Gottes").[60] During the ritornello the three ideas are combined in triple counterpoint, cycling between the oboes, recorders, and strings, respectively.

Not every work in the cycle is equally grand or complex. Bach used a relatively simple type of opening movement in the compositions for Epiphany and several succeeding Sundays after the Christmas 1724 season.

---

59 One might suppose a solo instrument to be an apt metaphor for John the Baptist, whose feast day it was, but Bach had included similar ritornellos in the opening movement of Cantata 83, performed some four months earlier for Purification. He would repeat the concerto idea three months later in Cantata 99, there with two solo parts (flute and oboe).

60 Another composition with two cantus firmi is Cantata 10, although that work, based on the German Magnificat, is a special case: it uses the *tonus peregrinus* in the opening movement, then derives the theme of the first aria from another of the chant formulas used for intoning the Magnificat text.

Even there, however, Bach's imaginative scoring could inspire delightful pictorial associations, as when a woodwind choir of two flutes and two oboes d'amore provides a pastoral setting of the chorale in BWV 123.[61] On the other hand, Bach sometimes persists in maintaining a striking melodic or harmonic pattern that is not beautiful or pleasant in conventional terms; this can produce an effect of vehemence, even hectoring. The opening ritornello of BWV 101 settles on a dissonant melodic figure that accompanies nearly every phrase of the chorale. The latter is a prayer for delivery from "harsh strife and great need" (*schwere Strafe und große Not*), but Bach focuses on the "negative" words "strife" and "need."

September and October 1724 saw the composition of what are now some of the most highly regarded of these cantatas. Seven of the ten new works performed during these months include challenging solo flute parts.[62] BWV 78, composed for September 10, may be the most frequently anthologized of all Bach's cantatas. Here, continuing the exploration of diverse genres in the opening choral movements, Bach begins the work with a passacaglia or chaconne (see Example 11.4). The duet that follows is a favorite with modern audiences, in part because of the pizzicato violone part, reminiscent of a jazz rhythm section.[63]

For the next five months Bach continued to write new works for almost every Sunday and holiday, all but a few of them indisputable masterpieces. Good Friday 1725 saw Bach's second version of the St. John Passion, updated to open with a chorale fantasia movement and thus, apparently, intended to be part of the chorale cantata cycle. Twelve new cantatas followed, but only two, BWV 68 and 128, open with chorale choruses, and subsequent movements in those cantatas do not derive from the same hymns. Evidently the collaboration that had produced the chorale cantatas had ended. Bach would ultimately write about a dozen further chorale cantatas, but most of these use the chorale text *per omnes versus* ("through all verses"), as in the early Cantata 4. Such works must

---

61 Bach would use similar scoring, with the addition of two tenor oboes, in Part 2 of the Christmas Oratorio.

62 BWV 78, 99, 8, 130, 114, 96, 180. BWV 96 and 180 also call for recorders, but not in the same movements as the flute. At least in BWV 96, for which Bach's original parts survive, it is clear that these instruments had separate players, as was evidently true also for one version of BWV 8 (see Rifkin 1989, 5–6).

63 Bach added the plucked double bass part for a later performance around 1740.

have fulfilled ambitions somewhat different from those that had originally inspired the chorale cantata cycle. Perhaps they resulted from the same urge to create pedagogical or exemplary compositions that apparently inspired other late compositions.[64]

Nine cantatas from spring 1725 are on texts by Mariane von Ziegler, Bach's only female librettist. They are often regarded as among the slighter of Bach's cantatas, yet they include several powerful, imaginative works. Among these is the first, BWV 103, an ambitious composition that opens with a dramatically conceived chorus. Here a solo part for *flauto piccolo* (a high recorder) seems to represent the "weeping and wailing" of the text. By the end, however, the instrument could just as well symbolize the "gladness" into which these plaints have been transformed (John 16:20).

Bach seems eventually to have grouped the Ziegler cantatas written in the weeks after Easter 1725 with his third annual cycle. But instead of commencing work on the latter immediately after Trinity Sunday, he departed from Leipzig on a trip to Gera, leaving performances at Leipzig in other hands. Upon his return he must have deliberately adopted a less intensive approach to cantata composition, despite the failure to have completed the cycle of chorale cantatas. This implies that he had found no new regular collaborator for the librettos. Not until fall 1726, and again during the first half of 1729 (when he wrote most of the known Picander settings), would Bach produce new cantatas at anything like the pace of the first two years at Leipzig.

A special feature of the works in Bach's third annual cycle is the prominence of so-called solo cantatas, without choral movements. Another is the re-use of music originally written for instruments alone, now incorporated into vocal compositions. For Cantata 110, performed at Christmas 1725, Bach added voices and wind parts to the overture of the Fourth Orchestral Suite (BWV 1069). The resulting overture-chorus recalls the opening movements of Cantatas 61 and 20, which were new compositions in the form of a French overture. Now, however, Bach added vocal parts to an existing instrumental piece, and the near future

---

64 Pfau (2015) provides evidence that four of these, BWV 97, 100, 117, and 192, were composed around 1730 for a special commission from Weissenfels, where Bach's music had been in demand since the early Hunt Cantata.

would see similar manipulations of movements from concertos and, possibly, a sonata.

The most famous instance of this occurs in BWV 146, composed for the third Sunday after Easter (Jubilate), although the year is uncertain.[65] The gospel reading for this day, on the transformation of sorrow into joy (John 16:16–23), had previously brought forth exceptional efforts from Bach, including Cantatas 12 and 103. Here the idea of "tribulation," perhaps expressed by the opening instrumental movement or sinfonia in D minor, is certainly symbolized by the second movement. The sinfonia is a straightforward arrangement of the first movement of the work known to us as the D-minor harpsichord concerto, substituting organ as the solo instrument. The following chorus reworks the second movement of the concerto, adding four voices to what was already a harmonically complex, darkly expressive Adagio.

Ingenious as this is, artistically the most successful of these works may be Cantata 49, which Bach performed on November 3, 1726. Its opening sinfonia, again with solo organ, is the concluding Allegro of the concerto on which Bach had drawn for the first two movements of Cantata 169, performed two weeks earlier. But unlike that work (a solo cantata for alto), BWV 49 is a dialog for soprano and bass.

Cantata 49 followed by one week the work for bass singer alone that might be Bach's best-known solo cantata, BWV 56. Cantata 56 is sometimes known as the "Kreuzstab" cantata, after the nautical instrument mentioned in its first line. That line was paraphrased from an earlier text by Neumeister, previously set by Telemann.[66] Bach incorporates the word into a fugue subject, stated respectively by voice, viola, and the two violin parts; the strings are doubled by oboes to produce a dark if not harsh sound appropriate to the text and the dissonant contrapuntal texture (see Example 11.5a).

---

65 As Dürr (2005, 314) argued, the most likely year is 1726, but 1727 and 1728 are also possibilities; the loss of original sources makes dating conjectural.

66 The *Kreuzstab* or cross-staff was a predecessor of the sextant; the likely librettist Birkmann, who wrote a dissertation on geometry, would have taken a professional interest in it. Neither he nor Bach is likely to have known Telemann's early cantata TWV 1:884, whose text by Neumeister uses the same nautical imagery. But they could have known Neumeister's poem, published in 1702 and reprinted in 1717 (see Poetzsch-Seban 2006, 280).

More conventionally beautiful than BWV 56 is Bach's second solo cantata for bass, BWV 82, heard about three months later on February 2, 1727. This must have been a favorite for Bach, who subsequently arranged it for soprano, substituting flute for the original oboe, which plays as a soloist alongside the singer.[67] Could the soprano version have been for a performance by Anna Magdalena, undertaken somewhere other than in the Leipzig churches? Her 1725 music book contains a shortened version of the famous aria "Schlummert ein," modeled on the slumber arias of Baroque opera; here it expresses the world-weariness typical of German sacred works. Sebastian evidently repeated this cantata in his last years, refining the organist's continuo part and adding an oboe da caccia.

Bach's subsequent cantatas on texts by Picander, although few in number, include similarly intimate compositions alongside large-scale works, the latter resembling the secular works on which the two also collaborated. The best known of these cantatas is probably BWV 156, a smaller work famous for its opening sinfonia, which was taken (probably) from a lost oboe concerto.[68] None of the few surviving sacred cantatas from after 1729 is on a text by Picander. The best known are two works that are as unlike as one could imagine, yet both were probably composed during the following two years. Cantata 51 resembles the solo motets that Vivaldi, Hasse, and others had been supplying for Catholic services at Dresden and elsewhere. BWV 140, on the other hand, is a chorale cantata, written in 1731 for the twenty-seventh Sunday after Trinity. This was a rare day in the church year that had not occurred since 1704 and would come only one more time during Bach's lifetime, in 1742.

Scored for solo soprano, trumpet, and strings, Cantata 51 lacks a specific liturgical assignment. Although possibly heard at Leipzig in

---

67 Bach may originally have conceived the cantata for alto, for, in his autograph composing score (Berlin, Staatsbibliothek, Mus. ms. Bach P 114), the vocal part in the first movement is written in alto clef; a note at the bottom of the first page dictates transposing it down an octave for bass. References to a version for mezzo-soprano are to a manuscript copy of the voice part that Bach converted back to the original C minor: he altered the key signature and changed the clef to the rarely used mezzo-soprano clef, also adding the word *mezo* [*sic*] to the original heading *Soprano* (in the hand of his pupil J. L. Krebs). The part never ranges above Bach's usual alto tessitura.

68 As established by Rifkin (1978); see also Rifkin (1983).

1730, it might have originated earlier.[69] One attractive idea, unfortunately without any documentary basis, is that Bach wrote it for Anna Magdalena and one of her trumpet-playing relatives. Nevertheless, the unusually high soprano part does imply performance somewhere other than in the Leipzig churches, as do the unique forms of the text and the individual movements. Particularly spectacular are the opening aria, a da capo form with an old-fashioned one-line reprise, and the concluding "Alleluja," which takes the form of a five-part fugue.

Whereas BWV 51 was probably composed for some special occasion, Bach wrote Cantata 140 in the course of his regular duties during fall 1731. A chorale cantata, BWV 140 shares the hallmarks of the most ambitious works of the second *Jahrgang*. Thus, for example, the opening chorale fantasia movement expands the ninth phrase of Nicolai's famous hymn ("Wachet auf") into a little fugue on the word *alleluia*. The ensuing duet for soprano and bass, alluding to the spiritual marriage celebrated in the Song of Songs, is perhaps Bach's most sensual movement of this type, accompanied by what may be his most ornately yet effortlessly florid violin part.[70]

Secular Cantatas

Even before 1730, Bach may have been putting less time and energy into new church works than into the "dramas," serenatas, and other works known today as secular cantatas. The few that survive, some fragmentarily, are remnants of a larger group of compositions that Bach created for various events. Many are known only from librettos or other documents, and musical traces of some survive in parody movements that Bach incorporated into other works; it is unclear how many complete compositions have been lost.[71] The distinction between sacred and

---

69 Bach at some point gave the work a title page indicating performance on the fifteenth Sunday after Trinity. That could have been September 17, 1730, but the first movement in his autograph score (Berlin, Staatsbibliothek, Mus. ms. Bach P 104) is a fair copy, implying an earlier origin.

70 Similar solo violin writing recurs, albeit to very different affect, in the aria "Ach, nun ist mein Jesu hin" which opens Part 2 of the St. Matthew Passion. An account of the duet in BWV 140 that represents the soprano as "whining" (McClary 1987, 53) is anachronistic; despite their distinct texts, the two dialoguing voices mostly share the same melodic ideas, neither being characterized musically as either strong ("male") or weak ("female").

71 The exact numbers are a matter of definition, but whereas Bach is known to have supplied music for close to fifty occasions during his Leipzig years (outside of regular church services), only seventeen works are fully extant, another dozen partly reconstructible.

secular cantatas is hardly airtight; a "secular" libretto for a wedding or for a ruler might employ religious language, and although they contain no full-fledged fugues, the secular works otherwise hardly differ in musical style. A composition used for one purpose could be readily adapted for another, as when portions of the 1725 birthday music for Duke Christian became a cantata for Easter a few weeks later and ultimately the Easter Oratorio.

Adaptations usually went from secular to sacred, if only because a sacred text was more likely to be used for more than a single performance. The low survival rate of Bach's secular vocal compositions stems in part from the ephemeral nature of their occasions, but it must also reflect the fact that Bach transformed many into sacred works—something he could have anticipated doing even as he composed the original, secular versions. To turn such a composition into a church piece, he needed to commission a new text, then make the minor revisions necessary for fitting the words of the arias and choruses into his existing score. He would also replace the recitatives and perhaps add a chorale harmonization at the end. Any unused music, especially simple recitatives, might simply have been discarded.

From the composer's point of view, the chief distinction between a secular and a sacred cantata was the absence of chorales and the tendency of choruses to follow aria or dance forms, not fugue or some other increasingly archaic design. The greatest number of the known secular works can be called "homage" cantatas, resembling the compositions written at Cöthen for the ruler's birthday and New Year celebrations. At Leipzig Bach wrote "homage" works for Duke Christian and several lesser aristocrats, but most were for the ruling elector and members of his family. Five of these survive intact out of at least thirteen that Bach is known to have composed.

Another dozen or so works can be designated "congratulatory" or "commemorative" cantatas for individuals or institutions, as when Bach provided music to celebrate the appointment of a university professor or the opening of the renovated St. Thomas School building. Cantatas for wedding celebrations constitute another group, as do the annual council election cantatas, although the latter, performed within formal church services, are usually counted as sacred works. Bach presumably provided music for all twenty-seven of the annual election services that took place during his time in Leipzig, but only six compositions survive. We have even fewer cantatas (five) for weddings, although like the election services some of these events might have involved repeats of existing works. Just three cantatas cannot be attributed to any special commission or occasion and might have been composed on Bach's own initiative for performance by the Collegium Musicum; among these was the famous Coffee Cantata.

There was not much difference, poetically or musically, between a "homage" piece for a ruler and a "congratulatory" or "commemorative" cantata. Bach's music for the rededication of the school building on June 5, 1732, does not survive, but the poem by his colleague Winckler falls into two parts, meant respectively to be sung before and after a spoken address (*Rede*). Its design thus resembles that of a two-part church cantata, framing a sermon. Whereas a church cantata might have lauded God, Winckler's poem repeats the praises of the "fathers of our city of linden trees"[72]—that is, the Leipzig city council, who doubtless were in attendance and whose authority over the school was thus underlined.

Such a composition was, then, a political work, written to a libretto by a highly placed member of the city community in praise of and to encourage submission to higher authorities. The choruses with trumpets and drums that open many of these compositions symbolize grandeur and power through the same musical imagery used in sacred cantatas for triumphal feast days. Indeed, identical music might be used, as when Bach formed his Christmas Oratorio largely out of music previously composed to honor the elector and his family. A few of those congratulatory works were performed publicly for the ruler himself; a greater number, to judge from newspaper announcements, were presented by the Collegium Musicum as concert pieces, constituting expressions of loyalty rather than direct homage. Those celebrating weddings and other private events presumably were performed in the homes of the well-off local families that commissioned them.

Bach could receive more than 50 Taler—half his annual base salary—on the most lavish of these occasions. Out of that, however, he presumably had to pay for expenses—everything from paper and instrument

---

72 "Väter unsrer Linden-Stadt," from the printed libretto (edited online on Bach-Digital).

transport to fees for the performers.[73] It is unknown whether Sebastian charged more when he supplied original music, as Emanuel would do at Hamburg. If so, many private patrons were probably content to have Bach repeat something that had been heard previously, and this could explain why so few distinct wedding and congratulatory pieces survive.[74] Bach seems to have written only a few secular cantatas during the first years at Leipzig, when he was pressed to supply works for the church. The greatest number are documented from the years 1725–1736, the best-known ones falling toward the end of the period or even later.

Among these are the "Coffee" and "Peasant" cantatas, as well as the satirical work entitled *Der Streit zwischen Phoebus und Pan* (The Contest of Apollo and Pan, BWV 201). All three reveal Bach as a comedian, as when he has the violins "paint" the donkey ears pinned by the poet onto a philistine judge, who has praised a mediocre performance by the forest god Pan (Example 11.6). The famous Coffee Cantata is less scathing, although it too is a satire, good-naturedly pointing up the young Lieschen's reaction to caffeine as well as her father's stolidness, the latter represented by a pedantic continuo aria (Example 11.7). Bach gave himself a quasi-solo role in Lieschen's last aria in the form of an elaborated version of the continuo part for the harpsichord (Example 11.8).

These works belong to a larger group of dramatic and moralizing cantatas, all on librettos by Picander. Cantata 204, the earliest of these, is on the theme of moderation in life; in this, as in its setting for solo soprano, it resembles the church cantata BWV 84 from perhaps the same year (1727). The Coffee Cantata may be a little later, but we can imagine Anna Magdalena participating in both, although the pleasant image of her singing at Zimmermann's coffee house is probably a figment, in view of the municipal ban on women entering there.[75] BWV 201, believed

---

73 As noted in NBR, 167 (the sentence, which should apply to no. 172, is misplaced). We have receipts in connection with royal visits for 50 Taler paid on October 14, 1734 (BD 1:196 [no. 119]) and 58 Taler on May 5, 1738 (BD 1:198 [no. 122]).

74 Several are known to have been repeated. Many more receipts survive from Emanuel Bach at Hamburg than from Sebastian at Leipzig; Emanuel's show different rates of pay depending on whether he had to compose new music (see Enßlin and Wolf 2007, 147–49).

75 Hübner (2018, 55–56) argues that documents previously seen as evidence for the presence of women during concerts at Zimmermann's have been misinterpreted. Yearsley (2019,

Example 11.6 *Der Streit zwischen Phoebus und Pan*, BWV 201, mvt. 11, mm. 108–12 (bracket marks "braying" motive):

Denn nach meinen beiden Ohren   For according to my two ears

to date from 1729, recalls, on the other hand, the large-scale homage and "congratulation" cantatas on which Picander and Bach had been collaborating since at least 1725.

With the Coffee and Peasant cantatas (BWV 211 and 212), Bach clearly entered the field of comedy, which had begun to flourish on the German stage during the decades before he set these two librettos by Picander. Bach's was not the first "coffee cantata." As early as 1703, the French composer Bernier had published a cantata whose text praised coffee in mock-classical style.[76] Bach's work has a sharper satirical point, implicitly criticizing a type of woman who refuses to marry, or at least is not

154) interprets this evidence less literally but repeats Katherine Goodman's suggestion that BWV 211 could have been performed elsewhere (at Mariane von Ziegler's salon).

76 *Le caffé*, in his *Cantates françoises*, Book 3 (Paris); this was also one of the first published works of any type to include a transverse flute part.

Example 11.7   *Schweigt stille, plaudert nicht* ("Coffee Cantata"), BWV 211, mvt. 6, mm. 7–10
(with editorial continuo realization):

Mädchen, die von harten Sinnen,   Girls of stubborn mind
Sind nicht leichte zu gewinnen,   Are not easy to win over,

as interested in doing so as she ought to.[77] Picander's text, published in
1732, was evidently popular; at least two other settings are known.[78] Only
Bach's, however, includes the final aria, in which the girl seems to get

77   Nevertheless, Picander's text has been described as being less opposed to female autonomy
and agency than a work by the supposed feminist Gottsched; see Potter (2012, Chapter 2).
Yearsley (2013) offers a similar reading.

78   One of these settings, attributed to "Sigr. Buchberg" (presumably Johann Sigismund
Buchberger, organist at Löbau, east of Dresden), is in Dresden, Sächsische Landesbibliothek—
Staats- und Universitätsbibliothek, Mus. ms. 2426-L-500 (available online). An anony-
mous setting in Berlin, Staatsbibliothek, Mus. ms. anon. 708, was edited by Erhard Franke
(Leipzig: Deutscher Verlag für Musik, 1966).

Example 11.8 *Schweigt stille, plaudert nicht* ("Coffee Cantata"), BWV 211, mvt. 8, mm. 20–25 (without strings):

Heute noch,   Even today,
Lieber Vater, thut es doch.   Dear Father, make it so.

the better of the father (see Example 11.8 above). Bach was also the only composer to continue with the concluding terzet, which allows the tenor narrator to join the two interlocutors in a final dance song—a comic version of the moralizing chorus that typically ended a serious opera.

The Peasant Cantata is a different kind of work. Bach's last precisely datable vocal composition, it probably fulfilled a commission or request from Picander to honor the royal chamberlain (*Kammerherr*) Carl Heinrich von Dieskau—who oversaw Picander's day job as a tax collector.[79] In 1742 Dieskau inherited the manor (*Rittergut*) of Kleinzschocher, now a part of the city of Leipzig. The cantata is thought to have been performed on August 30, Dieskau's birthday, when he first received the traditional tribute from the village.

79 The famed baritone Dietrich Fischer-Dieskau (1925–2012) claimed descent from this patron, according to his Wikipedia page.

Picander's text flatters his boss by painting the latter as a generous and sympathetic overseer of a peasant couple, who comprise the sole characters. Their first duet is in Saxon dialect—hence the odd incipit "Mer hahn en neue Oberkeet"—and Bach's music quotes a number of folk tunes. On the whole, however, both words and music are sophisticated evocations of country life, meant to appeal not to real peasants but to their social superiors. Bach, like Telemann in a number of ostensibly rustic works, writes for a small instrumental ensemble of just violin, viola, and continuo, joined by flute and horn respectively in several movements. The juxtaposition of high and low, or city and country, styles would have entertained those in Bach's audience who knew the melodies quoted in the arias and recitatives and in the medley that serves as an overture.

Motets

Bach's motets constitute another important, if small, group of vocal works. Like the secular cantatas, these were composed for special occasions, probably on commission. Yet they are entirely different from his other vocal music. Lacking independent instrumental parts, they could not incorporate the recitatives, chorale "fantasias," and other types of movement found in his cantatas. Instead they revert to an older approach to music making that must have appealed to both Bach and the musically sophisticated patrons for whom he wrote these works. As examples of old-fashioned vocal polyphony, they resemble the shorter and simpler motets by earlier composers that were a regular part of the Leipzig liturgy. Yet Bach's motets are less consistently archaic in style, modernizing and diversifying the musical language of the genre.

Most if not all were for the funerals of wealthy or notable citizens. Performed in the nineteenth and twentieth centuries as "a cappella" choral works, Bach's motets were originally executed at least with organ continuo, in some cases with instruments doubling all the vocal parts. Independent instrumental parts are present only in the unique work *O Jesu Christ, meins Lebens Licht*, published in the nineteenth century as Cantata 118 but designated a motet in Bach's autograph score.[80] Only five of the nine other motets attributed to Bach have undisputed credentials.

---

80 The doubtful motet BWV 230 also has a continuo part that is occasionally independent of the vocal bass. Further discussion in Hofmann (2000).

These are BWV 225–29, each of which was probably composed for a specific occasion at Weimar or Leipzig and subsequently revised. They apparently remained in the repertory of the St. Thomas School into the later eighteenth century, when Mozart, among others, reportedly heard them performed.[81]

The five undisputed motets are certainly the great works, revealing diverse approaches to what by the 1720s was an outmoded genre, although one with which Sebastian must have been familiar from the many examples by his older relatives.[82] We know the original occasion for only one of these works: BWV 226, which Bach wrote for the burial service of J. H. Ernesti, rector of the St. Thomas School, on October 20, 1729. This took place at the university church, as Ernesti was also a professor there. Bach must have composed the work quickly, engaging students and family members to copy out the performing parts. These are for eight singers divided into two choirs; the first choir is doubled by strings, the second by woodwinds.[83] Only conjectures have been offered about the origin or performance circumstances of the other motets, at least one of which, BWV 228, probably originated at Weimar.[84]

Today it seems odd to contemplate these austere compositions, written for funerals, in the context of Bach's Coffee and Peasant cantatas. Yet a city music director had to be prepared to produce both types of music. Bach continued to do so in later years, even as he diverted his attention away from the everyday church music that so occupied him when he first came to Leipzig.

---

81 Mozart supposedly heard BWV 225 during a visit to Leipzig in 1789; he certainly owned a manuscript copy. The story of the visit is from the unreliable Friedrich Rochlitz (quoted in NBR, 488), but Mozart's copy survives in Vienna, Gesellschaft der Musikfreunde, III 31685—bearing Mozart's note that it should be scored for full orchestra.

82 Among these were his father-in-law J. M. Bach and his Eisenach cousin J. C. Bach, whose works of this type are preserved chiefly in the Old Bach Archive. Sebastian may not have acquired the latter before the mid-1730s (see Wollny 2002, 51); hence his arrangements of several works from it for performance at Leipzig probably postdate his own contributions to the genre.

83 The parts (Berlin, Staatsbibliothek, Mus. ms. Bach St 121) are in the hands of J. S., A. M., and C. P. E. Bach, as well as J. L. Krebs and another student; the performance date was recorded by the local chronicler Sicul (see NBA 3/1, KB, 81).

84 As argued by Melamed (1995, 101ff.). His book remains a useful source on the motets, despite having been rendered out of date on certain matters by subsequent findings.

CHAPTER TWELVE

Leipzig

LATER YEARS (1731–1750)

T HE LAST FOUR MONTHS OF 1730 MAY HAVE BEEN ANXIOUS ONES FOR
Bach. We have no evidence of any response to Bach's "sketch"
(*Entwurff*) concerning church music, which he had addressed to the Leipzig
city council in August. Nor is there evidence of new compositions for the
Leipzig churches.[1] Indeed, we have little documentation of any kind con-
cerning Bach until the following March, when his daughter Christiana
Dorothea was born; among the godparents was her namesake Christiana
Dorothea Hebenstreit, wife of the conrector of the St. Thomas School.[2]
As the latter was Bach's higher-ranking colleague, this suggests that for the
time being he continued to maintain cordial relationships with his fellow
instructors. He had, however, been reprimanded in August for failing to
teach the singing class; one council member complained "not only was
the cantor doing nothing, but he would not even give a reason for this."[3]

---

1 It is possible that BWV 51 and 192 date from this period, but neither appears to have been
composed originally for a regular church performance. Cantata 51 is a solo cantata for soprano (also with a solo trumpet part; see Chapter 11); the fragmentary BWV 192 is an unusual chorale cantata *per omnes versus*.

2 BD 2:208 (no. 286); Hebenstreit would leave before the end of 1731. On October 30, 1730,
Bach had also stood beside the widow of the former rector J. H. Ernesti as godparent to
Johann Martin Wilde (BD 2:207 [no. 283]).

3 "es thue der Cantor nichts, sondern wolle sich auch diesfals nicht erklären, halte die
Singestunden nicht" (BD 2:205 [no. 280]). *Singestunden* (trans. as "the singing class" in NBR,
145 [no. 150a]) were presumably group lessons for the boys who sang chorales. Four years

Bach. David Schulenberg, Oxford University Press (2020). © Oxford University Press.
DOI: 10.1093/oso/9780190936303.001.0001

Another, as we have seen, described him as "incorrigible," leading to a decision to limit his supplemental income (see Chapter 10). Three weeks later it was reported that Bach had "little interest in work," probably meaning that he was still neglecting his duties in the School.[4] This came just two days after he signed and dated the *Entwurff*, which could have been intended in part as a defense against complaints that were not new.

The one exception to the dearth of documentation during this period, and it is a major one, is the famous letter that Bach addressed on October 28, 1730, to his old friend Georg Erdmann, with whom he had gone to school at Lüneburg. Together with the *Entwurff*, this has been taken as evidence of a major life crisis relating to Bach's turn away from composing sacred vocal music for the churches. Erdmann was now a diplomat representing the Russian empress Anna in the city of Danzig (Gdańsk) on the Baltic seacoast. Bach's letter is a unique surviving instance in which the composer writes at length about his career and family.[5] Its main purpose, however, was to ask Erdmann for help in finding a new position in his city.[6]

Bach had previously—at Weimar—ceased composing sacred music and sought a change of venue when his situation became untenable. Now the pattern was repeating. In his letter to Erdmann, he summarizes his career since leaving Weimar (evidently where the two had last seen one another). He then explains why he took the position at Leipzig and how it has proved to be a disappointment. He ends by bringing Erdmann up to date on his "domestic situation," summarily mentioning the death of his first wife, his remarriage, and his living children. He does not even give their names, but he does add that

later, on November 2, 1734, the council received a similar report that Bach still was "not doing what he was supposed to do in the school" ("derselbe gar nicht in der Schuhle thäte, was ihme zu thun obliege," BD 2:252 [no. 355]).

4 "der aber schlechte lust zur arbeit bezeige," BD 2:206 (no. 281), NBR, 145 (no. 150b).

5 Bach had written previously to Erdmann, but his letter of July 28, 1726 (trans. in NBR, 125–26 [no. 121]) looks like a tentative contact after years of no communication. Erdmann's biography is summarized on BD 1:69 (commentary to no. 23).

6 Had Bach become aware of a lucrative opening at the city's church of St. John, taken in 1730 by Daniel Magnus Gronau? The latter's previous position at St. Mary's was filled in 1732, according to Williams (2016, 497).

they are all born musicians, and I can assure you that I can already form an ensemble both vocal and instrumental within my family, particularly as my present wife sings a pure soprano, and my eldest daughter joins in not badly.

This information would not have been irrelevant to a job search, for it implies that Bach could rely on family members for assistance (as indeed he did). There can be little doubt that Bach was telling the truth when he complained that his income was less than he had been led to expect and that Leipzig was "very expensive." The lines that follow are frequently quoted, as they seem to express Bach's unhappiness in a poignantly uncharacteristic way. Yet how to interpret them is far from clear:

the authorities are whimsical and have little respect for music, so that I must live surrounded by almost constant annoyance, jealousy, and persecution, to the point that I will be forced to seek my fortune elsewhere, with God's help.[7]

Whether Erdmann was sympathetic or helpful to Bach is unknown; no reply survives. But Bach remained in Leipzig—fortunately for him and his family, as Danzig would suffer depredation after choosing the wrong side in the war that was about to break out.

The *Missa*

Meanwhile Bach's work with the Collegium continued, although like the church music this came to a halt during the mourning period for elector Friedrich August I (King Augustus II in Poland). His death on February 1, 1732, had momentous political consequences, for his son's campaign to succeed him as king of Poland led to the War of the Polish Succession. Friedrich August II would not be unchallenged as Polish king until well after his coronation at Kraków in January 1734. After a period of diplomatic maneuvering, hostilities commenced in October 1733, pitting Austria, Saxony, Prussia, and Russia against France and Spain for the next two years. The war was fought mostly in Italy and the Rhineland; hence the consequences for the people of Leipzig were probably minimal. Yet echoes of the war raging elsewhere can be detected in the librettos of the secular cantatas with which Picander and Bach paid

---

7 BD 2:67–68 (no. 23); NBR, 152 (no. 152). "Whimsical" is Williams's (2016, 496) rendering of *wunderlich*.

homage to the ruling house during these years. Cantata 205a, which marked the coronation, opened with the chorus "Sound the alarm, you enemies!" (*Blast Lärmen, ihr Feinde*). The king, reading a copy of the libretto sent to Dresden, would not have known that this was a parody of the "Chorus of the Winds" written nine years earlier to honor the academic August Müller.

The new ruler granted special dispensation for Collegium performances to start up again in June 1733, before the end of the mourning period for his father. These began with the first of the season's Wednesday summer concerts in Zimmermann's garden. The program is unknown, but the event featured a new harpsichord, "the likes of which [had] never been heard previously."[8] What was so special about the instrument is not recorded; one imagines that it must have been used for something more than continuo playing, presumably concertos or sonatas with obbligato keyboard. The instrument probably belonged not to Bach but to Zimmermann, who would have been the one who obtained the princely concession and released the news to the press. Bach, however, might have facilitated its purchase—likely from Zacharias Hildebrandt, who had moved to Leipzig from Sangerhausen by the following year and must have already known Bach.[9] Hildebrandt had built the organ that Bach dedicated at nearby Störmthal in 1723, and he would later make a lute-harpsichord to Bach's specifications; he could not have obtained his appointment as court organ maker at Weissenfels in 1730 without Bach's recommendation.

Regular church music did not resume at Leipzig until July 2 (the feast of the Visitation), when Bach may have repeated his Magnificat. During the mourning period, Sebastian had sent at least two letters (both dated June 7) to Dresden in the name of Wilhelm Friedemann, who was applying for a position as organist in the capital city. These

8 "ein neuer Clavicymbel, dergleichen allhier noch nicht gehöret worden" (BD 2:237–38 [no. 331]; NBR, 156 [no. 160]). Zimmermann's coffee garden had opened regularly for summer performances since at least 1723; see Spitta (1873–80, 2:768, citing the local advertiser *Der jetzt lebende und florirende Leipzig* for 1723, 59).

9 A suggestion that the instrument was an early type of piano is refuted by Koster (1996, 76). It could have been a harpsichord with a 16-foot rank or some unusual disposition, like the harpsichord by Hildebrandt offered for sale at Leipzig in 1775 but probably built there during Bach's lifetime, as suggested by Heyde (1985, 76).

letters—even the signatures—are in the hand of Sebastian, who also corrected Emanuel's unsuccessful application two months later for another organist position in Naumburg.[10] Presumably it was Sebastian who decided which son would apply for the more prestigious job in the capital city, which the one in what was now a provincial outpost, with an older if larger organ.[11] He must also have been thinking about employment possibilities for himself, especially under the new Saxon ruler. Friedemann competed successfully on June 22 for the position at the church of St. Sophia in Dresden. He apparently received the keys to both church and organ on July 11, although he did not take up his position until August 1.[12]

By then Sebastian had submitted an application of his own for a court title at Dresden. Dated July 27, this was accompanied by a set of performing parts for a *Missa*, that is, a Kyrie and Gloria. The purpose of this composition, which Bach later incorporated into the work known today as the B-Minor Mass, was to demonstrate the "small accomplishment in that learning which I have attained in music," as he put it in his dedicatory letter to the elector.[13]

In fact the *Missa* was, with the exception of the two passions, Bach's largest work to date. It is possible that he had been working on it since word had reached Leipzig of the previous elector's death. Yet the *Missa* was probably not ready in April, when Friedrich August II visited Leipzig to receive the city's homage during two days of ceremonies. These included a service on April 21 in the St. Nicholas church, but

10 The letters for Friedemann are in BD 1:71–73 (nos. 25–26). Emanuel's application for St. Wenceslaus's in Naumburg is dated August 8, 1733 (see BD 1:271, no. 5). Two other Bach pupils (J. T. and J. L. Krebs) also competed for the latter position, which went to one Johann Christian Kluge; he would, however, be succeeded by Altnickol in 1748.

11 Naumburg, once a residence of the dukes of Saxe-Zeitz, had reverted to electoral Saxony after the death of the last duke. The organ, originally built in 1613, would be replaced by a splendid Hildebrandt instrument before Altnickol gained the position.

12 Bitter (1868, 2:354–55) reproduces the relevant documents. Why the keys were handed over on July 11, three weeks before the organ itself was *übergeben* is unclear; Rifkin (1988, 793) supposes that this was "to inspect the organ." The date given by Wolff and Zepf (2008, 16) for changes to the temperament of the organ by Hildebrandt's son, 1733, is an error for 1773.

13 "derjenige Wissenschaft, welche ich in der Musique erlanget." BD 1: 74 (no. 27); NBR, 158 (no. 162).

there is no record of the elector's attendance or whether Bach provided any music. Nor is it entirely certain when and where the parts that Bach eventually submitted were copied out.[14] The music is mostly parody, demonstrating Bach's "accomplishment" through a selection of movements composed during the past few years in both strict and *galant* styles. The *Missa* could have been prepared quickly, perhaps even after Friedemann played his audition at Dresden, receiving his appointment the next day.[15]

It was probably during this time—in any case before the end of 1733— that Bach acquired the publication known as the "Calov Bible": three massive volumes incorporating the complete Old and New Testaments, with commentary by the Lutheran theologian Abraham Calov.[16] Published in 1681–1682, this was the most impressive of the learned but somewhat old-fashioned religious tractates that Bach seems to have been collecting and reading during this period. One of only two books to have survived from Bach's personal collection, his copy of the Calov Bible has become famous because of numerous handwritten additions in it that have been identified as being in the composer's hand.[17] Many are corrections of typographical errors and the like, and some merely underline passages that mention music or that Bach apparently considered important for other

14 The parts, written by Sebastian together with Magdalena, Friedemann, Emanuel, and another pupil (see Wollny 2016, 73–76), are on paper that was previously believed to have been obtained in Dresden—hence the older supposition that Sebastian traveled there with the four other copyists during July (as in Wolff 2000, 369). Recurring speculation that at least a portion of the work had already been performed at Leipzig is not based on any evidence.

15 See Falck (1913, 14). More likely is that the parts, and therefore the *Missa* itself, were prepared before Friedemann left Leipzig.

16 The year is established by Bach's dated possessor's mark in each volume, although Leaver (1985, 72) repeats the warning given by Gerhard Herz that this was not necessarily the date of acquisition.

17 That even underlinings and similar small markings were made by Bach is supported by technical analysis undertaken in the 1980s (see Cox 1985, 1–11 and 31–42). A complete facsimile edition has been published by Uitgeverij Van Wijnen (Franeker, Netherlands, 2017). Other theological titles from Bach's library, which included books by Luther, Olearius, and Neumeister, are known from Section 12 of Bach's estate inventory (BD 2:494–96 [no. 627]; NBR, 253–54 [no. 279]). Bach's only surviving music book is his copy of Fux's *Gradus ad Parnassum* in its original 1725 Latin edition (see BD 1:270).

reasons.[18] Several marginal annotations hint at concerns with numerology and money.

Four or five entries are of greater significance. These suggest that Bach found support in the bible and in Calov's commentaries for his view of music as a form of divine service—even that a musician such as himself could be the equal of a pastor or preacher. For instance, against Calov's heading and comment for 1 Chron. 25, Bach added in the margin: "This chapter is the true foundation of all church music pleasing to God." The following verses list the musicians working for King David; the genealogical information included here might have inspired Bach to draw up a genealogy of his own family two years after he inscribed his initials in the book.[19] At the end of Chapter 28, David tells his son Solomon: "With you in all the work will be every willing man who has skill for any kind of service." Here Bach adds in the margin: "Splendid proof that, besides other arrangements of the service of worship, music too was instituted by the Spirit of God through David."[20] The use of music in worship thus had divine authorization, in Bach's view, and he underlines Calov's description of the musician Asaph—who is called a "prophet"—as "the Capellmeister of David." In this way Bach implicitly identified himself and his family with those who served the royal author of the psalms.[21]

Family Matters

Although Bach had not yet received the royal title that he had requested, he might have felt that things were looking up by the end of 1734, when he gave the first performance of the Christmas Oratorio. This was largely parody, like the *Missa*, incorporating an even greater quantity of music

---

18 Bach also wrote "NB" into the margin alongside more than a dozen passages. Leaver (1985) lists all of Bach's entries, followed by transcriptions, facsimiles, and commentaries for his marginal annotations.

19 As argued by Greer (2008).

20 Translation from Leaver (1985, 95), who argues that Bach took this as evidence that music is an essential element of worship and that he saw himself as called or ordained to divine service, like the Levite priests mentioned in the same verse (among whom were David's musicians).

21 As observed by Leaver (1985, 100), noting that Bach held the same title of Capellmeister when he acquired the book.

from homage cantatas for the royal family. Those cantatas must have been received enthusiastically in their performances by the Collegium, which was "still flourishing steadily," as Bach's pupil and friend Lorenz Mizler would report in 1736.[22] In addition, Part 2 of Bach's *Clavierübung* came out during 1735, after which he must have begun preparing his contributions to Schemelli's songbook, published the following year. Although Friedemann had abandoned his university career after receiving the call to Dresden, Emanuel, disappointed in the organ audition at Naumburg in summer 1733, was now continuing his university studies at Frankfurt (Oder). He had matriculated there in September 1734 and was soon leading a collegium musicum—as his godfather Telemann had done while a university student at Leipzig. Moving to Frankfurt had taken Emanuel out of his father's immediate sphere, but they exchanged music, including the Coffee Cantata.[23] Whether Emanuel made the 250-mile round trip to visit home during this period is unknown; Friedemann, however, may have visited regularly, staying for four weeks during summer 1739.[24]

Bach's two younger surviving sons, however, were doing less well. By the mid-1730s Gottfried Heinrich, born in 1724, must have been exhibiting the intellectual deficit that led Emanuel to describe him as "a great talent who, however, did not develop."[25] Sebastian's original indication that he "inclines toward music, especially the keyboard," suggests that Heinrich received elementary musical training and possessed some ability at the clavichord and harpsichord, perhaps as much as any other young Bach. But although his hand was once seen in some manuscript copies, these are now assigned to others; evidently he was unable to learn some of the basic tools of the trade. He could not be admitted to the St. Thomas School, and in 1741 Elias Bach, who had been serving in the household as a sort of secretary and general assistant, described Heinrich

---

22 BD 2:277–78 (no. 387), trans. in NBR, 185–86 (no. 187); the passage refers to Görner's as well as Bach's collegium.

23 As documented by manuscript copies; see Wollny (1996, 9).

24 On this occasion traveling with the lutenists Weiss and Kropffgans, according to a letter by Elias Bach (BD 2:366 [no. 448]; NBR 204 [no. 29]).

25 "War ein großß Genie, welches aber nicht entwickelt ward." BD 1:267 (annotation to no. 184, entry 48); NBR, 293 (no. 303).

as needing "steady and regular guidance."[26] After Sebastian's death he was placed in the care of his younger sister Friederica, by then married to Altnickol and living in Naumburg, where he died in 1769. Emanuel, incidentally, described Friederica as "musical," but that is practically all we know about her.[27]

As sad as Heinrich's case may have been, that of Sebastian's third son, Bernhard, must have been devastating.[28] Born in 1715, a year after Emanuel, he had followed his two older brothers into the St. Thomas School, performing alongside them in the Collegium Musicum.[29] Yet like Heinrich he left no firmly identified manuscript copies. This cannot have been due to incapacity, for in June 1735 he left Leipzig to audition successfully as organist at Mühlhausen.[30] Could he not be trusted to make accurate copies? was he too lazy? too careless? Barely twenty when he departed—three years younger than Friedemann at the time of his first appointment—he was a good enough player to win the position at Mühlhausen's main church, St. Mary's. Sebastian wrote two letters to urge his son's consideration on local authorities.[31] He then traveled there with Bernhard for the audition, taking the opportunity to advise the local organ builder C. F. Wender on the new organ whose construction was now underway.[32] Yet within two years Bernhard would leave

---

26 "eine solide und treue Unterweisung," letter draft of January 28, 1741, quoted in BD 2:363 (commentary to no. 443). Johann Elias Bach was Sebastian's first cousin once removed, grandson of his uncle Georg Christoph Bach of Schweinfurth. The suggestion that Heinrich was the composer of the little minuet song BWV 515 (Wolff 2000, 398–99) in his mother's second keyboard book must be considered speculative.

27 BD 1:267 (annotation to no. 184, entry 49); NBR, 293 (no. 303). Emanuel does not even give the name of his half-sister—but then the Genealogy mentions no women at all after the generation of Sebastian's parents.

28 Kulukundis (2016) provides the only critical examination of Bernhard's short life.

29 As established by Stählin's account, in BD 5:235 (no. C895b).

30 Wollny (1996, 11) suggested that Bernhard might have been the copyist of BWV 510, a chorale melody with a (mostly) unfigured bass in Magdalena's second music book, and of manuscript parts for the trio sonata BWV 1039 (in Berlin, Staatsbibliothek, Mus. ms. Bach St 431). But at least the first of these conjectures is now regarded as "unlikely and unsubstantiated" (Kulukundis 2016, 266n26).

31 BD 1:79–81 (nos. 30–31), trans. in NBR, 167–69 (nos. 175–76).

32 As compensation they received "a little supper" (*eine kleine Mahlzeit*, BD 2:257–58 [no. 365]). Christian Friedrich Wender was son of the late Johann Friedrich Wender, whom

his prestigious position for another; a year later he would abandon that one as well, having racked up debts which Sebastian was forced to pay. He died in May 1739, a few months after ostensibly beginning university studies at Jena.

Scheibe, Prefects, and the Collegium Musicum

Soon Sebastian himself was to suffer from a series of professional "insults" probably worse than those of which he had previously complained. Not all was bad: his son Friedrich, born in 1732, was by 1739 being tutored by Elias. Although another son (Abraham) had died a day after his birth in November 1733, Johann Christian, born in September 1735, was evidently healthy and growing. From 1736 to 1739, however, Sebastian must have been preoccupied, first, by a dispute with the new rector of the St. Thomas School over the selection of the students responsible for leading the four choirs; this has come to be known (with some irony) as the "Battle of the Prefects." A second controversy began with a critique of Bach and his music published by Johann Adolph Scheibe, son of the city organ builder. A reply by one of Bach's supporters led to further polemics that continued to the end of Bach's life. A third matter was Bach's temporary resignation (or removal) from directorship of the Collegium for a period of about two years.

The ground for the "Battle of the Prefects" was laid in 1734, when Bach's friend Gesner left Leipzig and Johann August Ernesti replaced him as rector of the St. Thomas School. This Ernesti—only remotely related to the previous rector Johann Heinrich Ernesti—had studied at the universities of Wittenberg and Leipzig. In the year of his appointment he issued the first of many publications: *Initia doctrinae solidioris*, a massive textbook covering subjects from arithmetic to zoology—but not music. J. A. Ernesti would eventually receive the university appointment that was denied to Gesner, becoming a major figure in classical and biblical scholarship. Already three years earlier, in 1731, he had been appointed conrector at the School, despite being just twenty-four years old. He enjoyed, however, the support of Christian Ludwig Steiglitz, a member of the city council since 1715 and six times mayor, whose children Ernesti

---

Sebastian had advised on the renovation of the organ at St. Blasius's, Mühlhausen, while organist there.

had tutored while a student in the university.[33] Ernesti was tasked with modernizing the school curriculum, which meant, among other things, reducing the emphasis on music and rewarding students for their general academic achievement. The prefects, although still expected to lead the chorales and other music in the churches, would no longer be chosen primarily for their musical abilities.

As late as September 1735, when Ernesti stood as godfather to Johann Christian Bach, Sebastian evidently maintained good relations with his younger superior. But tensions must have been growing, breaking into open hostility during the following summer, a few weeks after the start of the new school year (which began on Pentecost). The immediate point of contention was the selection of the first prefect, that is, the boy honored by his selection to substitute for the cantor in directing performances of motets and chorales (but not the cantata) by the first choir. Bach sought to replace Johann Gottlob Krause, a boy favored by Ernesti, after finding him unable to beat time properly. Ernesti refused to go along, citing the school rules promulgated shortly after Bach's arrival in 1723. These left the final decision in the rector's hands. Apparently the previous two rectors, J. H. Ernesti and Gesner, had always given tacit approval to Bach's decisions. J. A. Ernesti did not. Bach made a scene, taking over leadership of the motet himself during two church services when none of the students dared do so themselves; they had been threatened by Ernesti with punishment if any of them followed Bach's appointee. A series of complaints and counter-complaints followed, but the council evidently had no wish to oppose Steiglitz. Bach appealed first to the consistory—which, as the governing body for the churches, had a somewhat ambiguous oversight responsibility in this case—and then to the elector. Each appeal led to the same inconclusive result, the decision being left to the council, which had already ruled in favor of Ernesti.[34]

As enervating as the "Battle of the Prefects" may have been, it was less consequential for Bach's place in the larger world than the Scheibe

---

33 Leaver (2017, 186–87) writes, "It is clear that Steiglitz and Ernesti were in league with each other," the latter being granted privileges not accorded Bach and other instructors.

34 Wolff (2000, 350) suggests that "the affair was settled in favor of the court composer," but in fact the elector's decree of December 17, 1737, instructed the consistory to do "as they saw fit" (*nach Befinden*). There is no record that they did anything, certainly not to overturn the council's decision to uphold Ernesti.

controversy, which affected perceptions of Bach and his music across northern Europe. Bach, strictly speaking, was not a party to the dispute, as it involved writings by others. But he knew the authors on both sides and could have felt betrayed by the increasingly personal attacks from a probable former student. The episode began when J. A. Scheibe published a few paragraphs critical of Bach in his serial publication *Der critische Musicus* (The Critical Musician). Issues comprising eight pages each appeared at Hamburg every two weeks; in the sixth issue, dated May 14, 1737, Scheibe published a purported letter from a traveling musician who gave accounts of twelve contemporary composers. Only two whose music was praised, Hasse and C. H. Graun, were identified by name, but the ten others were recognizable to knowledgeable contemporaries.[35] The seventh was Bach, whom Scheibe's fictional correspondent described as

> the most prominent music maker in [Leipzig]. He is an extraordinary performer on stringed keyboard instruments [*Clavier*] and at the organ, and . . . would be the admiration of entire nations if he were more agreeable, if he did not deprive his pieces of that which is natural by giving them a pretentious, muddled style, and if he did not obscure their beauty through all too much cleverness. . . . He requires singers and players to do with their throats and instruments what he can play at the keyboard; this, however, is impossible.

Scheibe goes on to explain that Bach writes out ornaments that other composers leave to be improvised by the performer, and that the contrapuntal character of his music makes it impossible to make out the "leading part" (*Hauptstimme*). He concludes by comparing Bach to Lohenstein, an outmoded seventeenth-century poet. Scheibe claims that "in both one is surprised by the burdensome labor and exceptional difficulty that are, however, deployed in vain, for they strive against nature."[36]

---

35 Maul (2013b) identifies the others, based on entries that Walther entered by hand into a copy of the original publication. These were Stölzel, J. T. Römhild, Christoph Förster, the Leipzig organists Gerlach, Schneider, and Görner, the latter's brother J. V. Görner (then in Hamburg), plus Bach, Paganelli, and Hurlebusch.

36 From Scheibe (1738, 46–47), ed. in BD 2:286–87 (no. 400); NBR, 338 (no. 343).

Many came to Bach's defense. Gesner, the former rector, wrote a Latin account praising Bach's performance of the Funeral Ode (BWV 198).[37] Mizler, who had dedicated his Leipzig dissertation to Bach,[38] wrote in 1739 that Scheibe "must either not have listened carefully to anything by Capellmeister Bach or not yet have had any mature knowledge of music when he did hear it." He adds that "whoever heard the music performed by the students [that is, the Collegium] at the Easter Fair in Leipzig last year . . . must admit that it was written entirely in accordance with the most up-to-date style."[39] It is possible that Bach did enter the fray himself by repeating his satirical Cantata 201. Evidence for a reperformance during the 1730s is equivocal, but if one did take place it might have been aimed at Scheibe.[40] Bach later had it repeated with clearly polemical intentions.[41]

The best-known response to Scheibe appeared as "Impartial Remarks on a Doubtful Passage in the Sixth Issue of *The Critical Musician*." Published anonymously, this was soon revealed to be by Johann Abraham Birnbaum, *Magister* and *Dozent* for rhetoric at the Leipzig university. Bach previously seems to have had little reluctance to engage verbally with better-educated superiors. In this instance, however, he either sought assistance

---

37 Maul (2013b, 135) interprets this as a response to Scheibe. Gesner's account, published in 1738, appears in BD 2:331–32 (no. 432), trans. in NBR, 328–29 (no. 328).

38 Mattheson is also named in the dedication, as well as two others; see BD 2:247 (no. 349). Mizler implies that he has received instruction (*informatio*) from Bach; his dissertation earned Mizler the rank of *Magister* (not a doctorate, which he gained later at Erfurt as a physician).

39 BD 2:336 (no. 436), trans. from NBR, 350 (no. 346). Mizler refers to the lost homage cantata BWV Anh. 13, with libretto by Gottsched; regarding the latter, Nisbet (1969, 220) wrote that "Scheibe, for one, was completely overawed by him, even if Mizler, a more sceptical spirit, had some inkling that rationalism always ended up with an unanalysable residue in its attempts to account for works of art."

40 As was long ago supposed by Spitta (1873–1880, 2:478–79). Some of Bach's manuscript performing parts for the work show handwriting characteristics that have been dated to the later 1730s (see BC 4:1617).

41 A revival in 1749 with revised text is thought to have been a response to Johann Gottlieb Biedermann, rector at Freiberg, who had inveighed against the teaching of music in schools (see BD 1:122, commentary to Bach's letter of December 10, 1749, trans. in NBR, 241–42 [no. 268]). Bach is unlikely to have directed this final performance (as noted in NBA 1/40, KB, p. 137), but a bad pun in the altered text probably referred to Count Brühl, whose favorite Harrer had just been named Bach's successor (see Wolff 2000, 445).

or preferred to stand above the fray. Birnbaum responded point by point to Scheibe's criticisms of Bach, writing at length in a manner that can only reflect discussions with Bach himself. Birnbaum pays particular attention to some of Scheibe's word choices, such as *Musicant* (translated above as "music maker"). Birnbaum considers this disrespectful; he would prefer the term *virtuoso*.[42] He similarly seizes upon Scheibe's use of the words "agreeability," "pretentious," and "muddled."[43] This element of Birnbaum's argument today seems pedantic, yet it might have been the best way to reach the university-educated professionals who were his chief readership. Birnbaum did justify some of Bach's musical decisions, noting, for example, that certain older French composers were similarly explicit in notating ornaments. Many readers, however, probably knew little about such music, sharing Scheibe's preference for the easier style of Telemann, Hasse, or Graun. Hence Birnbaum appealed rather to his readers' respect for learning and connoisseurship in the arts generally.

Turning toward Berlin

Bach finally received the title of Saxon court composer during the fall of 1736. This might have cheered him as the "Battle of the Prefects" raged on. Yet during the next few years there are signs of disillusionment with Dresden as well as Leipzig. His last known visit to Dresden occurred late in 1741, undertaken perhaps to present a copy of the Goldberg Variations to Count Keyserlingk.[44] This, however, was preceded and followed by at least two trips to Berlin, where Emanuel had been living since his graduation from the Frankfurt university in 1738. Sebastian's last known performance of a homage cantata for the Saxon dynasty was in 1742, the previous new one having been composed for the Easter fair four years

---

42 Birnbaum likens Scheibe's use of the word *Musicanten* to "calling a thoroughly learned man the best member of the top class of schoolboys" (BD 2:299 [no. 409], trans. in NBR, 341 [no. 344]). The reference to schoolboys echoes the issue of the prefects, of which Birnbaum undoubtedly knew from conversations with Bach.

43 *Annehmlichkeit, schwülstig,* and *verworren* (BD 2:286 [no 400]); the words are rendered as "amenity," "turgid," and "confused" in NBR, 338 (no. 343).

44 Keyserlingk was the Russian imperial ambassador to Saxony; on the Goldberg Variations, see Chapter 13. Elias Bach reports traveling with Sebastian and staying with Keyserlingk in a letter dated January 13, 1742 (BD 2:399 [no. 502]); earlier letters place the trip in the previous November (BD 2:396–97 [nos. 497–98]).

earlier.[45] Having gained nothing concrete from his court title, Bach might have sought advancement elsewhere, if not for himself then for his sons. In 1746 Friedemann would leave the Saxon capital for Halle, a Prussian possession. The three younger composer sons, as well as a grandson, would also be associated with Prussian or Prussian-allied courts, none with Saxony.[46] Sebastian's last "homage" work, the Musical Offering, was famously dedicated to the youthful King Frederick "the Great" of Prussia, who was not only an accomplished musician but a genuine intellectual, statesman, and military leader; if only nominally Protestant, at least he was not Catholic, as was the elector in Dresden.[47]

Bach had traveled to Berlin during the Cöthen years; he made a return visit in 1741, presumably in connection with his son Emanuel's appointment as a royal Prussian chamber musician. His final journey to Berlin took place in 1747, in the course of which he met King Frederick, to whom he subsequently dedicated his Musical Offering. This visit became one of the best-known episodes in his life. Bach had previously met many rulers, among them possibly the Saxon elector and Polish king. He was certainly familiar with the ritualized protocol and conspicuous consumption of even minor German courts. But Frederick was his own sort of monarch, secure in his position and accustomed to meeting with officers and musicians in relatively informal settings.

The oft-related encounter of the aging Sebastian with the much younger Frederick II took place in Potsdam, then a country town about twenty miles outside Berlin, at the new palace of Sanssouci.[48] It was probably no coincidence that the famous father of one of the king's chamber musicians came to visit just as the small, jewel-like residence was being given its final touches. The music room had already received its paintings by Antoine Pesne and exquisite decoration (incorporating

---

45 BWV Anh. 13, followed by a repeat of BWV 206 and a parody of the early BWV 208.

46 Even J. C. Bach, after studying in Berlin with Emanuel, eventually worked in England, a Prussian ally, as music master for Queen Charlotte. She was originally a princess of Mecklenburg-Strelitz, which, like Anhalt-Cöthen, bordered on Prussian territory.

47 The Hohenzollern family was Calvinist, like Prince Leopold of Cöthen, but Frederick "the Great" was agnostic or atheist. Religion played no role in his thinking; Catholics and even Jews enjoyed greater tolerance in his kingdom than in most of Protestant Europe.

48 That is, not at the larger Potsdam city castle, as is sometimes supposed; this and the following information about the king's palaces and instruments are from Oleskiewicz (2017, 42).

musical motifs) by Johann Michael Hoppenhaupt. During the month of Bach's visit, the king's flute teacher and chamber composer Quantz was reimbursed for acquiring a new fortepiano by Silbermann. Previously, in 1740 or 1741, Emanuel Bach had had the honor of accompanying Frederick's first flute solo as king at Charlottenburg Palace in Berlin.[49] Now Sebastian gave the first publicly acknowledged performance on one of the king's pianos. The latter resembled instruments that Bach himself would soon be handling as dealer, if he was not doing so already.

The king was reportedly in the middle of one of his famous private concerts when Bach arrived. In later years even distinguished visitors were rarely admitted into the king's music room (Figure 12.1).[50] Bach, however, was let in at once; the king himself "condescended" to play a theme at the keyboard, Bach elaborating it extemporaneously into a fugue. Bach let it be known that he would soon turn the improvised fugue into a written one; the "Prussian fugue," as he called it, would quickly grow into the collection to which he gave the title Musical Offering (*Musicalisches Opfer*).[51] The day after meeting the king, Bach went to the Holy Ghost Church in town to play the organ there, built in 1730 by Joachim Wagner, the leading Brandenburg maker. Frederick may have heard this performance too, for many years later he was able to tell the diplomat and fellow music-lover Baron van Swieten that Friedemann, although also a "great organist named Bach," did not equal his father.[52] That evening Sebastian certainly played again for the king, this time a six-part fugue on his own subject.

49 As he indicated in his autobiography (inserted into the German version of Burney 1775), leaving the exact date ambiguous (as noted by Exner 2012).

50 For instance, the English visitor Charles Burney had to listen in the antechamber through the door, according to the later Capellmeister Reichardt (see Oleskiewicz 2007a, 255). The present account of Bach's visit follows the contemporary newspaper report published at Berlin on May 11, 1747 (BD 2:434–35 [no. 554]; NBR, 224 [no. 239]). A more elaborate version given by Forkel probably reflects embellishments of the story by Friedemann, including the doubtful reference to Sebastian's playing multiple Silbermann instruments in various palace rooms (see Oleskiewicz 2017, 69).

51 The word *Opfer*, which here means something like "tribute," can also mean a ritual offering, hence the bizarre translation of the title in some nineteenth-century editions as "Musical Sacrifice."

52 Swieten, letter of July 26, 1774, in BD 3:276 (no. 790).

Figure 12.1 The Music Room at Sanssouci, Potsdam, with fortepiano by Silbermann and flute by Quantz (in display case); murals by Pesne, music stand by Kambly. Photo: Janstoecklin, from Wikimedia.

Afterward, in Berlin, Emanuel showed Frederick's new opera house to his father. According to Emanuel, Sebastian immediately recognized its acoustic properties as well as those of the so-called whispering gallery in the banquet hall of the same building.[53] Sebastian also would have met his two-year-old grandson Johann Adam; at the time, Emanuel's wife was expecting again, and their daughter Anna Carolina Philippina would be born in September. Another son would follow a year later; this was Johann Sebastian Bach the Younger, who in his short life would make a name for himself not as a musician but as a painter and draftsman.

During previous trips home, Bach might have considered job prospects; on this one he would have planned the promised publication of his "Prussian fugue." By July 7 he had signed the printed dedication to the king of the Musical Offering, which now comprised two fugues (called ricercars), a trio sonata, and multiple canons. A year after having it printed, Bach answered a request for a copy by saying that he could not oblige, having given away most of what he had had printed "to good friends."[54] In fact he seems to have had different numbers of copies printed of the work's various components, probably because he expected to send different parts to different people. The king, naturally, got a complete copy, printed on special paper, although possibly not received all at once.[55]

On the way back to Leipzig, Bach might also have been considering a second musical offering: to the Corresponding Society of Musical Sciences, founded nine years earlier by Mizler. Mizler's society at the time comprised just thirteen handpicked men, including Telemann, Stölzel, and C. H. Graun. Members agreed to circulate "packets" among themselves; sent twice a year, these contained compositions and writings.[56] Bach might have been reluctant to commit himself to the regular creation and distribution of contributions that, coming from him, would take

53 As Emanuel related to Forkel in 1774 (BD 3:285 [no. 801]; NBR, 397 [no. 394]).

54 Letter of October 6, 1748, to Johann Elias Bach, BD 1:117–18 (no. 49); trans. in NBR, 234 (no. 257).

55 This summary of the work's history mainly follows Butler (2002).

56 The chief source regarding the Correspondierende Societät der musicalischen Wissenschaften is Mizler's Musikalische Bibliothek (1738–1754), in which were published the society's guidelines as well as some of the items from the Pakete.

the form of musical compositions rather than verbal documents. On the other hand, the idea of musical "science" or learning could have appealed to him at a time when the mere possibility of such a thing was apparently denied by the powers that be in Leipzig.

Mizler himself passed through Leipzig that June, apparently convincing Bach to join his society, perhaps by assuring Bach that compositions alone would suffice. Bach told him that he would send the membership an engraved copy of "the fugue he played before the king."[57] The only offerings that Bach is known to have sent, however, were samples of stricter, more ostentatiously learned, music: the Canonic Variations for organ, probably in a manuscript version that fully realized each movement, and a sheet containing the little canon BWV 1076.[58] Mizler duly reprinted the latter in the *Musikalische Bibliothek*, but although clever enough—it incorporates the first eight notes of the Goldberg Variations bass line—it is not much more than a token. Indeed, that is literally its function in the other place where it appears: as a symbol of Bach's musical vocation in the portrait by Haussmann, executed the year before (Figure 12.2).

Final Months

Until 1749 Bach is not known to have suffered any serious illnesses or injuries. Yet during the preceding years he seems to have withdrawn from many of his duties, even leaving the direction of the main "musical" performances in the churches to two prefects named Bammler and Fleckeisen. In January 1749 Bach saw his daughter Friederica married at Leipzig to his pupil Altnickol, now organist at Naumburg—surely a proud moment for her mother and father, though a bittersweet one for her much older unmarried half-sister Catharina Dorothea.[59] That June, however, the Leipzig authorities were effectively ordered to give

---

57 This was how Mizler put it in a letter, BD 2:437 (no. 557); NBR, 228 (no. 247).

58 The "fully worked out" (*vollständig ausgearbeitet*) variations sent to members of the society are mentioned at the end of Bach's Obituary (BD 3:89 [no. 666]; NBR, 307 [no.306]). This implies that they were given in a form more explicit than the "puzzle" format in which they were printed and published. Milka (2014) argues that Bach also intended the incomplete *Fuga a 3 soggetti* from the Art of Fugue as an offering to Mizler's society.

59 Bach mentioned the upcoming wedding, which took place on January 20 (BD 2:454 [no. 579a]), in a letter to Elias (BD 1:119 [no. 50], trans. in NBR, 235 [no. 258]). Maul

Figure 12.2 Portrait of Bach, oil on canvas by Elias Gottlob Haussmann (1746). Altes
Rathaus, Leipzig. Seemingly less finished than the same artist's version of 1748 (apparently
an idealized copy), this image may give a better idea of what the composer was really like
around the time of his sixtieth birthday. From Wikimedia.

an audition to Gottlob Harrer, composer for the private *Capelle* of the Saxon prime minister Heinrich von Brühl, "in case the Capellmeister and cantor Bach should die." The command was couched in the form of a letter of introduction, but it followed up a "recommendation" that Count Brühl, the most powerful man in Saxony, had made to the council during a visit to Leipzig. If there remained any members of the Leipzig city council who still inclined toward Bach, even they would have understood this as an order to provide Harrer with a formal document assuring him of his future appointment.[60]

It has been surmised that Bach had suffered some sort of incapacitation during 1749. Emanuel, however, claimed that his father was in good health until he underwent two procedures to relieve a condition that must have been seriously hampering his eyesight.[61] The operations took place between March 28 and April 4, 1750, just days after a presumed visit by Emanuel and performances of the latter's Magnificat, as well as Sebastian's St. John Passion.[62] Sebastian's eyesight, which according to the Obituary had always been weak due to long hours copying and playing music, was clearly failing by the end of 1749, and his handwriting had gotten very shaky.[63] Whether the latter was due solely to visual problems is uncertain; these must, however, have been very serious for Bach even to contemplate submitting to surgery at the end of March 1750.

If Bach indeed repeated his St. John Passion that month, doing so might have constituted pious personal preparation for an arduous,

(2017) revealed Bach's apparent replacement by an assistant in liturgical performances for a period during the mid-1740s.

60 Brühl's letter of June 2, 1749, directs the council to prepare an "aufrichtige Kennzeichnen derjenigen Hochachtung," BD 2:456 (no. 583), trans. in NBR, 240 (no. 265). A second letter followed on August 9, 1750, after Bach's death (BD 2:481 [no. 616]).

61 Emanuel's account in the Obituary (BD 3:85 [no. 666]; NBR, 303 [no. 306]) must be based on what he learned subsequently from Friedemann and Christian.

62 Dates are established by contemporary newspaper reports: BD 2:468–69 (nos. 598–99); NBR, 243–44 (nos. 269a–b); as Easter fell on March 29, the operation is unlikely to have taken place before the next day. On Emanuel's visit and the possible performance of his Magnificat (W. 215), see Wollny (2011, 44–46).

63 Bach's last known autographs, listed by Kobayashi (1988, 61–64), reveal increasing difficulty in the formation and alignment of notes, eventually even of simple letters.

potentially deadly medical procedure.[64] The roving English surgeon John Taylor has been described as "a rare combination of a man of serious science and a charlatan in daily practice."[65] He was, however, a good enough marketer, through public lectures and printed notices, to find two prominent clients in Leipzig besides Bach, and he would later operate (or so he claimed) on Handel.[66] Neither the procedure performed on Bach nor the results were described with any medical precision, even by the standards of the time. Newspaper reports indicate that at first his vision improved, but after a second operation (the reason for which is unclear) Bach not only became effectively blind but also suffered general pain. There ensued a rapid and serious physical decline.[67]

As with any operation of the time, carried out without anesthesia or antiseptics, Bach doubtless experienced trauma and subsequent infection. He might well have reconciled himself to blindness or death even before the procedures, knowing that the majority of surgeries at the time were unsuccessful. Yet he survived for another four months, despite pain that the Obituary attributed, in part, to "harmful medications," likely including mercury. Old ideas that Bach dictated an organ chorale or that he died while trying to finish a movement of the Art of Fugue almost certainly reflect misunderstandings.[68] As late as May 1750 the

64 Glöckner (2008, 194–95) suggests that Bach might have continued to direct church music through Easter Sunday (March 29) 1750.

65 Zegers (2005, 1429), whose evaluation of Bach's condition and treatment remains the most comprehensive by a qualified ophthalmologist.

66 Taylor's 1761 memoir provides the only documentation that he also operated on Handel.

67 Taylor's account is confused; he seems to claim temporary success in Bach's case, followed by failure due to a "paralytic disorder" discovered after "drawing the curtain," that is, couching or displacing a cataract (BD 3:171 [no. 712]; NBR, 244 [no. 270]). Bach's death has been attributed to "intractable secondary glaucoma" following couching (Tarkkanen 2013, 192). But whether Bach in fact suffered from cataracts is uncertain, nor is it clear exactly how the operation or subsequent treatment led to his death (as pointed out by Grzybowski 2013).

68 The so-called deathbed chorale, BWV 668a, differs only in a few details from the version incorporated into the "Great Eighteen" (BWV 668). The archaic style of both implies that they antedate the embellished "monodic" setting of the same chorale melody in the *Orgelbüchlein* (BWV 641). Emanuel Bach's claim that BWV 668a was "dictated on the spur of the moment" and that his father "died over" the incomplete *Fuga a 3 soggetti* cannot have been meant literally (see Schulenberg 2006, 421).

organist Johann Gottfried Müthel arrived as a pupil, apparently joining J. C. Kittel in the Bach household. By this point, however, instruction might have consisted only in being granted access to Bach's manuscripts, for copying.

The Obituary reported that Bach suddenly recovered his vision on July 18. This, however, has been interpreted as a possible hallucination, and a stroke reportedly followed, although, again, exactly what that meant is unknown.[69] On July 22 Bach received communion for the last time, and he died six days later.[70] He would not have been alone, and we can imagine Anna Magdalena, Catharina Dorothea, Heinrich, Christian, Carolina, and Regina Susanna all helping him prepare for death through the singing of hymns and other spiritual exercises, as recommended by Lutheran pastors.[71]

Sixty-five years and four months of age at his death, Bach was not unusually old for an upper-middle-class professional who had survived childhood and early adulthood. Although this was well past the average life expectancy of the time, many contemporaries, including Telemann and his own son Emanuel, were healthy and active creatively well into their seventies. Three of Bach's four composer sons had longer lives, as did his first and last daughters. As a composer he had been highly prolific, but again not unusually so; Graupner and Telemann, among others, wrote greater numbers of compositions, probably at a steadier pace. Bach, however, placed greater artistic demands on himself, and any evaluation of his health at the end of his career must take into consideration the effects of an exhausting regimen during earlier periods of high productivity. These seem to have been relatively short, however, followed by periods of comparative inactivity. Bach clearly had a robust constitution, but sheer exhaustion, creative as well as physical, might explain the fallow periods of his career, especially after he passed the age of fifty.

69 As Zegers (2005, 1430) suggests.

70 As recorded in BD 2:472 (no. 605). At Leipzig Bach normally took communion two or three times a year (see BD 2:124–26 [no. 605]); this was the first time since December 14, 1749.

71 Described by Yearsley (2002, Chapter 1).

It has often been remarked that Bach was no stranger to the pleasures of the world, enjoying good food and drink, apparently also tobacco, and fathering twenty children from 1708 to 1742.[72] An appreciation for sensual things is also manifest in his music, which includes exquisitely and sometimes luxuriously scored passages for organ and for variegated instrumental ensembles. The prodigious energy and physical vitality that Bach displayed during his prime years must have been sustained by greater than average intake of high-calorie foods; the aging Bach probably retained his appetite for the latter even as his physical activity diminished. That this led to obesity is clear from the Haussmann portrait; he certainly had all the risk factors for diabetes, which may well have contributed to his final decline and illness. The Haussmann portrait also provides some supporting evidence for Bach's reported myopia, although what looks like squinting might be only a mild congenital ptosis.[73]

Haussmann, who had previously depicted the trumpeter Reiche and the writer L. A. V. Gottsched, among other prominent residents of Leipzig, is usually said to have painted Bach in 1746, making a copy two years later (see Figure 12.2).[74] A companion portrait of Anna Magdalena, later owned by Emanuel along with the 1746 portrait of his father, no longer survives.[75] There are many other purported portraits of Sebastian, but, as none is fully authenticated or universally accepted, it would be rash to draw conclusions about the composer's personal character or health from them. However penetrating the subject's scrutiny of his

---

72 The children include one short-lived set of twins. Receipts for Bach's food, drink, and tobacco while traveling are often cited, for example, trips to Halle and Gera in 1713 and 1724, respectively; see Wollny (1994, 32), trans. in NBR, 65–66 (no. 46b), and BD 2:143–44 (nos. 183–84).

73 That is, a drooping of the eyelids, especially over the right eye, which has also been observed in portraits of other family members; see Towe (2001, 9), online at http://www.bach-cantatas.com/thefaceofbach/QCL09.htm.

74 Towe (2001) argues that the "copy" was done from life; he also argues plausibly for the authenticity of several other portraits, including a "Weydenhammer" portrait (named for a recent owner) that he identifies with a lost depiction once owned by Kittel.

75 A figure of a woman playing a clavichord, on the title page of a 1736 songbook by the poet Sperontes, has been claimed as a possible portrait of Anna Magdalena, but it would seem unlikely for a cantor's wife to be depicted in this manner—and what is one to make of the satyr beneath the table who is lifting up her skirt?

viewer in the Haussmann picture, there is also something remote, inscrutable about him. Yet this portrait probably depicts Bach as he wanted to be seen toward the end of his life. If so, it confirms what we can deduce from other sources—that he wished to be known as strong but modest, intelligent and musically accomplished yet not ostentatiously so, as he respectfully offers the viewer a small sample of his work: the canon that two years later he would circulate to his fellow members of Mizler's Corresponding Society.

CHAPTER THIRTEEN

Bach the Teacher

PUBLICATIONS AND PEDAGOGY

MORE THAN ANY OTHER MAJOR COMPOSER OF HIS DAY, BACH WAS and is known as a teacher. Handel, Telemann, and other German contemporaries took students. Yet only in Italy, with Vivaldi and Alessandro Scarlatti, do we encounter composers of comparable stature who were also famous specifically as teachers. The guild-like culture into which Bach and other German composers were born guaranteed that a master composer would serve as a model and instructor for a certain number of students and assistants. The cantorial roles filled by so many of them, including Telemann, incorporated elementary musical training among their responsibilities. Yet no major contemporary approached Bach in the degree to which teaching shaped his output as a composer. This was not necessarily because Bach deliberately created pedagogic pieces, that is, compositions intended to exercise the fingers or the mind in specific ways. Rather, much of Bach's output seem to have been meant to comprise examples of good composition, illustrating diverse ways of writing music that uses a particular type of instrumentation or scoring, belongs to a particular genre, or employs particular compositional techniques. This approach was made explicit after his death, when Emanuel Bach advertised "the Art of Fugue in twenty-four examples."[1]

---

[1] "Die Kunst der Fuga, in 24. Exempeln," from a lengthy description of the work published at Berlin on May 7, 1751 (Wilhelmi 1992; trans. in NBR, 256 [no. 281]), repeated in shorter form on June 1 at Leipzig (BD, 3:8–9 [item 639]; NBR, 258 [no. 282]).

Bach. David Schulenberg, Oxford University Press (2020). © Oxford University Press.
DOI: 10.1093/oso/9780190936303.001.0001

Something similar could be said of certain works by Bach's contemporaries, but his far surpass theirs in variety, compositional craft, and challenges for the performer or student. Many predecessors, especially Italians from Frescobaldi to Corelli, published systematically organized collections of pieces that demonstrated how to compose fugues, sonatas, or other types of compositions. These earlier sets of exemplary pieces were probably directed primarily to other professional musicians. Bach, living at a time when publication of music had begun to extend to the amateur market, might instead have focused his printed output on relatively small, unchallenging compositions, as Telemann did. Nothing compelled him to produce collections as unconventional as the Musical Offering or as massive and challenging as Part 3 of the *Clavierübung*. The title of the latter indicated that its purpose was at least partly the "spiritual delight" of "music lovers," yet that delight was "especially for connoisseurs of these things."[2] Recreation in the modern sense of mindless escape was hardly the point of Bach's collections, whose appeal, however, is not limited to connoisseurs who might enjoy puzzling over a double canon or tracing the contrapuntal manipulations of the subject in a fugue. These are expressive and often exciting virtuoso compositions as well. Nevertheless, Bach evidently saw value in the study and performance of intellectually challenging or instructive music. It is therefore fitting to conclude this survey of his output by examining the collections assembled during his later years in the context of his status as a teacher.

Bach and His Pupils

Although he taught throughout his career, only at Leipzig did Bach hold a position, as cantor, that was fundamentally educational. Although at times neglecting to teach the musically "useless" students at the St. Thomas School, from Leipzig he sent forth pupils who included some of the century's leading composers and performers, as well as some of its most important writers on music. His sons were the most significant of these, followed by Altnickol and Agricola, J. L. Krebs, Kittel, and Kirnberger.

---

2 "Denen Liebhabern, und besonders denen Kenner von dergleichen Arbeit, zur Gemüths Ergezung." Facsimile and translation in NBR, 202–3 (no. 206). Appeals to "*Kenner* and *Liebhaber*" would later appear on the title pages of collections published by Emanuel Bach, among others.

Many others less well known today held locally significant positions, training further generations of musicians and perpetuating the Bach tradition. Another group close to Bach includes those such as Mizler and Marpurg, who might not have studied with him formally but performed beside him in the Collegium or "discussed certain matters pertaining to fugue."[3] Their writings, influenced by or incorporating ideas gained from contact with Bach, also helped shape the musical thought of the time. Indeed, the number of writers on music who came out of Bach's orbit is remarkable. Bach himself might not have counted as learned in the eyes of someone like J. A. Ernesti. Yet even before his arrival at the university city of Leipzig, the learned character of his compositions and his professional closeness to pastors, or to a musician-scholar such as Walther, would have made study or conversation with him desirable for musically knowledgeable intellectuals as well as students.

The ways in which one might have studied with Bach were various. At Weimar, family members such as Johann Bernhard and Johann Lorenz Bach lived as members of the household. They must have gained knowledge and experience through daily apprentice-like work, whether copying music, pumping organ bellows, or moving and tuning instruments. Johann Elias's duties at Leipzig were an extension of this sort of assistance, although his employment as both family tutor and personal secretary seems to have been unique. Other pupils, such as the elder Krebs at Weimar and Altnickol, Agricola, and other university students at Leipzig, were already musical professionals, or at least had received advanced musical training, before beginning private study with Bach. J. T. Krebs, born in 1690, was one of several early students of Bach who were not much younger than he was. Organist at nearby Buttstädt from 1710, Krebs is supposed to have made twice-weekly trips into Weimar, but one wonders whether these were primarily for lessons in the modern sense or rather for copying music. At Leipzig, students such as the younger Krebs probably also performed in the Collegium and, when needed, in church cantatas—which therefore must also be counted among the venues in which learning (if not actual instruction) took place. Those unable to

---

3 "Ich habe ihn selbst einsmals, als ich bey meinem Aufenthalte in Leipzig mich über gewisse Materien, welche die Fuge betrafen, mit ihm besprach" (letter no. 33 of February 9, 1760, in Marpurg 1760–63, 1:266; NBR, 363 [no. 357a]).

pay cash for instruction—or for the right to copy manuscripts—might have provided other services. Two pupils, Balthasar Schmid and Johann Gotthilf Ziegler, have been plausibly identified as the engravers of Bach's harpsichord partitas, perhaps carrying out the work in Bach's own house.[4]

Not all Bach's adult pupils were university students. Courts and municipalities sometimes sent promising young musicians to study abroad. Some lucky Germans were sent to Italy, as were Schütz and later Quantz and Heinichen. Others had to settle for study with Bach. Among these were Philipp David Kräuter, who studied with Bach at Weimar, and G. H. L. Schwanberg, already chamber musician at the court of Wolfenbüttel when he arrived at Leipzig in 1727.[5] A capable violinist, Schwanberg owned copies made by Anna Magdalena of the unaccompanied violin and cello pieces. If he was able to play these, he might also have performed many of the solos in Bach's cantatas during his time in Leipzig.[6] In his later years, as Bach grew increasingly famous, he must have supplemented his income substantially by giving lessons to visitors such as these, as well as to the occasional noble amateur.[7] A third category of pupils were the students at the St. Thomas School to whom Bach was supposed to provide elementary musical training. Whether someone taught only to carry a chorale tune should be considered a "Bach pupil" is debatable. But the musically "useful" students probably learned valuable lessons in all sorts of practical subjects, as did members of the Collegium fortunate enough to play or sing alongside so exceptional a musician.

Despite the large number of Bach pupils, we know surprisingly little about what he actually taught them, or how. Some clues might be gleaned from what is known about other teachers, such as Pachelbel, who had taught Bach's older brother.[8] But Sebastian was largely self-taught and could not have based his approach to teaching on any one model. The

4 As Butler (1986) argues, also naming a third engraver, J. G. Schübler, as a Bach pupil.

5 Schulze (1984, 95–101) traces Schwanberg's career, summarized by Butler (2016, 83). The name also appears as Schwanenberg and Schwanenberger.

6 He was there at least through May 1729. Schwanberg's copies are in Berlin, Staatsbibliothek, Mus. ms. Bach P 268; he also copied the violin part of the violin "trios" in St 162.

7 Heber (2017, 120) counts no fewer than seventy-one private students at Leipzig, including a count who paid 6 Taler for a single lesson—6 percent of Bach's annual base salary.

8 Welter (2008, esp. 10–11) describes older teaching traditions going back to Sweelinck through Pachelbel.

few primary sources for his teaching consist chiefly of a handful of anecdotal accounts, written long after the fact, plus the brief letters of recommendation that Bach wrote, testifying to students' mastery of various musical skills.

E. L. Gerber explained how his father, arriving at Leipzig for university studies, spent six months listening to church music and concerts before obtaining an introduction to Bach. He then proceeded to study the inventions, suites, and Well-Tempered Clavier in turn, concluding his studies with figured bass realization. Yet exactly what this "study" comprised is unexplained. As we have seen, Gerber's father "counted among his happiest hours those when Bach, under the pretext of not feeling in the mood to teach, sat down at one of his fine instruments and turned these hours into minutes."[9] This suggests that Bach (like Chopin later) often taught by demonstration, although we also have the younger Gerber's manuscript copies of Sebastian's keyboard compositions, as well as a written-out continuo part for a violin sonata by Albinoni, corrected by Bach.[10]

Emanuel Bach, in response to questions from Forkel, confirmed that his father used his own keyboard music for teaching. By this he evidently meant study of performance, as pupils did not begin the study of composition unless Sebastian "detected talent [*Genie*]" in their work, by which Emanuel meant the "invention of ideas."[11] The latter might have become apparent in the course of improvised figured bass realization and chorale harmonization. These were required skills for any organist, and capable pupils must have advanced to these after more basic keyboard studies, as Gerber did. On the other hand, training in fugue, which "started with two-part ones," might have been reserved for more talented students,

9 E. L. Gerber (1790–1792, Vol. 1, cols. 491–92), trans. in NBR, 321 (no. 315). Strangely, Gerber omitted this material (indeed the entire entry for his father) in the expanded version of his musical lexicon published in 1812–1814.

10 H. N. Gerber's continuo part (for Albinoni's op. 6, no. 6) is in Berlin, Staatsbibliothek, Mus. ms. 455. It is notable for its full four-part harmony except where the bass rests (in which passages the realization doubles the violin), and for the absence of "improvisatory" melodic or contrapuntal additions. On the place of chorales in Bach's teaching, see Leaver and Remeš (2018).

11 "Erfindung der Gedancken," letter of January 13, 1775, in BD 3:289 (no. 803), trans. in NBR, 399 (no. 395).

incorporating performance of examples by Bach as well as composition of original pieces. Emanuel added that his father "omitted all the strict types of counterpoint given by Fux and others."[12] Yet he must have known that his father owned a copy of Fux's counterpoint treatise and that Mizler had made a German translation of the Latin original. Emanuel's comments, recorded fifty years after the fact, might reflect his own limited interest in strict counterpoint. Other pupils, even his older brother Friedemann, might have received different training.[13]

The only contemporaneous account of Bach's teaching known today comes from Kräuter, who paid 80 Taler for a year's instruction as well as lodging. This was subsidized by the school council (*Scholarchat*) of his home town of Augsburg, to which he reported in several letters describing his studies. Kräuter explained that these included six hours of daily "instruction" *(Information)* in composition and keyboard playing. He also was allowed to "look through . . . all of [Bach's] pieces" and, apparently, to copy them for his own use.[14] Not all his copying was for himself, however, as Kräuter also assisted Sebastian in preparing the score of the motet *Ich lasse dich nicht* (BWV Anh. 159); this remained with the Bach family. Kräuter also mentions being able to hear Bach's organ playing—perhaps while pumping the bellows for him?—as well as "much fine Italian and French music," which would aid him in his own writing of "concertos and overtures."[15] Returning to Augsburg, Kräuter was appointed cantor and music director of the Lutheran church there. By 1725 he had produced at least three annual cycles of church pieces—about as many as Bach had written—although these seem not to survive.[16]

If Kräuter really spent six hours a day under Bach's "guidance," this must have consisted in some part of directed keyboard practice or copying

---

12 "aller der trockenen Arten von Contrapuncten, wie sie in Fuxen u. andern stehen." The word *trocken*, usually translated as "dry," could be used in eighteenth-century references to counterpoint without the derogatory implications understood today.

13 As argued in Schulenberg (2010, 27–30, and 2014, 14–16).

14 "die übrige Zeit wende ich vor mich allein zum exerciren und decopiren an, dann derselbe mir alle Musik Stücke, die ich verlange, communiciert, habe auch die Freyheit alle seine Stück durchzusehen," letter of April 30, 1712, in BD 5:117 (no. B53b), first published in Krautwurst (1986, 180–81), trans. in NBR, 318 (no. 312b).

15 Letter of April 10, 1713, BD 5:121 (no. B57a), trans. in NBR, 319 (no. 312c).

16 Krautwurst (1986, 178, 182).

manuscripts. The time available for actual instruction must have been limited even at Weimar, more so as Bach's responsibilities grew in number at Leipzig. Although Bach's pupils did not have to prepare for "juries" and recitals, like those in modern conservatories, auditions for church, court, and civic positions would have loomed ahead for the more advanced students. Private lessons must have included appropriate preparation for these; Bach, having both played and heard many high-level auditions, surely could advise students better than anyone else on this matter. First lessons, on the other hand, might have been given to family members by Maria Barbara and later Anna Magdalena, or by older siblings. As in the teaching of grammar, religion, and other subjects, rote memorization and the verbatim reproduction of models, whether written (as in manuscript copying) or aural (as in playing), are likely to have been the basis of instruction, at least at the beginning stages. However original Sebastian's composing and playing, he cannot be assumed to have taken anything resembling a modern approach to education, and not everyone could have profited equally from study with Bach.

The music that Bach most clearly intended to serve his students takes the form of keyboard compositions. Another substantial group of potentially pedagogical works is composed of four-part chorale settings. Other vocal compositions, including the Latin church that so deeply occupied Bach in his later years, were probably not conceived in the first instance as teaching pieces. Yet these too might serve for instruction, if not in the usual sense then as exemplary models of composition, like the mass movements included in Fux's *Gradus ad Parnassum*.

Bach as Editor and Collector of His Own Works

Keeping all this music in neat, well-organized, correctly written scores would have become a priority as Bach gained increasing numbers of pupils, especially if their studies included making copies of these compositions for their own use or for sale. It is therefore impossible to separate Bach's teaching from his work as editor and compiler of his own music. How he used the growing stockpile of exemplary compositions must have evolved with his teaching, driven not only by practical pedagogic needs but by Bach's urge toward compositional "perfection." Both impulses would have pushed him toward providing students with polished scores free of elementary notational and compositional errors (such as parallel fifths). They would also have encouraged him to ensure that every detail was carefully notated—including the ornaments and embellishments appropriate to the French or Italian style, respectively, of a given piece. Bach must also have derived some measure of personal satisfaction from the production of well-ordered collections of masterpieces, especially if "perfecting" them was, in his eyes, a form of religious service or devotion.

The fact that Bach frequently revised older compositions suggests that, like his son Emanuel, he aimed at leaving a corpus of works that was sufficiently complete and finished to place before students and the public, not only during his own lifetime but afterwards.[17] Unrevised old compositions might have been deliberately discarded or, at least, confined to his own use. Among these was most of his vocal music, for whereas Telemann had substantial selections from his cantatas and oratorios printed and published, Bach's compositions of this type circulated, if at all, only in manuscript copies; the only cantatas to appear in print during his lifetime were the two or three very early ones for the Mühlhausen council. Of the early vocal works, only Cantata 4 seems to have been revised and repeated at Leipzig. But much of Bach's vocal output for Weimar was re-used, and many equally old keyboard pieces held their place in his repertory for performance or teaching. Even Part 2 of the Well-Tempered Clavier includes at least a few movements that probably go back to the Weimar years, and the same is true for the chorale settings that were revised for inclusion in the "Great Eighteen." An even earlier work, the G-minor organ praeludium (BWV 535), may also have been polished up for student use during the 1740s.[18]

Bach's Late Collections

Not every revised work became part of a carefully ordered collection, like those described in Chapter 9, but Bach continued to assemble further sets to the end of this life. To what degree these were intended for

---

17 Emanuel codified his decisions in a list of works that was eventually published after his death as part of his estate catalog (C. P. E. Bach 1790). There is no evidence that Sebastian ever kept such a list, although the tabulation of compositions in the Obituary might represent Emanuel's attempt to generate one.

18 To judge from probable autograph corrections in a copy made during Bach's last decade; see the description of source **LEm** in the author's edition, *J. S. Bach: Organ Works*, Vol. 2 (Wiesbaden: Breitkopf & Härtel, 2014), 12.

performance, as opposed to study, is unclear, although the absence of performance opportunities for at least one late compilation, the B–Minor Mass, has long been recognized. It could be that Bach, having put his musical affairs into a grand but inaudible order, died in the sad belief that his greatest achievements would never be heard or appreciated by fellow mortals.

Yet Bach's later collections contain some of his most famous and most frequently performed works. They include the ambitious pieces for harpsichord and for organ that Bach published in four volumes modestly entitled *Clavierübung* (Keyboard Practice): six large suites or partitas as well as an Italian concerto and French overture for harpsichord; a series of chorale settings together with a great prelude and fugue for organ; and the Goldberg Variations for double-manual harpsichord. Two somewhat smaller organ publications based on chorales followed, together with the extraordinary demonstrations of contrapuntal craft that make up the Musical Offering and Art of Fugue. Alongside these must also be considered vocal works ranging from "simple" chorale settings to the great passions and oratorios and the Latin church music. All served simultaneously as demonstrations of compositional technique and examples of profoundly expressive text setting.

Bach was not the only eighteenth-century composer to use the title *Clavierübung*. It is attached to a suite published in 1728 by Vincent Lübeck (in clear imitation of Bach) and to later publications by Bach's pupil J. L. Krebs and by Georg Andreas Sorge, who also issued a set of sonatinas with an admiring dedication to Bach.[19] Bach's title aligned his work with suites that Kuhnau, Graupner, and others had been publishing in Germany since the last decades of the seventeenth century. Yet the opening movements of the partitas in the first part of Bach's *Clavierübung* are of unprecedented diversity. Among them are extended two- and three-part inventions (called "Fantasia" and "Praeludium," respectively), a French overture, and a toccata. The following movements, although representing the traditional dances of the French harpsichord

---

19 Remarkably, the dedication of Sorge's "Third Half-Dozen Sonatinas" (*Drittes halbes Dutzend Sonatinen*, ca. 1745) praises Bach's personal character, not his music; see BD 2:412–13 (no. 526), trans. in NBR, 35 (no. 339). Sorge's *Clavierübung*, which included preludes in all twenty-four keys, came out in five volumes during the 1730s and 1740s.

suite, also departed from convention, as indeed those of Rameau and other composers were doing by this time—but, again, Bach goes farther, and no two examples of any one dance in the set much resemble one another.

Some movements, such as the "Aria" of Partita no. 4 and the corrente of no. 5, are really abstract sonata allegros. Indeed, the corrente of Partita no. 6 probably originated as a movement in an early version of the sixth sonata for violin and keyboard (BWV 1019a). The Second Partita closes not with the usual gigue but with a fugal capriccio. The latter title traditionally served for abstruse, through-composed contrapuntal music, as in examples by Froberger that Bach probably knew.[20] This capriccio, however, is in binary form, with an explosively vivacious subject that is genuinely capricious (unlike more conventional examples). The other partitas close with the usual gigue, but that of the First Partita is a unique etude in hand-crossing. On the other hand, the gigue that brings the collection to a conclusion is an austere chromatic fugue.

Contemporaries who had been purchasing the individual partitas as they came out—they were published in installments, prior to the collected edition of all six in 1730 or 1731—might have wondered at the growing complication and difficulty of the pieces. These had progressed from the relatively simple and decidedly non-contrapuntal First Partita in B-flat to the rigorous and highly contrapuntal Sixth, in the diametrically opposed key of E minor. Beyond mere difficulty or complexity, however, was a more fleeting characteristic of this music: its failure to be contained, an audacious refusal to be confined by conventions of how one should write a suite for harpsichord, of what "keyboard practice" (*Clavierübung*) might *be*.

Nevertheless, the "Italian concerto" and "French overture" that make up the second volume of the *Clavierübung*, published in a single installment in 1735, belong to seemingly well-established genres.[21] The supposedly antithetical national characters of the two components of the

---

20 See Schulenberg (2017).

21 The date is documented by an announcement given by the engraver and publisher, Christoph Weigel, at Nuremberg on July 1, 1735 (BD 2:258 [no. 366]). Butler (1990, 27ff.), however, argues that some editions could actually have been printed at Leipzig during the fairs.

volume are reflected in their tonalities, again contrasted by mode and the interval of a tritone.[22] Yet both are for a harpsichord with two manuals— a type associated only with French music—while drawing heavily on Italian style. Even the "French" overture has a fugue in concerto style, after the initial "dotted" section. Both pieces in fact represent specifically German varieties of their respective genres, the concerto abandoning the manner of Vivaldi's earlier works for a lyrical *galant* style character- istic of the next generation, including such composers as Pisendel and Gottlieb Graun.

When Bach continued the series in fall 1739, it was with a volume of music for organ, not further harpsichord pieces.[23] At that point the Scheibe controversy had been ongoing for more than two years, and Part 3 of the *Clavierübung*, with its mixture of strict and *galant* elements, could have been a response.[24] While reflecting elements of Frescobaldi's *Fiori musicali* and various French organ books, the volume is unlike any- thing previously published, in this respect surpassing Parts 1 and 2. Those volumes reinvented writing for harpsichords of one and two manuals, respectively; Part 3 offered "practice" for two-manual organ with pedals. Not every movement requires all three keyboards; perhaps conceived in- itially as a series of *pedaliter* chorale settings, it ultimately incorporated a full range of organ pieces both with and without pedals.[25]

The order of movements in Part 3 of the *Clavierübung* has been described as an ideal recital program, comprising as it does both a large praeludium and a series of organ chorales.[26] More surely it is a Lutheran

---

22 F major and B minor; that this was intentionally symbolic is evident from Bach's changing the key of the overture from its original C minor, in the version copied by Magdalena (BWV 831a).

23 The date is established by a newspaper announcement of September 30, 1739 (BD 2:370 [no. 456]). Earlier that year, on January 10, Johann Elias had written in a letter that Sebastian was planning to issue a volume of pieces "mainly for organists" ("hauptsächlich vor die Herrn Organisten") that would come out during the Easter fair; apparently publication was delayed.

24 As suggested by Butler (1990, 17 and 19).

25 The complicated history of the expansion, engraving, and printing of the volume as reconstructed by Butler (1990, esp. 79–82) is summarized by Werner Breig in the intro- duction to his edition (Wiesbaden: Breitkopf und Härtel, 2010), 8–9 (English translation, 15–16).

26 As Wolff (1986, 288) suggested.

version of a French *livre d'orgue*, such as Bach knew from his manuscript copying of organ books by Grigny and (probably) Dumage. Bach's
volume consists of an opening prelude followed by ten chorales, ordered
liturgically; each melody appears in settings with and without pedals.
Echoing publications by Grigny and d'Anglebert, the volume ends with
"free" contrapuntal pieces: four *manualiter* duets, plus a five-part fugue
(with pedals) that forms a pair with the opening prelude.[27]

Today the opening prelude and the closing fugue are regarded as a
single composition, yet the initial movement, like several in the WTC,
already resembles a self-contained prelude and fugue. The volume
concludes with the "Five-part fugue for full organ."[28] The piece clearly
complements the opening praeludium and is just as clearly *not* a conventional fugue. Rather it resembles canzoni from the previous century by
Frescobaldi and Froberger, comprising three sections based on versions
of the same subject in different meters. That subject is based in turn on
a motive that also occurs in the opening phrase of the Anglican hymn
known as "Saint Anne"—hence the use of the latter as a nickname for
the fugue itself, although similar subjects occur in earlier pieces.

The same combination of archaic and modern features characterizes
the publication that is always regarded as Part 4 of the *Clavierübung*, although the words *Vierter Theil* are absent from the title page. Published
two years after Part 3, in 1741, the Goldberg Variations, as the work is usually called, were actually entitled "Keyboard Practice consisting of an Aria
with diverse variations for the harpsichord with two keyboards, prepared
for the spiritual refreshment of music lovers."[29] Bach uses the word *aria* as
Pachelbel and other seventeenth-century composers had done, referring
to a movement in binary form that is then varied. Like Frescobaldi in his
Aria di Romanesca, Bach bases his variations not on the melody but the
bass, preserving the original tonal design (including a central double bar)
in each variation. On the other hand, few of the variations preserve any

---

27 Grigny's organ book includes a five-part fugue as the third piece from the end; the last
compositions in d'Anglebert's *Pièces de clavecin* are five organ fugues and a Kyrie.

28 *Fuga a 5 pro Organo pleno.*

29 *Clavier Ubung [sic] bestehend in einer Aria mit verschiedenen Veraenderungen vors Clavicimbal mit
2 Manualen denen Liebhabern zur Gemüths-Ergetzung verfertiget von Johann Sebastian Bach.* The
date was established by Butler (1988), arguing from the chronology of travels by Bach and
the identification of pupils associated with the work and its engraving.

thematic or rhythmic elements of the aria, which is a sarabande comparable to that of the Fifth French Suite (also in G major).

The popular title of the variations reflects Forkel's account of private performances by Johann Gottlieb Goldberg, a young pupil of J. S. (or W. F.) Bach, for his employer Count Keyserlingk. The latter is supposed to have enjoyed listening to the work when unable to sleep; Goldberg's reputation as a great keyboard player would have been well earned if he was indeed able to perform it on short notice in the middle of the night. The Variations as we have them follow a three-fold pattern, every third variation (starting with no. 3) being a canon at a different interval. Each canon is followed by a free variation of some sort, then a duet requiring the two keyboards of a double harpsichord. For this reason pianists can play this work only by adapting it to a single keyboard—not a straightforward task, given the freedom with which the two hands continually cross one another in the double-manual variations.

The cycling between three types of movement is reminiscent of the passions (see below). It is, however, more regular than their alternation between gospel, chorale, and aria. Still, just as one type of movement—the gospel recitatives—furnished the basic framework for the passions, here the canons provided the underlying structure. As in previous installments of the *Clavierübung*, variety is of the essence. The work incorporates many traditional types of movements: a gigue, a fughetta, a French overture, a "monodic" setting of a decorated sarabande melody. But by the last four or five variations, it has left behind the conventions of ordinary harpsichord music.

Bach's other canonic set of variations—*the* Canonic Variations, as they are known to organists—was a later and shorter work. It was probably conceived as an offering for Mizler's society—a version in large format of the little canons that were traditional tokens of friendship among musicians. Exactly when or in what form Bach originally composed the music is unknown. It clearly reflected his intensified interest during the 1740s in a compositional device that he had long associated with chorale settings, especially those for Christmas.[30]

---

30 The work's history, reconstructed by Butler (1990), became more complicated with the same author's subsequent argument (2000) that variation 4 was not engraved until sometime in 1747. This would have been after the other variations had been engraved, even

Bach's other late printed work for organ, known as the "Schübler chorales," came out around the same time as the Canonic Variations (probably slightly earlier). Originally entitled "Six chorales of various types," it is now known after Bach's pupil Johann Georg Schübler. He had studied both engraving and organ playing and was entrusted with the engraving and publication of the new work, probably during 1748.[31] All but one of the six chorale settings is known to be a *pedaliter* transcription of a chorale movement from one of the cantatas.

The Musical Offering

Among the most remarkable of all Bach's works is the unique publication that emerged from his last trip into Prussian territory. By the time of his last two organ publications—the "Schübler" chorales and the Canonic Variations—Bach probably had already made his final visit to Berlin and seen his Musical Offering engraved and printed by his former pupil Johann Georg Schübler. This work, the product of his encounter with Frederick "the Great" in Potsdam, has been discussed from religious, political, and biographical viewpoints.[32] The king was a composer and flutist of professional capability, practically the equal musically of the virtuosos who accompanied him in his private concerts. The latter were already legendary during his lifetime, but Sebastian would have learned many useful details from Emanuel, who by 1747 had probably accompanied much of the king's repertory of flute sonatas and concertos composed up to that point. Thus Sebastian would have known that the king not only was capable of playing the most advanced passagework in difficult keys but was a superb performer of adagios, rivaled in this only by Emanuel himself.[33] Although the king doubtless favored *galant*

---

after variation 4 had been added at the end of Bach's manuscript copy—which gives later versions at least for the first three variations.

31 The date is based in part on the apparent improvement in Schübler's engraving work as compared with that of the Musical Offering, which is known to date from 1747 (Kobayashi 1988, 59). That Schübler studied with Bach is known from an autobiographical sketch of his brother Johann Heinrich, also an engraver; see Butler (2002, 311).

32 See, for example, Marissen (1995a).

33 And by the violinist Franz Benda, leader of the palace concerts, according to the king's later accompanist Carl Fasch (see Schulenberg 2014, 194). Adverse reports about Frederick's playing or repertory reflect conditions two or three decades after Sebastian's visit.

music, at least during his early days he also cultivated contrapuntal pieces, playing sonatas as well as concertos that included fugal movements.[34]

Sebastian would have known, too, that Quantz, Frederick's chief chamber musician, furnished the king not only with flute music but with instruments, including special two-keyed flutes made by Quantz himself. These facilitated fine intonation in previously difficult tonalities. They also possessed a strong low register, especially when played at the low chamber pitch—more than a whole step beneath modern concert pitch—which was still favored for chamber music in the mid-eighteenth century.[35] In publishing an "offering" for a musical king, Bach could hardly avoid taking into consideration the instruments, performance practices, and musical styles favored by the Prussian ruler. At the same time he paid tribute to the latter's interest in the sciences by including a substantial "learned" element in the form of strict fugues and canons.[36]

Unlike the Canonic Variations and the Goldberg Variations, the Musical Offering is not an integrated work, rather a sort of compendium—a musical equivalent of the journals containing essays, poems, and other writings that were then being published at Berlin and elsewhere. Peculiarities in the printed format of the work, such as the use of different-sized sheets of paper for different components, have given rise to speculation about the intended ordering or meaning of its contents.[37] These may not, in fact, have been meant to fall in any particular sequence. Yet they are readily understood as comprising (1) two fugues for performance or study by individual keyboard players; (2) a trio sonata for performance by small groups; and (3) ten canons in "puzzle" notation, for realization either by a copyist in a manuscript score or by several players as a form of musical entertainment. Each item is based on the same subject: the theme that

---

34 On Frederick's cultivation of contrapuntal music, see Oleskiewicz (1999, 80–84).

35 Oleskiewicz (1999, 89–102) discusses these aspects of instrumentation at Berlin.

36 Bach's dedication, dated July 7, 1747, refers to the king's fame "in all the disciplines of war and peace, but particularly in music" (*allen Kriegs- und Friedens-Wissenschaften, also auch besonders in Musik*). This could reflect Frederick's establishment in 1744 of the Prussian Academy of Sciences, which in the following year began publishing annual volumes of writings on the sciences, philosophy, and literature.

37 In particular, Kirkendale (1980) proposed ordering the work's sections by analogy to classical rhetoric, but this proved unpersuasive due to the weak connection with the actual music.

Example 13.1 Musical Offering, BWV 1079, forms of the royal theme as it appears in: (a) three-part ricercar; (b) sonata (mvt. 2, mm. 161–69, flute); (c) canon *per augmentationem, contrario motu*

the king had played for Bach at their initial meeting (Example 13.1). As much was already clear from the original newspaper announcement of the work. From this it is evident that the two fugues for solo keyboard, called ricercars within the publication itself, retained priority as a souvenir of Bach's original improvisation on the royal theme.[38]

In its use of a single theme for every component, the work is comparable to the two variation sets that Bach also published during these years and to the Art of Fugue that would follow—although neither the latter nor the Musical Offering is a set of variations as such. The idea of treating the same subject in different rhythmic forms went back to the Renaissance; Bach had previously used it in the "St. Anne" fugue from

38 The announcement of September 30, 1747, is edited in BD 3:656 (no. 558a), trans. in NBR, 229 (no. 248).

Part 3 of the *Clavierübung*.[39] The same device made possible the myriad contrapuntal manipulations to which he routinely subjected chorale melodies. The fugue subject that the king gave Bach is unlikely to have been made up on the spot; it could have been suggested by examples from works by Quantz and Zelenka. The king himself had composed a flute sonata in the same key that includes a vaguely similar fugue subject.[40]

As impressive as the two ricercars may be in a good performance, the sonata is the great work of the set. Bach's only trio sonata to survive in its original form, it is much later in date and more mature in style than the other examples. The four movements, in the order slow-fast-slow-fast, correspond to what is now called a church sonata—a type long out of fashion by this date, as Bach knew. Yet the two slow movements draw on the so-called *empfindsam* style—the expressive version of the *galant* favored at Berlin—while falling into highly symmetrical versions of sonata form.[41] The quick movements are fugues of contrasting form and character.

The Art of Fugue

Both the contrapuntal devices and the expressive effects exemplified by the Musical Offering are developed with greater intensity and variety in the Art of Fugue. Although sometimes viewed as Bach's last work, the Art of Fugue mostly predates his visit to Potsdam and Berlin. One or two movements, however, were among Bach's last entirely new compositions, and another may never have been finished. Bach meant to publish the work as his contribution to the literature of counterpoint, and as his health declined while the music remained unprinted, he must have wondered whether the wider world would ever receive his final musical testament. The music was largely composed, however, by the early 1740s, when Bach wrote out the existing autograph manuscript, some of

---

39 Bach also used this device in the Canzona BWV 588, an early work perhaps from the first years at Weimar more directly modeled on examples by Frescobaldi and Froberger.

40 See Oleskiewicz (1999, 85–86 and Ex. 1). Frederick's theme belonged to a conventional type, but that it was a direct offshoot of any particular fugue subject, let alone an example by Handel (as argued by Sassoon 2003), is unlikely.

41 Both slow movements employ "subdominant recapitulations." The first movement falls into three sections of sixteen measures each (with double bar after the first); the third movement is only slightly less symmetrical, dividing into sections of 7½, 10½, and 12 measures.

it copied from still earlier drafts. Details of the work's history remain enigmatic, and it was published after his death in an incomplete form that did not entirely reflect his intentions. The identities of its engravers and its status as *manualiter* keyboard music are now clear.[42] But whether Bach ever completed the "Fugue with three subjects" and whether this was to have been followed by a mirror fugue with four subjects—as Emanuel indicated in his father's Obituary—are among the questions unlikely ever to be resolved.[43]

What we do have of the work is so compelling that regrets over whatever may be missing are almost impertinent. As with other works, Bach expanded on his original plan, producing a wealth of music that admits multiple arrangements. Hence the Art of Fugue, like the Musical Offering, remains a heterogeneous set of separate pieces, all based on a single theme but standing in no unique order.[44] Indeed, the Musical Offering was really a second, smaller realization of the same fundamental plan, combining long fugal movements with shorter canonic ones. The canons of the Art of Fugue, however, are fewer in number and much larger—full-fledged compositions, not vignettes added at the ends of pages not already filled by other music.

Although the Art of Fugue is keyboard music, most of Bach's autograph manuscript is notated in open score (Figures 13.1, 13.2). It therefore looks similar on the page to the seventeenth-century contrapuntal works by Frescobaldi and Froberger that were among its main models. The

42 Leonhardt (1952) made the case for keyboard performance, after arrangements for instrumental ensemble had become the norm earlier in the twentieth century (following Graeser 1924). That the first edition, like that of the Musical Offering, was engraved chiefly by the brothers Johann Georg and Johann Heinrich Schübler was established by Butler (2008), refining earlier work by Wiemer (1979).

43 "The last [piece] . . . was to contain four themes and to have been afterward inverted note for note in all four voices" ("die letzte, welche 4 Themata enthalten, und nachgehends in allen 4 Stimmen Note für Note umgekehret werden sollte"), BD 3:86 (no. 666), trans. in NBR, 304 (no. 306). It is possible that these lines reflected a misunderstanding and that a sketch for the final section of the unfinished fugue was mistaken for a separate composition.

44 Tatlow (2015, 243–51) and Milka (2017, esp. 79ff.) offer reconstructions of Bach's changing formal scheme for the work as a whole; they follow different principles but agree with earlier scholars that Bach revised the "ground plan" alluded to by a cryptic rubric (*ein andere Grund Plan*) added in the autograph manuscript.

Figure 13.1 Contapunctus 1 from the Art of Fugue (BWV 1080/1), opening, from Bach's autograph manuscript score of ca. 1742 (Berlin, Staatsbibliothek, Mus. ms. Bach P 200). From Bach-Digital.

Figure 13.2 Contapunctus 1 from the Art of Fugue (BWV 1080/1), opening, as printed (Berlin, Staatsbibliothek, Mus. O. 17364 Rara). From Bach-Digital.

Example 13.2   Art of Fugue, BWV 1080, various forms of the main subject: (a) from
Contrapunctus 1, mm. 1–5; (b) inversion, from Contrapunctus 4, mm. 1–5; (c) inversion in
rhythmic diminution, with dotted rhythm, from Contrapunctus 6, mm. 2–4

theme as first presented in the opening movement is archaic in its large
note values and quasi-vocal style, avoiding the lively motives and dance
rhythms of so many later Baroque fugues. The idea of varying the subject for subsequent movements came from the multi-sectional canzoni
and recercars of earlier composers such as Froberger and Buxtehude
(Example 13.2). Yet no one previously had written such a monumental
compendium of self-contained compositions based on a single theme,
which, alone or combined with additional subjects, was ultimately the
basis of eighteen movements—six more counting alternate versions.

The individual movements, most of them fugues in four parts
(entitled *contrapuncti*), exemplify increasingly sophisticated contrapuntal
devices, such as inversion, stretto, and invertible counterpoint at different
intervals. There are also four canons in two parts. The work in its en-
tirety is thus comprised of "demonstration counterpoint," although this
did not rule out expressive gestures and bravura virtuoso writing. Some
movements bear titles describing the particular types of counterpoint
that they demonstrate, but the collection is inconsistent in this matter.
Thematic diminution and augmentation, both named in the title of
movement 7 (as published), also occur in no. 6. Invertible counterpoint
at the octave is so fundamental to Bach's compositions that it is present
in every piece although named in the title of only one. Two contrasting
mirror fugues (Contrapuncti 12 and 13), playable both in their "original"
forms and with every melodic interval in every part inverted, perhaps
constitute the most dazzling examples of contrapuntal technique. The
expressive climax of the set, however, occurs in Contrapunctus 11, one of

two triple fugues whose third subject incorporates the letters of Bach's name (BACH). Bach had been using this device since at least his Weimar days (see Example 7.11; it also occurs in the bass line of Brandenburg Concerto no. 2). Here he uses it to "sign" two of his most intricate and overwhelming compositions.

Songs and Chorale Harmonizations

It is possible that Bach saw works like the Art of Fugue as his most important legacy—hence the focus on publication of contrapuntal keyboard music during his last decade. Yet for a Lutheran teacher and church musician, vocal music, especially chorales, was at the center of professional life. Although Bach's most important vocal compositions remained unpublished for more than half a century after his death, he did see a few examples of his vocal music in print during his lifetime, and he may have gathered his four-part chorale harmonizations into some sort of "official" manuscript collection.

To everyday listeners the chorale harmonizations may not seem very exciting, but for close to three centuries they have served serious music students as models of ingenious and expressive part writing (see Example 7.5). Bach probably regarded his chorale arrangements not as present-day music students do—as abstract exercises in recherché harmony—but as sacred songs, that is, *Lieder:* settings of strophic poetry, distinct from operatic arias in their straightforward syllabic melodies and relatively homophonic textures. Most are for four-part polyphonic ensemble, but Bach arranged some hymn tunes for solo voice and continuo, and there are also a few secular songs for voice and continuo. Today art songs or lieder for voice and piano are associated with nineteenth-century Romantic composers, like Schubert and Schumann. But German composers had been publishing collections of songs, sacred as well as secular, since the sixteenth century. During Sebastian's lifetime the genre began to see a revival, to which Emanuel Bach would be an important contributor.[45] Although secular songs make up an insignificant portion of Sebastian's output, his chorale harmonizations were a transformative contribution to a genre that was of vital significance for any Lutheran

45 C. P. E. Bach's first published songs appeared in anthologies during the early 1740s; Youngren (2003) surveys them in massive detail.

cantor and his students, even if only a handful, at most, of the melodies are his own.

Passions and Oratorios

Most of Bach's four-part chorale settings were eventually published after his death in an edition by his pupils Kirnberger and Emanuel Bach. The majority were taken from cantatas, but some came from Sebastian's larger sacred works, the passions and oratorios. The five such works that survive originated at Leipzig. Whether or not they were preceded by earlier examples (as is sometimes thought), Bach, while completing the St. John Passion during Lent 1724, must have recognized that what he was creating was greater by an order of magnitude than anything of the type previously composed. At the end of his life, a quarter century later, Bach appears to have regarded the passions and oratorios as the high points of his work in the sphere of vocal music, worthy of preservation in newly prepared revision scores. In this they are comparable to the "exemplary" instrumental works of his last two decades.

These passions and oratorios are more than simply expanded versions of Bach's regular sacred cantatas. They were also responses to interest across western Europe in the dramatization of biblical history. Handel's English oratorios, on which work began in earnest with the expanded version of *Esther* in 1732, were another manifestation of this. Closer to Bach was Hasse's *Cantico de' tre fanciulli*, performed for the Dresden court on Good Friday 1734. On that same day, Bach was performing a passion oratorio by Stölzel, another manifestation of the same trend.[46] Leipzig had previously heard a "Joseph" oratorio, performed by Schott's collegium some time before the latter's departure in 1729.[47] These works were of varying length and took various shapes, some retaining biblical texts for part or all of the music, others paraphrasing or entirely eliminating them. Some have named characters, whereas in others the soloists are limited to narration and reflection.

---

46 Later during 1734–1735 Bach apparently performed an entire annual cycle of cantatas by Stölzel; see Pfau (2008).

47 The music is lost, the composer unknown. Maul (2007, 71–75) reports this as well as a performance by Görner of a secular *Klage* (lament) for Phaeton; the anonymous libretto was printed by Breitkopf in 1726.

Bach's own passions and oratorios are similarly diverse, although they remain close stylistically to his cantatas. But in place of the lyrical or contemplative texts of the cantatas, whose drama is entirely metaphorical—taking place in the mind of the individual listener—the librettos of these works explicitly recount episodes from the New Testament. As such they are descended from seventeenth-century *historiae*, and they were genuinely historical for congregations to whom these were true accounts of real events. The word *passion* comes from Latin *patior* (I suffer), and in principle a passion is simply a *historia* for Good Friday, recounting the arrest, trial, and crucifixion of Jesus. But the special traditions associated with that day, the most solemn of the church year, led Bach and other Lutheran composers to write distinctive music for it. Bach's two extant passions, based on the gospels of Matthew and John, respectively, are his most important oratorios and arguably his greatest individual works. During the 1730s Bach extended the concept to oratorios for Christmas, Easter, and Ascension. These days memorialized the three other most significant points in the New Testament narrative: Jesus's birth, resurrection, and ascension as heavenly king.

The basic element in Bach's passions (and in two of the three oratorios) is the gospel narrative, mainly set as recitative. There are also short duets and so-called *turba* (crowd) choruses, used respectively when pairs of characters and when larger groups of people (such as the disciples) speak. This narration is interspersed with the same types of additional matter that was incorporated into Bach's church cantatas: chorale stanzas and "madrigalian" verse, that is, recitatives and arias. In some librettos, including that of Bach's lost St. Mark Passion, the extra-biblical component consists mainly of chorales. In the St. John and St. Matthew Passions, however, the arias are the main shaping elements, as in opera of the period. The recitatives that precede most of the arias are set as accompanied ariosos, distinguishing them from the simple ("secco") recitative used for most of the gospel narrative.

The combination of biblical narration, reflective recitatives and arias, and chorales representing congregational responses makes for a complicated alternation or cycling of movement types over the course of each work. The "action" and dialog of the gospel passages lead sometimes to a chorale, sometimes to an arioso-aria pair. Both chorales and arias reflect on events narrated in a preceding gospel passage. But the madrigalian ariosos and arias—which can be scored for multiple soloists, or even antiphonal choruses—sometimes offer drama as intense as any *turba* chorus, especially in several examples in the St. Matthew Passion.

Bach's Obituary mentions five passions, but only two survive.[48] Both were conceived for somewhat larger performing forces than usual, including eight vocal parts. In the St. John Passion these comprise concertists and ripienists; in the later St. Matthew Passion the eight voices have become two distinct four-part choruses, each with its own orchestra. Yet the second chorus and orchestra of the latter work have a lesser role than the first; the "double-chorus" element, like the double-manual harpsichord writing in Part 2 of the *Clavierübung*, is less essential than is usually supposed.[49] The two passions have complicated, intertwined histories, leaving many questions unresolved. In particular, the librettist of the St. John Passion remains uncertain, although a substantial portion derives from the famous passion text by Brockes, apparently adapted by the Leipzig theology student Birkmann. Uncertain, too, are Bach's precise intentions for its final form, most modern performances being based on an edition that conflates matter from its first and last versions.[50]

The St. John Passion (BWV 245) was first performed on Good Friday 1724. Suspicions that some movements were taken from an earlier "Weimar" or "Gotha" passion have never been substantiated, but the loss of the original score and most of the performing parts for the first Leipzig performance prevents any definitive conclusion.[51] Bach repeated

---

48 The authors of the Obituary might have counted the anonymous St. Luke Passion (BWV 246) or several pastiche passions. Dürr (2000, 233n. 2) argued that C. P. E. Bach is unlikely to have considered BWV 246 as one of his father's works, but he included pastiche passions in a posthumously published list of his own compositions.

49 See Melamed (2004, drawing on Rifkin 2000a, 207), who shows that the instrumental complement needed for both passions was not much larger than usual. Although the writing for two-manual harpsichord was noted on the title page of the Italian Concerto and French Overture, it is not an integral element of either as it is in the Goldberg Variations (see Schulenberg 2006, 348–49, 352, 356).

50 On the librettist, see Blanken (2015, 51–55). Arthur Mendel's 1973 edition in the NBA (Vol. 2/4) is to be replaced by new volumes presenting the versions of 1725 and 1749 separately.

51 Dürr (2000, 5–6) notes that the one sure borrowing from a previous work, the chorus "Christe, du Lamm Gottes," added for the 1725 version, can be traced only as far back as Cantata 23, one of Bach's test-pieces from 1723. Another movement included in the 1725

the work in 1725 with substantial changes; further revisions took place around 1732 and perhaps again in 1739, when Bach started making a fair-copy score. The latter was completed only around 1749 by a copyist, at which time Bach made further changes. These returned the work to something close to its original version, at least in terms of its large design.[52] Meanwhile Bach had composed the St. Matthew Passion (BWV 244) for performance in 1727. It was possibly repeated in 1729, certainly in 1736, and probably in 1742, each time with changes, but none as substantial as in the St. John Passion.[53]

The fundamental question regarding both works is, When did Bach arrive at the idea of creating liturgical passions of such magnitude, comparable in size to an opera or to a non-liturgical work such as the Brockes-Passion of Telemann? The latter had been performed at Frankfurt, Hamburg, and other places, possibly including Leipzig, by 1717.[54] It was, however, a different sort of work, paraphrasing selected gospel passages rather than presenting a continuous narrative extracted from a single book. It contained only a few chorales, making it more suitable for performance as a concert work; in this it resembled later oratorios of the same type, such as Telemann's *Seliges Erwägen*. Today the familiarity of Bach's two passions makes their dimensions seem normal, but they are much more ambitious than other liturgical passions of the period, including the "Keiser" passion which Bach copied out and probably performed during his Weimar years. If he did compose a passion of

---

version, the chorale aria "Himmel, reiße," uses a distinct form of the hymn tune "Jesu, deine Passion" that suggests a pre-Leipzig origin.

52 Bach never reconciled many small discrepancies between the 1749 score and individual performing parts. Hence the work remained not quite finished, much like WTC2, which also survives in slightly distinct revised versions.

53 Old views of the St. Matthew Passion as having originated in 1729 or even 1731 were refuted by Rifkin (1975). He showed that the text of the 1729 funeral music for Prince Leopold (BWV 244a) parodied that of BWV 244, which in turn drew on an earlier passion text by Picander (*Erbauliche Gedanken*) for several numbers.

54 Glöckner (1990, 79) asserts that Telemann's Brockes-Passion was the passion cantata known from a contemporary chronicle to have been performed at Leipzig on Good Friday 1717, and that this took place at the New Church. Telemann himself had mentioned (without giving details) a Leipzig performance in his autobiography, written in 1718 as a letter to Mattheson but published by the latter only in 1731 (178).

his own during that period, it was not necessarily a monumental composition like the two surviving ones.

The St. John Passion as we know it must have been composed largely during the six-week Lenten period preceding Good Friday 1724. Bach repeated it the following year, perhaps because it had previously been heard only at St. Nicholas's, and in 1725 the passion performance moved to St. Thomas.[55] To be sure, the 1725 version differed substantially, opening with a new chorale chorus that perhaps was meant to align it with the cycle of chorale cantatas, underway since the end of the previous May.[56] The work as a whole is built around Chapters 18 and 19 from the gospel of John; those words are set mostly as simple recitative for the tenor concertist.[57] The three remaining soloists sing the words of Jesus and others. The words of groups, such as the disciples and priests, are presented as short four-part choruses, accompanied by the full instrumental ensemble of two flutes, two oboes, strings, and continuo. Into this narrative are inserted eight arias and ten chorales, the latter all in "simple" four-part harmonizations; there are also two framing choruses in aria form at beginning and end.[58]

The majority of listeners today probably find the St. John Passion, with its single chorus and orchestra, relatively austere by comparison with the St. Matthew Passion. The latter not only calls for somewhat larger forces but is also longer and more theatrical, at least in the sense of presenting Jesus as a human character in a drama. Those differences probably reflect intentional distinctions made as Picander

---

55 This was a departure from the practice with cantatas, which were performed in the morning at one church, then repeated in the afternoon at the other. Passion performances for 1723–1738 were recorded by the sexton of St. Thomas's; see BD 2:141 (no. 180).

56 The cycle would not continue after Easter, however, and Bach eventually moved the chorale chorus "O Mensch, bewein" to the end of the first half of the St. Matthew Passion.

57 There are also two brief inserts from Matthew, one within no. 12c (from "Da gedachte Petrus"), the other comprising the whole of no. 33 ("Und siehe da"). The latter replaced a verse from Mark (15:38), but Bach's setting of this is lost together with other music from the 1724 version.

58 Not counted in these totals are the concluding chorale and the ariosos that precede two of the arias. "Durch dein Gefängnis" (no. 22) is counted as a chorale because that is how Bach treats it musically, using the hymn tune "Mach's mit mir, Gott, nach deiner Güt." Its text, however, originated as an aria in a passion libretto by Christian Heinrich Postel.

and Bach collaborated on the later work. Yet Bach's inventiveness is, if anything, more astounding in the St. John Passion. For here the composer effectively reinvented the oratorio passion, radically surpassing anything by his contemporaries, just as he had previously done in his church cantatas. It is nearly arbitrary to select individual passages or movements for special attention. But one would not want to miss such things as the deep contrast between the opening movement—a choral aria characterized by the harsh dissonances and swirling tumult of its ritornello—and the comforting penultimate aria. The latter, a dialogue between bass soloist and a choral sung by the three other voices, points toward the double-choral conception of the later passion (Examples 13.3, 13.4).

As in any passion of this type, the movements inserted into the gospel text shape and interpret the latter, which could be divided in several ways. The traditional division of the passion narrative was into five "acts,"[59] corresponding with (1) Jesus's arrest in the garden; (2) his interrogation by the priests; (3) his trial by Pilate; (4) the crucifixion; and (5) the burial. The first two "acts" precede the sermon; the last three follow it. As a result, the work is asymmetrical, for the second half is not only longer but more harrowing emotionally. Each "act" ends with a chorale,[60] yet the great variation in the lengths of the acts (dependent in part on the number of inserted arias and additional chorales) suggests that the *actus* division was secondary to other considerations for Bach and his librettist.

One potential shaping device within the first three "acts" is the grouping of certain numbers into sequences that begin and end with choral movements and remain in closely related keys.[61] Another such grouping, within the fourth ("crucifixion") *actus*, begins and ends with complementary statements of the same chorale melody, sung to

59 From Latin *actus*, meaning more "actions" or "events" than the acts of a play. The five-fold division is set out clearly by Dürr (2000, 51), following Martin Petzoldt.

60 Dürr 2000 (2000, 51).

61 These comprise nos. 1–3, 11–14, and 15–17, respectively. (The present numbering follows the NBA, in which the various solo, duo, and *turba* segments of each gospel portion are considered a single numbered unit, subdivided by letter suffixes, as no. 2a. Older editions, including the BG, numbered each such segment separately, resulting in a greater total number of units.)

Example 13.3   Saint John Passion, BWV 245, no. 1, mm. 19–20:

Herr, unser [Herrscher,]   Lord, our [ruler,]

Example 13.4 Saint John Passion, BWV 245, no. 32, mm. 24–28:

Ist aller Welt Erlösung da . . .   Is the redemption of all the world here?
Als zu dir, der mich versühnt, . . .   but to you who atones for me,

different stanzas; these mark off something like a small cantata within the larger work.[62] Better known is the so-called core section or heartpiece (*Herzstück*) within the third or "trial" *actus*. This segment is

---

62 This comprises nos. 28–32, incorporating settings of the chorale "Jesu, deine Passion."

articulated by the symmetrical placement of *turba* choruses in an arch form around the chorale-like "Durch dein Gefängnis" (no. 22).[63] Yet, as in the St. Matthew Passion, where something similar occurs, the symmetry created by the re-use of music for similar *turba* speeches is inexact. Several other *turba* choruses and chorale melodies also recur over the course of the work, but at points that are not easily related to an overall scheme.

Bach's recitative setting of the gospel narration is always expressive. For most listeners, however, the most compelling music lies in the arias (including the framing choral arias) and in several of the *turba* choruses. The latter, following a tradition that went back to the Renaissance, sometimes resemble little imitative motets. Thus, when the priests explain the law ("Wir haben ein Gesetz"), the idea of law is expressed by fugue or imitation.

The eight arias for solo singers are divided equally between the concertists, although the tenor and bass also sing one arioso or accompanied recitative each. Both arioso-aria pairs fall in the second half, following particularly dramatic moments. They respond, first, to the selection of Barabbas over Jesus for release, then to the earthquake that follows the crucifixion. Both are intensely sad or meditative, as reflected in their special, quiet instrumentation. The first pair originally included two violas d'amore, with obbligato lute later replacing the keyboard continuo at least in the arioso.[64] In the second pair, the entire instrumental ensemble accompanies the arioso, where the strings play in unison to represent thunder. These drop out for the aria, where the deeply "flat" key of F minor (rare even in late-Baroque ensemble music) gives the woodwinds a particularly dark sound.[65] The poems of both of these arias are based on "flowing" imagery—blood, then tears—and Bach finds similar musical symbolism for each.

---

63 The *Herzstück* in the St. John Passion, first described by Smend (1926), minimally comprises the section bounded by the choruses nos. 21b and 25b ("Sei gegrüßet" and "Schreibe nicht"), which use the same music.

64 Bach's precise original intentions are unclear due to the loss of his performing parts. The lute was eventually replaced by obbligato organ and harpsichord (for different performances), the violas d'amore with muted violins.

65 The scoring of the aria no. 35 is uncertain; it might originally have been for the same violas d'amore used in nos. 19–20. The participation of both flutes and oboes (as indicated in some editions) is unlikely.

One aspect of Bach's St. John Passion that cannot be avoided in any modern discussion is the role of the Jewish priests and the Jewish people in the passion story. Their treatment has led to accusations of anti-Semitism, if not against the evangelists themselves, then against the authors of eighteenth-century librettos based on their writings. Bach's librettists clearly intended his congregations to identify with the "people" as a whole; it is sinful humanity, not any one group, that was responsible for Jesus's death. Yet this could not rule out the possibility of bigoted responses to the story.

Whether Bach's passion *settings* should be regarded as "anti-Judaic" might depend on how his music treats relevant expressions in the text. A composer could emphasize certain words, as by repeating the syllables *der Jüden* (of the Jews) in the *turba* chorus "Gegrüßet seist du" (no. 53b in the St. Matthew Passion). Sebastian never does that. In the St. John Passion, the chorus "Sei gegrüsset, lieber Judenkönig" (no. 21b) offered a similar opportunity to focus on the "Jüden" element in the text. Yet Bach fails to do so here or in the corresponding chorus "Schreibe nicht: der Jüden König" (no. 25b), which uses essentially the same music.

The occasional dialoguing between concertists and ripienists in the St. John Passion has been seen as a precursor to the "expanded ripieno practice" of the St. Matthew Passion.[66] The latter, however, differs fundamentally in that its libretto is the work of a single author: Picander, with whom Bach had been collaborating for at least the previous two years, mainly on commissioned secular cantatas. By spring 1727, moreover, Bach's pace in composing sacred cantatas had considerably slowed. He had written twelve new church pieces between Advent 1723 and Lent 1724—the period immediately preceding the St. John Passion. But only four or five cantatas are known for the corresponding period three years later, and several of them are small-scale solo works. Of course there were other compositions and performances, but the St. Matthew Passion was planned and realized during a relatively fallow period, and this could be one reason it required fewer subsequent alterations than the John Passion. Yet Bach did revise it, making changes that strengthened its character as a double-chorus work, even if

66 Melamed (2004, 13).

the second chorus remained distinctly secondary.[67] When he prepared a new fair-copy manuscript of the score in 1736—a massive clerical undertaking—he could do so confidently and with such attention to detail that verses from the gospel could be set off with red ink. Anna Magdalena would later call this the "great" Passion.[68] Arguably Bach's last major church work, it consisted mainly if not entirely of new composition (not parody) and was also the one that he "appears to have prized beyond any of his other music."[69]

Like Brockes's text, that of the St. Matthew Passion includes allegorical characters alongside those of the biblical narrative: a "Daughter of Zion" and "Believers" (*Tochter Zion* and *Gläubigen*). Picander, in the printed text included in a volume of his poetry, names these figures in nine dialog numbers. Bach scores eight of these movements for two alternating choruses, as in the opening number (Example 13.5).[70] Elsewhere the two ensembles usually perform either in unison or alone, although the double-chorus scoring remains dramatically clear in the most imposing dialog movements. These include the opening movement as well as the duet with chorus "So ist mein Jesus nun gefangen" (Example 13.6). Both are settings of aria texts:[71] the opening chorus is musically a through-composed da capo form (ABA'), the duet-chorus a bipartite (AB) form that becomes a raging double chorus in its second section. These are arguably Bach's most sublime settings of their respective types of texts. In each, Bach achieves high drama through the vivid musical realization of the dialog already explicit in Picander's text.

---

67 This is the conclusion of Melamed (2004, esp. 46–47).

68 In a note on a part for the basso continuo; see NBA, Vol. 2/5, KB, 61.

69 Rifkin (1975, 387).

70 Numbers 1, 19, 20, 27 (a and b), 30, 60, 67, and 68 (see Melamed 2004, Table 3 on p. 12). Melamed (2011, 20–21) suggests that other movements might also have been understood as representing the voice of "Zion," but this is not explicit in the printed poem, where "Z" is repeated at the beginning of each dialog, subsequently followed by "G." Besides Brockes, Picander's sources included poems by Franck and a book of passion sermons by the seventeenth-century pastor Heinrich Müller, first identified by Axmacher (1978). The German phrase *Tochter Zion* is more literally rendered "daughter Zion," and Picander probably understood it as distinct from *Tochter Zions* (daughter of Zion), as it is in Luther's translation of the bible, although not in older English versions.

71 So designated in *Picanders Ernst-Schertzhaffte und Satyrische Gedichte: Anderer Theil* (Leipzig: Boetius, 1729), 101ff.

Example 13.5 St. Matthew Passion, BWV 244, opening chorus, mm. 26–30, voices only (omitting flutes, oboes, strings, and basso continuo of both orchestras):

Sehet. Wen? den Bräutigam!   See! Whom? The bridegroom;
Seht ihn. Wie? Als wie ein Lamm.   See him? Like what? Like a lamb.

Example 13.6   St. Matthew Passion, BWV 244, no. 27, mm. 17–22 (without flutes of chorus 1 and flutes, oboes, strings, and continuo of chorus 2):

So ist mein Jesus nun gefangen.   Thus is my Jesus now captured.
Laßt ihn! haltet! bindet nicht!   Release him! stop! do not bind him!

The grander conception of Bach's St. Matthew Passion, as compared to his earlier St. John Passion, extends to the recitatives setting the words of Jesus, which are accompanied by strings and not continuo alone. The sheer amount of gospel text set in this passion is also somewhat greater: although both works set, essentially, two complete chapters, those from Matthew contain a significantly greater number of verses. Even more consequential for the lengthening of the work, however—by nearly an hour, to judge from recent recordings—is the greater number of arias and arioso-aria pairs for soloists.[72] These paired movements, moreover, more closely resemble conventional recitative-aria sequences than do the pairs in the earlier work; now both movements of each pair call for the same singer, and they usually employ the same accompanying instruments.

Six arias, including the opening and closing choral arias, involve dialogs between singers of both choirs, that is, between "Zion" and the "Believers," as do two of the ariosos. Two dialog movements also incorporate chorales: the opening choral aria, and the arioso no. 19 ("O Schmerz"). The remaining solo arias are distributed unevenly between the two groups of singers, those of the first choir predominating.[73] Clearly Bach planned the work to be performable with a second group of less accomplished soloists, who under other circumstances would have served as ripienists. Modern conductors often assign all the arias to a single group of four soloists, even while employing masses of singers in the choral movements. This distorts the formal and expressive design of the work, which retains the intimacy of chamber music.

During the years that followed the completion of the St. Matthew Passion, Bach continued to produce major vocal works, albeit chiefly through parody and revision of existing ones. For Good Friday 1731 he prepared the lost St. Mark Passion (BWV 247). To judge from Picander's libretto, this was considerably shorter than the two extant passions, its music consisting largely of parody. The libretto, dated 1731, was published the following year, and some of the music can be reconstructed from it. But Bach's settings of the gospel recitatives and *turba* choruses are completely lost, although this has not prevented reconstructions even of these sections from being published and recorded.

---

72 The "ariosos" are designated *recitatives* in Picander's libretto and in Bach's manuscript score and parts.

73 Details in Melamed (2004, 21).

It has been suggested that, after completing three passions, Bach planned a cycle of three oratorios for Christmas, Easter, and Ascension.[74] If so, this might have been a response to the passion oratorio by Stölzel performed on Good Friday 1734. But unlike Telemann, Handel, and, later, Emanuel Bach, Sebastian did not also write oratorios for use in public concerts. Nor did he share those composers' interest in performing large works on subjects from the Hebrew Bible. His oratorios, like his passions, are essentially liturgical and limited to the most important Christian themes.

Precisely what the term *oratorium* meant for Bach is uncertain, as usage of the word was in flux when he created these works. Telemann's annual cycle of cantatas for 1730–1731 was called the "Oratorical" due to the presence of named allegorical figures in its librettos. Bach, however, seems to have understood the term as implying a narrative, and each of his three oratorios relates an episode from New Testament history. Yet the three works vary considerably in form and extent. Only the one for Christmas, completed by January 1735, is comparable in both size and structure to the two passions. The six parts of the Christmas Oratorio, however, were composed for performance on six days spread over the Christmas season, from Christmas Day itself through Epiphany thirteen days later. The oratorio for Ascension, which followed in May 1735, is comparable to a single part of the Christmas work. The Easter Oratorio, which probably dates only from 1737 or 1738, is an expanded version of a regular cantata and lacks any gospel narrative.[75] The Easter Oratorio is thus a unique example in Bach's output of the new type of contemplative oratorio, made fashionable by Brockes's frequently set libretto. Rather than forming a cycle, Bach's three oratorios could be viewed as comprising a single large work for Christmas (complementing the passions) alongside a pair of shorter works that demonstrate alternative ways of celebrating the related feasts of Easter and Ascension.[76]

---

74 Wolff (2011).

75 An earlier cantata version of the Easter Oratorio bears no separate BWV number.

76 As implied by Tatlow (2015, 336–53), who discusses the work for Christmas, on the one hand, and the pair for Easter and Ascension, on the other, as two distinct "personalised oratorio projects."

It is the Christmas Oratorio that is famous today and which makes the deepest impression in performance, although this may be simply due to its greater length and diversity of content. Its division into six parts was a practical response to the absence of any place in the liturgy for a full-length Christmas oratorio on a single day. Multiday performances of oratorios were not unheard of, but the clearest antecedents for Bach's procedure could be found in passions that were likewise spread out over several days.[77] Each part of Bach's work, however, had to serve as the regular liturgical cantata for a particular day of the church year, starting with Christmas; because cantatas alternated between the two principal Leipzig churches, neither one would hear all six parts during the main service.[78]

Hence the Christmas Oratorio is a unique work in which Bach solved a compositional problem in a characteristically creative way. Each part remains a distinct cantata, opening with a large chorus or (in one case) a sinfonia such as occurs typically only at the beginning of other oratorios of the period. Yet the individual parts differ from ordinary cantatas in their inclusion of narration and dialog; they also incorporate more than the usual number of four-part hymn settings, although only Part 5 *ends* with a "simple" chorale harmonization. Presumably this was because it was for a regular day in the church year, the Sunday after New Year's.[79] Four of the other parts end with more elaborate chorale choruses, the final chorale of Part 6 (and of the oratorio as a whole) being particularly grand. It features the same solo writing for the first trumpet that marks the opening chorus of this part. Part 3, on the other hand, concludes with a repeat of its opening choral aria. That might be because this part would otherwise have ended with a stanza from the rather somber minor-key chorale "Wir Christenleut'," as dictated by the libretto.

As in the St. Mark Passion, most of the work's arias—including the grand choral arias that open Parts 1, 3, and 4—are parodies. The

---

77 Melamed (2014, 226–32) describes a multiday performance of a passion by Keiser that took place at Erfurt probably during the 1730s. This was Keiser's setting of the libretto by Brockes, not the "Keiser" passion with an anonymous text that Bach performed.

78 Further on this in Rathey (2016, 125). Bach presumably also performed Part 1 within the "old service" at the university church (St. Paul's).

79 There is no "part" for the Sunday after Christmas because December 25, 1734, was a Saturday and the following day was observed as the second day of Christmas.

majority of those whose models have been identified came from just two works: homage cantatas for the Saxon ruling dynasty that Bach had performed during fall 1733.[80] The gospel narrative and the chorale harmonizations were doubtless newly written, as were at least the opening chorus of no. 5 and (probably) one further aria. But the remaining music must comprise parodies from lost works, to judge from their neat and largely faultless handwriting in Bach's autograph manuscript.

Works with Latin Texts

As important as parody and pastiche were for Bach's oratorios, they were even more fundamental in his sacred works on Latin texts. The Lutheran service had never excluded music with Latin texts. Just as pastors continued to be described as "priests," the main service could be properly called a mass, its parts clearly derived from medieval Catholic practice even if transformed by Luther and his successors. Latin was still understood by most educated European men, including Protestants, and in the conservative university city of Leipzig it was a regular part of Sunday services. At the two main city churches these usually began with seventeenth-century Latin "introits" sung by the student choristers. More elaborate music with Latin texts was also sung, particularly for the Kyrie, Gloria, or Sanctus, and especially on holidays. On those occasions a polyphonic Magnificat might also be heard at Vespers. The Sanctus was usually a single movement, lacking the "Osanna" and "Benedictus." But complete Kyrie-Gloria pairs comprising multiple subsections were not uncommon; by convention, these are now described by the Latin term *missa*.

Throughout his career as a church musician Bach had reason to collect and perform Latin polyphony. His own music of this type is mostly from late in his career and based on pre-existing works; of the examples from Leipzig, only the Magnificat and one or two Sanctus settings appear to be wholly original compositions. The other composers whose Latin works he copied or performed were older than he, most of them significantly so. Performing their music might have been viewed as educational;

---

80 One aria comes from a third homage cantata, BWV 215, which had just been performed in October 1734.

certainly Bach's own Latin works served as exemplary demonstrations of counterpoint and composition—vocal counterparts of the *Clavierübung* and other keyboard collections. Although they are not uniformly in archaic styles, certain movements in these compositions, as in the Art of Fugue, reflected Bach's interest in contrapuntal music of the past. He appears to have pursued this interest with increased enthusiasm after 1730, making his most important contributions to this repertory only after ceasing to compose cantatas on a regular basis.

Personal interest in Latin church music was not necessarily the only motivation for this shift in focus. Changes in the Leipzig church repertory may have been a response to the accession of Augustus III in 1733, aligning practices at the main Lutheran churches more closely with those of the Catholic court church in Dresden.[81] Because most of the Latin works that Bach performed were by composers of previous generations, Bach may also have understood this music in relation to the Old Bach Archive, which he assembled or acquired during the same period; both could provide lessons not only in composition but in music history as understood at the time.

The Magnificat and the B-Minor Mass are Bach's best-known works with Latin texts. The Magnificat was one of his first Leipzig compositions. The mass was not completed until near the end of his life, although it incorporates music from throughout his maturity. A Latin work designed not for a specific day but for repeated use on festive occasions, the Magnificat differs fundamentally from the cantatas, above all in its use of five rather than four vocal parts. The original version, in E-flat, was the major new work for Visitation 1723 (July 2), when it was heard alongside a revised version of the Weimar cantata BWV 147a. This may not have been Bach's first Latin composition for Leipzig, if the short but grand Sanctus in C, BWV 237, was in fact written for the preceding St. John's Day (June 24). But Bach returned to the Magnificat that Christmas, when it was probably heard alongside the smaller Sanctus in D (BWV 238). Into the Magnificat Bach now inserted four extra movements, somewhat old-fashioned polyphonic arrangements of Christmas songs. These "Christmas interpolations" were a bow to Leipzig tradition; Bach's predecessor Kuhnau had included settings of the same songs in

81 As argued by Sposato (2018, esp. 91ff.).

a Magnificat of his own. Naturally Bach develops them at far greater length. Unfortunately, they are rarely heard today, as they are in keys that do not fit into the revised version of the Magnificat in D major that Bach created perhaps in 1733.

The word *Magnificat* opens the text, which, according to the gospel of Luke, Mary sang upon learning that she would give birth to Jesus ("My soul *magnifies* the lord"). This is one of the three canticles of the New Testament, resembling the psalms of the Hebrew Bible. In both Catholic and Protestant traditions it is sung at the afternoon or evening service (Vespers), typically in a form similar to that used for a psalm, ending with a doxology ("Glory to the father . . ."). In its simplest musical form it was chanted to one of several melodies that resembled the so-called psalm tones. Lutherans adopted one of the latter as their standard melody, and Bach made this the basis of BWV 10 in the cycle of chorale cantatas.[82] That work was for Visitation, one of the so-called Marian feasts; these were (and are) still observed by Lutherans, but their focus shifted from veneration of Mary to contemplation of some aspect of Jesus.

The loss of Bach's original performing materials for both versions of the Magnificat leaves us in the dark as to how the parts were distributed, nor is it clear why he wrote the original version of this work in E-flat rather than D. The latter was the usual key for works with trumpets and drums, such as this one; when he revised the Magnificat for performance in the early 1730s he transposed it to D major.[83] The rushing string figuration and slow harmonic rhythm of the opening chorus recall Italianate movements like the one that begins Vivaldi's popular Gloria in D (R. 589). The opening music returns at the end of the Magnificat for the "Sicut erat": As it was in the beginning. The musical pun was used by composers of psalms from Monteverdi to Vivaldi.

Bach sets the ten verses of the canticle in as many sections. Modern editions divide the third verse into two numbered movements, with a change of tempo for the second. This is not how Bach and his contemporaries understood it, as doing so separates the verb *dicent* (will

---

82 This chant formula, known as the *tonus peregrinus* for its "wandering" tonality—the two phrases end on different pitches—is the subject of Lundberg (2011).

83 He also added flutes, which replaced the recorders in "Esurientes" as well as the trumpets in two exceptionally high passages; there are many other changes of detail.

call me) from its subject *omnes generationes* (all generations).[84] The original disposition of movements places the chorus "Fecit potentiam" at the
center of the work, framed by solos, a duet, and a trio. Some of these
movements resemble arias; nos. 2, 6, 8, and 9 all open with ritornellos
that include the usual symbolic themes and instrumentation. Thus "Et
exsultavit spiritus meus" (My spirit exults) begins with a rising motive,
"Deposuit potentes" (He put down the mighty) with a falling one. These
are both accompanied by strings, the latter employing unison violins,
as in a virtuoso opera aria of the period; no. 9 ("Esurientes") expresses
the idea of feeding the hungry through the "empty" sound of two flutes
(originally recorders), accompanied by pizzicato bass.

At Christmas a year later (1724) Bach introduced not only the chorale
cantata BWV 91—a rather thoughtful, quiet work, after its magnificent
opening chorus—but a new Sanctus in D that far surpassed his and anyone else's settings of this text in size and grandeur. Bach's only six-voice
composition,[85] it also adds a third oboe to the instrumental forces used
in Bach's first Sanctus. More important, it is a full-fledged prelude and
fugue, unlike the perfunctory examples that were apparently the norm
for this part of the service. Bach would eventually incorporate it into
the B-Minor Mass, but even as a standalone piece this would have been
a splendid complement to the cantata performed earlier in the service.

Until Bach conceived the idea of assembling a complete mass—
perhaps not until after arranging three movements from the Gloria as
Cantata 191 in the early 1740s—a Sanctus would have seemed, to a
Lutheran, a distinct entity from a *missa* such as Bach submitted to the
elector in summer 1733. By then Bach had probably made manuscript
copies of several such works by other composers, including Antonio
Lotti, whose opera *Teofane* had received a famous performance at
Dresden in 1719. Lotti's *Missa sapientiae* (Mass of Wisdom), as it is called
in a manuscript copy by Zelenka, was an ambitious and apparently much

---

84 Cammarota (2001) demonstrates conclusively that the break between "movements" and
change of tempo at this point represent an anachronistic modern tradition. References
here follow the customary numbering of the individual movements.

85 The Gloria of Lotti's *Missa sapientia* (see below) also calls for as many as six vocal parts, but
"T[tutti]" and "Solo" markings in Bach's copy of the latter (Berlin, Staatsbibliothek, Mus.
ms. 13161) imply performance by eight singers (concertists and ripienists).

Table 13.1   Bach's Masses

BWV	Key	Source*	Date	Known Parallel Works (BWV/Movement)
232¹	b	P	1733	29/2, 46/1
234	A	A	ca. 1738	67/6, 179/5, 79/2, 136/1
236	G	A	ca. 1738–1739	179/1, 79/1, 138/4, 79/5, 179/3, 17/1
233	F	S	ca. 1747–1748	233a, 102/3, 102/5, 40/1
235	g	S	ca. 1747–1748	102/1, 72/1, 187/4, 187/3, 187/5, 187/1
232ᴵᴵ⁻ᴵⱽ	D	A	ca. 1748–1749	171/1, 12/2, 120a/1, 215/1, 11/4, 232¹/7

*A = manuscript score partly or entirely in Bach's hand
P = manuscript performing parts in the hand of Bach or known copyists working for him
S = manuscript score in the hand of a Bach pupil or associated copyist
Dates given are those of the principal sources, not necessarily of origin. "Parallel works" are mostly independent parodies of lost original versions.

admired Kyrie-Gloria pair.[86] Opening in G minor, it is older in style and quite unlike the music Bach was writing when he began assembling his own first *missa*. Nevertheless Bach followed Lotti in using an antique-style fugue for the second "Kyrie" and a more modern one to end the Gloria. Hence Lotti's composition might at least have ratified, if it did not inspire, Bach's decision to create an ambitious work of this type that opened in a minor key.

Between 1733 and around 1748 Bach assembled five *missae*, finally expanding the first of these into a complete mass (see Table 13.1). After submitting the first one to Dresden, Bach seems to have suspended further activity of this type at least until he received his court title. He created at least two more such works in the late 1730s, then paused until near the end of his life, when the full B-Minor Mass was probably his last major project. It is uncertain whether Bach performed any of these works integrally during his lifetime. Original performing parts survive only for the *missae* in A and B minor, parts for the latter having accompanied Bach's

86 Bach's copy, in Berlin, Staatsbibliothek, Mus. ms. 13161, appears to have been made directly from the one owned by Zelenka (Dresden, Sächsische Landesbibliothek, Mus. ms. 2159-D-4); Stockigt (2013, 45) dates the latter "ca. 1729." Curiously, there is also a partial copy by Handel in the British Library (R.M.20.g.10).

petition to the court in 1733.[87] Yet performances of Latin church music by other composers are well documented and would continue under his successor Harrer.[88]

The majority of movements in these masses have been identified as parodies from sacred cantatas. Among these are the complete contents of the masses in G and G minor, the latter drawing extensively on Cantata 187. Most of the movements that have no known sources look like parodies taken from lost works. For instance, the Domine Deus of the A-major Mass clearly originated as a regular da capo aria.

Bach's use of parody no longer scandalizes commentators, as it did in the nineteenth century, but it still raises questions about how the music relates to the text—in both the original and the parody versions. In the Gloria of the A-major Mass, a phrase originally sung to the words "Friede sei mit euch" (peace be with you) now sets the text *et in terra pax* (and peace on earth). This alternates with very different music that originally represented battle ("Jesus helps us fight"), now heavenly glory (*gloria in excelsis*). In this case the verbal ideas are closely related, but elsewhere there may be only a very approximate parallelism of affect. Two psalm verses that praise divine generosity in the opening chorus of Cantata 187 (Ps. 104:27–28) became the "Cum sancto spiritu" of the G-minor mass. The lively counterpoint seems equally appropriate to both, but only because it lacks signs or figures that an eighteenth-century listener might have recognized as distinctly meaningful or symbolic.

The B-Minor Mass

Whereas models are known for all but four movements in the short masses, relatively few have been identified for the B-Minor Mass. This

---

87 The sole part known for the A-major Mass is a transposed and figured continuo part in Bach's hand from the mid-1740s. For this, as for the works in G and D, Bach's autograph score also survives; for the masses in F and G minor we have only copies of the scores by Altnickol. Dates for the surviving copies and parts cannot be assumed to correspond with dates of origin.

88 See the list of works by German as well as Italian composers, including Palestrina as well as Telemann, in Kollmar (2006, 126–27).

is unlikely to have been a coincidence. The work's origin as part of a petition to the Saxon court made it reasonable to appropriate music from now-lost works that had honored the ruler. The *missa* portion, moreover, is on a larger scale than the other Kyrie-Gloria pairs. When Bach extended it into a full mass, he gave the latter an unprecedented monumentality, incorporating the six-voice Sanctus from 1724 and a double-chorus movement originally performed for the elector.[89]

After the death of Emanuel Bach, his father's manuscript score of the B-Minor Mass, which he owned, was described as "the Great Catholic Mass." *Catholic* could have meant "universal," referring not to a religious denomination but to the work's completeness or its presumed relevance to any Christian; Lutherans, too, confess belief in a "holy catholic church."[90] To be sure, the original version, comprising Kyrie and Gloria, was presented to a Catholic ruler. Yet there is no evidence that it ever entered the repertory of his court chapel. It differs from masses actually performed there in its enormous length, the absence of ripieno parts, and the division of the Gloria into a greater than usual number of movements.[91] Small departures from the standard text raise the question whether Bach could have expected the work to be used liturgically at Dresden.[92] It may be hard to believe that he never performed the *missa* portion himself, but any evidence for such a performance is lost.

89 This is the "Osanna," whose music also occurs in the opening movement of BWV 215, performed on October 5, 1734 (see BD 2:249–51 [nos. 351–53], the first trans. in NBR, 164 [no. 171], facsimile on p. 165). The latter was already a parody from the lost BWV Anh. 11, composed two years earlier.

90 "Die große catholische Messe" is listed in C. P. E. Bach's estate catalog (1790, 72).

91 As shown by Stockigt (2013, 48–53). Maul (2013a) provides an ingenious argument that the finished mass might have been intended for and performed on St. Cecilia's Day 1749 (November 22) by a Musicalische Congregation at Vienna. Among the members of the latter was Johann Adam von Questenburg, who corresponded with Bach in that year.

92 These include the addition of the word *altissime* after "Domine fili unigenite, Jesu Christe" and *gloria eius* in place of *gloria tua* in the Sanctus (noted by Smend in NBA, Vol. 2/1, KB, 190ff.). Bach's readings corresponded with Lutheran as opposed to Catholic usage, but there is no significant difference in meaning, and old notions about the "Lutheran" as opposed to "Catholic" nature (or vice versa) of Bach's work are laid to rest by Leaver (2013a).

Bach and his heirs understood the expanded work as comprising four parts: the *Missa*, Credo (called "Symbolum Nicenum"), and Sanctus, plus the remaining subsections ("Osanna," "Benedictus," "Agnus Dei," and "Dona nobis pacem").[93] Nothing in principle would have prevented performance of any of these parts within a Lutheran service, although "concerted" performances of the Credo and the last four subsections were rare. Still, as Bach prepared the final manuscript score in the late 1740s, he undoubtedly viewed it more as an ideal than a practical compilation. In this it resembled the late keyboard collections rather than the passions, which were single items for actual liturgical use. The work nevertheless constitutes an integrated whole, at least to some degree. The sequence of keys—organized as much around D major as its relative B minor—and the recurrence of the music for the "Gratias" in the final "Dona nobis pacem" assure a basic coherence. The latter sort of musical repetition was common in mass compositions, as in the "Osanna" from Kerll's *Missa superba* (whose Sanctus Bach arranged as BWV 241).

Other symmetries in the work are equally conventional, yet its plan also reflects Bach's tendency to create pairs of movements that are complementary rather than strictly parallel. The two fugal "Kyrie" movements for chorus, in minor keys, frame a "Christe" in D major for the two sopranos. The Gloria opens and closes with grand choruses also in D major; smaller choruses in related keys are spaced evenly within. The Credo similarly begins and ends with pairs of choral movements, all but one of which is fugal. At the center is the "Crucifixus," a chorus of a very different kind, built on a ground bass or ostinato. In each case the paired or complementary movements, such as the two Kyries, are of distinct types. The first Kyrie is a fugue, but one whose choral expositions are framed by ritornellos; the second Kyrie is in *stile antico* without independent instrumental parts (other than basso continuo). Yet their subjects are equally chromatic and expressive (Example 13.7). Only the concluding part of the work looks like a miscellany. The presence of two successive choral fugues in D major, both in 3/8 meter (the "Pleni sunt coeli" and the

---

93 The division into four parts, each with its own title page, is clear in the autograph score and from the way it was listed by C. P. E. Bach (1790).

Example 13.7 B-Minor Mass, BWV 232, (a) Kyrie 1, subject (tenor, mm. 30–32); (b) Kyrie 2, subject (bass, mm. 1–3):

Kyrie eleison.   Lord have mercy.

"Osanna"), may be the clearest indication that Bach did not anticipate integral performances of the Mass, or at least of the sections following the Credo.[94]

The B-Minor Mass contains a greater proportion of choral to solo writing than the cantatas and the other masses. This was doubtless by design, as choruses provided more opportunities to demonstrate sophisticated counterpoint and harmony—here mostly in five parts rather than the usual four. One result is that Bach's manuscript for the completed mass is his largest, exceeding in size even that of the St. Matthew Passion.[95] The opening Kyrie is among Bach's most astounding efforts, not least for the slow, majestic fugal expositions in which its discursive subject unfolds (see Example 13.7a). The chorus that opens the Gloria achieves even greater monumentality. The opening section sounds like another adaptation of something that once glorified the Saxon monarch. But in place of the customary middle section comes a fugue whose quiet theme, representing peace on earth (*et in terra pax*), first emerges in the voices alone. The great crescendo that follows culminates in an entry by the first trumpet, ascending to high d‴.[96] The remainder of the Gloria

94 The "Osanna" and "Benedictus" were often omitted in Lutheran services; see Leaver (2013a, 31–32).

95 Bach's score of the Mass (Berlin, Staatsbibliothek, Mus. ms. Bach P 180) contains 188 numbered pages, that of the St. Matthew Passion (P 25) 163.

96 This entry is doubled by soprano 2, presumably added for the parody.

offers lessons in instrumentation as well as counterpoint, featuring several colorful wind solos.

The Credo postdates the original *Missa* by some fifteen years. Comprising mostly choral numbers, it includes only two movements for soloists (a duet and a solo aria). The "Crucifixus" at its center was originally the A section in the first vocal movement of Cantata 12, Bach's second work after being named concertmaster at Weimar. This makes the "Crucifixus" the earliest identified component of the Mass, demonstrating (among other things) the use of chaconne or passacaglia style. It leads, after several intervening movements, to one of Bach's last creative efforts, the "Confiteor," which appears to be one of the few entirely original portions of the Mass. A five-voice fugue whose only independent instrumental part is the basso continuo, the "Confiteor" returns to the key and the antique style of the second Kyrie. Moreover, as a double fugue (with two subjects), the "Confiteor" demonstrates a compositional technique employed previously in the "Gratias agimus" of the Gloria. For this final exemplification of fugue and faith, Bach adds a new contrapuntal element: a *cantus firmus* introduced about halfway through, sung in canon between the bass and alto.

This cantus firmus, or pre-existing melody, is from the same chant used by Lutherans for singing the complete Credo.[97] Bach had already used this melody as the subject of the fugal intonation that opens this section of the Mass ("Credo in unum Deum"). Now it serves as the closest thing possible, within the stylistic possibilities of a Latin mass, to the type of chorale cantus firmus around which Bach had constructed the great choruses of his second annual cycle of cantatas. To symbolize the hoped-for resurrection of the dead, the "Confiteor" ends by passing miraculously through keys as remote as E-flat minor, eventually arriving in D major, which is the true tonality of the "B-minor" Mass as a whole. The ecstatic "Et expecto" follows in that key.[98]

97 As given in the standard collection of the time, the *Neu Leipziger Gesangbuch* of Gottfried Vopelius (Leipzig: Klinger, 1682), 497–500.

98 Bach's precise intentions for this crucial passage have been obscured by the illegibility of his own manuscript, as well as the subsequent attempts of Emanuel Bach and perhaps others to clarify it; see Rifkin (2002a and 2011).

Even if Bach never expected the Mass as a whole to be performed integrally, modern concert performances show that the complete work leaves no impression of redundancy, even as the final section turns repeatedly to grand repurposed choruses in D major. The re-use of music from the "Gratias agimus" for the closing movement is a demonstration of parody technique within a compilation of parodies. With it Bach brought the Mass, and in a real sense his life work, to an end.

Like the anonymous sculptors who made exquisite stone portraits of ancient Egyptian pharaohs, only to see them entombed out of human sight, Bach labored here on music of extraordinary refinement and complexity that he expected no one to hear or understand as he did in his own mind. Joshua Rifkin, describing the later portions of Bach's manuscript score, points out how the "cramped, labored" writing shows "errors of alignment that suggest weakened spatial perception." Not only was the expansion of the *Missa* "Bach's last major creative undertaking," but his autograph score reveals "evidence of how much effort and determination that undertaking cost him on just about every page."[99]

The motivations for that effort might have included selfish or self-aggrandizing ones, including a desire—entirely excusable in Bach's case—to memorialize his own monumental achievement. He would have justified himself as serving "God and his neighbor," in the standard phrase of organists' contracts. The ferocious commitment to musical perfection evident throughout Bach's work came at substantial costs to himself—including his eyesight—and doubtless also to those around him. We can only guess what sacrifices and allowances his wives, children, pupils, and colleagues made on his behalf—for accomplishments such as Bach's are not those of the composer alone. Somehow, however, his society's hopes, expectations, and demands for music—not only for its own sake, but for instruction and the elevation of the spirit—percolated through his unique psyche to generate his endlessly inventive music. The precise nature of that process must remain a mystery, although every writer or thinker on Bach will imagine different ways in which it might have occurred. And the unparalleled challenges that Bach's music makes on listeners and performers will continue to inspire creative responses from anyone who takes it seriously.

99 Rifkin (1988, 787).

CHAPTER FOURTEEN

Legacy

B ACH'S LEGACY—TO FAMILY, STUDENTS, AND THE WIDER WORLD—
was not limited to his music, nor, of course, to his material possessions.
The latter were not insubstantial; at death Bach was reasonably well off by
the standards of the time. He owned a considerable collection of not only
music but also instruments and books, as well as personal and household
effects typical of a prosperous German middle-class professional of the
time. Because he left no will, most of his possessions were inventoried
after his death prior to distribution to surviving members of his family.
The list of his possessions is included in a document dated November 11,
1750, some three and a half months after his death. From this we know
that Bach had a net worth of a little under a thousand Taler, ten times
his base salary but only a fraction above his typical annual earnings. The
most valuable portion of the list comprised musical instruments, followed
by silverware and a few small gold objects. In addition, he owned cash
and medals—some of the latter probably received after performing for
members of the nobility—and a share in a Saxon silver mine. A list of
theological books included two editions of Luther's complete works, but
there is no account of music books, scores, or parts.[1]

---

1 The undated *Specification der Hinterlassenschaft* appears in BD 2:490–99 (no. 627); NBR, 250–
   55 (no. 279). The date given above for the division of Bach's estate is from the account of
   its distribution between the heirs (BD 2:498–512 [no. 628]). Yearsley (2019, 192–93), citing
   Reinhard Szeskus, concludes that Bach's net worth at death placed his family at only "the

Bach. David Schulenberg, Oxford University Press (2020). © Oxford University Press.
DOI: 10.1093/oso/9780190936303.001.0001

The distribution of Bach's estate took place about six weeks after Harrer's formal installation as cantor.[2] In the interim, prefects presumably took charge of the city church music, as they had done during the months preceding Bach's arrival. The period after Bach's death was shorter, as his successor had already been named. Word of Bach's passing reached Berlin by August 6, when a notice appeared in the local newspaper.[3] Presumably Emanuel and his brothers learned details about the funeral and burial from family members still in Leipzig. All that is known today is that that the service took place three days after his death, following a procession headed by the School faculty and entire student body; and that his body was buried on July 30 or 31.[4] Remains believed to have been those of Sebastian were exhumed from the graveyard outside St. John's Church and examined in 1894.[5] These were subsequently moved to St. Thomas's, where they are marked by a modern plaque inscribed simply with his name.

Of the surviving sons, Friedrich had departed less than a year earlier for far-off Bückeburg. He could hardly have returned in time for the funeral or to participate in negotiations over the estate. Emanuel, who had visited Leipzig only the past spring, likewise stayed away and was represented at the division of the estate by Friedemann, traveling from Halle. He afterwards took Christian to Berlin, where the latter would live with Emanuel for five years. Presumably they brought with them

lowest border of the Leipzig middle class," and he argues that the mine share was actually a liability due to associated fees.

2 This took place on October 2; Kollmar (2006, 326 [no. 28]) gives the official report from the city archive.

3 BD 2:476 (no. 612); NBR, 245 (no. 273).

4 Wolff (2000, 451) describes the procession, based on what was in 2000 a newly discovered source; there is no record of what music, if any, was performed, but Wolff suggests that it included a motet by J. C. Bach of Eisenach that Sebastian had worked over during his last months, perhaps specifically for use at his own funeral. Uncertainty over the date of the burial reflects conflicting sources; see BD 2:474–75 (nos. 609–11); NBR, 244–45 (nos. 271–72).

5 As reported by Wilhelm His; see Yearsley (2002, 210–24). His's report was the basis of the portrait sculpture by Carl Seffner (1908) that stands in the St. Thomas Church Square, Leipzig, and more recently of a forensic reconstruction claimed to be "around 70% accurate" (*Guardian*, March 3, 2008, online at https://www.theguardian.com/music/2008/mar/04/classicalmusicandopera.germany).

the two-manual clavichord with pedals, used for practicing organ music, which Christian claimed to have received as a gift from Sebastian while the latter was still living.[6] The mentally handicapped Heinrich remained for a time in Leipzig, afterwards living in Naumburg with his sister Elisabeth Juliana Friederica.[7] Their younger sisters Johanna Carolina and Regina Susanna stayed with their mother in Leipzig; there they were eventually re-joined by their half-sister Catharina Dorothea (after Friedemann's departure from Halle) and Friederica (after the death of her husband Altnickol).

Pupils and Family

Among the less tangible parts of Bach's legacy were his teaching and influence, passed on in various ways and degrees to his many pupils, including family members. A lesser teacher might have imposed his own ways on his students. Bach evidently inspired his best pupils less to imitate his style than to follow his professional model, first by perfecting their craft, then by pursuing an original manner of composition. Forkel reported that both Friedemann and Emanuel "confessed frankly that they had been necessarily obliged to choose a style of their own because they could never have equaled their father in his."[8] In developing styles of "their own," Friedemann and Emanuel also avoided imitating one another. The music of Christian is equally distinct from that of Sebastian and his two older half-brothers.

Any list of Bach's students must be headed by his sons Emanuel and Christian. Born twenty-one years apart, to Maria Barbara and Anna Magdalena, respectively, they were to be among the most influential European musicians of their two successive generations. Emanuel would become the leading German composer, first of keyboard sonatas and

---

6 This had to be proved by offering sworn testimony from Anna Magdalena and two others (see BD 2:504 [no. 628, para. 8]), but nothing further is known about the instrument. It might eventually have come into Emanuel's possession if the latter purchased Christian's share of the inheritance (as Wolff 2000, 459, plausibly suggests was the case with Christian's copies of their father's music).

7 Gottfried Heinrich did not go immediately to the home of his brother-in-law Altnickol, as previously thought; see Blanken (2018, 134n. 4).

8 Forkel (1802, 44); trans. in NBR, 458.

concertos, then of songs and sacred vocal music. Christian would, in ef-fect, invent the style that was adopted and further developed by Wolfgang Amadeus Mozart. Neither wrote music bearing obvious similarities to their father's, yet neither could have composed what he did without the early training and models furnished by Sebastian. The two other com-poser sons, Friedemann and Friedrich, were less influential, but in his relatively small number of works Friedemann maintained Sebastian's standards of craftsmanship and originality, albeit in a notably idiosyn-cratic style. Friedrich was a more distinctly minor composer—as was his son, whom Sebastian never knew. Yet Friedrich wrote prolifically, at first in a manner probably inspired by Emanuel, then in a more Classical style resembling that of Christian, beginning around the time of a visit to the latter at London in 1778.

Afterward

The large number of Bach's pupils assured that at least his keyboard music continued to be used during the half century after his death, albeit more for study than public recitals. Performances of his vocal music during this period were rare although not unknown. Friedemann directed some of the sacred cantatas during his time as organist at Halle, in his own arrangements. Among these was an adaptation of two movements from Cantata 80, to which Friedemann added trumpets and timpani. When the work was edited in the nineteenth century, these were taken to be Sebastian's own, and the cantata became widely known in this hybrid form.[9] At Hamburg Emanuel similarly adapted portions of his father's vocal music, including some of the chorale settings and fragments of the gospel narration from the St. Matthew Passion, worked into a pastiche.[10]

It has been suggested that Harrer, after succeeding Bach, may have repeated several of the latter's cantatas, but the performances in question were probably led by prefects after Harrer's early death in 1756.[11] Harrer's successor, Bach's pupil Doles, is more likely to have performed at least

---

9 On Friedemann's arrangements of his father's cantatas generally, see Wollny (1995). Melamed (2008) traces the later history of BWV 80.

10 Hill (2015) provides a detailed study of Emanuel's pastiche practice.

11 As supposed by Kollmar (2006), 124.

a few of Bach's cantatas. Under Doles the motets also continued to be sung, although perhaps more for pedagogic than liturgical use; when Mozart visited Leipzig in 1789, he reportedly heard *Singet dem Herrn* (BWV 225) performed by students of the St. Thomas School.[12] There is also limited evidence for a continuing tradition of playing Bach's organ music, especially by his pupils (and *their* pupils). As with the motets, however, study of these works may sometimes have reflected more respect for their pedagogic value, or for the technical challenges that they offered, than enthusiasm for the music itself.[13]

During the later eighteenth century, Bach was frequently contrasted to his contemporary Handel. The common view was that the latter, whose music was more popular and more widely known, was up-to-date and expressive, whereas Bach was old-fashioned, his music primarily of technical interest for its elaborate counterpoint. This view was not discouraged by Bach's own focus on works like the Art of Fugue during his last years. Yet it could have been held only by those who had not heard his performances, whether as an organ virtuoso or leading those vocal works which even Scheibe had praised for their *galant* attractions.[14]

Mozart encountered some of Bach's contrapuntal keyboard music, possibly through the same intermediary as Beethoven: the diplomat Baron van Swieten, who had known King Frederick "the Great" and perhaps Bach's pupil Kirnberger in Berlin. Mozart arranged some of Bach's keyboard and organ fugues for string trio and quartet, but this was presumably for private use only.[15] Both Viennese composers also knew the music of C. P. E. Bach; Mozart performed the latter's Resurrection Cantata, and Beethoven attended a performance of Emanuel's *Israelites* oratorio and polychoral *Heilig* (a German Sanctus) on Christmas Day

---

12 Sposato (2018, 117–18) relates information about performances under Doles, although much comes from the unreliable Rochlitz.

13 This is the implication of Burney's (1775, 2:206) report of hearing a performance of a "most learned and difficult double fugue" by Sebastian for organ with pedals; this took place during his visit to Berlin in 1771.

14 Schulenberg (1992) discusses the relationship of the Bach tradition to Handel.

15 Mozart's fugue arrangements, most of them later published with preludes of uncertain origin, include the eleven works listed as the sets K. 404a and 405.

1817.[16] But Mozart never orchestrated any of Sebastian's vocal music for concert use, as he did Handel's *Messiah* and other works.

Meanwhile Sebastian's sacred music was not entirely forgotten; wealthy collectors were commissioning manuscript copies of the B-Minor Mass before the end of the eighteenth century.[17] But concert programming of vocal music by Sebastian Bach would not become commonplace until much later in the nineteenth century. This could reflect the fact that, until the Romantic generation of 1810 (including Schumann and Mendelssohn) reached maturity, few sensed an expressive element in Bach's music comparable to what eighteenth-century listeners already felt in Handel's. Only when this had changed could J. S. Bach be viewed unequivocally as comparable in stature to his great contemporary.

Still, by the beginning of the nineteenth century it could not have been unusual for serious European musicians to study the Well-Tempered Clavier, which had come out in no fewer than three different editions around 1801. One of these was edited by Beethoven's teacher Neefe, with whom the composer studied the work as a boy.[18] During the following decades, further Bach works appeared in print, although those for organ or keyboard predominated. In 1829, however, the young Mendelssohn conducted a famous Berlin performance of the St. Matthew Passion, in his own heavily altered and abbreviated version. Within a few years, other vocal works began to emerge from obscurity. For this reason the so-called Bach Revival is often regarded as starting with Mendelssohn's concert. Already by then, however, other musicians had also begun to adopt (and adapt) Bach's music as their own, a process that continued through the twentieth century. A work such as Chopin's densely chromatic Mazurka

16 This took place as part of the same program during which Beethoven directed his own Eighth Symphony. In view of his worsening deafness, it is uncertain how much he actually heard. See Thayer (1969, 691).

17 See Boomhower (2017). Such copies probably reflected interests similar to those that led to printed editions in score of Graun's *Te Deum* and C. P. E. Bach's *Heilig;* performances of such large-scale works would have been few and far between, but collectors evidently relished having scores as souvenirs.

18 Lockwood (2003, 34) describes Neefe's assignment of Bach's music to his pupil "as a profession of faith in J. S. Bach as a supreme musical model." Early study of this music would have encouraged a young genius to ignore convention, as well as convenience for the player, in his own compositions for keyboard instruments. On Neefe's edition, see Tomita (2005).

op. 17, no. 4, or the same composer's twenty-four preludes in all major and minor keys, deeply reflects his early study of Bach's music.

In closing, we might return to the questions posed at the beginning of this book: What made it possible for Bach to create what he did? How could a politically fragmented, provincial region of Europe produce such a composer? Bach came from a family that had reliably produced capable musicians for generations, yet none before him had been particularly notable; not even the "expressive" organist and composer Christoph Bach of Eisenach stood much above the routine of the time. Yet no other musical family then or since—not the Couperins, the Mozarts, or the Bendas and the Grauns (who are still producing artists)—did as the Bachs, generating not only J. S. Bach but three exceptional composers among his sons.

Clearly, many factors came together to help a lucky member of an artist family rise to the highest level that a musician might attain. Bach himself probably believed that, just as the great military-aristocratic dynasties of the Ascanians, Wettins, Hohenzollerns, and others had been divinely appointed, he and his relatives had been chosen by God to serve their "neighbors" through music. This belief probably continued at least into the next generation. Emanuel Bach's famous collection of musician portraits included a depiction of King David; a contemporary artist portrayed Emanuel standing in front of this picture, alongside one of the Hamburg pastors.[19] This suggests that Emanuel shared with his father the belief that a cantor was a colleague of the clergy, with a divinely approved mission.

Such a conviction might have provided motivation but could hardly assure brilliance or recognition by others. Persistent family tradition, a micro-culture of diligent training and mastery of musical craftsmanship, surely played a role in preparing members of the Bach family for their profession. But there is also a workmanlike character, an avoidance of anything too artistically challenging, in the compositional output of family members prior to Sebastian. On the other hand, not every creative contemporary came from a musical background, as Telemann, Handel, and Quantz showed. Each of these, growing up in the same region as Bach, nevertheless benefited from a culture, an economic and social system,

---

19 Andreas Stöttrup's drawing of Emanuel Bach with pastor Christoph Christian Sturm dates from 1784 and has been widely reproduced; further discussion in Schulenberg (2014, 167).

even geography that somehow seems to have specially favored musical creativity among members of his generation. Still, the particular combination of old and new—respect for tradition as well as for the innovations of his contemporaries—that characterizes Sebastian perhaps reflected his origin in a great musical family. His emergence out of a sea of lesser Bachs could have reflected his difficult yet stimulating early life, as well as the good luck of being consistently recognized by patrons who provided support despite his challenging music and (it would seem) personality.

Anyone convinced of the values of a democratic, egalitarian society must confess that Bach arose within a culture that was less just, less governed by the rule of law, and less free of bigotry than that toward which his and other parts of the world continued to evolve for some two and half centuries after his death. It may even be that his peculiar brand of music, like his particular sort of life and career, could never have emerged in a society that purported to prize democracy, equality, or freedom for all. It goes without saying that Bach's music was a unique product of the time, place, and society in which he lived. Yet the individual artist, Bach, was a nexus within which the patterns and influences of his environment melded in unforeseeable ways. The result was a miracle that can never be repeated but whose products, his compositions, will be with us as long as there remains the will and the ability to perform, hear, and interpret them.

Calendar

Year	Age	Bach	Contemporaries and Events
1685		Born March 21 at Eisenach to Johann Ambrosius (age 40) and Maria Elisabeth Lämmerhirt (41), baptized March 23.	Emperor Leopold I (reigned 1658–1705); King Louis XIV of France (r. 1643–1715); Duke Johann Georg I of Saxe-Eisenach (r. 1672–86). Handel and Domenico Scarlatti born. Reinken age 62, Lully 53, Buxtehude 48, Corelli 32, Pachelbel 32, Fux 25, Kuhnau 25, Alessandro Scarlatti 25, Böhm 24, F. Couperin 17, Keiser 11, Vivaldi 7, Mattheson 4, Telemann 4, Heinichen 2, Rameau 2.
1690	5	Enters German school at Eisenach.	J. T. Krebs born near Weimar.
1693	8	Enters Latin School at Eisenach.	
1694	9	Mother dies (buried May 3); father marries Barbara Margaretha Bartholomaei (Keul) November 27.	
1695	10	Father dies (February 20). Bach and brother Johann Jacob go to live with their brother Johann Christoph at Ohrdruf, entering Lyceum there.	
1697	12		Quantz born. Duke-Elector Friedrich August I "the Strong" of Saxony elected king of Poland as Augustus II.
1699			Hasse born.
1700	15	Leaves Ohrdruf (March 15), enrolls at St. Michael School, Lüneburg.	

Year	Age	Bach	Contemporaries and Events
1702	17	Applies successfully for but is not granted post of organist at Sangerhausen.	
1703	18	"Lackey" at Weimar (January–June); appointed organist at New Church, Arnstadt (August 9).	Carl Henrich Graun born (or in 1704).
1704	19	Brother Johann Jacob enters service of King Charles XII of Sweden.	
1705	20	Altercation with Geyersbach (August); travels to Lübeck to hear music by Buxtehude (November).	Leopold I dies (May 5), succeeded by Joseph I as emperor.
1706	21	Returns to Arnstadt and is reprimanded (February 21) by church consistory.	Pachelbel (52) dies.
1707	22	Audition at St. Blasius Church, Mühlhausen (April 24, appointed June 15); marries Maria Barbara Bach (age 23) at Dornheim (October 17).	Buxtehude (ca. 70) dies.
1708	23	First publication, BWV 71 (February?). Appointed organist and chamber musician to Duke Wilhelm Ernst of Weimar (June). First child Catharina Dorothea born (December 29).	J. A. Scheibe born at Leipzig.
1709	24	Visits Mühlhausen to perform lost work (February 4, also in 1710).	Sweden defeated by Russia at Poltava; King Charles XII escapes to Bender in Moldavia.
1710	25	Organ inspection at Traubach (October 26). Son Wilhelm Friedemann born (November 22).	Pergolesi born.
1713	28	At Weissenfels to perform "Hunt Cantata" for Duke Christian (February 21–22). Visits Ohrdruf for baptism of brother Johann Christoph's son Johann Sebastian (September 7). Competes for organist position at Halle (November 28–December 15).	Corelli dies. J. L. Krebs (son of Bach's pupil J. T. Krebs) born. Frederick William I becomes king of Prussia, soon dismisses most court musicians.

Year	Age	Bach	Contemporaries and Events
1714	29	Declines Halle position (February 19), is promoted to concertmaster at Weimar (March 2), and begins regular composition of church cantatas (March 25). Son Carl Philipp Emanuel born (March 8).	
1715	30	Son Johann Gottfried Bernhard born (May 11).	Prince Johann Ernst of Weimar dies (August 1; mourning period through November 3).
1716	31	Organ inspections at Halle (April 29–May 2) and Erfurt (July 31). Weimar Capellmeister Drese dies (December 1).	Marriage of Duke Ernst August of Weimar to Eleonore Wilhelmine of Anhalt-Cöthen (January 24).
1717	32	Directs a passion at Gotha (March 26); in Dresden for competition with Marchand (October–November). Signs contract as Capellmeister for Cöthen (August 5), but Duke Wilhelm Ernst imprisons him (November 6). Leaves Weimar (December 2), inspects organ at Leipzig (December 16), arrives at Cöthen (December 29).	
1718	33	Travels (May–July) to Carlsbad with Prince Leopold, who is godson to Bach's seventh child Leopold August (November 17; dies September 26, 1719).	
1719	34	Travels to Berlin (March) to purchase harpsichord for Cöthen court.	
1720	35	Dedicates *Clavierbüchlein* to son Wilhelm Friedemann (January 22). While he visits Carlsbad with Prince Leopold (May–July), Maria Barbara dies and is buried (July 7). Auditions at Hamburg (November) but declines post as organist.	Future pupil Agricola born; future son-in-law Altnikol baptized (January 1).

Year	Age	Bach	Contemporaries and Events
1721	36	Brother Johann Christoph dies (February 22). Brandenburg Concertos dedicated to Margrave Christian Ludwig (March 24). Travels to Schleiz (August) via Gera, Weissenfels, and Zeitz (?), marries Anna Magdalena (Wilcke) at Cöthen (December 3).	Prince Leopold of Cöthen marries Princess Henrietta of Anhalt-Bernburg (December 11; she dies April 4, 1723).
1722	37	Brother Johann Jacob dies (April 16).	Kuhnau (62) and Reinken (80?) die.
1723	38	Requests dismissal from Cöthen (April 13), leaves for Leipzig and gives first performances there (May 16 and 30). Inspects organ at Störmtal (November).	
1724	39	Son Gottfried Heinrich born (February 26). St. John Passion performed (April 7).	
1725	40	Performs at Weissenfels (February 23), Dresden (September 19–20), and Cöthen (November 30–December 15, also July?); examines organ at Gera (June 25). First petitions to Elector Frederick August I (September 14, November 3, December 31).	
1726	41	Announces publication of first harpsichord partita (November 1), launching *Clavierübung* series.	
1727	42	Performances of St. Matthew Passion (April 11), *Trauerode* BWV 198 (October 17).	
1728	43	At Cöthen for New Year's celebration.	Prince Leopold of Cöthen dies (November 19), age 33.
1729	44	Visits Weissenfels (February 12), appointed titular Capellmeister there; visits Cöthen to perform memorial music for Prince Leopold (March 23–24). Assumes direction of Collegium Musicum (March). St. Thomas School rector J. H. Ernesti dies (October 16).	Heinichen dies, age 46.

Year	Age	Bach	Contemporaries and Events
1730	45	Submits memo on church music to town council (August 23); writes to Erdmann about possible employment in Danzig (October 28).	
1731	46	In Dresden to give organ concerts and attend Hasse's *Cleofide* (September). Major renovation of St. Thomas School building begins (May).	
1732	47	Son Johann Christoph Friedrich born (June 21); examines organs at Stöntzsch and Kassel (September 22–28).	Joseph Haydn born.
1733	48	Writes son Wilhelm Friedemann's successful letter of application for appointment (June 23) as organist at Dresden, visits there to present *Missa* BWV 232¹ to Elector Friedrich August II (June 27).	F. Couperin (64) and Böhm (71) die. Friedrich August I dies, succeeded by Friedrich August II as duke-elector of Saxony; War of Polish Succession begins.
1734	49	Son Carl Philipp leaves for Frankfurt on the Oder (September 9). J. A. Ernesti installed as rector of St. Thomas School (November 21). Christmas Oratorio performed (December 25–).	
1735	50	Publishes Part 2 of *Clavierübung* (BWV 971, 831); examines organ at Mühlhausen, where son Gottfried Bernhard is appointed organist (June 16). Son Johann Christian born (September 5).	
1736	51	"Battle of the Prefects" with J. A. Ernesti begins (July). Appointed Dresden court composer, gives organ recital there (December 1).	Pergolesi (26) dies.
1737	52	Suspends directorship of Collegium Musicum (March?); son Johann Gottfried Bernhard appointed organist at Sangerhausen (April 4); where Bach visits (May?). Scheibe publishes critique of Bach (May 14).	

Year	Age	Bach	Contemporaries and Events
1738	53	Birnbaum publishes defense of Bach (January 8), who visits Dresden (May).	
1739	54	Cancels performance of St. John Passion (March 27). Scheibe publishes satire on Bach (April). Son Johann Gottfred Bernhard dies (May 27) after quitting Sangerhausen post. Bach gives organ concert at Altenburg and publishes Part 3 of *Clavierübung* (fall). Resumes directing the Collegium Musicum (October 2), visits Weissenfels with Anna Magdalena (November 7–14).	Performance of Passion by Scheibe at the New Church (March 27).
1740	55	Visits Halle (April) and Dresden (November). Son Carl Philipp Emanuel appointed chamber musician to King Frederick II at Berlin (possibly in 1741).	Emperor Charles VI dies, succeeded by daughter Maria Theresa. Frederick II "the Great" becomes king "in" Prussia.
1741	56	Visits Berlin (July–August) and Dresden (November); publishes Goldberg Variations (fall).	Vivaldi (63) and Fux (ca. 80) die at Vienna, where Haydn is chorister.
1742	57	Last child Regina Susanna baptized (February 22). Performs BWV 212 at Kleinzschocher (August 30).	
1744	59		Second Silesian War (continuation of War of Austrian Succession, through 1745). Prussia defeats coalition including Saxony; Leipzig occupied (November 30–December 25, 1745).
1746	61	Son Wilhelm Friedemann moves from Dresden to Halle (April); Bach examines organs at Zschortau (August 7) and Naumburg (September 27).	
1747	62	Visits Potsdam and Berlin, performs for King Frederick II "the Great" (May 7–8); composes and publishes Musical Offering and Canonic Variations.	

Year	Age	Bach	Contemporaries and Events
1748	63	Schübler chorales published (1747?).	Walther dies (age 63).
1749	64	Harrer auditions for St. Thomas cantoriate (June 8); B-Minor Mass finished, Art of Fugue prepared for publication.	
1750	65	Son Johann Christoph Friedrich appointed chamber musician at court of Bückeburg (January); son Carl Philipp Emanuel visits and performs his Magnificat (March?). Eye surgery by John Taylor (March 28–April 8). Following an apparent stroke, receives last communion (July 22), dies (July 28), and is buried (July 31).	Albinoni age 79; Telemann 69; Rameau 67; Handel and Domenico Scarlatti 65; Pisendel 63; J. T. Krebs 60; Quantz 53; Hasse 51; W. F. Bach 40; King Frederick II of Prussia 38; J. L. Krebs 37; C. P. E. Bach and Gluck 36; Leopold Mozart 31; Agricola and Altnickol 30; Kirnberger 29; Haydn 18; J. C. Bach 15; Boccherini 7.
1751		Art of Fugue published at Berlin (2d edition, by Marpurg, 1752).	
1754		Obituary by C. P. E. Bach and Agricola published. Bach's second wife Anna Magdalena lives until 1760, age 59; his surviving children: Gottfried Heinrich (d. 1763, age 39, at Naumburg); Catharina Dorothea (d. 1774, age 65, Leipzig); Johanna Carolina (d. 1781, age 43, Leipzig); Elisabeth Juliane Friederica Altnickol (d. 1781, age 55, Leipzig); Johann Christian (d. 1782, age 46, London); Wilhelm Friedemann (d. 1784, age 73, Berlin); Carl Philipp Emanuel (d. 1788, age 74, Hamburg); Johann Christoph Friedrich (d. 1795, age 63, Bückeburg); Regina Susanna (d. 1809, age 67, Leipzig).	

List of Works

This list of J. S. Bach's works is ordered by the "BWV" numbers in Wolfgang Schmieder's *Bach-Werke-Verzeichnis*. For vocal works it also shows "BC" numbers from the *Bach Compendium*. Gaps in the sequence are due to the skipping of spurious and lost works and to irregularities in the numbering; a few compositions of ambiguous classification (such as BWV 11) are listed twice for ease of finding. Most works with "BWV Anh." (appendix) numbers are excluded.

Those unfamiliar with the BWV numbers may find the following summary of the major divisions helpful. *Alphabetical indexes of cantatas and keyboard chorales by title or first line can be found in the online supplement.*

Summary of BWV Numbers

1 Sacred cantatas (BWV 1–200)
2 Secular cantatas (BWV 201–16, etc.)
3 Motets, passions, and oratorios (BWV 225–30, 244–49)
4 Latin sacred music (BWV 232–43)
5 Chorales, songs, and miscellaneous vocal music (BWV 250–524)
6 Music primarily for organ
   (a) "Free" compositions:
      sonatas (BWV 525–30)
      preludes, fugues, and related pieces (BWV 531–90, etc.)
      transcriptions and arrangements (BWV 592–96, etc.)
   (b) Chorale compositions
      Orgelbüchlein (BWV 599–644)
      "Schubler" chorales (BWV 645–51)
      "Great Eighteen" ("Leipzig") chorales (BWV 651–68)
      chorales from *Clavierübung*, Part 3 (BWV 669–89)
      miscellaneous chorales (BWV 690–743, etc.)
      chorales from the "Neumeister" manuscript (BWV 1090–1119, etc.)
      chorale variations (BWV 766–70, etc.)
7 Other keyboard ("clavier") music
   inventions and sinfonias (BWV 772–801)
   suites and related compositions (BWV 806–33, etc.)
   preludes, fugues, and related compositions (BWV 846–963)
   transcriptions and arrangements (BWV 964–87)

   miscellaneous compositions (BWV 988, etc.)
 8 Music for solo lute, violin, cello, and flute (BWV 995–1013)
 9 Music for instrumental ensemble
   sonatas and other chamber works (BWV 1014–39, etc.)
   concertos and orchestral suites (BWV 1041–69)
10 Canons and related contrapuntal works (BWV 1072–80, etc.)

Notes

Titles are regularized for easy finding and do not necessarily correspond to those in sources.

Librettists' names are given in parentheses following titles of vocal works, where known; the abbreviation *et al.* ("and others") signifies that the work as performed by Bach incorporated anonymous additions or modifications to an original text.

Lost, doubtful, fragmentary, and misattributed works are included selectively. Works of uncertain authorship are indicated by an asterisk (*), whereas those known not to be by Bach are listed in brackets [like this]. The abbreviation "frag." is used for all works that survive incompletely, whether due to loss of parts, Bach's failure to complete a composition, etc.

Keys: uppercase letters indicate major keys, lowercase minor keys (C = C major; c = C minor).

Liturgical occasions in Advent and Lent are abbreviated as Advent 1, meaning the First Sunday in Advent; otherwise the number signifies a Sunday *after* the named one, as Christmas 1 is the Sunday after Christmas, Trinity 22 is the Twenty-second Sunday after Trinity.

Dates for vocal works are abbreviated as 1 Jan 1723 and are usually for the earliest known or presumed performances; for instrumental works published during Bach's lifetime, dates are of publication. Most dates for remaining works are highly approximate and apply to the first complete version of the work as listed (not to revisions or to alternate versions).

Editions: the relevant volume numbers in the two complete editions (*Bachgesamtausgabe* and *Neue Bach-Ausgabe*) are given in the rightmost columns. A few works are found only in appendices or supplements to the listed volumes.

Abbreviations: arrgt., arr. = arrangement, arranged by; attr. = attributed to; b.c. = basso continuo; ed. = edited by; frag. = fragment; publ. = published

1 Sacred Cantatas

BWV	BC	Text Incipit (Text Author)	Occasion	Date	BG	NBA
1	A 173	Wie schön leuchtet der Morgenstern	Annunciation	25 Mar 1725	i	I/28.2
2	A 98	Ach Gott, vom Himmel sieh darein	Trinity 2	18 Jun 1724	i	I/16
3	A 33	Ach Gott, wie manches Herzeleid	Epiphany 2	14 Jan 1725	i	I/5

BWV	BC	Text Incipit (Text Author)	Occasion	Date	BG	NBA
4	A 54	Christ lag in Todesbanden	Easter	24 Apr 1707	i	I/9
5	A 145	Wo soll ich fliehen hin	Trinity 19	15 Oct 1724	i	I/24
6	A 57	Bleib bei uns, denn es will Abend	Easter Monday	2 Apr 1725	i	I/10
7	A 177	Christ unser Herr zum Jordan kam	St. John	24 Jun 1724	i	I/29
8	A 137	Liebster Gott, wenn werd ich sterben?	Trinity 16	24 Sep 1724	i	I/23
9	A 107	Es ist das Heil uns kommen her	Trinity 6	ca. 1732	i	I/17.2
10	A 175	Meine Seele erhebt den Herren	Visitation	2 Jul 1724	i	I/28.2
11	D 9	Lobet Gott in seinen Reichen	Ascension	19 May 1735	ii	II/8
12	A 68	Weinen, Klagen, Sorgen, Zagen (Franck)	Easter 3	22 Apr 1714	ii	I/11.2
13	A 34	Meine Seufzer, meine Tränen (Lehms)	Epiphany 2	20 Jan 1726	ii	I/5
14	A 40	Wär Gott nicht mit uns diese Zeit (Luther)	Epiphany 4	30 Jan 1735	ii	I/6
[15		Denn du wirst meine Seele, by J. L. Bach	Easter]			
16	A 23	Herr Gott, dich loben wir (Lehms)	New Year	1 Jan 1726	ii	I/4
17	A 131	Wer Dank opfert, der preiset mich	Trinity 14	22 Sep 1726	ii	I/21
18	A 44	Gleichwie der Regen und Schnee (Neumeister)	Sexagesima	?24 Jan 1715	ii	I/7
19	A 180	Es erhub sich ein Streit (Picander)	St. Michael	29 Sep 1726	ii	I/30
20	A 95	O Ewigkeit, du Donnerwort	Trinity 1	11 Jun 1724	ii	I/15

BWV	BC	Text Incipit (Text Author)	Occasion	Date	BG	NBA
21	A 99	Ich hatte viel Bekümmernis (Franck?)	Trinity 3	17 Jun 1714	v/1	I/16
22	A 48	Jesus nahm zu sich die Zwölfe (Lange?)	Quinquagesima	7 Feb 1723	v/1	I/8.1
23	A 47	Du wahrer Gott und Davids Sohn (Lange?)	Quinquagesima	7 Feb 1723	v/1	I/8.1
24	A 102	Ein ungefärbt Gemüte (Neumeister)	Trinity 4	20 Jun 1723	v/1	I/17.1
25	A 129	Es ist nichts Gesundes an meinem Leibe	Trinity 14	29 Aug 1723	v/1	I/21
26	A 162	Ach wie flüchtig, ach wie nichtig	Trinity 24	19 Nov 1724	v/1	I/27
27	A 138	Wer weiss, wie nahe mir mein Ende	Trinity 16	6 Oct 1726	v/1	I/23
28	A 20	Gottlob! nun geht das Jahr zu Ende (Neumeister)	Christmas 1	30 Dec 1725	v/1	I/3
29	B 8	Wir danken dir, Gott	council election	27 Aug 1731	v/1	I/32.2
30	A 178	Freue dich, erlöste Schar (Picander?)	St. John	24 Jun 1738	v/1	I/29
31	A 55	Der Himmel lacht! (Franck)	Easter	21 Apr 1715	vii	I/9
32	A 31	Liebster Jesu, mein Verlangen (Lehms)	Epiphany 1	13 Jan 1726	vii	I/5
33	A 127	Allein zu dir, Herr Jesu Christ	Trinity 13	3 Sep 1724	vii	I/21
34	A 84	O ewiges Feuer, O Ursprung der Liebe	Pentecost	?1 Jun 1727	vii	I/13
34a	B 13	O ewiges Feuer, O Ursprung der Liebe	wedding	1726		I/33
35	A 125	Geist und Seele wird verwirrct (Lehms)	Trinity 12	8 Sep 1726	vii	I/20

BWV	BC	Text Incipit (Text Author)	Occasion	Date	BG	NBA
36	A 3	Schwingt freudig euch empor (Picander?)	Advent 1	2 Dec 1731	vii	I/1
37	A 75	Wer da gläubet und getauft wird	Ascension	18 May 1724	vii	I/12
38	A 152	Aus tiefer Not schrei ich zu dir	Trinity 21	29 Oct 1724	vii	I/25
39	A 96	Brich dem Hungrigen dein Brot	Trinity 1	23 Jun 1726	vii	I/15
40	A 12	Darzu ist erschienen der Sohn Gottes	2nd day of Christmas	26 Dec 1723	vii	I/3
41	A 22	Jesu, nun sei gepreiset	New Year	1 Jan 1725	x	I/4
42	A 63	Am Abend aber desselbigen Sabbats	Easter 1	8 Apr 1725	x	I/11.1
43	A 77	Gott fähret auf mit Jauchzen (Helm?)	Ascension	30 May 1726	x	I/12
44	A 78	Sie werden euch in den Bann tun	Exaudi	21 May 1724	x	I/12
45	A 113	Es ist dir gesagt, Mensch	Trinity 8	11 Aug 1726	x	I/18
46	A 117	Schauet doch und sehet	Trinity 10	1 Aug 1723	x	I/19
47	A 141	Wer sich selbst erhöhet (Helbig)	Trinity 17	13 Oct 1726	x	I/23
48	A 144	Ich elender Mensch	Trinity 19	3 Oct 1723	x	I/24
49	A 150	Ich geh und suche mit Verlangen (Birkmann?)	Trinity 20	3 Nov 1726	x	I/25
★50	A 194	Nun ist das Heil und die Kraft			x	I/30
51	A 134	Jauchzet Gott in allen Landen!	Trinity 15 (?)	?17 Sep 1730	xii/2	I/22
52	A 160	Falsche Welt, dir trau ich nicht	Trinity 23	24 Nov 1726	xii/2	I/26
[53		Schlage doch, gewünschte Stunde, by Hoffmann]				

BWV	BC	Text Incipit (Text Author)	Occasion	Date	BG	NBA
54	A 51	Widerstehe doch der Sünde (Lehms)	?Lent 3	?4 Mar 1713	xii/2	I/18
55	A 157	Ich armer Mensch, ich Sündenknecht	Trinity 22	17 Nov 1726	xii/2	I/26
56	A 146	Ich will den Kreuzstab gerne tragen (Birkmann?)	Trinity 19	27 Oct 1726	xii/2	I/24
57	A 14	Selig ist der Mann (Lehms)	2nd day of Christmas	26 Dec 1725	xii/2	I/3
58	A 26	Ach Gott, wie manches Herzeleid	New Year 1	5 Jan 1727	xii/2	I/4
59	A 82	Wer mich liebet (Neumeister)	Pentecost	?16 May 1723	xii/2	I/13
60	A 161	O Ewigkeit, du Donnerwort	Trinity 24	7 Nov 1723	xii/2	I/27
61	A 1	Nun komm, der Heiden Heiland (Neumeister)	Advent 1	2 Dec 1714	xvi	I/1
62	A 2	Nun komm, der Heiden Heiland	Advent 1	3 Dec 1724	xvi	I/1
63	A 8	Christen, ätzet diesen Tag (?Heineccius)	Christmas	?25 Dec 1714	xvi	I/2
64	A 15	Sehet, welch eine Liebe (Knauer)	3rd day of Christmas	27 Dec 1723	xvi	I/3
65	A 27	Sie werden aus Saba alle kommen	Epiphany	6 Jan 1724	xvi	I/5
66	A 56	Erfreut euch, ihr Herzen	Easter Monday	10 Apr 1724	xvi	I/10
67	A 62	Halt im Gedächtnis Jesum Christ	Quasimodogeniti	16 Apr 1724	xvi	I/11.1
68	A 86	Also hat Gott die Welt geliebt (Ziegler)	Monday after Pentecost	21 May 1725	xvi	I/14
69	B 10	Lobe den Herrn (after Knauer)	council election	ca. 1742–1748	xvi	I/32
69a	A 123	Lobe den Herrn (Knauer)	Trinity 12	15 Aug 1723	xvi	I/20

BWV	BC	Text Incipit (Text Author)	Occasion	Date	BG	NBA
70	A 165	Wachet! betet! betet! wachet! (Franck et al.)	Trinity 26	21 Nov 1723	xvi	I/27
71	B 1	Gott ist mein König	council election	4 Feb 1708	xviii	I/32.1
72	A 37	Alles nur nach Gottes Willen (Franck)	Epiphany 3	27 Jan 1726	xviii	I/6
73	A 35	Herr, wie du willt, so schicks mit mir	Epiphany 3	23 Jan 1724	xviii	I/6
74	A 83	Wer mich liebet (Ziegler)	Pentecost	20 May 1725	xviii	I/13
75	A 94	Die Elenden sollen essen (Lange?)	Trinity 1	30 May 1723	xviii	I/15
76	A 97	Die Himmel erzählen die Ehre Gottes (Lange?)	Trinity 2	6 Jun 1723	xviii	I/16
77	A 126	Du sollt Gott, deinen Herren, lieben (Knauer)	Trinity 13	22 Aug 1723	xviii	I/21
78	A 130	Jesu, der du meine Seele	Trinity 14	10 Sep 1724	xviii	I/21
79	A 184	Gott der Herr ist Sonn und Schild	Reformation	31 Oct 1725	xviii	I/31
80	A 183	Ein feste Burg ist unser Gott (Franck et al.)	Reformation	?ca. 1731	xviii	I/31
81	A 39	Jesus schläft, was soll ich hoffen?	Epiphany 4	30 Jan 1724	xx/1	I/16
82	A 169	Ich habe Genung	Purification	2 Feb 1727	xx/1	I/28.1
83	A 167	Erfreute Zeit im neuen Bunde	Purification	2 Feb 1724	xx/1	I/28.1
84	A 43	Ich bin vergnügt mit meinem Glücke (Picander?)	Septuagesima	9 Feb 1727	xx/1	I/7
85	A 66	Ich bin ein guter Hirt	Misericordias	15 Apr 1725	xx/1	I/11.1
86	A 73	Wahrlich, wahrlich, ich sage euch	Rogate	14 May 1724	xx/1	I/12

BWV	BC	Text Incipit (Text Author)	Occasion	Date	BG	NBA
87	A 74	Bisher habt ihr nichts gebeten (Ziegler)	Rogate	6 May 1725	xx/1	I/12
88	A 105	Siehe, ich will viel Fischer aussenden	Trinity 5	21 Jul 1726	xx/1	I/17.2
89	A 155	Was soll ich aus dir machen, Ephraim?	Trinity 22	24 Oct 1723	xx/1	I/26
90	A 163	Es reisset euch ein schrecklich Ende	Trinity 25	14 Nov 1723	xx/1	I/27
91	A 9	Gelobet seist du, Jesu Christ	Christmas	25 Dec 1724	xxii	I/2
92	A 42	Ich hab in Gottes Herz und Sinn	Septuagesima	28 Jan 1725	xxii	I/7
93	A 104	Wer nur den lieben Gott lässt walten	Trinity 5	9 Jul 1724	xxii	I/17.2
94	A 115	Was frag ich nach der Welt	Trinity 9	6 Aug 1724	xxii	I/19
95	A 136	Christus, der ist mein Leben	Trinity 16	12 Sep 1723	xxii	I/23
96	A 142	Herr Christ, der einge Gottessohn	Trinity 18	8 Oct 1724	xxii	I/24
97	A 189	In allen meinen Taten	uncertain	1734	xxii	I/34
98	A 153	Was Gott tut, das ist wohlgetan	Trinity 21	10 Nov 1726	xxi	I/25
99	A 133	Was Gott tut, das ist wohlgetan	Trinity 15	17 Sep 1724	xxii	I/22
100	A 191	Was Gott tut, das ist wohlgetan (Rodigast)	uncertain	?ca. 1735	xxii	I/34
101	A 118	Nimm von uns, Herr, du treuer Gott	Trinity 10	13 Aug 1724	xxiii	I/19
102	A 119	Herr, deine Augen sehen nach dem Glauben	Trinity 10	25 Aug 1726	xxiii	I/19
103	A 69	Ihr werdet weinen (Ziegler)	Jubilate	22 Apr 1725	xxiii	I/11.2
104	A 65	Du Hirte Israel, höre	Misericordias	23 Apr 1724	xxiii	I/11.1

BWV	BC	Text Incipit (Text Author)	Occasion	Date	BG	NBA
105	A 114	Herr, gehe nicht ins Gericht	Trinity 9	25 Jul 1723	xxiii	I/19
106	B 18	Gottes Zeit ist die allerbeste Zeit ("Actus tragicus")	funeral?	ca. 1708–1710	xxiii	I/34
107	A 109	Was willst du dich betrüben	Trinity 7	23 Jul 1724	xxiii	I/18
108	A 72	Es ist euch gut (Ziegler)	Kantate	29 Apr 1725	xxiii	I/12
109	A 151	Ich glaube, lieber Herr	Trinity 21	17 Oct 1723	xxiii	I/25
110	A 10	Unser Mund sei voll Lachens (Lehms)	Christmas	25 Dec 1725	xxiii	I/2
111	A 36	Was mein Gott will, das g'scheh allzeit	Epiphany 3	21 Jan 1725	xxiv	I/6
112	A 67	Der Herr ist mein getreuer Hirt (Meuslin)	Misericordias	8 Apr 1731	xxiv	I/11.1
113	A 122	Herr Jesu Christ, du höchstes Gut	Trinity 11	20 Aug 1724	xxiv	I/20
114	A 139	Ach, lieben Christen, seid getrost	Trinity 17	1 Oct 1724	xxi	I/23
115	A 156	Mache dich, mein Geist, bereit	Trinity 22	5 Nov 1724	xxiv	I/26
116	A 164	Du Friedefürst, Herr Jesu Christ	Trinity 25	26 Nov 1724	xxiv	I/27
117	A 187	Sei Lob und Ehr dem höchsten Gut	uncertain	?ca. 1731	xxiv	I/34
118	B 23	O Jesu Christ, mein Lebens Licht (motet)	memorial?	1736–37	xxiv	III/1
119	B 3	Preise Jerusalem, den Herrn	council election	30 Aug 1723	xxi	I/32.1
120	B 6	Gott, man lobet dich in der Stille	council election	?29 Aug 1729	xxiv	I/32.2
120a	B 15	Herr Gott, Beherrscher aller Dinge	wedding	?1729	xli	I/33

BWV	BC	Text Incipit (Text Author)	Occasion	Date	BG	NBA
121	A 13	Christum wir sollen loben schon	2nd day of Christmas	26 Dec 1724	xxv	I/3
122	A 19	Das neugeborne Kindelein	Christmas 1	31 Dec 1724	xxvi	I/3
123	A 28	Liebster Immanuel, Herzog der Frommen	Epiphany	6 Jan 1725	xxvi	I/5
124	A 30	Meinen Jesum lass ich nicht	Epiphany 1	7 Jan 1725	xxvi	I/5
125	A 168	Mit Fried und Freud ich fahr dahin	Purification	2 Feb 1725	xxvi	I/28.1
126	A 46	Erhalt uns, Herr, bei deinem Wort	Sexagesima	4 Feb 1725	xxv	I/7
127	A 49	Herr Jesu Christ, wahr' Mensch und Gott	Quinquagesima	11 Feb 1725	xxvi	I/8.1
128	A 76	Auf Christi Himmelfahrt (Ziegler)	Ascension	10 May 1725	xxvi	I/12
129	A 93	Gelobet sei der Herr, mein Gott (Olearius)	uncertain	?1727	xxvi	I/15
130	A 179	Herr Gott, dich loben alle wir	St. Michael	29 Sep 1724	xxvi	I/30
131	B 25	Aus der Tiefen rufe ich, Herr (Eilmar?)	uncertain	?1708	xxvii	I/34
132	A 6	Bereitet die Wege (Franck)	Advent 4	22 Dec 1715	xxviii	I/1
133	A 16	Ich freue mich in dir	3rd day of Christmas	27 Dec 1724	xxviii	I/3
134	A 59	Ein Herz, das seinen Jesum lebend weiss	Easter Tuesday	11 Apr 1724	xxviii	I/10
135	A 100	Ach Herr, mich armen Sünder	Trinity 3	25 Jun 1724	xxviii	I/16
136	A 111	Erforsche mich, Gott, und erfahre	Trinity 8	18 Jul 1723	xxviii	I/18
137	A 124	Lobe den Herren, den machtigen (Neander)	Trinity 12	19 Aug 1725	xxviii	I/20

BWV	BC	Text Incipit (Text Author)	Occasion	Date	BG	NBA
138	A 132	Warum betrübst du dich, mein Herz	Trinity 15	5 Sep 1723	xxvii	I/22
139	A159	Wohl dem, der sich auf seinen Gott	Trinity 23	12 Nov 1724	xxviii	I/26
140	A 166	Wachet auf, ruft uns die Stimme	Trinity 27	25 Nov 1731	xxviii	I/27
[141		Das ist je gewisslich wahr, by Telemann]				
[142		Uns ist ein Kind geboren, perhaps by Kuhnau	Christmas]			
★143		Lobe den Herrn, meine Seele	New Year	?1709	xxx	I/4
144	A 41	Nimm was dein ist, und gehe hin	Septuagesima	6 Feb 1724	xxx	I/7
145	A 60	Ich lebe, mein Herze [Auf, mein Herz] (Picander)	Easter Tuesday	?19 Apr 1729	xxx	I/10
146	A 70	Wir müssen durch viel Trübsal	Jubilate	?12 May 1726	xxx	I/11.2
147	A 174	Herz und Mund und Tat und Leben (Franck et al.)	Visitation	2 Jul 1723	xxx	I/28.2
148	A 140	Bringet dem Herrn Ehre (Picander et al.?)	Trinity 17?	?19 Sep 1723	xxx	I/23
149	A 181	Man singet mit Freuden (Picander)	St. Michael	?29 Sep 1728	xxx	I/30
150	B 24	Nach dir, Herr, verlanget mich	uncertain	?by 1708	xxx	I/41
151	A 17	Süsser Trost, mein Jesus kömmt (Lehms)	3rd day of Christmas	27 Dec 1725	xxxii	I/3
152	A 18	Tritt auf die Glaubensbahn (Franck)	Christmas 1	30 Dec 1714	xxxii	I/3
153	A 25	Schau, lieber Gott, wie meine Feind	New Year 1	2 Jan 1724	xxxii	I/4

BWV	BC	Text Incipit (Text Author)	Occasion	Date	BG	NBA
154	A 29	Mein liebster Jesus ist verloren	Epiphany 1	9 Jan 1724	xxxii	I/5
155	A 32	Mein Gott, wie lang, ach lange (Franck)	Epiphany 2	19 Jan 1716	xxxii	I/5
156	A 38	Ich steh mit einem Fuss im Grabe (Picander)	Epiphany 3	?23 Jan 1729	xxxii	I/6
157	A170	Ich lasse dich nicht (Picander)	memorial	6 Feb 1727	xxxii	I/34
158	A 61	Der Friede sei mit dir	Easter Tuesday	?15 Apr 1727	xxxii	I/10
159	A 50	Sehet, wir gehn hinauf (Picander)	Quinquagesima	?27 Feb 1729	xxxii	I/8, 1
[160		Ich weiss, dass mein Erlöser lebt, by Telemann]				
161	A 135	Komm, du süsse Todesstunde (Franck)	Trinity 16	27 Sep 1716	xxxiii	I/23
162	A 148	Ach! ich sehe, itzt, da ich zu Hochzeit gehe (Franck)	Trinity 20	25 Oct 1716	xxxiii	I/25
163	A 158	Nur jedem das Seine (Franck)	Trinity 23	24 Nov 1715	xxxiii	I/26
164	A 128	Ihr, die ihr euch von Christo nennet (Franck)	Trinity 13	26 Aug 1725	xxxiii	I/21
165	A 90	O heilges Geist- und Wasserbad (Franck)	Trinity	16 Jun 1715	xxxii	I/15
166	A 71	Wo gehest du hin?	Cantate	7 May 1724	xxxiii	I/12
167	A 176	Ihr Menschen, rühmet Gottes Liebe	St. John	24 Jun 1723	xxxiii	I/29
168	A 116	Tue Rechnung! Donnerwort (Franck)	Trinity 9	29 Jul 1725	xxxiii	I/19

BWV	BC	Text Incipit (Text Author)	Occasion	Date	BG	NBA
169	A 143	Gott soll allein mein Herze haben	Trinity 18	20 Oct 1726	xxxiii	I/24
170	A 106	Vergnügte Ruh, beliebte Seelenlust (Lehms)	Trinity 6	28 Jul 1726	xxxiii	I/17.2
171	A 24	Gott, wie dein Name, so ist auch dein Ruhm (Picander)	New Year	?1 Jan 1729	xxxv	I/4
172	A 81	Erschallet, ihr Lieder (?Franck)	Pentecost	20 May 1714	xxxv	I/13
173	A 85	Erhöhtes Fleisch und Blut	Monday after Pentecost	?29 May 1724	xxxv	I/14
174	A 87	Ich liebe den Höchsten (Picander)	Monday after Pentecost	6 Jun 1729	xxxv	I/14
175	A 89	Er rufet seinen Schafen mit Namen (Ziegler)	Tuesday after Pentecost	22 May 1725	xxxv	I/14
176	A 92	Es ist ein trotzig, und verzagt Ding (Ziegler)	Trinity	27 May 1725	xxxv	I/15
177	A 103	Ich ruf zu dir, Herr Jesu Christ (J. Agricola)	Trinity 4	6 Jul 1732	xxxv	I/17.1
178	A 112	Wo Gott, der Herr, nicht bei uns hält	Trinity 8	30 Jul 1724	xxxv	I/18
179	A 121	Siehe zu, dass deine Gottesfurcht	Trinity 11	8 Aug 1723	xxxv	I/20
180	A 149	Schmücke dich, O liebe Seele	Trinity 20	22 Oct 1724	xxxv	I/25
181	A 45	Leichtgesinnte Flattergeister	Sexagesima	13 Feb 1724	xxxvii	I/7
182	A 53	Himmelskönig, sei willkommen (?Franck)	Palm Sunday	25 Mar 1714	xxxvii	I/8.2
183	A 79	Sie werden euch in den Bann tun (Ziegler)	Exaudi	13 May 1725	xxxvii	I/12

BWV	BC	Text Incipit (Text Author)	Occasion	Date	BG	NBA
184	A 88	Erwünschtes Freudenlicht	Tuesday after Pentecost	30 May 1724	xxxvii	I/14
185	A 101	Barmherziges Herze der ewigen Liebe (Franck)	Trinity 4	14 Jul 1715	xxxvii	I/17.1
186	A 108	Ärgre dich, o Seele, nicht (Franck et al.)	Trinity 7	11 Jul 1723	xxxvii	I/18
187	A 110	Es wartet alles auf dich	Trinity 7	4 Aug 1726	xxxvii	I/18
188	A 154	Ich habe meine Zuversicht (Picander)	Trinity 21	?17 Oct 1726	xxxvi	I/25
[189		Meine Seele rühmt und preist, by Hoffmann]				
190	A 21	Singet dem Herrn (frag.)	New Year	1 Jan 1724	xxxvii	I/4
191	E 16	Gloria in excelsis Deo	?Christmas	?25 Dec 1742	xli	I/2
192	A 188	Nun danket alle Gott (frag.)	?Reformation	?31 Oct 1730	xli	I/34
193	B 5	Ihr Tore zu Zion (frag.)	council election	25 Aug 1727	xli	I/32.1
194	B 31	Höchsterwünschtes Freudenfest	organ dedication	2 Nov 1723	xxix	I/31
195	B 14	Dem Gerechten muss das Licht	wedding	by 3 Jan 1736	xii/1	I/33
196	B 11	Der Herr denket an uns	uncertain	?ca. 1708–1710	xiii/1	I/33
197	B 16	Gott ist unsre Zuversicht	wedding	1736–1737	xiii/1	I/33
197a	A 11	Ehre sei Gott in der Hohe (Picander) (frag.)	Christmas	?25 Dec 1728	xli	I/2
199	A 120	Mein Herze schwimmt im Blut (Lehms)	Trinity 11	?12 Aug 1714		I/20

BWV	BC	Text Incipit (Text Author)	Occasion	Date	BG	NBA
200	A 192	Bekennen will ich seinen Namen (aria by Stölzel, arr. Bach)		?1735		I/28.1
223	A 186	Meine Seele soll Gott loben (incipit only)	unknown			
1083	B 26	Tilge, Höchster (Pergolesi, *Stabat mater*, parody arr. Bach)	unknown	1745–1746		I/41

2 Secular Cantatas

BWV	BC	Text incipit (text author)	Occasion/ Honoree	Date	BG	NBA
30a	G 31	Angenehmes Wiederau (Picander)	homage to J. C. Hennicke	28 Sep 1737	v/1, xxxiv	I/39
36b	G 38	Die Freude reget sich	J. F. Rivinus installed as university rector?	?Oct 1735	xxxiv	I/38
36c	G 35	Schwingt freudig euch empor	birthday?	?spring 1725	xxxiv	I/39
134a	G 5	Die Zeit, die Tag und Jahre macht (Hunold)	New Year	1 Jan 1719	xxix	I/35
173a	G 9	Durchlauchtster Leopold	birthday, Pr. Leopold	?10 Dec 1722	xxxiv	I/35
198	G 34	Trauerode: Lass, Fürstin, lass noch (Gottsched)	memorial, Electress Christiane Eberhardine	17 Oct 1727	xiii/3	I/38
201	G 46	Der Streit zwischen Phoebus und Pan: Geschwinde, ihr wirbelnden (Picander)		?1729	xi/2	I/40

BWV	BC	Text incipit (text author)	Occasion/ Honoree	Date	BG	NBA
202	G 44	Weichet nur, betrübte Schatten	wedding?	?by 1715	xi/2	I/40
203	G 51	Amore traditore	unknown	?1717–1723	xi/2	I/41
204	G 45	Ich bin in mir vergnügt (Hunold et al.)	unknown	1727–1728	xi/2	I/40
205	G 36	Zerreisset, zersprenget (Picander)	name day, A. F. Müller	3 Aug 1725	xi/2	I/38
206	G 23, G 26	Schleicht, spielende Wellen	birthday, Elector Friedrich August II	7 Oct 1736	xx/2	I/36
207	G 37	Vereinigte Zwietracht der wechselnden Saiten	installation, Professor G. Kortte	?11 Dec 1726	xx/2	I/38
207a	G 22	Auf, schmetternde Tone	name day, Friedrich August II	?3 Aug 1735	xx/2	I/37
208	G I, 3	Was mir behagt [Hunt Cantata] (Franck)	birthday, Duke Christian of Weissenfels	?23 Feb 1713	xxix	I/35
209	G 50	Non sa che sia dolore	unknown	?ca. 1735	xxix	I/41
210	G 44	O holder Tag, erwünschte Zeit	wedding	ca. 1738–1741	xxix	I/40
211	G 48	Schweigt stille, plaudert nicht [Coffee Cantata] (Picander)	unknown	?1734	xxix	I/40
212	G 32	Mer hahn en neue Oberkeet [Peasant Cantata] (Picander)	homage to C. H. von Dieskau	30 Aug 1742	xxix	I/39
213	G 18	Hercules auf dem Scheidewege: Lasst uns sorgen (Picander)	birthday, Pr. Friedrich Christian of Saxony	5 Sep 1733	xxxiv	I/36
214	G 19	Tönet, ihr Pauken! Erschallet Trompeten!	birthday, Electress Maria Josepha	8 Dec 1733	xxxiv	I/36
215	G 21	Preise dein Glücke, gesegnetes Sachsen (Clauder)	anniversary, Augustus III as Polish king	5 Oct 1734	xxxiv	I/37

BWV	BC	Text incipit (text author)	Occasion/ Honoree	Date	BG	NBA
216	G 43	Vergnügte Pleisenstadt (frag.) (Picander)	wedding	5 Feb 1728		I/40

3 Motets, Passions, and Oratorios

BWV	BC	Text Incipit (Text Author)	Occasion	Date	BG	NBA
Motets						
118	B 23	O Jesu Christ, mein Lebens Licht	funeral procession?	1736–1737	xxiv	III/1
225	C 1	Singet dem Herrn		1726–1727	xxxix	III/1
226	C 2	Der Geist hilft unser Schwachheit auf	funeral, J. H. Ernesti	20 Oct 1729	xxxix	III/1
227	C 5	Jesu, meine Freude		?before 1723	xxxix	III/1
228	C 4	Fürchte dich nicht		?before 1717	xxxix	III/1
229	C 3	Komm, Jesu, komm! (Thymich)		before 1732	xxxix	III/1
★230	C 6	Lobet den Herrn alle Heiden			xxxix	III/1
★	C 9	Ich lasse dich nicht (BWV Anh. 159)		?before 1714	xxxix	III/1
Passions						
244	D 3	St. Matthew Passion (Picander)	Good Friday	11 Apr 1727	iv	II/5
245	D 2	St. John Passion	Good Friday	7 Apr 1724	xii/1	II/4
[246		St. Luke Passion, anonymous]				
247	D 4	St. Mark Passion (Picander) (lost)	Good Friday	23 Mar 1731		
1084	D 5b/6	O hilf Christe (chorale harmonization inserted in "Keiser" passion)	Good Friday	19 Apr 1726		II/9
1088	D 10/2	So heb ich denn mein Auge (arioso, inserted in pasticcio passion)	Good Friday	?after 1731		I/41

BWV	BC	Text Incipit (Text Author)	Occasion	Date	BG	NBA
Oratorios						
11	D 9	Ascension Oratorio	Ascension	19 May 1735	ii	II/8
248	D 7	Christmas Oratorio (?Picander)	Christmas, etc.	1734–1735	v/2	II/6
249	D 8	Easter Oratorio (?Picander)	Easter	?1737 or 1738	xxi/3	II/7

4 Latin Sacred Music

BWV	BC	Title	Date	BG	NBA Vol.
232[a]		*Missa* in b	1733		
232	E 1	Mass in b	ca. 1747–49	vi	II/1
233a	E 7	Kyrie in F	?ca. 1715	xli	II/2
233	E 6	*Missa* in F	ca. 1747–48	viii	II/2
234	E 3	*Missa* in A	ca. 1738, 1743–1749	viii	II/2
235	E 5	*Missa* in g	ca. 1747–1748	viii	II/2
236	E 4	*Missa* in G	ca. 1738–1739	viii	II/2
237	E 10	Sanctus in C	?24 Jun 1723	xi	II/2
238	E 11	Sanctus in D	?25 Dec 1723	xi/1	II/2
239		Sanctus in d, by Caldara, ?arr. Bach	ca. 1738–1741	xi/1	II/9
240		Sanctus in G, anon., arr. Bach	ca. 1738–1741	xi/1	II/9
241		Sanctus in D, by Kerll, arr. Bach	1742	xi/1	II/9
242	E 8	Christe eleison	ca. 1727–1732	xli	II/2
243a	E 13	Magnificat in E-flat	25 Dec 1723		II/3
243	E 14	Magnificat in D	?1733	xi/1	II/3
1081	E 9	Credo (for Bassani mass)	ca. 1747–1748		II/2
1082	E 15	Suscepit Israel (for Caldara Magnificat)	1745–1746		II/9

5 Chorales, Songs, and Miscellaneous Vocal Music

BWV	Item	BG	NBA
250–52	3 wedding chorales	xiii/1	III/2.1
253–438	186 harmonized chorales, publ. Leipzig, 1784–1787, ed. Kirnberger and C. P. E. Bach	xxxix	III/2.1–2
439–507	69 hymns for voice, b.c., in Schemelli's *Musicalisches Gesang-Buch*, publ. Leipzig, 1736 (mostly arr. Bach?)	xxxix	III/2.1
509–18	songs (etc.) in 1725 *Clavierbüchlein* for A. M. Bach (not all by J. S. Bach)	xxxix	V/4
★524	Quodlibet (frag.), ca. 1707		I/41
1089	Da Jesus an dem Kreuze stund		III/2.2
1122–26	5 chorale settings		III/2.1, III/2.2
1127	Alles mit Gott (strophic aria, 1713)		supplement (2011)

6 Music primarily for organ

(a) "Free" Compositions

BWV	Title or Genre	Key	Date	BG	NBA
Sonatas					
525–30	Six sonatas	E-flat, c, d, e, C, G	1723–1731	xv	IV/7
★583	Trio	d		xxxviii	IV/7
Preludes, Fugues, and Related Pieces					
531	Praeludium ("prelude and fugue")	C	?by 1708	xv	IV/5
532	Praeludium ("prelude and fugue")	D	?by 1714	xv	IV/5
533	Praeludium ("prelude and fugue")	e	?by 1708	xv	IV/5
[534	Praeludium ("prelude and fugue")	f		xv	IV/5]

BWV	Title or Genre	Key	Date	BG	NBA
535	Praeludium ("prelude and fugue")	g	?by 1708	xv	IV/5
536	Praeludium ("prelude and fugue")	A	?by 1708	xv	IV/5
537	Praeludium ("prelude and fugue")	c	?after 1723	xv	IV/5
538	Toccata and Fugue ("Dorian")	d	by 1717	xv	IV/5
*539	Praeludium ("prelude and fugue")	d		xv	IV/5
540	Toccata and Fugue	F	by 1717	xv	IV/5
541	Praeludium ("prelude and fugue")	G	after 1723	xv	IV/5
542	Fantasia and Fugue	g	?by 1723	xv	IV/5
543	Praeludium ("prelude and fugue")	a	?by 1714	xv	IV/5
544	Praeludium ("prelude and fugue")	b	after 1723	xv	IV/5
545	Praeludium ("prelude and fugue")	C	by 1717	xv	IV/5
546	Praeludium ("prelude and fugue")	c	?after 1723	xv	IV/5
547	Praeludium ("prelude and fugue")	C	?after 1723	xv	IV/5
548	Praeludium ("prelude and fugue," "Wedge")	e	1727 or later	xv	IV/5
549	Praeludium ("prelude and fugue")	c (d)	?by 1707	xxxviii	IV/5
550	Praeludium ("prelude and fugue")	G	?by 1714	xxxviii	IV/5
*551	Praeludium ("prelude and fugue")	a		xxxviii	IV/6
552	Prelude, fugue ("St. Anne," publ. in *Clavierübung*, Part 3)	E-flat	1739	iii	IV/6
[553–60	[8] preludes and fugues	C, d, e, F, G, g, a, B-flat		xxxviii	IV/11]
562	Fantasia and Fugue (fugue = frag.)	c	ca. 1740–1745	xxxviii	IV/5

BWV	Title or Genre	Key	Date	BG	NBA
563	Fantasia	b	?by 1707	xxxviii	IV/6
564	Toccata, Adagio and Fugue	C	?by 1717	xv	IV/6
[565	"Toccata and Fugue," by Kellner?	d		xv	IV/6]
566	Praeludium ("toccata")	E (C)	?by 1708	xv	IV/6
[568	Praeludium	G		xxxviii	IV/6]
569	Praeludium	a	?by 1708	xxxviii	IV/6
570	Fantasia	C	?by 1707	xxxviii	IV/6
★571	Fantasia	G		xxxviii	IV/11
572	Pièce d'orgue ("fantasia")	G	?by 1714	xxxviii	IV/7
573	Fantasia (frag.)	C	ca. 1722	xxxviii	IV/6
574	Fugue ("on theme by Legrenzi")	c	?by 1708	xxxviii	IV/6
★575	Fugue	c		xxxviii	IV/6
★577	Fugue	G		xxxviii	IV/11
578	Fugue	g	by 1714	xxxviii	IV/6
579	Fugue on theme by Corelli	b	by 1714	xxxviii	IV/6
582	Passacaglia [and Fugue]	c	by 1714	xv	IV/7
★583	Trio	d		xxxviii	IV/7
588	Canzona	d	?by 1708	xxxviii	IV/7
★589	Alla breve	D		xxxviii	IV/7
590	Pastorella	F	?after 1723	xxxviii	IV/7
[591	Kleines harmonisches Labyrinth	C		xxxviii	IV/11]
[598	Pedal exercise (frag.), probably by C. P. E. Bach	g		xxxviii	IV/11]
802–5	[4] Duets (publ. in *Clavierübung*, Part 3)	e, F, G, a	1739	iii	IV/6
1121	Fantasia (follows BWV 921)	c	?by 1708		IV/11

Transcriptions and Arrangements

★585	Fasch, Trio FWV N c2 (2 mvts.)	c			IV/8
★586	Anon., Trio	G			IV/8
★587	F. Couperin, Sonata La Convalescente (1 mvt.)	F			IV/8

BWV	Title or Genre	Key	Date	BG	NBA
592	Prince Johann Ernst, Concerto	G	?ca. 1714	xxxviii	IV/8
593	Vivaldi, Concerto op. 3, no. 8 (R. 522)	a	?ca. 1714	xxxviii	IV/8
594	Vivaldi, Concerto R. 208a ("Il grosso Mogul")	C	?ca. 1714	xxxviii	IV/8
595	Prince Johann Ernst, Concerto	C	?ca. 1714	xxxviii	IV/8
596	Vivaldi, Concerto op. 3, no. 11 (R. 565)	d	?by 1717		IV/8

(b) Chorale Compositions

Not shown here are numerous doubtful works that have been attributed to Bach by copyists or editors on various grounds; *some are listed in the online supplement.* Here, "2 kb., ped." = two keyboards and pedal; "c.f." = cantus firmus; sop. = soprano; ten. = tenor.

BWV	Title

Orgelbüchlein (mostly ca. 1713–1716), in BG xxv/2, NBA IV/1

599–644	Forty-six chorale preludes *(for individual titles, see supplement)*

"Schubler" Chorales (publ. 1748 or 1749), in BG xxv/2, NBA IV/1

645	Wachet auf, ruft uns die Stimme
646	Wo soll ich fliehen hin
647	Wer nur den lieben Gott lässt walten
648	Meine Seele erhebt den Herren
649	Ach bleib bei uns, Herr Jesu Christ
650	Kommst du nun, Jesu, vom Himmel

"Great Eighteen" ("Leipzig") chorales (mostly 1708–1717, later revised), in BG xxv/2, NBA IV/2

651	Komm, heiliger Geist (fantasia)
652	Komm, heiliger Geist (2 kb., ped.)
653	An Wasserflüssen Babylon (2 kb., ped.)
654	Schmücke dich, o liebe Seele (2 kb., ped.)
655	Herr Jesu Christ, dich zu uns wend (trio)
656	O Lamm Gottes, unschuldig (3 *versus*)
657	Nun danket alle Gott (2 kb., ped., c.f. in sop.)
658	Von Gott will ich nicht lassen (c.f. in ped.)
659	Nun komm, der Heiden Heiland (2 kb., ped.)

BWV	Title
660	Nun komm, der Heiden Heiland (trio)
661	Nun komm, der Heiden Heiland (c.f. in ped.)
662	Allein Gott in der Höh' sei Ehr'(2 kb., ped., c.f. in sop.)
663	Allein Gott in der Höh' sei Ehr'(2 kb., ped., c.f. in ten.)
664	Allein Gott in der Höh' sei Ehr' (trio)
665	Jesus Christus, unser Heiland (sub comm.)
666	Jesus Christus, unser Heiland (alio modo)
667	Komm, Gott Schöpfer, heiliger Geist
668	Vor deinen Thron tret' ich (frag.)

Chorales from Clavierübung, *Part 3 (published 1739), BG iii, NBA IV/4*

669	Kyrie, Gott Vater in Ewigkeit
670	Christe, aller Welt Trost
671	Kyrie, Gott heiliger Geist
672	Kyrie, Gott Vater in Ewigkeit *(manualiter)*
673	Christe, aller Welt Trost *(manualiter)*
674	Kyrie, Gott heiliger Geist *(manualiter)*
675	Allein Gott in der Höh' sei Ehr' *(manualiter)*
676	Allein Gott in der Höh' sei Ehr' (trio)
677	Allein Gott in der Höh' sei Ehr' (fughetta)
678	Dies sind die heil'gen zehn Gebot
679	Dies sind die heil'gen zehn Gebot (fughetta)
680	Wir glauben all' an einen Gott
681	Wir glauben all' an einen Gott (fughetta)
682	Vater unser im Himmelreich
683	Vater unser im Himmelreich *(manualiter)*
684	Christ, unser Herr, zum Jordan kam
685	Christ, unser Herr, zum Jordan kam *(manualiter)*
686	Aus tiefer Not schrei ich zu dir
687	Aus tiefer Not schrei ich zu dir *(manualiter)*
688	Jesus Christus unser Heiland
689	Jesus Christus unser Heiland *(manualiter)*

Miscellaneous chorales, mostly in BG xl, NBA IV/3 (doubtful works in NBA IV/9)

690–743, 758, 764, 1128	Various chorale settings, mostly short, some spurious or doubtful *(for individual titles see supplement)*

BWV	Title
Chorales from the "Neumeister" manuscript (most probably before 1710), in NBA V/9	
957, 1090–1119	Thirty short chorale settings of various types *(for individual titles see supplement)*
Chorale variations (all except BWV 769 probably before 1710)	
*758	O Vater, allmächtiger Gott (NBA IV/11)
766	Christ, der du bist der helle Tag (BG xl, NBA IV/1)
767	O Gott, du frommer Gott (BG xl, NBA IV/1)
768	Sei gegrüsset, Jesu gütig (BG xl, NBA IV/1)
769	Vom Himmel hoch, da komm' ich her, publ. 1747 (BG xl, NBA IV/2)
*770	Ach, was soll ich Sünder machen (BG xl, NBA IV/1)

7 Other Keyboard ("Clavier") Music

BWV	Title or genre	Key	Date	BG	NBA
Inventions and Sinfonias					
772–86	[15] Inventions	C, c, D, d, E-flat, E, e, F, f, G, g, A, a, B-flat, b	ca. 1720–1723	iii, xlv	V/3, V/5
787–801	[15] Sinfonias (three-part inventions)	C, c, D, d, E-flat, E, e, F, f, G, g, A, a, B-flat, b	ca. 1720–1723	iii	V/3, V/5
802–5	[4] Duets (publ. in *Clavierübung*, Part 3)	e, F, G, a	1739	iii	IV/6
Suites and Related Compositions					
806–11	[6] English Suites	A, a, g, F, e, d	ca. 1714–1723	xlv/1	V/7
812–17	[6] French Suites	d, c, b, E-flat, G, E	ca. 1717–1725	xlv/1	V/8
818	Suite	a	?ca. 1708–1717	xxxvi	V/8
819	Suite	E-flat	?ca. 1714–1723	xxxvi	V/8
820	*Ouverture*	F	?by 1708	xxxvi	V/x
821	Suite	B-flat	?by 1708	xlii	V/12
822	*Ouverture*	g	?by 1708		V/10
823	Suite	f	?by 1708	xxxvi	V/10
825–30	[6] Partitas (publ. in *Clavierübung*, Part 1)	B-flat, c, a, D, G, e	1726–1731	iii	V/1, V/4

BWV	Title or genre	Key	Date	BG	NBA
831	*Ouverture* (publ. in *Clavierübung*, Part 2)	b	1735	iii	V/2
832	*Partie* (suite)	A	?by 1708	xlii	V/10
833	*Praeludium et partita* (suite)	F	?by 1708		V/10
841–43	[3] Minuets	G, g, G	ca. 1720–1723	xxxvi	V/5

Preludes, Fugues, and Related Compositions

BWV	Title or genre	Key	Date	BG	NBA
846–69	Well-Tempered Clavier, Part 1 (24 preludes and fugues)	C, c, C-sharp, etc.	by 1722	xiv	V/6.1
870–93	Well-Tempered Clavier, Part 2 (24 preludes and fugues)	C, c, C-sharp, etc.	?by ca. 1740	xiv	V/6.2
894	Praeludium ("prelude and fugue")	a	?by 1717	xxxvi	V/9.2
895	Praeludium ("prelude and fugue")	a	?by 1714	xxxvi	V/9.2
896	Praeludium ("prelude and fugue")	A	?by 1708	xxxvi (fugue)	V/9.2
899–902	[4] Prelude-fughetta pairs	d, e, F, G	?by 1717	xxxvi	V/6.2
903	Chromatic fantasia and fugue	d	?by 1717	xxxvi	V/9.2
904	Fantasia and fugue	a	?by 1717	xxxvi	V/9.2
★905	Fantasia and fugue	d		xxxvi	V/12
906	Fantasia (and fugue, fragment)	c	?after 1723	xxxvi	V/9.2
★907–8	[2] Fantasia-fughetta pairs (*partimenti*)	B-flat, D		xlii	V/12
910–16	[7]Toccatas	f-sharp, c, D, d, e, g, G	by 1714	iii, xxxvi	V/9.1
917	Fantasia (2 subjects)	g	?by 1708	xxxvi	V/9.2
918	*Fantaisie sur un rondeau*	c	?after 1723	xxxvi	V/9.2
921	Praeludium (cf. BWV 1121)	c	?by 1708	xxxvi	V/9.2
922	Praeludium (fantasia)	a	?by 1707	xxxvi	V/9.2
923	Prelude	b	?by 1717	xlii	V/9.2

BWV	Title or genre	Key	Date	BG	NBA
924–32	[9] Preludes and other pieces in the *Clavierbüchlein* for W. F. Bach (the last is frag.)	C, D, d, F, F, g, g, a, e	?ca. 1720–1723	xxxvi	V/5
933–38	[6] Preludes	C, c, d, D, E, e	?after 1723	xxxvi	V/9.2
939–43	[5] Preludes	C, d, e, a, C	?by 1723	xxxvi	V/9.2
944	Fugue (with short fantasia)	a	by 1714	iii	V/9.2
946	Fugue (subject by Albinoni)	C	?by 1708	xxxvi	V/9.2
★947–48	Fugues	a, d		xxxvi	V/12,V /9.2
949	Fugue	A	by 1708	xxxvi	V/9.2
950–51	Fugues (subjects by Albinoni)	A, b	?by 1714	xxxvi	V/9.2
952–53	Fugues	C, C	by 1723	xxxvi	V/9.1
954	Fugue (subject by Reinken)	B-flat	?by 1708	xlii	V/11
955	Fugue (subj. attr. Erselius)	B-flat	?by 1708	xlii	V/11
957	Fughetta (on the chorale "Machs mit mir, Gott")	G	?by 1708	xlii	IV/9
961	Fughetta (fugue)	c	?by 1723	xxxvi	V/9.2
963	Sonata	D	?by 1707	xxxvi	V/10
993	Capriccio	E	?by 1707	xxxvi	V/10

Transcriptions and Arrangements

BWV	Title or genre	Key	Date	BG	NBA
592a	Prince Johann Ernst, Concerto	G	?ca. 1714	xxxviii	V/11
964	Bach, Violin Sonata no. 2	d	?after 1723	xlii	V/12
965–66	Reinken, sonata movements from *Hortus musicus*	a, C	?by 1714	xlii	V/11
968	Bach, Violin Sonata no. 3 (frag.)	G	?after 1723	xlii	V/12
972	Vivaldi, Concerto op. 3, no. 9 (R. 230)	D	ca. 1714	xlii	V/11

BWV	Title or genre	Key	Date	BG	NBA
973	Vivaldi, Concerto op. 7, no. 8 (R. 299)	G	ca. 1714	xlii	V/11
974	?A. Marcello, Oboe concerto	d	ca. 1714	xlii	V/11
975	Vivaldi, Concerto R. 316a	g	ca. 1714	xlii	V/11
976	Vivaldi, Concerto op. 3, no. 12 (R. 265)	C	ca. 1714	xlii	V/11
977	Anon., Concerto	C	ca. 1714	xlii	V/11
978	Vivaldi, Concerto op. 3, no. 3 (R. 310)	F	ca. 1714	xlii	V/11
979	?Vivaldi (also attr. Torelli), Concerto	b	ca. 1714	xlii	V/11
980	Vivaldi, Concerto R. 381	G	ca. 1714	xlii	V/11
981	B. Marcello, Concerto op. 1, no. 2	C	ca. 1714	xlii	V/11
982	Prince Johann Ernst, Concerto op. 1, no. 1	B-flat	ca. 1714	xlii	V/11
983	Anon., Concerto	g	ca. 1714	xlii	V/11
984	Prince Johann Ernst, Concerto	C	ca. 1714	xlii	V/11
985	Telemann, Concerto	g	ca. 1714	xlii	V/11
986	Anon., Concerto	G	ca. 1714	xlii	V/11
987	Prince Johann Ernst, Concerto op. 1, no. 4	d	ca. 1714	xlii	V/11

Miscellaneous Compositions

BWV	Title or genre	Key	Date	BG	NBA
691	Wer nur den lieben Gott	a	?by 1723	xl	IV/3, V/4, V/5
[692a, 693	Ach Gott und Herr, two settings, probably by Walther]	C		xl	IV/11
728	Jesus, meine Zuversicht	C	?by 1723	xl	IV/3, V/4
753	Jesu, meine Freude (frag.)	d	?by 1723	xl	V/v
967	Sonata	a	?by 1707	xlv/1	V/9.2

BWV	Title or genre	Key	Date	BG	NBA
971	Italian concerto (publ. in *Clavierübung*, Part 2)	F	1735	iii	V/2
988	"Goldberg"Variations (publ. in *Clavierübung*, Part [4])	G	1741	iii	V/2
989	Aria variata	a	by 1714	xxxvi	V/10
★990	*Sarabande con partitis*	C	?by 1707	xxxvi	V/10
991	Air [with variations, fragment]	c	?after 1723	xliii	V/iv
992	Capriccio sopra la lontananza de il fratro dilettissimo	B-flat	?by 1707	xxxvi	V/10
993	Capriccio	E	?by 1707	xxxvi	V/10
994	Applicatio (fingering prelude)	C	?ca. 1720	xxxvi	V/v
1121	Fantasia (follows BWV 921)	c	?by 1708		IV/11

8 Music for Solo Lute, Violin, Cello, and Flute

BWV	Title or genre	Key	Date	BG	NBA
995	Suite, lute	g	1727–1731		V/10
996	Suite, lute	e	?ca. 1708–1717	xlv/1	V10
997	Suite, lute	c	by 1738–1744	xlv	V/10
998	Prelude, fugue, allegro, lute	E	by ca. 1735	xlv/1	V/10
999	Prelude, lute	c	ca. 1720?	xxxvi	V/10
1000	Fugue, lute	g	?after 1720		V/10
1001–6	Solos: [3] sonatas and [3] partitas, violin	g, a, C, and b, d, E	by 1720	xxvii/1	VI/1
1007–12	[6] Suites, cello	G, d, C, E-flat, c, D	?by 1717	xxvii/1	VI/2
1013	Partita, flute	a	?by 1723		VI/3

9 Music for Instrumental Ensemble

BWV	Title or Genre	Key	Date	BG	NBA
Sonatas and Other Chamber Works					
1014–19	[6] Sonatas, violin, harpsichord	b, A, E, c, f, G	?by 1725	ix	VI/1
[1020	Sonata, violin (flute?), harpsichord, ?by C. P. E. Bach]	g		ix	
1021	Sonata, violin, b.c.	G	by 1733		VI/1
1023	Sonata, violin, b.c.	e	?ca. 1714–1717	xliii/1	VI/1
1025	Trio, violin, harpsichord (arrgt. of suite by Weiss)	A	?ca. 1746–1747	ix	VI/5
1026	Fugue, violin, b.c.	g	?ca. 1712–1717	xliii/1	VI/4
1027	Sonata, gamba, harpsichord	G	by ca. 1742	ix	VI/4
1028	Sonata, gamba, harpsichord	D	?after 1723	ix	VI/4
1029	Sonata, gamba, harpsichord	g	?ca. 1717–1723	ix	VI/4
1030	Sonata, flute, harpsichord	b	by ca. 1736–1737	ix	VI/3
[1031	Sonata, flute, harpsichord	E-flat		ix]	
1032	Sonata, flute, harpsichord (frag.)	A	?after 1736	ix	VI/3
[1033	Sonata, flute, b.c.	C		xliii/1]	
1034	Sonata, flute, b.c.	e	after 1717	xliii/1	VI/3
1035	Sonata, flute, b.c.	E	?1741	xliii/1	VI/3
[1037	Trio sonata, flute, violin, b.c., by Goldberg]	C		ix	
1038	Trio sonata, flute, violin, b.c. (composed jointly with C. P. E. Bach?)	G	by ca. 1732–1735	ix	VI/5
1039	Trio sonata, 2 flutes, b.c.	G	?ca. 1736–1741	ix	VI/3
1040	Trio, oboe, violin, b.c.	F	1713	xxix	I/35
Concertos and Suites (all except BWV 1048, 1051, and 1061a include strings, continuo)					
1041	Concerto, violin	a	by ca. 1730	xxi/1	VII/3
1042	Concerto, violin	E	?by ca. 1730	xxi/1	VII/3
1043	Concerto, 2 violins	d	by ca. 1730	xxi/1	VII/3

BWV	Title or Genre	Key	Date	BG	NBA
★1044	Concerto, flute, violin, harpsichord	a		xvii	VII/3
1046–51	[6] Brandenburg concertos:		by 1721	xix	VII/2
1046	no. 1, 2 horns, 3 oboes, bassoon, violin	F			
1047	no. 2, trumpet, recorder, oboe, violin	F			
1048	no. 3, 3 violins, 3 violas, 3 cellos, b.c.	G			
1049	no. 4, violin, 2 recorders	G			
1050	no. 5, flute, violin, harpsichord	D			
1051	no. 6, 2 violas, 2 gambas, cello, b.c.	B-flat			
1052–58	[7] Concertos, harpsichord (?all arrgts. of earlier concertos)	d, E, D, A, f, F, g	ca. 1738	xvii	VII/4
1059	Concerto, harpsichord, oboe (frag.)	d	ca. 1738	xvii	VII/4
1060	Concerto, 2 harpsichords	c	by 1744–1748	xxi/2	VII/5
[1061	Concerto, 2 harpsichords, arrgt. of BWV 1061a, by W. F. Bach?]	C		xxi/2	VII/5
1061a	Concerto, 2 harpsichords	C	ca. 1732–1733		VII/5
1062	Concerto, 2 harpsichord	c	by 1736	xxi/2	VII/5
1063	Concerto, 3 harpsichords	d	?by ca. 1733	xxxi/3	VII/6
1064	Concerto, 3 harpsichords	C	?by ca. 1733	xxxi/3	VII/6
1065	Concerto, 4 harpsichords, arrgt. of Vivaldi, op. 3, no. 10 (R. 580)	a	ca. 1730	xliii/1	VII/6
1066	Suite, 2 oboes, bassoon	C	?by 1723	xxxi/1	VII/1
1067	Suite, flute	b	by 1738–1739	xxxi/1	VII/1
1068	Suite, 3 trumpets, timpani, 2 oboes	D	ca. 1730	xxxi/1	VII/1
1069	Suite, 3 trumpets, timpani, 3 oboes, bassoon	D	by 1725	xxxi/1	VII/1
[1070	Suite, by W. F. Bach?	g		xlv/1]	

10 Canons and Related Contrapuntal Works

BWV	Title	Date	BG	NBA
1072	Canon trias harmonica		xlv/1	VIII/1
1073	Canon a 4 perpetuus	2 Aug 1713	xlv/1	VIII/1
1074	Canon a 4	1727	xlv/1	VIII/1
1075	Canon a 2 perpetuus	10 Jan 1734		VIII/1
1076	Canon triplex (in Haussmann portrait)	by ca. 1746	xlv/1	VIII/1
1077	Canone doppio sopr'il soggetto	15 Oct 1747		VIII/1
1078	Canon super fa mi a 7	1 Mar 1749	xlv/1	VIII/1
1079	Musical Offering	publ. 1747	xxxi/2	VIII/1
1080	Art of Fugue	publ. 1751	xxv/1	VIII/2.1–2
1086	Canon concordia discors			VIII/1
1087	[14] Canons on the first 8 bass notes of BWV 988	1741–1746		V/2

Personalia

Abel, Carl Friedrich (1723–1787), gambist and composer, son of the following, friend and colleague of Johann Christian Bach.

Abel, Christian Ferdinand (ca. 1683–1737), string player, colleague of Johann Jacob and J. S. Bach.

Adlung, Jacob (1699–1762), Erfurt organist and writer on music.

Agricola, Johann Friedrich (1720–1774), composer and writer on music; pupil of Bach at Leipzig and of Quantz at Berlin.

Ahle, Johann Georg (1651–1706), organist and composer at Mühlhausen, son of the following.

Ahle, Johann Rudolf (1625–1673), organist and composer at Mühlhausen.

Albinoni, Tomaso Giovanni (1671–1751), Italian (Venetian) composer, known especially for his violin and oboe concertos, one of which Bach transcribed for solo keyboard.

Altnickol, Johann Christoph (1720–1759), organist and composer, pupil of Bach, whom he assisted as singer and music copyist at Leipzig.

Altnickol, Johann Sebastian (1749), infant son of the above, grandson of J. S. Bach.

Anglebert, Jean-Henri d' (1629–1691), French composer and keyboard player; Bach probably knew his *Pièces de clavecin* (Paris, 1689).

Anna Amalie, Princess of Prussia (1723–1787), sister of King Frederick "the Great," composer and collector of music, including Bach's; his pupil Kirnberger was her librarian.

Augustus II, *see* Friedrich August I.

Augustus III, *see* Friedrich August II.

Bach (relationship to Johann Sebastian follows given names; maiden name in parentheses)

    Anna Carolina Philippina, granddaughter (1747–1804), daughter of Carl Philipp Emanuel.

    Anna Magdalena (Wilcke), second wife (1701–1760), court singer at Cöthen, also worked as music copyist for J. S. Bach and presumably helped train their children, including her sons Johann Christoph Friedrich and Johann Christian.

    Barbara Margaretha (Keul), stepmother (b. 1658).

    Carl Philipp Emanuel, son (1714–1788), composer, keyboard player, and writer on music, chamber musician to King Frederick "the Great," then cantor and music director at Hamburg.

    Catharina Dorothea, daughter (1731–1732).

    Christian Gottlieb, son (1725–1728).

    Christiana Sophia Henrietta Bach, daughter (1713).

    Christoph, grandfather (1613–1661), court and town musician, serving at Weimar, Erfurt, and Arnstadt.

Elisabeth Juliana Friederica, daughter (1726–1781), married Sebastian's pupil Altnickol.

Friedelena Margaretha Bach, sister-in-law (1675–1729).

Friederica Sophia, granddaughter (b. 1757), daughter of Wilhelm Friedemann; her descendants emigrated to the United States.

Georg Christoph, paternal uncle (1642–1697), composer and organist, cantor at Schweinfurt.

Gottfried Heinrich, son (1724–1763), said to have been talented, but mentally disabled.

Heinrich, uncle (1615–1692), composer, organist and court and church musician at Arnstadt.

Johann, great uncle (1604–1673), composer, organist at Erfurt.

Johann Adam, grandson (1745–1789), son of Carl Philipp Emanuel, lawyer at Berlin.

Johann Ambrosius, father (1645–1695), court and town musician at Eisenach.

Johann August Abraham, son (1733).

Johann Balthasar, brother (1673–1691), apprenticed to his father as town musician at Eisenach.

Johann Bernhard, nephew (1700–1743), organist, succeeded his father at Ohrdruf.

Johann Bernhard, second cousin (1676–1749), organist and court keyboard player at Eisenach.

Johann Christian, son (1735–1782), keyboard player and composer, served as organist at Milan, later lived in London; wrote sacred music, Italian operas, and many sonatas, concertos, etc.

Johann Christoph, first cousin once removed (1642–1703), son of Heinrich, court organist at Arnstadt before becoming city organist and court keyboard player at Eisenach, described by Sebastian as "profound."

Johann Christoph, uncle (1645–1693), twin brother of Sebastian's father Johann Ambrosius, court and town musician at Arnstadt.

Johann Christoph, brother (1671–1721), organist and schoolteacher at Ohrdruf, where he took in Sebastian after their parents' death.

Johann Christoph, son (1713).

Johann Christoph Friedrich, son (1732–1795), chamber musician at Bückeburg, wrote numerous sonatas, concertos, and vocal works.

Johann Elias, first cousin once removed (1705–1755), pupil of Bach at Leipzig, tutoring the younger children and serving as personal assistant, later cantor at Schweinfurt.

Johann Ernst, first cousin (1683–1739), organist at Arnstadt, succeeding Sebastian.

Johann Friedrich Bach, second cousin (1682–1730), organist at Mühlhausen, succeeding Sebastian.

Johann Gottfried Bernhard, son (1715–1739), briefly organist at Mühlhausen, then Sangerhausen; died shortly after beginning legal studies at Jena.

Johann Günther, first cousin once removed (1653–1683), organist and instrument maker at Arnstadt.

Johann Jacob, second cousin (1668–1692), apprentice and journeyman for Bach's father.

Johann Jacob, brother (1682–1722), "oboist" (military musician) and later chamber musician for the royal Swedish court.

Johann Lorenz, first cousin once removed (1695–1773), pupil of Bach at Weimar, later organist and cantor at Lahm.

Johann Ludwig (1677–1631), Meiningen Capellmeister, an important early composer of sacred cantatas, many of them performed by Sebastian at Leipzig; their relationship uncertain, presumably distant cousins.

Johann Michael, first cousin once removed (1648–1694), organist at Arnstadt, later Gehren, like his brother Johann Christoph a significant composer of motets and organ music; father of Maria Barbara, Sebastian's first wife.

Johann Nicolaus, second cousin (1669–1753), composer, organist, and instrument maker at Jena.

Johann Rudolf, brother (1670).

Johann Sebastian, grandson (1748–1778), son of Carl Philipp Emanuel, painter, died young at Rome.

Johanna Carolina, daughter (1737–1781).

Johanna Dorothea (Vonhof), sister-in-law (1674–1745), wife of Johann Christoph, older brother of Johann Sebastian.

Johanna Judith, sister (1680–1686).

Johannes Jonas, brother (1675–1685).

Leopold August, son (1718–1719), godson of Prince Leopold of Cöthen.

Maria Barbara (Bach), second cousin and first wife (1684–1720), mother of Wilhelm Friedemann, Carl Philipp Emanuel, and Johann Gottfried Bernhard.

Maria Elisabeth (Lämmerhirt), mother (1644–1694).

Maria Sophia, daughter (1713).

Marie Salome (later Wiegand), sister (1677–1728).

Regina Johanna, daughter (1728–33).

Veit (16th cent.), great-great-grandfather said to have been a baker.

Wilhelm Friedemann, son (1710–1784), composer and keyboard player, organist at Dresden and Halle, later lived at Berlin; an original if idiosyncratic writer of sonatas, concertos, and church cantatas.

Wilhelm Friedrich Ernst, grandson (1759–1845), son of Johann Christoph Friedrich, court musician and composer at Berlin.

Bach, August Wilhelm (1796–1869), organist and composer (no known relationship to J. S. Bach).

Bammler, Johann Nathanael, pupil of Bach at Leipzig, substituted for him as director of church music during the 1740s.

Biber, Heinrich Ignaz Franz (von) (1644–1704), Bohemian violinist and composer, the most influential virtuoso on and writer for his instrument of his time.

Biffi, Antonio (1666–1733), singer, composer, *maestro di cappella* at St. Mark's, Venice.

Birkmann, Christoph, Leipzig university student, thought to have been a librettist for and performer in some of Bach's cantatas.

Birnbaum, Johann Abraham (1702–1748), instructor at the Leipzig university, defender of Bach against Scheibe.

Böhm, Georg (1661–1733), organist and composer; Bach studied with (or at least knew) him at Lüneburg.

Bordoni, Faustina (1697–1781), Italian (Venetian) soprano; married Hasse, performing the title role in his *Cleofide* and other works at Dresden, Vienna, and elsewhere.

Brauns, Friedrich Nicolaus (1637–1718), composer, cantor at Hamburg.

Breitkopf, Bernhard Christoph (1695–1777), publisher, founder of what is now the Leipzig firm of Breitkopf und Härtel.

Brockes, Barthold Heinrich (1680–1747), poet and member of the Hamburg senate, author of a passion oratorio text set by Handel, Telemann, and others, portions used in Bach's St. John Passion.

Brühl, Heinrich Count von (1700–1763), Saxon prime minister and effectively regent for Friedrich August II.

Buffardin, Pierre-Gabriel (ca. 1690–1768), French flutist, teacher of Johann Jacob Bach, later of Quantz while both were chamber musicians at Dresden.

Buttstett, Johann Heinrich (1666–1727), Erfurt organist, pupil of Pachelbel and teacher of Walther, related by marriage to Bach; author of a treatise disparaged by Mattheson.

Buxtehude, Dieterich (ca. 1637–1707), the pre-eminent composer of keyboard and vocal music of his generation in Germany, organist at Lübeck.

Christian, duke of Saxe-Weissenfels (1682–1736), patron of Bach, who served him as external Capellmeister, composing several cantatas (BWV 208, 210a, 249a).

Christian Ludwig, margrave of Brandenburg (1677–1734), great-uncle of King Frederick "the Great" and nominal overlord of Schwedt, dedicatee of Bach's Brandenburg Concertos.

Christiane Eberhardine of Brandenburg-Bayreuth (1671–1727), Saxon electress and queen of Poland (from 1694), wife of Friedrich August I, memorialized in Bach's *Trauerode* (BWV 199).

Corelli, Arcangelo (1653–1713), Italian violinist and composer, worked at Bologna, later Rome.

Couperin, François (1668–1733), French keyboard player and composer, famed for his four books of harpsichord pieces.

Doles, Johann Friedrich (1715–1797), composer, pupil of Bach at Leipzig and his successor as cantor (after Harrer).

Drese, Adam (ca. 1620–1701), composer and string player, Capellmeister at Weimar, Jena, and finally Arnstadt.

Drese, Johann Samuel (ca. 1644–1716), Capellmeister at Weimar during Bach's time there; a cousin of the preceding.

Drese, Johann Wilhelm (1677–1745), composer, son of the preceding, whom he succeeded as Capellmeister at Weimar.

Eberlin, Daniel (1647–1715), composer and official, Capellmeister at Eisenach during Bach's time there; Telemann married his daughter Amalie Louise Juliane.

Effler, Johann (ca. 1640–1711), Bach's predecessor (and briefly colleague) as Weimar court organist.

Eichentopf, Johann Heinrich (1678–1769), woodwind instrument maker at Leipzig during Bach's time there; his products included the oboes da caccia called for in Bach's Leipzig cantatas.

Eilmar, Georg Christian (1665–1715), pastor at St. Mary's, Mühlhausen, and compiler of the libretto for Cantata 131; godfather of Catharina Dorothea and Wilhelm Friedemann Bach.

Erdmann, Georg (1682–1736), Bach's fellow student at Orhdruf and traveling companion to Lüneburg, later a diplomat in Russian service.

Ernesti, Johann August (1707–1781), philologist and theologian; as conrector, later rector, of the St. Thomas School, Leipzig, he opposed Bach's efforts to keep music a focus of educational activity there.

Ernesti, Johann Heinrich (1652–1729), Lutheran theologian and poet, rector of the St. Thomas School, Leipzig, and professor at the university during Bach's first years there.

Ernst August I (1688–1748), duke of Saxe-Weimar, patron and supporter of Bach.

Fasch, Johann Friedrich (1688–1758), Capellmeister at Zerbst, an important and prolific composer of cantatas, concertos, and other works.

Fleckeisen, Gottfried Benjamin (b. 1719), pupil of Bach at Leipzig, evidently substituted for the latter as director of church music for an extended period during the 1740s.

Flemming, Count Jacob Heinrich von (1667–1728), military commander and official; Bach's musical contest with Marchand was to have taken place at his palatial home in Dresden.

Flemming, Johann Friedrich (1665–1740), older brother of the preceding, governor of Leipzig during Bach's time there.

Forkel, Johann Nicolaus (1749–1818), organist and writer on music, Bach's first biographer, studied and later taught at Göttingen; knew or corresponded with W. F. and C. P. E. Bach.

Franck, Salomo (1659–1725), poet and court official at Weimar, author of librettos for many of Bach's cantatas composed there.

Frederick II "the Great" (1712–1786), king of Prussia (from 1740), patron of the arts and sciences and an amateur composer and flutist of professional capabilities.

Friedrich August I (1670–1733), duke of Saxony and elector of the Holy Roman Empire, king of Poland as Augustus II.

Friedrich August II, duke of Saxony and elector of the Holy Roman Empire, king of Poland as Augustus III, son of the preceding.

Gesner, Johann Matthias (1691–1761), classicist, rector of the St. Thomas School, Leipzig during Bach's time there (serving between J. H. and J. C. Ernesti).

Gerber, Ernst Ludwig (1746–1819), organist and music lexicographer, son of the following.

Gerber, Heinrich Nicolaus (1702–1775), organist and court musician at Sondershausen, pupil of Bach at Leipzig, where he copied numerous music manuscripts.

Gerlach, Carl Gotthelf (1704–1761), organist of the New Church, Leipzig, during Bach's time there, probably also a pupil of the latter and later director of the Collegium Musicum.

Görner, Johann Gottlieb (1697–1778), composer, pupil of Kuhnau, organist at the university church, Leipzig, and director of a competing Collegium Musicum during Bach's time there.

Goldberg, Johann Gottlieb (1727–1756), keyboard player and composer, probably a pupil of J. S. or W. F. Bach.

Gottsched, Johann Christoph (1700–1766), poet and important literary theorist and critic, professor at Leipzig during Bach's time there; wrote three cantata libretti set by the latter.

Gottsched, Luise Adelgunde Victorie (Kulmus) (1713–1772), author of stage comedies, translations, and other writings, wife of the preceding; admirer of Bach's music.

Graupner, Christoph (1683–1760), Capellmeister at Darmstadt, prolific composer of cantatas, concertos, and many other works; competed with Bach for the Leipzig cantoriate.

Handel, George Frideric (1685–1759), composer of operas, oratorios, and instrumental music; Bach performed at least one of his cantatas and probably knew his setting of the passion text by Brockes.

Harrer, Gottlob (1703–1755), composer, Bach's successor as Leipzig cantor.

Hasse, Johann Adolf (1699–1783), prolific and influential composer of operas and sacred music, Capellmeister at Dresden.

Haussmann, Elias Gottlob (1695–1774), painter at Dresden, later Leipzig, known for his portraits of Bach and others in his circle.

Heinichen, Johann David (1683–1729), composer and music theorist, Capellmeister at Dresden.

Henrici, Christian Friedrich, known as Picander (1700–1764), poet, author of librettos of Bach's St. Matthew Passion and other works, especially secular cantatas, including BWV 211–12.

Hildebrandt, Zacharias (1688–1757), important organ builder, apprenticed to Silbermann, later worked at Leipzig during Bach's time.

Hunold, Christian Friedrich, known as Menantes (1680–1721), writer based in Halle; Bach set several librettos by him in his Cöthen secular cantatas.

Hurlebusch, Conrad Friedrich (1691–1765), keyboard player and composer, later organist at Amsterdam; visited Leipzig and presented one of his publications to Bach.

Johann Ernst, prince (*Prinz*) of Saxe-Weimar (1696–1715), son of Duke Johann Ernst III, amateur composer; Bach arranged at least five of his concertos for solo keyboard.

Johann Ernst III, duke of Saxe-Weimar (1664–1707), father of Bach's patron Duke Ernst August.

Johann Georg II, duke of Saxe-Eisenach (1665–1698), ruler of Eisenach at the time of Bach's birth, employer of his father and other family members.

Kayser, Bernhard Christian (1705–1758), pupil of Bach at Cöthen and Leipzig, important copyist of his keyboard music.

Keiser, Gottfried (d. before 1732), organist, father of the following.

Keiser, Reinhard (1674–1739), composer, chiefly of operas, at Brunswick, Weissenfels, and especially Hamburg.

Kellner, Pauline (d. 1736), singer at Zeitz and elsewhere, presumed teacher of Anna Magdalena Bach.

Keyserlingk, Herrmann Carl von (1697–1764), diplomat representing Russia at Dresden and Berlin, knew and patronized Bach and his older sons.

Kirchhoff, Gottfried (1685–1746), keyboard player and composer, organist at Halle; succeeded Handel's teacher Zachow, followed by Wilhelm Friedemann Bach.

Kirnberger, Johann Philipp (1721–1783), composer and music theorist, studied with Bach at Leipzig; an early collector and editor of Bach's music as librarian for Princess Anna Amalie.

Kittel, Johann Christian (1732–1809), keyboard player and composer, one of Bach's last pupils at Leipzig, later organist at Erfurt; an important copyist of Bach's music and author of a book on organ playing.

Kräuter, Philipp David (1690–1741), pupil and copyist for Bach at Weimar, later cantor at Augsburg.

Krebs, Johann Ludwig (1713–1780), keyboard player and composer, pupil of Bach at Leipzig, later organist at Altenburg; son of the following.

Krebs, Johann Tobias (1690–1762), composer and organist at Buttstädt near Weimar, where he studied with Bach.

Kuhnau, Johann (1660–1722), Bach's predecessor as cantor at Leipzig and an important composer of church cantatas and keyboard music.

Kuhnau, Johann Andreas (b. 1703), nephew of the preceding, pupil and copyist for Bach at Leipzig.

Lange, Gottfried (1672–1748), Leipzig city council member and burgomaster, instrumental in Bach's appointment; wrote librettos for vocal works, including at least a few of Bach's cantatas.

Lehms, Georg Christian (1684–1717), poet, worked at Darmstadt; published librettos for sacred cantatas by Telemann, Bach, and other composers.

Leopold, prince (*Fürst*) of Anhalt-Cöthen (1694–1728), employed Bach as Capellmeister, patron of his Cöthen works.

Lully, Jean-Baptiste (1632–1687), Florentine-born French composer, among the most influential figures of Baroque music, known for operas, ballets, and sacred music.

Marcello, Alessandro (1669–1747), Italian (Venetian) composer, brother of the following; Bach transcribed an oboe concerto for keyboard.

Marcello, Benedetto (1686–1739), prolific Italian (Venetian) composer of vocal and instrumental music, also a writer; Bach transcribed one of his violin concertos for keyboard.

Marchand, Louis (1669–1732), French keyboard player and composer; Bach was to have met him in a musical contest at Dresden.

Marpurg, Friedrich Wilhelm (1718–1795), composer and prolific and influential critic and music theorist, familiar with J. S. and W. F. Bach.

Mattheson, Johann (1681–1764), singer, composer, and prolific writer on music; music director at Hamburg, where he knew Handel and later must have met Bach.

Mietke, Michael (d. 1719?), court harpsichord maker at Berlin, built an instrument for the Cöthen court on Bach's recommendation.

Mizler von Kolof, Lorenz Christoph (1711–1778), mathematician and writer on music, a university student at Leipzig where he knew Bach.

Neumeister, Erdmann (1671–1756), theologian and poet, pastor at Weissenfels, later Hamburg, author of numerous cantata librettos set especially by Telemann, only a few by Bach.

Neumeister, Johann Gottfried (1757–1840), organ pupil of Sorge and owner and presumed copyist of a manuscript containing early chorale preludes, many of them attributed to Bach.

Olearius, Johann Christoph (1668–1747), theologian and musician, deacon at Arnstadt during Bach's time there, published a collection of hymns (text only); son of the following.

Olearius, Johann Gottfried (1635–1711), theologian and musician, church superintendent at Arnstadt during Bach's time there.

Pachelbel, Johann (1653–1706), keyboard player and important composer of organ music and sacred vocal works; held positions at Vienna, Eisenach, Stuttgart, and Erfurt, where he taught Bach's brother Johann Christoph.

Pezold, Carl Friedrich (1675–1731), instructor (*tertius*), later conrector, at St. Thomas School, Leipzig, during Bach's time there.

Pezold, Christian (1677–?by 1733), Dresden organist, composer of a minuet erroneously attributed to Bach.

Picander, *see* Christian Friedrich Henrici.

Pisendel, Johann Georg (1687–1755), violinist and composer, apparently met and shared music with Bach at Weimar; eventually concertmaster at Dresden, where he taught Quantz.

Quantz, Johann Joachim (1697–1773), composer, especially of numerous sonatas and concertos for flute; worked at Dresden and later Berlin, wrote an important treatise on flute playing, also made flutes characterized by several innovations including a second key.

Reiche, Gottfried (1667–1734), trumpeter and town musician at Leipzig, where he probably played most of the virtuoso brass parts written there by Bach.

Reinken (Reincken), Johann Adamszoon (?1643–1722), keyboard player and composer, organist at Hamburg.

Scheibe, Johann (ca. 1680–1748), organ builder, worked at Leipzig during Bach's time there.

Scheibe, Johann Adolph (1708–1776), composer and writer on music, studied at the St. Nicolaus School and then the university at Leipzig, later royal Danish Capellmeister; son of the preceding.

Schemelli, Georg Christian (ca. 1676–1762), cantor at Zeitz, edited a volume of sacred songs to which Bach contributed.

Schmid, Balthasar (1705–1749), pupil of Bach at Leipzig, later music engraver and publisher.

Schneider, Johann (1702–1788), organist at St. Nicholas, Leipzig, during and after Bach's time there.

Scholze, Johann Sigismund, known as Sperontes (1705–1750), poet, worked at Leipzig, where he edited a series of songbooks to which Bach may have contributed.

Schott, Georg Balthasar (1686–1736), organist of the New Church, Leipzig, and director of the Collegium Musicum there at the time of Bach's arrival, afterwards cantor at Gotha.

Schubart, Johann Martin (1690–1721), pupil of Bach at Weimar, where he succeeded the latter as court organist.

Schübler, Johann Georg (b. ca. 1725), pupil of Bach at Leipzig, afterwards music engraver and publisher of the "Schübler" chorales (BWV 645–50).

Silbermann, Gottfried (1683–1753), instrument builder active in Saxony, made organs, harpsichords, and fortepianos.

Stieglitz, Christian Ludwig (1677–1758), Leipzig city councilor and burgomaster (mayor), favored J. A. Ernesti in the "Battle of the Prefects."

Stölzel, Georg Heinrich (1690–1749), Capellmeister at Gera, a significant composer of cantatas and other works, also wrote librettos and treatises.

Stricker, Augustin Reinhard (d. after 1720), composer, chamber musician at Berlin before becoming Bach's predecessor as Capellmeister at Cöthen.

Swieten, Baron Gottfried van (1733–1803), Dutch-born diplomat based in Vienna, where he helped introduce Bach's music to Mozart.

Taylor, John (1703–1772), English surgeon, today regarded as a charlatan; performed unsuccessful ocular surgery on Bach and Handel.

Telemann, Georg Philipp (1681–1767), the pre-eminent German composer of his day, Capellmeister at Eisenach and Frankfurt, then music director at Hamburg; a prolific and influential composer in every genre of the time, especially church cantatas.

Trebs, Heinrich Nicolaus (1678–1748), Weimar court organ builder; Bach was godfather to his oldest son Johann Gottfried.

Vetter, Daniel (1657 or 1658–1721), organist at St. Nicholas, Leipzig; published collections of simple keyboard chorales.

Vivaldi, Antonio (1678–1741), Italian (Venetian) composer of numerous concertos and other works, profoundly influenced German composers including Bach.

Vogler, Johann Caspar (1696–1763), keyboard player and composer, pupil of Bach at Arnstadt and Weimar, where he later served as court organist and mayor.

Vogler, Johann Gottfried (1691–after 1733), organist of the New Church, Leipzig, before Bach's time there; preceded Schott as director of the Collegium Musicum.

Volumier (Woulmyer), Jean-Baptiste (ca. 1670–1728), violinist and composer of Flemish origin, concertmaster at Berlin, then at Dresden.

Walther, Johann Gottfried (1684–1748), composer and musical lexicographer, Bach's second cousin and organist at Weimar during Bach's time there.

Weiss, Christian (1671–1736), pastor of St. Thomas's Church, Leipzig, Bach's father confessor.

Weiss, Sylvius Leopold (?1686–1750), composer and lutenist, worked at Dresden.

Weldig, Adam Immanuel (1667–1716), singer and master of the pages at Weimar, godfather of Carl Philipp Emanuel Bach.

Wender, Christian Friedrich (d. after 1768), organ builder at Mühlhausen, son of the following.

Wender, Johann Friedrich (1655–1729), organ builder based in Mühlhausen, where J. S. Bach played his instruments.

Werckmeister, Andreas (1645–1706), organist and writer on music, author of numerous publications on organs and related subjects, including tuning and temperament.

Westhoff, Johann Paul von (1656–1705), violinist and composer, court musician at Weimar.

Wilcke, Johann Caspar (d. 1731), court trumpeter at Zeitz, later Weissenfels; father of Anna Magdalena Bach.

Wilcke, Johann Caspar (1691–1766), court trumpeter at Zerbst, son of the preceding.

Wilhelm Ernst, duke of Saxe-Weimar (1662–1728), Bach's employer at Weimar.

Witt, Christian Friedrich (ca. 1660–1717), composer, Capellmeister at Gotha.

Zachow, Friedrich Wilhelm (1663–1712), composer and organist at Halle, Handel's teacher.

Zelenka (Xelenka), Jan Dismas (1679–1745), Czech composer and court violone player at Dresden.

Ziegler, Johann Gotthilf (1688–1747), keyboard player and composer, organist at Halle; briefly a pupil of Bach at Weimar, he later engraved the latter's Partitas for harpsichord.

Ziegler (Romanus), Mariane von (1695–1760), poet and librettist, author of texts for nine of Bach's sacred cantatas; daughter of the disgraced Leipzig burgomaster Franz Conrad Romanus.

Zimmermann, Gottfried (d. 1741), entrepreneur at Leipzig, sponsored Bach's performances with the Collegium Musicum at his coffee house.

Bibliography

"Ed." = edited by; edition. "Rev." = revised by. "Trans." = translated by. *See Appendix D in the online supplement for a concise guide to sources and further reading.*

Frequently Cited Reference Sources

AmB   Amalienbibliothek (a collection within D B, the Staatsbibliothek zu Berlin)

BC   *Bach-Compendium: Analytisch-bibliographisches Repertorium der Werke Johann Sebastian Bachs.* 1985–. Ed. Hans-Joachim Schulze and Christoph Wolff. Leipzig and Dresden: Peters.

BD 1   *Bach-Dokumente I: Schriftstücke von der Hand Johann Sebastian Bachs.* 1963. Ed. Werner Neumann and Hans-Joachim Schulze. Kassel: Bärenreiter.

BD 2   *Bach-Dokumente II: Fremdschriftliche und gedruckte Dokumente zur Lebensgeschichte Johann Sebastian Bachs.* 1969. Ed. Werner Neumann and Hans-Joachim Schulze. Kassel: Bärenreiter.

BD 3   *Bach-Dokumente III: Dokumente zum Nachwirken Johann Sebastian Bachs.* 1972. Ed. Hans-Joachim Schulze. Kassel: Bärenreiter.

BG   *Johann Sebastian Bach: Werke.* 46 vols. 1851–1900. Ed. the Bach-Gesellschaft. Leipzig: Breitkopf und Härtel. Numerous reprints, most content online at imslp.org.

BJ   *Bach-Jahrbuch.* Volumes more than five years old are online at https://oa.slub-dresden. de/ejournals/bjb/issue/archive.

BuxWV   Karstädt, Georg. 1974. *Thematisch-systematisches Verzeichnis der musikalischen Werke von Dietrich Buxtehude: Buxtehude-Werke-Verzeichnis.* Wiesbaden: Breitkopf & Härtel.

BWV   Schmieder, Wolfgang. 1990. *Thematisch-systematisches Verzeichnis der musikalischen Werke Johann Sebastian Bachs: Bach-Werke-Verzeichnis.* 2d ed. Wiesbaden: Breitkopf und Härtel. Originally published Leipzig: Breitkopf & Härtel, 1950.

D B   Berlin, Staatsbibliothek zu Berlin–Preußischer Kulturbesitz, Musikabteilung.

F.   Falck, Martin. 1913. *Wilhelm Friedemann Bach: Sein Leben und seine Werke.* Leipzig: Kahnt. 2d ed., 1919.

HWV   *Händel-Handbuch.* 1978–. 5 vols. Kassel: Bärenreiter.

KB   *Kritischer Bericht* (critical commentary volume for the NBA; see below).

NBA   Bach, Johann Sebastian, 1954–. *Neue Ausgabe sämtlicher Werke.* Ed. the Johann-Sebastian-Bach-Institut, Göttingen, and the Bach-Archiv, Leipzig. Kassel: Bärenreiter. *Kritische Berichte* (editorial reports) appear in separate volumes. Many volumes (music only) are now available at imslp.org.

NBR   *New Bach Reader, The: A Life of Johann Sebastian Bach in Letters and Documents.* 1998. Ed. Hans T. David and Arthur Mendel. Revised and enlarged by Christoph Wolff. New York: Norton.

TWV   Ruhnke, Martin, ed. 1984. *Georg Philipp Telemann: Thematisch-Systematisches Verzeichnis seiner Werke. Instrumentalwerke.* Band 1. Kassel: Bärenreiter.

W.   Wotquenne, Alfred. 1905. *Catalogue thématique des oeuvres de Charles Philippe Emmanuel Bach (1714–1788).* Leipzig: Breitkopf & Härtel. Reprints, 1964, 1972, as *Thematisches Verzeichnis der Werke von Carl Philipp Emanuel Bach.*

Works Cited

Adlung, Jakob. 1768. *Musica mechanica organoedi.* Ed. Lorenz Albrecht with additional annotations by Johann Friedrich Agricola. Berlin: Birnstiel.

Ahrens, Christian. 2007. "Neue Quellen zu J. S. Bachs Beziehungen nach Gotha." *BJ* 93: 45–60.

Ahrens, Christian. 2014. "Johann Sebastian Bach, Johann Heinrich Eichentopf, und die Hautbois d'amour in Leipzig." *BJ* 100: 45–60.

Altschuler, Eric Lewin. 2001. "J. S. Bach and the Reiche Portrait: Trumpet Major?" *Musical Times* 142: 29–31.

Axmacher, Elke. 1978. "Ein Quellenfund zum Text der Matthäus-Passion." *BJ* 64: 181–91.

Bach, Carl Philipp Emanuel. 1753–1762. *Versuch über die wahre Art das Clavier zu spielen.* 2 vols. Berlin. Ed. Tobias Plebuch in *Carl Philipp Emanuel Bach: The Complete Works,* vols. 7/1–3. Los Altos: Packard Humanities Institute, 2011. Trans. William J. Mitchell as *Essay on the True Art of Playing Keyboard Instruments.* New York: Norton, 1949.

Bach, Carl Philipp Emanuel. 1790. *Verzeichniß des musikalischen Nachlasses des verstorbenen Capellmeisters Carl Philipp Emanuel Bach.* Hamburg: Schniebes. Annotated facsimile ed. Rachel Wade as *The Catalog of Carl Philipp Emanuel Bach's Estate: A Facsimile of the Edition by Schniebes, Hamburg, 1790.* New York: Garland Publishing, 1981. Transcription online at http://www.cpebach.org/pdfs/resources/NV-1790.pdf.

Beißwenger, Kirsten. 1992. *Johann Sebastian Bachs Notenbibliothek.* Kassel: Bärenreiter.

Besseler, Heinrich. 1956. "Markgraf Christian Ludwig von Brandenburg." *BJ* 43: 18–35.

Bitter, Carl Herrmann. 1868. *Carl Philipp Emanuel und Wilhelm Friedemann Bach und deren Brüder.* 2 vols. Berlin: Wilhelm Müller.

Blanken, Christine. 2015. "Christoph Birkmanns Kantatenzyklus 'Gott-geheiligte Sabbaths-Zehnden' von 1728 und die Leipziger Kirchenmusik under J. S. Bach in den Jahren 1724–1727." *BJ* 101: 13–74.

Blanken, Christine. 2018. "Neue Dokumente zur Erbteilung nach dem Tod Johann Sebastian Bachs." *BJ* 104: 133–53.

Blume, Friedrich. 1963. "Outlines of a New Picture of Bach." Trans. Stanley Godman. *Music & Letters* 44: 214–27.

Bojanowski, Paul von. 1903. *Das Weimar Johann Sebastian Bachs.* Weimar: Hermann Bölhaus Nachfolger.

Boomhower, Daniel F. 2017. "Zur handschriftlichen Überlieferung der h-Moll-Messe in Berlin und Wien in der zweiten Hälfte des 18. Jahrhunderts." *BJ* 103: 11–31.

Boyd, Malcolm, ed. 1999. *Oxford Composer Companions: J. S. Bach.* Oxford and New York: Oxford University Press.

Boyd, Malcolm. 2006. *Bach.* 3d ed., electronic version. New York: Oxford University Press. Issued in print in 2000.

Braatz, Thomas. 2009. "Johann Sebastian Bach's Performance Environment in the *Nicolaikirche* from 1723 to 1750." Accessed June 3, 2018. http://www.bach-cantatas.com/Articles/Nikolaikirche-Braatz.pdf.

Breig, Werner. 1976. "Bachs Violinkonzert d-moll: Studien zu seiner Gestalt und seiner Entstehungsgeschichte." *BJ*: 7–34.

Breig, Werner. 1998. "Bach und Marchand in Dresden: Eine überlieferungskritische Studie." *BJ* 84: 7–18.

Bund, Conrad. 1984. "Johann Ludwig Bach und die Frankfurter Kapellmusik in der Zeit Georg Philipp Telemanns." *BJ* 70: 117–29.

Bunge, Rudolf. 1905. "Johann Sebastian Bachs Kapelle zu Cöthen und deren nachgelassene Instrumente." *BJ* 2: 14–47.

Burney, Charles. 1775. *The Present State of Music in Germany, the Netherlands, and United Provinces.* 2d ed., corrected, 2 vols. London.

Burrows, Donald. 2012. *Handel.* New York: Oxford University Press.

Butler, Gregory G. 1986. "The Engraving of J. S. Bach's 'Six Partitas'." *Journal of Musicological Research* 7: 3–27.

Butler, Gregory G. 1988. "Neues zur Datierung der Goldberg-Variationen." *BJ* 74: 219–23.

Butler, Gregory G. 1990. *Bach's Clavier-Übung III: The Making of a Print. With a Companion Study of the Canonic Variations on "Vom Himmel hoch."* Durham, NC: Duke University Press.

Butler, Gregory G. 1995. "J. S. Bach's Reception of Tomaso Albinoni's Mature Concertos." In *Bach Studies 2*, ed. Daniel R. Melamed, 20–46. Cambridge: Cambridge University Press.

Butler, Gregory G. 2000. "J. S. Bachs Kanonische Veränderungen über 'Vom Himmel hoch' (BWV 769): Ein Schlußstrich unter die Debatte um die Frage der 'Fassung letzter Hand'." *BJ* 86: 9–34.

Butler, Gregory G. 2002. "The Printing History of J. S. Bach's *Musical Offering:* New Interpretations." *Journal of Musicology* 19: 306–31.

Butler, Gregory G. 2016. "The Choir Loft as Chamber: Concerted Movements by Bach from the Mid- to Late 1720s." In *Bach Perspectives*, vol. 10, ed. Matthew Dirst, 76–86. Urbana: University of Illinois Press.

Cammarota, Robert M. 2001. "On the Performance of 'Quia respexit . . . omnes generations' from J. S. Bach's *Magnificat*." *Journal of Musicology* 18: 458–89.

Chafe, Eric. 2014. *J. S. Bach's Johannine Theology: The St. John Passion and the Cantatas for Spring 1725.* Oxford: Oxford University Press.

Clark, Stephen L., trans. and ed. 1997. *The Letters of C. P. E. Bach.* Oxford: Clarendon Press.

Claus, Rolf Dietrich. 1998. *Zur Echtheit von Toccata und Fuge d-moll BWV 565.* 2d ed. Cologne: Dohr.

Cortens, Evan. 2015. "'Durch die Music gleichsam lebendig vorgestellet': Graupner, Bach, and *Mein Herz schwimmt im Blut.*" *BACH Journal* 46/1: 74–110.

Cox, Harvey H., ed. 1985. *The Calov Bible of J. S. Bach.* Ann Arbor, MI: UMI Research Press.

Czok, Karl. 1982. "Sächsischer Landesstaat zur Bachzeit." *Beiträge zur Bachforschung* 1: 25–31.

Dadelsen, Georg von. 1958. *Beiträge zur Chronologie der Werke Johann Sebastian Bachs.* Trossingen: Hohner.

Dadelsen, Georg von. 1963. "Zur Entstehung des Bachschen Orgelbüchlein." In *Festschrift Friedrich Blume zum 70. Geburtstag*, ed. Anna Amalie Abert and Wilhelm Pfannkuch, 74–79. Kassel: Bärenreiter.

Dirksen, Pieter. 2008. "J. S. Bach's Violin Concerto in G Minor." In *Bach Perspectives*, vol. 7, ed. Gregory Butler, 21–54. Urbana: University of Illinois Press.

Dirksen, Pieter. 2010. "Zur Echtheit der Johann Christoph Bach (1642–1703) zugeschriebenen Clavierwerke." *BJ* 96: 217–48.

Dreyfus, Laurence. 1987. *Bach's Continuo Group: Players and Practices in His Vocal Works.* Cambridge, MA: Harvard University Press.

Dürr, Alfred. 1976. *Zur Chronologie der Leipziger Vokalwerke J. S. Bachs.* 2d ed. Kassel: Bärenreiter. Originally published in *BJ* 44 (1957): 5–162.

Dürr, Alfred. 1992. "Zur Parodiefrage in Bachs h-moll-Messe: Eine Bestandsaufnahme." *Die Musikforschung* 45: 117–38.

Dürr, Alfred. 2000. *Johann Sebastian Bach: St. John Passion: Genesis, Transmission, and Meaning.* Trans. Alfred Clayton. Oxford: Oxford University Press.

Dürr, Alfred. 2005. *The Cantatas of J. S. Bach with Their Librettos in German–English Parallel Text.* Rev. and trans. Richard D. P. Jones. Oxford: Oxford University Press.

Engelke, Bernhard. 1908. *Johann Friedrich Fasch: Sein Leben und seine Tätigkeit als Vokalkomponist.* Halle: Kämmerer.

Enßlin, Wolfram, and Uwe Wolf. 2007. "Die Prediger-Einführungsmusiken von C. P. E. Bach: Materialien und Überlegungen zu Werkbestand, Entstehungsgeschichte, und Aufführungspraxis." *BJ* 93: 139–78.

Exner, Ellen. 2012. "C. P. E. Bach at His Word: A Reconsideration of the Early Berlin Years." *Eighteenth-Century Music* 9: 253–60.

Exner, Ellen. 2016. "The Godfather: Georg Philipp Telemann, Carl Philipp Emanuel Bach, and the Family Business." *BACH Journal* 47/1: 1–20.

Falck, Martin. 1913. *Wilhelm Friedemann Bach.* Leipzig: C. F. Kahnt Nachfolger. 2d ed., 1919.

Feld, Ulrike, and Ulrich Leisinger, eds. 2003. *Musik am Meininger Hofe.* Denkmäler mitteldeutscher Barockmusik, vol. 1/2. Leipzig: Friedrich Hofmeister.

Forkel, Johann Nicolaus. 1802. *Ueber Johann Sebastian Bachs Leben, Kunst, und Kunstwerke.* Leipzig: Hoffmeister und Kühnel. Facsimile, Frankfurt am Main: H. L. Grahl, 1950. Edited by Walther Vetter. Kassel: Bärenreiter, 1968. Translation in NBR, 417–82.

Freyse, Conrad. 1956. "Johann Christoph Bach (1642–1703)." *BJ* 43: 36–51.

Freyse, Conrad. 1959. "Das Porträt Ambrosius Bachs." *BJ* 46: 149–55.

Fritz, Barthold. 1757. *Anweisung, wie man Claviere, Clavecins, und Orgeln . . . gleich rein stimmen könne.* 2d ed. Leipzig: Breitkopf. The first edition appeared the previous year.

Geck, Martin. 2006. *Johann Sebastian Bach: Life and Work.* Trans. John Hargraves. New York: Harcourt. Originally *Johann Sebastian Bach: Leben und Werk.* Reinbek: Rowohlt, 2000.

Gerber, Ernst Ludwig. 1790–1792. *Historisch-Biographisches Lexicon der Tonkünstler.* 2 vols. Leipzig: Breitkopf.

Gerber, Ernst Ludwig. 1812–1814. *Neues historisch-biographisches Lexikon der Tonkünstler.* 4 vols. Leipzig: Kühnel.

Glöckner, Andreas. 1985. "Zur Chronologie der Weimarer Kantaten Johann Sebastian Bachs." *BJ* 71: 159–64.

Glöckner, Andreas. 1990. "Die Musikplege an der Leipziger Neukirche zur Zeit Johann Sebastian Bachs." *Beiträge zur Bachforschung* 8: 1–170.

Glöckner, Andreas. 1995. "Neue Spuren zu Bachs 'Weimarer' Passion." *Leipziger Beiträge zur Bach-Forschung* 1: 33–46.

Glöckner, Andreas. 2008. "Johann Sebastian Bach und die Universität Leipzig: Neue Quellen (Teil I)." *BJ* 94: 159–95.

Górny, Tomasz. 2019. "Estienne Roger and His Agent Adam Christoph Sellius: New Light on Italian and French Music in Bach's World. *Early Music* 47: 361–70.

Graeser, Wolfgang. 1924. "Bachs 'Kunst der Fuge'." *BJ* 21: 1–104.

Greer, Mary Dalton. 2008. "From the House of Aaron to the House of Johann Sebastian: Old Testament Roots for the Bach Family Tree." In *About Bach*, ed. Gregory G. Butler et al., 15–32. Urbana: University of Illinois Press.

Grychtolik, Alexander Ferdinand. 2013. "Anmerkungen zu den Aufführungsstätten J. S. Bachs in Weimar." *BJ* 99: 309–18.

Grzybowski, Andrzej. 2013. "John Taylor and Johann Sebastian Bach: More Information Still Needed." *Acta Ophthalmologica* 91: e250–52.

Heber, Noelle. 2017. "Bach and Money: Sources of Salary and Supplemental Income in Leipzig from 1723 to 1750." *Understanding Bach* 12: 111–25.

Helmbold, Hermann. 1930. "Die Söhne von Johann Christoph und Johann Ambrosius Bach auf der Eisenacher Schule." *BJ* 27: 49–55.

Henze-Döhring, Sabine. 2009. *Markgräfin Wilhelmine und die Bayreuther Hofmusik.* Bamberg: Heinrichs.

Heyde, Herbert. 1985. "Der Instrumentenbau in Leipzig zur Zeit Johann Sebastian Bachs." In *300 Jahre Johann Sebastian Bach* (exhibition catalogue, Internationale Bachakademie, Staatsgalerie, Stuttgart, 1985), 73–88. Tutzing: Hans Schneider.

Hill, Moira. 2015. "Carl Philipp Emanuel Bach's Passion Settings: Context, Content, and Impact." PhD diss., Yale University.

Hill, Robert, ed. 1991. *Keyboard Music from the Andreas Bach Book and the Möller Manuscript.* Harvard Publications in Music, 16. Cambridge, MA: Department of Music, Harvard University (distributed by Harvard University Press).

Hilse, Walter. 1973. "The Treatises of Christoph Bernhard." In *Music Forum*, vol. 3, ed. William Mitchell and Felix Selzer, 1–196. New York: Columbia University Press.

Hobohm, Wolf. 1973. "Neue 'Texte zur Leipziger Kirchen-Music'." *BJ* 59: 5–32.

Hofmann, Klaus. 1993. "Neue Überlegungen zu Bachs Weimarer Kantaten-Kalendar." *BJ* 79: 9–29.

Hofmann, Klaus. 2000. "Die Motette 'Lobet den Herrn, alle Heiden' (BWV 230): Alte und neue Probleme." *BJ* 86: 35–50.

Hofmann, Klaus. 2002. "Anmerkungen zum Problem 'Picander-Jahrgang'." *BJ* 88: 69–87.

Hofmann, Klaus. 2013. "Anmerkungen zu Bachs Kantate 'Mein Herze schwimmt im Blut' (BWV 199)." *BJ* 99: 206–21.

Hofmann, Klaus. 2015. "Anmerkungen zu Bachs Kantate 'Ich hatte viel Bekümmernis' (BWV 21)." *BJ* 101: 168–76.

Hübner, Maria. 2006. "Neues zu Johann Sebastian Bachs Reisen nach Karlsbad." *BJ* 92: 93–107.

Hübner, Maria. 2018. "Die Kaffeehäuser von Gottfried Zimmermann und Enoch Richter in Leipzig." *BJ* 104: 43–67.

Ishii, Akira. 2013. "Johann Sebastian Bach, Carl Philipp Emanuel Bach, and Johann Jacob Froberger: The Dissemination of Froberger's Contrapuntal Works in Late Eighteenth-Century Berlin." *BACH Journal* 44/1: 46–133.

Jauernig, Reinhold. 1950. "Bach in Weimar." In *Bach in Thüringen: Festgabe zum Gedenkjahr 1950*, 49–105. Weimar: Thüringer Volksverlag.

Kevorkian, Tanya. 2017. "Households." In *The Routledge Research Companion to Johann Sebastian Bach*, ed. Robin A. Leaver, 99–115. Abingdon: Routledge.

Kirkendale, Ursula. 1980. "The Source for Bach's *Musical Offering*: The *Institutio oratoria* of Quintilian." *Journal of the American Musicological Society* 33: 88–141.

Kobayashi, Yoshitake. 1988. "Zur Chronologie der Spätwerke Johann Sebastian Bachs Kompositions- und Aufführungstätigkeit von 1736 bis 1750." *BJ* 84: 7–72.

Kobayashi, Yoshitake. 1989. "Zur Teilung des Bachschen Erbes." In *Acht kleine Präludien und Studien über Bach*, ed. Kirsten Beißwänger, 66–76. Wiesbaden: Breitkopf & Härtel.

Kobayashi, Yoshitake. 1995. "Quellenkundliche Überlegungen zur Chronologie der Weimarer Vokalwerke Bachs." In *Das Frühwerk Johann Sebastian Bachs: Bach-Kolloquium Rostock 1990*, ed. Karl Heller and Hans-Joachim Schulze, 290–308. Cologne: Studio.

Koch, Ernst. 2006. "'Jakobs Kirche': Erkundungen im gottesdienstlichen Arbeitsfeld Johann Sebastian Bachs in Weimar." *BJ* 92: 37–64.

Kollmar, Ulrike. 2006. *Gottlob Harrer (1703–1755), Kapellmeister des Grafen Heinrich von Brühl am sächsisch-polnischen Hof und Thomaskantor in Leipzig: Mit einem Werkverzeichnis und einem Katalog der Notenbibliothek Harrers.* Beeskow: Ortus.

Koster, John. 1996. "The Quest for Bach's *Clavier*: An Historiographical Interpretation." *Early Keyboard Journal* 14: 65–84.

Koster, John. 1999. "The Harpsichord Culture in Bach's Environs." In *Bach Perspectives*, vol. 4, ed. David Schulenberg, 57–77. Lincoln: University of Nebraska Press. Reprinted in *Baroque Music*, ed. Peter Walls, 41–61. Farnham: Ashgate, 2011.

Kottick, Edward L. 2003. *A History of the Harpsichord.* Bloomington and Indianapolis: Indiana University Press.

Kraft, Günther. 1956. "Zur Entstehungsgeschichte des 'Hochzeitsquodlibet' (BWV 524)." *BJ* 43: 140–54.

Krautwurst, Franz. 1986. "Anmerkungen zu den Augsburger Bach-Dokumentation." In *Festschrift Martin Ruhnke zum 65. Geburtstag.* Ed. Institute für Musikwissenschaft of the University of Erlangen-Nürnberg. Neuhausen-Stuttgart: Hänssler.

Kulukundis, Elias N. 2016. "Johann Gottfried Bernhard Bach: Fact and Fiction—A Remembrance and Birthday Tribute." In *The Sons of Bach: Essays for Elias N. Kulukundis,* ed. Peter Wollny and Stephen Roe, 260–69. Ann Arbor, MI: Steglein.

Küster, Konrad. 1996. *Der junge Bach.* Stuttgart: Deutsche Verlagsanstalt. Consulted in the electronic ed., Endeavour Press, 2015.

Küster, Konrad. 1996a. "'Der Herr denket an uns' BWV 196: Eine frühe Bach-Kantate und ihr Kontext." *Musik und Kirche* 66: 86–96.

Langusch, Steffen. 2007. "'. . . auf des Herrn Capellmeisters Bach recommendation . . .': Bachs Mitwirken an der Besetzung des Kantorats der Altstadt Salzwedel 1743/44." *BJ* 93: 9–43.

Leaver, Robin A., ed. 1985. *J. S. Bach and Scripture: Glosses from the Calov Bible.* St. Louis: Concordia.

Leaver, Robin A.. 2010. "Bach's Organ Music in the Context of the Liturgy." *Keyboard Perspectives* 3: 147–60.

Leaver, Robin A.. 2013. "Bachs lateinische Kantate 'Gloria in excelsis Deo' BWV 191 und eine lateinische Rede über Lukas 2:14." *BJ* 99: 329–34.

Leaver, Robin A.. 2013a. "Bach's Mass: 'Catholic' or 'Lutheran'?" In *Exploring Bach's B-Minor Mass,* ed. Yo Tomita et al., 21–38. Cambridge: Cambridge University Press.

Leaver, Robin A.. 2016. "Bach's Choral-Buch? The Significance of a Manuscript in the Sibley Library." In *Bach Perspectives,* vol. 10, ed. Matthew Dirst, 16–38. Urbana: University of Illinois Press.

Leaver, Robin A.. 2017. "Churches." In *The Routledge Research Companion to Johann Sebastian Bach,* ed. Robin A. Leaver, 142–90. Abingdon: Routledge.

Leaver, Robin A., and Derek Remeš. 2018. "J. S. Bach's Chorale-Based Pedagogy: Organs and Continuity." *BACH Journal* 49/1: 116–50.

Ledbetter, David. 2009. *Unaccompanied Bach: Performing the Solo Works.* New Haven: Yale University Press.

Leonhardt, Gustav. 1952. *The Art of Fugue, Bach's Last Harpsichord Work: An Argument.* The Hague: Nijhoff.

Lockwood, Lewis. 2003. *Beethoven: The Music and the Life.* New York: Norton.

Lundberg, Mattias. 2011. *Tonus Peregrinus: The History of a Psalm-Tone and Its Use in Polyphonic Music.* Farnham: Ashgate.

Marissen, Michael. 1995. "The Theological Character of J. S. Bach's Musical Offering." In *Bach Studies 2,* ed. Daniel R. Melamed, 85–106. Cambridge: Cambridge University Press.

Marpurg, Friedrich Wilhelm. 1760–1763. *Kritische Briefen über der Tonkunst*. 2 vols. Berlin: Birnstiel.

Marshall, Robert L. 1972. *The Compositional Process of J. S. Bach: A Study of the Autograph Scores of the Vocal Works*. 2 vols. Princeton: Princeton University Press.

Marshall, Robert L. 1986. "Organ or 'Klavier'? Instrumental Prescriptions in the Sources of Bach's Keyboard Works." In *J. S. Bach as Organist: His Instruments, Music, and Performance Practices*, ed. George Stauffer and Ernest May, 212–39. Bloomington: Indiana University Press.

Mattheson, Johann. 1717. *Das beschützte Orchestre*. Hamburg: Schiller.

Mattheson, Johann. 1719. *Exemplarische Organisten-Probe im Artikel vom General-Bass*. Hamburg: Schiller.

Mattheson, Johann. 1722–1723 and 1725. *Critica musica*. 2 vols. Hamburg: Wierings Erben.

Mattheson, Johann. 1731. *Grosse General-Bass-Schule oder Organisten-Probe*. Hamburg: Kißner.

Mattheson, Johann. 1739. *Der vollkommene Capellmeister*. Hamburg: Christian Herold.

Mattheson, Johann. 1740. *Grundlage einer Ehren-Pforte*. Hamburg: Author. Consulted in the quasi-facsimile edition by Max Schneider. Berlin: Liepmannssohn, 1910. Reprint, Kassel: Bärenreiter, 1994.

Maul, Michael. 2004. "Johann Sebastian Bachs Besuche in der Residenzstadt Gera." *BJ* 90: 101–19.

Maul, Michael. 2006. "Überlegungen zu einer Magnificat-Paraphrase und dem Leiter der Leipziger Kantatenaufführungen im Sommer 1725." *BJ* 92: 109–25.

Maul, Michael. 2007. "Neues zu Georg Balthasar Schott, seinem Collegium musicum, und Bachs Zerbster Geburtstagskantate." *BJ* 93: 61–103.

Maul, Michael. 2013. "'welche ieder Zeit aus den 8 besten Subjectis bestehen muß: Die erste 'Cantorey' der Thomasschule: Organisation, Aufgaben, Fragen." *BJ* 99: 11–77.

Maul, Michael. 2013a. "'The Great Catholic Mass': Bach, Count Questenberg, and the Musicalische Congregation in Vienna." In *Exploring Bach's B-Minor Mass*, ed. Yo Tomita et al., 84–104. Cambridge: Cambridge University Press.

Maul, Michael. 2013b. "Bach versus Scheibe: Hitherto Unknown Battlegrounds in a Famous Conflict." In *Bach Perspectives*, vol. 9, ed. Andrew Talle, 120–43. Urbana: University of Illinois Press.

Maul, Michael. 2017. "'Having to Perform and Direct the Music in the Capellmeister's Stead for Two Whole Years': Observations on How Bach Understood His Post During the 1740s." *Understanding Bach* 12: 37–58.

Maul, Michael. 2018. *Bach's Famous Choir: The Saint Thomas School in Leipzig, 1212–1804*. Translation by Richard Howe of *"Dero berühmter Chor": Die Leipziger Thomasschule und ihre Kantoren, 1212–1804* (Leipzig: Lehmstedt, 2012). Woodbridge: Boydell Press.

Maul, Michael, and Peter Wollny. 2003. "Quellenkundliches zu Bach-Aufführungen in Köthen, Ronneburg, und Leipzig zwischen 1720 und 1760." *BJ* 89: 97–141.

May, Ernest. 1996. "Connections between Breitkopf and J. S. Bach." In *Bach Perspectives*, vol. 2, ed. George B. Stauffer, 11–26. Lincoln: University of Nebraska Press.

McClary, Susan. 1987. "The Blasphemy of Talking Politics during Bach Year [1985]." In *Music and Society: The Politics of Composition, Performance, and Reception*, ed. Richard Leppert and Susan McClary, 13–62. Cambridge: Cambridge University Press.

Melamed, Daniel R. 1995. *J. S. Bach and the German Motet*. Cambridge: Cambridge University Press.

Melamed, Daniel R. 1999. "Constructing Johann Christoph Bach (1642–1703)." *Music & Letters* 80: 345–65.

Melamed, Daniel R. 2004. "The Double Chorus in J. S. Bach's *St. Matthew Passion* BWV 244." *Journal of the American Bach Society* 57: 3–50.

Melamed, Daniel R. 2005. *Hearing Bach's Passions.* Oxford: Oxford University Press.

Melamed, Daniel R. 2008. "The Evolution of 'Und wenn die Welt voll Teufel wär'." In *The Century of Bach and Mozart: Perspectives on Historiography, Composition, Theory, and Performance*, ed. Sean Gallagher and Thomas Forrest Kelly, 189–205. Cambridge, MA: Harvard University Department of Music (distributed by Harvard University Press).

Melamed, Daniel R. 2011. "Johann Sebastian Bach and Barthold Heinrich Brockes." In *Bach Perspectives*, vol. 8, ed. Daniel R. Melamed, 13–41. Urbana: University of Illinois Press.

Melamed, Daniel R. 2012. "Johann Sebastian Bach, Johann Gottfried Walther, und die Musik von Giovanni Pierluigi da Palestrina." *BJ* 98: 74–93.

Melamed, Daniel R. 2014. "Multi-Day Passions and J. S. Bach's *Christmas Oratorio*, BWV 248." *Eighteenth-Century Music* 11: 215–34.

Melamed, Daniel R., and Michael Marissen. 1998. *An Introduction to Bach Studies.* New York: Oxford University Press.

Milka, Anatoly. 2014. "Warum endet die *Fuga a 3 soggetti* BWV 1080/19 in Takt 239?" *BJ* 100: 11–26.

Milka, Anatoly. 2017. *Rethinking J. S. Bach's* The Art of Fugue. Trans. Marina Ritzarev. Ed. Esti Sheinberg. Abingdon and New York: Routledge.

Mizler von Kolof, Lorenz Christoph. 1738–1754. *Musikalische Bibliothek, oder Gründliche Nachricht nebst unpartheyischem Urtheil von alten und neuen musikalischen Schriften und Büchern.* 3 vols. in multiple parts, issued serially. Leipzig.

Neumann, Werner. 1960. "Das 'Bachische Collegium Musicum'." *BJ* 47: 5–27.

Neumann, Werner, ed. 1974. *Sämtliche von Johann Sebastian Bach vertonte Texte.* Leipzig: VEB Deutscher Verlag für Musik.

Niedt, Friedrich Erhardt. 1721. *Musicalische Handleitung: Andere Theil.* Ed. Johann Mattheson. Hamburg. Originally published as *Handleitung zur Variation* (vol. 2 of *Musicalische Handleitung*). Hamburg: Schiller, 1706.

Nisbet, Hugh Barr (Barry). 1969. Review of Joachim Birke, *Christian Wolffs Metaphysik und die zeitgenössische Literatur- und Musiktheorie: Gottsched, Scheibe, Mizler.* In *Modern Language Review* 64: 220–21.

Oleskiewicz, Mary. 1998. "Quantz and the Flute at Dresden: His Instruments, His Repertory, and Their Significance for the *Versuch* and the Bach Circle." PhD diss., Duke University.

Oleskiewicz, Mary. 1999. "The Trio in Bach's Musical Offering: A Salute to Frederick's Tastes and Quantz's Flutes?" In *Bach Perspectives*, vol. 4, ed. David Schulenberg, 79–110. Lincoln: University of Nebraska Press.

Oleskiewicz, Mary. 2000. "The Flutes of Quantz: Their Construction and Performing Practice." *Galpin Society Journal* 53: 201–20.

Oleskiewicz, Mary. 2007. "'For the Church as well as for the Orchestra': J. S. Bach, the *Missa*, and the Dresden Court, 1700–1750." *BACH Journal* 38/2: 1–38.

Oleskiewicz, Mary. 2007a. "Like Father, Like Son? Emanuel Bach and the Writing of Biography." In *Music and Its Questions: Essays in Honor of Peter Williams*, ed. Thomas Donahue, 253–79. Richmond, VA: Organ Historical Society Press.

Oleskiewicz, Mary. 2011. "The Court of Brandenburg-Prussia." In *Music at German Courts, 1715–1760: Changing Artistic Priorities*, ed. Samantha Owens et al., 79–130. Woodbridge: Boydell and Brewer.

Oleskiewicz, Mary. 2017. "Keyboards, Music Rooms, and the Bach Family at the Court of Frederick the Great." In *Bach Perspectives*, vol. 11, ed. Mary Oleskiewicz, 24–82. Urbana: University of Illinois Press.

Otto, Rüdiger. 2007. "Ein Leipziger Dichterstreit: Die Auseinandersetzung Gottscheds mit Christian Friedrich Henrici." In *Johann Christoph Gottsched in seiner Zeit: Neue Beiträge zu Leben, Werk, und Wirkung*, ed. Manfred Rudersdorf, 92–142. Berlin: De Gruyter.

Paczkowski, Simon. 2017. *Polish Style in the Music of Johann Sebastian Bach.* Trans. Piotr Szymcza. Lanham, MD: Roman & Littlefield.

Parrott, Andrew. 2000. *The Essential Bach Choir.* Woodbridge: Boydell Press.

Peters, Mark A. 2008. *A Woman's Voice in Baroque Music: Mariane von Ziegler and J. S. Bach.* Aldershot: Ashgate.

Petzoldt, Martin. 1998. "Bachs Prüfung vor dem Kurfürstlichen Konsistorium zu Leipzig." *BJ* 84: 19–30.

Pfau, Marc-Roderich. 2008. "Ein unbekanntes Leipziger Kantatentextheft aus dem Jahr 1735: Neues zum Thema Bach und Stölzel." *BJ* 91: 99–115.

Pfau, Marc-Roderich. 2015. "Entstanden Bachs vier späte Choralkantaten 'per omnes versus' für Gottesdienste des Weißenfelser Hofes?" *BJ*: 341–49.

Plichta, Alois. 1981. "Johann Sebastian Bach und Johann Adam Graf von Questenberg." *BJ* 64: 24–30.

Poetzsch-Seban, Ute. 2006. *Die Kirchenmusik von Georg Philipp Telemann und Erdmann Neumeister: Zur Geschichte der protestantischen Kirchenkantate in der ersten Hälfte des 18. Jahrhunderts.* Beeskow: Ortus.

Potter, Edward T. 2012. *Marriage, Gender, and Desire in Early Enlightenment German Comedy.* Rochester, NY: Boydell & Brewer.

Quantz, Johann Joachim. 1752. *Versuch einer Anweisung die Flöte traversiere zu spielen.* Berlin: Johann Friedrich Voß. Trans. Edward R. Reilly as *On Playing the Flute.* 2d ed. New York: Schirmer Books, 1985.

Ranft, Eva-Maria. 1985. "Ein unbekannter Aufenthalt Johann Sebastian Bachs in Gotha?" *BJ* 71: 165–66.

Rathey, Markus. 2006. "Zur Datierung einiger Vokalwerke Bachs in den Jahren 1707 und 1708." *Bach-Jahrbuch* 92: 65–92.

Rathey, Markus. 2012. "The Chorale Cantata in Leipzig: The Collaboration between Schelle and Carpzov in 1689–1690 and Bach's Chorale Cantata Cycle." *BACH Journal* 43/2: 46–92.

Rathey, Markus. 2016. *Johann Sebastian Bach's Christmas Oratorio: Music, Theology, Culture.* New York: Oxford University Press.

Rathey, Markus. 2016a. *Bach's Major Vocal Works: Music, Drama, Liturgy.* New Haven: Yale University Press.

Rathey, Markus. 2016b. "Printing, Politics, and 'A Well-Regulated Church Music': A New Perspective on J. S. Bach's Mühlhausen Cantatas." *Early Music* 44: 449–60.

Richter, Bernhard Friedrich. 1902. "Eine Abhandlung Joh. Kuhnaus." *Monatshefte für Musik-Geschichte* 34: 147–54.

Rifkin, Joshua. 1975. "The Chronology of Bach's Saint Matthew Passion." *Musical Quarterly* 61: 360–87.

Rifkin, Joshua. 1978. "Ein langsamer Konzertsatz Johann Sebastian Bachs." *BJ* 64: 140–47.

Rifkin, Joshua. 1982. "Bach's Chorus: A Preliminary Report." *Musical Times* 123: 747–54.

Rifkin, Joshua. 1983. Liner note to *J. S. Bach: Oboe Concertos.* The Bach Ensemble, directed by Joshua Rifkin. Minneapolis: Pro-Arte.

Rifkin, Joshua. 1988. Review of *Johann Sebastian Bach: Messe in h-moll: Faksimile-Lichtdruck des Autographs*, ed. Alfred Dürr and Hans-Joachim Schulze. In *Notes* 44: 787–98.

Rifkin, Joshua. 1989. Liner note to *Johann Sebastian Bach: Cantata BWV 8 [etc.]*. The Bach Ensemble, directed by Joshua Rifkin. London: Decca.

Rifkin, Joshua. 1997. "Verlorene Quellen, verlorene Werke: Miszellen zu Bachs Instrumentalkompositionen." In *Bachs Orchesterwerke: Bericht über das 1. Dortmunder Bach-Symposion 1996*, ed. Martin Geck et al., 59–75. Witten: Klangrfarben.

Rifkin, Joshua. 1997a. "Besetzung—Entstehung—Überlieferung: Bemerkungen zur Ouvertüre BWV 1068." *BJ* 83: 170–76.

Rifkin, Joshua. 2000a. "Bach's Chorus." Appendix 6 in Andrew Parrott, *The Essential Bach Choir*, 189–211. Woodbridge: Boydell Press.

Rifkin, Joshua. 2000. "Siegesjubel und Satzfehler: Zum Problem von 'Nun ist das Heil und die Kraft' (BWV 50)." *BJ* 86: 68–86.

Rifkin, Joshua. 2002. *Bach's Choral Ideal*. Dortmund: Klangfarbes Musikverlag.

Rifkin, Joshua. 2002a. "Eine schwierige Stelle in der h-Moll-Messe." In *Bach in Leipzig—Bach und Leipzig: Bach-Konferenz Leipzig 2000*, ed. Ulrich Leisinger (Leipziger Beiträge zur Bachforschung, 5), 321–31. Hildesheim: Olms.

Rifkin, Joshua. 2007. "The 'B-Minor Flute Suite' Deconstructed: New Light on Bach's Ouverture BWV 1067." In *Bach Perspectives*, vol. 6, ed. Gregory G. Butler, 1–98. Urbana: University of Illinois Press.

Rifkin, Joshua. 2011. "Blinding Us with Science? Man, Machine, and the Mass in B Minor." *Eighteenth-Century Music* 8: 77–91.

Rifkin, Joshua. 2012. "Chorliste und Chorgröße bei Johann Sebastian Bach: Neue Überlegungen zu einem alten Thema." *BJ* 98: 121–43.

Rosen, Charles. 1997. *The Classical Style: Haydn, Mozart, Beethoven*. Expanded ed. New York: Norton (originally published 1971).

Sardelli, Federico Maria. 2005. "Le opere giovanili di Antonio Vivaldi." *Studi vivaldiani* 5: 45–78.

Sassoon, Humphrey F. 2003. "Royal Peculiar: J. S. Bach's Musical Offering and the Source of Its Theme." *Musical Times* 144: 38–39.

Schabalina, Tatjana. 2008. "'Texte zur Musik' in Sankt Petersburg: Neue Quellen zur Leipziger Musikgeschichte sowie zur Kompositions- und Aufführungstätigkeit Johann Sebastian Bachs." *BJ* 94: 33–98.

Scheibe, Johann Adoph. 1738–40. *Der kritische Musicus*. 2 vols. Hamburg: Wierings Erben.

Schering, Arnold. 1902–1903. "Zur Bach-Forschung." *Sammelbände der Internationalen Musik-Gesellschaft* 4: 565–70.

Schering, Arnold, ed. 1918. *Sebastian Knüpfer, Johann Schelle, Johann Kuhnau: Ausgewählte Kirchenkantaten*. Denkmäler deutscher Tonkunst, vol. 58–59. Leipzig: Breitkopf und Härtel.

Schröder, Dorothea. 2012. *Johann Sebastian Bach*. Munich: Beck.

Schubart, Christoph. 1953. "Anna Magdalena Bach: Neue Beiträge zu ihrer Herkunft und ihren Jugendjahren." *BJ* 40: 29–50.

Schulenberg, David. 1992. "An Eighteenth-Century Composer Confronts Music History and Criticism: C. P. E. Bach and Handel." *Bach* 23/2: 5–30.

Schulenberg, David. 2006. *The Keyboard Music of J. S. Bach*. 2d ed. New York: Routledge.

Schulenberg, David. 2007. "Why We Know So Little about Bach's Early Works: A Case Study (Two Keyboard Fugues)." In *Music and Its Questions: Essays in Honor of Peter Williams*, ed. Thomas Donahue, 169–203. Richmond, VA: Organ Historical Society Press.

Schulenberg, David. 2008. "The *Sonate auf Concertenart*: A Postmodern Invention?" In *Bach Perspectives*, vol. 7, ed. Gregory Butler, 55–96. Urbana and Chicago: University of Illinois Press.

Schulenberg, David. 2008a. "Fugues, Form, and Fingering: Sonata Style in Bach's Preludes and Fugues." In *Variations on the Canon: Essays in Musical Interpretation from Bach to Boulez in Honor of Charles Rosen on His Eightieth Birthday*, edited by Robert Curry, David Gable, and Robert L. Marshall, 12–21. Rochester, NY: University of Rochester Press.

Schulenberg, David. 2010. *The Music of Wilhelm Friedemann Bach*. Rochester, NY: University of Rochester Press.

Schulenberg, David. 2010a. "An Enigmatic Legacy: Two Instrumental Works Attributed to Wilhelm Friedemann Bach." *Bach* 41/2: 24–60.

Schulenberg, David. 2010b. "Editing Bach's 'Preludes and Fugues' for Organ." *Organ Yearbook* 39: 59–72.

Schulenberg, David. 2011. "An Enigmatic Legacy: Organ Music and the Berlin Bach Traditions." *Keyboard Perspectives* 4: 153–74.

Schulenberg, David. 2014. *The Music of Carl Philipp Emanuel Bach*. Rochester, NY: University of Rochester Press.

Schulenberg, David. 2017. "Expression and *Discrétion*: Bach and Froberger." *Bach Notes*, no. 26: 5–8 (online).

Schulze, Hans-Joachim. 1984. *Studien zur Bach-Überlieferung im 18. Jahrhundert*. Leipzig: Peters.

Schulze, Hans-Joachim. 1984a. "Bachs Helfer bei der Leipziger Kirchenmusik." *BJ* 70: 46–52.

Schulze, Hans-Joachim. 1985. "Besitzstand und Vermögensverhältnisse von Leipziger Ratsmusikern zur Zeit Johann Sebastian Bachs." *Beiträge zur Bachforschung* 4: 33–46.

Schulze, Hans-Joachim. 1985a. "Johann Christoph Bach (1671–1721): 'Organist und Schul Collega in Ohrdruf,' Johann Sebastian Bachs erster Lehrer." *BJ* 71: 55–81.

Schulze, Hans-Joachim. 1985b. *Ey! wie schmeckt der Coffee süsse: Johann Sebastian Bachs Kaffee-Kantate in ihrer Zeit*. Leipzig: Verlag für die Frau.

Schulze, Hans-Joachim, ed. 1985c. *Die Thomasschule Leipzig zur Zeit Johann Sebastian Bachs: Ordnungen und Gesetze 1634, 1723, 1733*. Leipzig: Zentralantiquariat der Deutschen Demokratischen Republik.

Schulze, Hans-Joachim. 2008. "Johann Friedrich Schweinitz, 'A Disciple of the Famous Herr Bach in Leipzig'." In *About Bach*, ed. Gregory G. Butler et al., 81–88. Urbana and Chicago: University of Illinois Press.

Schulze, Hans-Joachim. 2013. "Anna Magdalena Wilcke: Gesangsschülerin der *Paulina*?" *BJ* 99: 279–95.

Seiffert, Max. 1907–8. "Die Chorbibliothek der St. Michaelisschule in Lüneburg zu Seb. Bach's Zeit." *Sammelbände der Internationalen Musikgesellschaft* 9: 593–621.

Siegele, Ulrich. 1983, 1984, 1985. "Bachs Stellung in der Leipziger Kulturpolitik seiner Zeit." *BJ* 69: 7–50; 70: 7–43; and 71: 63–77.

Smend, Friedrich. 1926. "Die Johannes-Passion von Bach auf ihren Bau untersucht." *Bach-Jahrbuch* 23: 105–28.

Smend, Friedrich. 1985. *Bach in Köthen*. Trans. John Page with annotations by Stephen Daw. St. Louis: Concordia. Originally *Bach in Köthen*. Berlin: Christlicher Zeitschriftenverlag, 1951.

Smend, Julius. 1921. "Predigt im Festgottesdienst in der St. Michaelis-Kirche zu Hamburg am Sonntag, den 5. Juni 1921, anläßlich des Neunten Deutschen Bachfestes." *BJ* 18: 1–8.

Smith, Mark. 1998. "Joh. Seb. Bachs Violoncello piccolo: Neue Aspekte—offene Fragen." *Bach-Jahrbuch* 84: 63–81.

Snyder, Kerala. 2007. *Dieterich Buxtehude: Organist in Lübeck*. Rev. ed. Rochester, NY: University of Rochester Press.

Speerstra, Joel. 2004. *Bach and the Pedal Clavichord: An Organist's Guide*. Rochester, NY: University of Rochester Press.

Spitta, Philipp. 1873–1880. *Johann Sebastian Bach*. 2 vols. Leipzig: Breitkopf & Härtel. Trans. Clara Bell and J. A. Fuller-Maitland as *Johann Sebastian Bach: His Life and Influence on the Music of Germany, 1685–1750*. 3 vols. London: Novello, 1889. Reprint in 2 vols. New York: Dover, 1952.

Sposato, Jeffrey S. 2018. *Leipzig after Bach: Church and Concert Life in a German City*. New York: Oxford University Press.

Stauffer, George B. 1996. "The Thomasschule and the Haus 'zum Goldenen Bären': A Bach-Breitkopf Architectural Connection." In *Bach Perspectives*, vol. 2, ed. George B. Stauffer, 181–203. Lincoln: University of Nebraska Press.

Stauffer, George B. 2008. "Music for 'Cavaliers et Dames': Bach and the Repertoire of His Collegium Musicum." In *About Bach*, ed. Gregory G. Butler et al., 135–56. Urbana and Chicago: University of Illinois Press.

Stevens, Jane R. 1971. "An Eighteenth-Century Description of Concerto First-Movement Form." *Journal of the American Musicological Society* 24: 85–95.

Stevens, Jane R. 2001. *The Bach Family and the Keyboard Concerto: The Evolution of a Genre*. Warren, MI: Harmonie Park Press.

Stiehl, Herbert. 1984. "Das Innere der Thomaskirche zur Amtszeit Johann Sebstian Bachs." *Beiträge zur Bachforschung* 3: 5–96.

Stinson, Russell. 1996. *Bach: The Orgelbüchlein*. New York: Schirmer Books.

Stockigt, Janice B. 2013. "Bach's *Missa* BWV 232^1 in the Context of Catholic Mass Settings in Dresden, 1729–1733." In *Exploring Bach's B-Minor Mass*, ed. Yo Tomita et al., 39–53. Cambridge: Cambridge University Press.

Suchalla, Ernst, ed. 1994. *Carl Philipp Emanuel Bach: Briefe und Dokumente: Kritische Gesamtausgabe*. 2 vols. Göttingen: Vandenhoeck & Ruprecht.

Tarkkanen, Ahti. 2016. "Blindness of Johann Sebastian Bach." *Acta Ophthalmologica* 91: 191–92.

Tatlow, Ruth. 2015. *Bach's Numbers: Compositional Proportion and Significance*. Cambridge: Cambridge University Press.

Telemann, Georg Philipp. 1972. *Briefwechsel: Sämtliche erreichbare Briefe von und an Telemann*. Ed. Hans Grosse and Hans Rudolf Jung. Leipzig: VEB Deutscher Verlag für Musik.

Terry, Charles Sanford. 1933. *Bach: A Biography*. 2d rev. ed. London: Oxford University Press.

Thayer, Alexander Wheelock. 1969. *Life of Beethoven*. Translated by Henry Edward Krehbiel. Revised and edited by Elliot Forbes as *Thayer's Life of Beethoven*. Princeton: Princeton University Press.

Tiggemann, Hildegard. 1994. "Unbekannte Textdrucke zu drei Gelegenheitskantaten J. S. Bachs aus dem Jahre 1729." *BJ* 80: 7–22.

Tomita, Yo. 2005. "The Simrock Edition of the Well-Tempered Clavier II." "First published on-line in April 2005; last revised on 25 November 2017." http://www.mu.qub.ac.uk/tomita/essay/simrock.

Towe, Teri Noel. 2001. "The Face of Bach: The Queens College Lecture of March 21, 2001." Online, multiple webpages linked from http://www.bach-cantatas.com/thefaceofbach/QCL09.htm.

Vanscheeuwijck, Marc. 2010. "Recent Re-evaluations of the Baroque Cello and What They Might Mean for Performing the Music of J. S. Bach." *Early Music* 38: 181–92.

[Voltaire, pen name of François-Marie Arouet]. 1764. *Essai sur l'histoire générale . . . nouvelle edition . . . tome second.* Amsterdam.

Walther, Johann Gottfried. 1732. *Musicalisches Lexicon.* Leipzig: Wolffgang Deer.

Walther, Johann Gottfried. 1955. *Praecepta der musicalischen Composition.* Ed. Peter Benary. Leipzig: VEB Breitkopf und Härtel. The original manuscript (Weimar, Landesbibliothek, Hs Q 341c) is dated March 1708.

Walther, Johann Gottfried. 1987. *Briefe.* Ed. Klaus Beckmann and Hans-Joachim Schulze. Leipzig: VEB Deutscher Verlag für Musik.

Welter, Kathryn. 2008. "A Master Teacher Revealed: Johann Pachelbel's *Deutliche Anweisung.*" In *About Bach*, ed. Gregory G. Butler et al., 3–13. Urbana and Chicago: University of Illinois Press.

Wiemer, Wolfgang. 1979. "Johann Heinrich Schübler, der Stecher der Kunst der Fuge." *BJ* 65: 75–96.

Wiermann, Barbara. 2002. "Bach und Palestrina: Neue Quellen aus Johann Sebastian Bachs Notenbibliothek." *BJ* 88: 9–28.

Wilhelmi, Thomas. 1992. "Carl Philipp Emanuel Bachs 'Avertissement' über den Druck der Kunst der Fuge." *BJ* 78: 101–5.

Williams, Peter. 1980. *A New History of the Organ from the Greeks to the Present Day.* Bloomington: Indiana University Press.

Williams, Peter. 1980–1984. *The Organ Music of J. S. Bach.* 3 vols. Cambridge: Cambridge University Press.

Williams, Peter. 1981. "BWV 565: A Toccata in D Minor for Organ by J. S. Bach?" *Early Music* 9: 330–37.

Williams, Peter. 1984. "Bach's G-Minor Sonata for Viola da Gamba and Harpsichord BWV 1029: A Seventh Brandenburg Concerto?" *Early Music* 12: 345–54.

Williams, Peter. 2003. *The Organ Music of J. S. Bach.* 2d ed. Cambridge: Cambridge University Press.

Williams, Peter. 2003a. "Is There an Anxiety of Influence Discernible in J. S. Bach's *Clavierübung I?*" In *The Keyboard in Baroque Europe* (Festschrift for Gustav Leonhardt), ed. Christopher Hogwood, 140–56. Cambridge: Cambridge University Press.

Williams, Peter. 2016. *Bach: A Musical Biography.* Cambridge: Cambridge University Press.

Wolff, Christoph. 1986. "Johann Sebastian Bach's Third Part of the *Clavier-Übung.*" In *Charles Brenton Fisk, Organ Builder.* Volume 1, *Essays in His Honor*, ed. Fenner Douglass, Owen Jander, and Barbara Owen, 283–91. Easthampton, Mass.: The Westfield Center for Early Keyboard Studies.

Wolff, Christoph. 1992. "The Identity of the 'Fratro Dilettissimo' in the Capriccio B-Flat Major [*sic*] and Other Problems of Bach's Early Harpsichord Works." In *The Harpsichord and Its Repertoire: Proceedings of the International Harpsichord Symposium Utrecht 1990*, ed. Pieter Dirksen, 145–56. Utrecht: STIMU: Foundation for Historical Performance Practice.

Wolff, Christoph. 2000. *Johann Sebastian Bach: The Learned Musician.* New York: Norton.

Wolff, Christoph. 2008. "Sicilianos and Organ Recitals: Observations on J. S. Bach's Concertos." In *Bach Perspectives*, vol. 7, ed. Gregory G. Butler, 97–114. Urbana: University of Illinois Press.

Wolff, Christoph. 2011. "Under the Spell of Opera? Bach's Oratorio Trilogy." In *Bach Perspectives*, vol. 8, ed. Daniel R. Melamed, 1–12. Urbana: University of Illinois Press.

Wolff, Christoph. 2016. "Did J. S. Bach Write Organ Concertos? Apropos the Prehistory of Cantata Movements with Obbligato Organ." In *Bach Perspectives*, vol. 10, ed. Matthew Dirst, 60–75. Urbana: University of Illinois Press.

Wolff, Christoph, and Markus Zepf. 2012. *The Organs of J. S. Bach: A Handbook.* Trans. Lynn Edwards Butler. Urbana: University of Illinois Press.

Wollny, Peter. 1994. "Bachs Bewerbung um die Organistenstelle an der Marienkirche zu Halle und ihr Kontext." *BJ* 80: 26–39.

Wollny, Peter. 1995. "Wilhelm Friedemann Bach's Halle Performances of Cantatas by His Father." In *Bach Studies 2,* ed. Daniel R. Melamed, 202–28. Cambridge: Cambridge University Press.

Wollny, Peter. 1996. "Zur Überlieferung der Instrumentalwerke Johann Sebastian Bachs: Der Quellenbesitz Carl Philipp Emanuel Bachs." *BJ* 82: 7–22.

Wollny, Peter. 1997. "Neue Bach-Funde." *BJ* 83: 7–50.

Wollny, Peter. 2001. "Neue Ermittlungen zu Aufführungen Bachscher Kirchenkantaten am Zertbster Hof." In *Bach und seine mitteldeutschen Zeitgenossen: Bericht über das Internationale Musikwissenschaftliche Kolloquium Erfurt und Arnstadt 13. bis 16. Januar 2000,* ed. Rainer Kaiser, 199–217. Eisenach: Wagner.

Wollny, Peter. 2002. "Geistliche Musik der Vorfahren Johann Sebastian Bachs: Das 'Altbachische Archiv'." *Jahrbuch des Staatlichen Instituts für Musikforschung Preussischer Kulturbesitz:* 40–59.

Wollny, Peter. 2011. "Fundstücke zur Lebensgeschichte Johann Sebastian Bachs 1744–1750." *BJ* 97: 35–50.

Wollny, Peter. 2013. "Eine unbekannte Bach-Handschrift und andere Quellen zur Leipziger Musikgeschichte in Weißenfels." *BJ* 99: 129–70.

Wollny, Peter. 2015. "Vom 'apparat der auserleßensten kirchen Stücke' zum 'Vorrath an Musicalien, von J. S. Bach und andern berühmten Musicis': Quellenkundliche Ermittlungen zur frühen Thüringer Bach-Überlieferung und zu einigen Weimarer Schülern und Kollegen Bachs." *BJ* 101: 99–154.

Wollny, Peter. 2016. "Neuerkenntnisse zu einigen Kopisten der 1730er Jahre." *BJ* 102: 63–99.

Wollny, Peter, and Michael Maul. 2008. "The Weimar Organ Tablature: Bach's Earliest Autographs." *Understanding Bach* 3: 67–74.

Yearsley, David. 2002. *Bach and the Meanings of Counterpoint.* Cambridge: Cambridge University Press.

Yearsley, David. 2007. "Women at the Organ: A Fragment." In *Music and Its Questions: Essays in Honor of Peter Williams,* ed. Thomas Donahue, 119–41. Richmond, VA: Organ Historical Society Press.

Yearsley, David. 2013. "Hoopskirts, Coffee, and the Changing Musical Prospects of the Bach Women." *Women and Music* 17: 27–58.

Yearsley, David. 2019. *Sex, Death, and Minuets: Anna Magdalena Bach and her Musical Notebooks.* Chicago: University of Chicago Press.

Youngren, William H. 2003. *C. P. E. Bach and the Rebirth of Strophic Song.* Lanham, MD, and Oxford: Scarecrow Press.

Zegers, Richard H. C. 2005. "The Eyes of Johann Sebastian Bach." *Archives of Ophthalmology* 123: 1427–30.

Zitellini, Rodolfo. 2013. "Das 'Thema Legrenzianum' der Fuge BWV 574: Eine Fehlzuschreibung?" *BJ* 99: 243–59.

Zohn, Steven. 2008. *Music for a Mixed Taste: Style, Genre, and Meaning in Telemann's Instrumental Works.* Oxford: Oxford University Press.

Index

Musicians contemporary to Bach who knew or influenced him are listed in preference to many others briefly mentioned in the book. Pages whose numbers are given in italic type show figures or music examples. Relatives of J. S. Bach are identified by parenthetical expressions following their names. Alternate versions of works signified by BWV numbers with letter suffixes (e.g., 951a) are usually indexed only under the primary number. Doubtful and misattributed compositions that have been assigned BWV numbers are included among the works listed under Bach's name. Umlauts are disregarded in the alphabetization of German words and names. Matter within tables and appendices is not indexed.